D0140872

Early China

"Early China" refers to the period from the beginning of human history in China to the end of the Han Dynasty in AD 220. The roots of modern Chinese society and culture are all to be found in this formative period of Chinese civilization. Li Feng's new critical interpretation draws on the most recent scholarship and archaeological discoveries from the past thirty years. This fluent and engaging overview of early Chinese civilization explores key topics including the origins of the written language, the rise of the state, the Shang and Zhou religions, bureaucracy, law and governance, the evolving nature of war, the creation of empire, the changing image of art, and the philosophical search for social order. Beautifully illustrated with a wide range of new images, this book is essential reading for all those wanting to know more about the foundations of Chinese history and civilization.

LI FENG is Professor of Early Chinese History and Archaeology at Columbia University. Both a historian and an archaeologist, his research interests extend from bronze inscriptions and Western Zhou history to broader issues such as the nature of early states, bureaucracy, comparative literacy, cross-region cultural relations, and theories of social development. He is also an active archaeologist with extensive fieldwork experience in China and Japan. Li's published English books include *Landscape and Power in Early China: The Crisis and Fall of the Western Zhou, 1045–771 BC* (2006), *Bureaucracy and the State in Early China: Governing the Western Zhou* (2008), and *Writing and Literacy in Early China: Studies from the Columbia Early China Seminar* (co-editor, 2011).

New Approaches to Asian History

This dynamic new series publishes books on the milestones in Asian history, those that have come to define particular periods or to mark turning points in the political, cultural, and social evolution of the region. The books in this series are intended as introductions for students to be used in the classroom. They are written by scholars whose credentials are well established in their particular fields and who have, in many cases, taught the subject across a number of years.

Books in the Series

1   Judith M. Brown, *Global South Asians: Introducing the Modern Diaspora*
2   Diana Lary, *China's Republic*
3   Peter A. Lorge, *The Asian Military Revolution: From Gunpowder to the Bomb*
4   Ian Talbot and Gurharpal Singh, *The Partition of India*
5   Stephen F. Dale, *The Muslim Empires of the Ottomans, Safavids, and Mughals*
6   Diana Lary, *The Chinese People at War: Human Suffering and Social Transformation, 1937–1945*
7   Sunil S. Amrith, *Migration and Diaspora in Modern Asia*
8   Thomas David DuBois, *Religion and the Making of Modern East Asia*
9   Susan L. Mann, *Gender and Sexuality in Modern Chinese History*
10   Tirthankar Roy, *India in the World Economy: From Antiquity to the Present*
11   Robin R. Wang, *Yinyang: The Way of Heaven and Earth in Chinese Thought and Culture*
12   Li Feng, *Early China: A Social and Cultural History*

Early China

A Social and Cultural History

Li Feng

Columbia University

CAMBRIDGE
UNIVERSITY PRESS

CAMBRIDGE
UNIVERSITY PRESS

University Printing House, Cambridge CB2 8BS, United Kingdom

One Liberty Plaza, 20th Floor, New York, NY 10006, USA

477 Williamstown Road, Port Melbourne, VIC 3207, Australia

314-321, 3rd Floor, Plot 3, Splendor Forum, Jasola District Centre, New Delhi - 110025, India

79 Anson Road, #06-04/06, Singapore 079906

Cambridge University Press is part of the University of Cambridge.

It furthers the University's mission by disseminating knowledge in the pursuit of
education, learning and research at the highest international levels of excellence.

www.cambridge.org
Information on this title: www.cambridge.org/9780521719810

© Cambridge University Press 2013

First published 2013
Reprinted with corrections 2014
3rd printing 2015

A catalogue record for this publication is available from the British Library

Library of Congress Cataloging in Publication data
Li, Feng, 1962–
Early China: a social and cultural history / Li Feng, Columbia University.
  pages cm
ISBN 978-0-521-89552-1 – ISBN 978-0-521-71981-0 (pbk.)
1. China – History – To 221 B.C.   2. China – History – Shang dynasty, 1766–1122
B.C.   3. China – History – Zhou dynasty, 1122–221 B.C.   4. China – History – Qin
dynasty, 221–207 B.C.   5. China – History – Han dynasty, 202 B.C.–220
A.D.   I. Title.
DS741.5.L45   2013
931–dc23

2013008431

ISBN   978-0-521-89552-1   Hardback
ISBN   978-0-521-71981-0   Paperback

Contents

List of figures   *page* ix
List of maps   xvi
Preface   xvii
Chronology of Early China   xx
Map of China   xxi

1   Introduction: Early China and its natural and cultural demarcations   1

2   The development of complex society in China   15

3   Erlitou and Erligang: early state expansion   41

4   Anyang and beyond: Shang and contemporary Bronze Age cultures   66

5   Cracking the secret bones: literacy and society in late Shang   90

6   Inscribed history: the Western Zhou state and its bronze vessels   112

7   The creation of paradigm: Zhou bureaucracy and social institutions   140

8   Hegemons and warriors: social transformation of the Spring and Autumn period (770–481 BC)   162

9   The age of territorial states: Warring States politics and institutions (480–221 BC)   183

10   Philosophers as statesmen: in the light of recently discovered texts   207

11   The Qin unification and Qin Empire: who were the terracotta warriors?   229

12   Expansion and political transition of the Han Empire   257

13   State and society: bureaucracy and social orders
     under the Han Empire   283

14   Ideological changes and their reflections in Han
     culture and Han art   304

     Index   325

Figures

Fig. 1.1   Temperature fluctuation in China, 11,000 BP to
present. (From Shi Yafeng and Kong Zhaozheng
et al., "Mid-Holocene Climates and Environments
in China," *Global and Planetary Change* 7 [1973],
219–233.)   *page* 4

Fig. 1.2   Pioneers of early sinology: (a) Édouard Chavannes,
(b) Wang Guowei. (From *Bulletin Archéologue du
Musée Guimet*, fasc. I [Paris: Librairie nationale d'art
et d'histoire, 1921]; Wang Guowei, *Haining Wang
Jingan xiansheng yishu*, vol. 1 [Shanghai:
Commerical Press, 1940].)   8

Fig. 1.3   Excavators at Anyang wearing bronze helmets
freshly excavated from the Shang royal tomb no.
1004; photograph taken in 1935 during the twelfth
excavation. (Courtesy of the Institute of History and
Philology, Academia Sinica.)   9

Fig. 2.1   The "Chinese Interaction Spheres." (From K. C.
Chang, *The Archaeology of Ancient China*, 4th edn.
[New Haven: Yale University Press, 1986], p. 108.)   19

Fig. 2.2   Peiligang and Jiahu. (1–4 from Peiligang, 5–6 from
Jiahu). (1, 3, from Institute of Archaeology, CASS,
Kaogu jinghua [Beijing: Kexue chubanshe, 1993],
p. 6; 2, 4, Institute of Archaeology, *Zhongguo
kaoguxue: Xin shiqi shidai juan* [Beijing: Zhongguo
shehui kexue chubanshe, 2010], pl. 2; 5, *Wenwu* 1
[1989], pl. 1; 6, *Kaogo* 12 [1996], pl. 8.)   23

Fig. 2.3   Earliest ceramic shards from southern China. (From
Institute of Archaeology, *Guilin Zengpiyan* [Beijing:
Wenwu chubanshe, 2003], pls. 5.1–2, 8.1–2.)   25

Fig. 2.4   Pottery types of the Yangshao culture. (From
Institute of Archaeology, *Kaogu Jinghua*, pp. 15, 17,
18, 19, 24, 25, 26.)   26

Fig. 2.5   The Jiangzhai village. (From Li Liu, *The Chinese Neolithic: Trajectories to Early States* [Cambridge: Cambridge University Press, 2004], p. 80.)   28

Fig. 2.6   Taosi town of the Longshan period. (From Liu, *The Chinese Neolithic: Trajectories to Early States*, p. 109.)   31

Fig. 2.7   Solar observatory discovered in the walled town in Taosi, Shanxi, 2003. (From *Chinese Archaeology* 5 [2005], 54.)   34

Fig. 2.8   The Longshan and Liangzhu town culture. (1–2, from Institute of Archaeology, *Kaogu jinghua*, p. 67; 3, *Kaogu* 12 [1984], pl. 3; 4–5, Kwang-chih Chang et al. [eds.], *The Formation of Chinese Civilization* [New Haven: Yale University Press, 2005], pp. 106, 133; 6, Zhongguo wenwu jiaoliu fuwu zhongxin, *Zhongguo wemwu jinghua* [Beijing: Wenwu chubanshe, 1990], pl. 15.)   35

Fig. 2.9   The earthquake site in Lajia and the earliest noodle in China. (From *Kaogu* 12 [2002], pl. 3.)   39

Fig. 3.1   The Erlitou site and its palace zone. (Left, from Li Liu and Xingcan Chen, *State Formation in Early China* [London: Duckworth, 2003], p. 61; right, from *Chinese Archaeology* 5 [2005], 2.)   45

Fig. 3.2   Bronze vessels and turquoise objects from Erlitou. (1–3, 5, 6, from Institute of Archaeology, *Kaogu jinghua*, pp. 118–121; 4, *Chinese Archaeology* 5 [2005], 11.)   46

Fig. 3.3   The Bingong *xu* and its inscription. (From *Zhongguo lishi wenwu* 6 [2002], 4.)   51

Fig. 3.4   The Shang king list. (Based on David Keightley, "The Shang," in Michael Loewe and Edward L. Shaughnessy [eds.], *The Cambridge History of Ancient China: From the Origins of Civilization to 221 BC* [Cambridge: Cambridge University Press, 1999], pp. 234–235.)   55

Fig. 3.5   The city of Yanshi. Circled numbers show excavation trenches 1996–8; inset shows palace foundations D1–D8 and D10. (Reworked based on Du Jinpeng, *Xia Shang Zhou kaogu xue yanjiu* [Beijing: Kexue chubanshe, 2007], pp. 372, 376.)   57

Fig. 3.6   The Shang city in Zhengzhou. (From Li Liu and Xingcan Chen, *State Formation in Early China*, p. 94.)   58

Fig. 3.7   Bronze vessel from Zhengzhou. (From *Zhongguo
           meishu quanji: Gongyi meishu bian: Qingtongqi 1*
           [Beijing: Wenwu chubanshe, 1985], p. 5.)   59

Fig. 3.8   Mining remains found in Tongling, Jiangxi. (From
           Jiangxi sheng wenwu kaogu yanjiusuo *et al.*, *Tongling
           gu tongkuang yizhi faxian yu yanjiu* [Nanchang:
           Jiangxi kexue jishu chubanshe, 1997], pls. 3, 5, 15,
           23, 40.)   65

Fig. 4.1   Anyang or the "Ruins of Yin." (From Institute of
           Archaeology, *Yinxu de faxian yu yanjiu* [Beijing:
           Kexue chubanshe, 1994], pl. 2.)   68

Fig. 4.2   The Shang royal palaces in Anyang. (From K. C.
           Chang, *Shang Civilization* [New Haven: Yale
           University Press, 1980], p. 94.)   70

Fig. 4.3   1, Plan of the Shang royal cemetery; 2, royal tomb
           no. 1001. (1, from Institute of Archaeology, *Xin
           Zhongguo de kaogu faxian he yanjiu* [Beijing: Wenwu
           chubanshe, 1984], p. 231; 2, *Cambridge History of
           Ancient China: From the Origins of Civilization to 221
           BC*, p. 190.)   72

Fig. 4.4   Zuoce Ban's turtle. (From *Zhongguo lishi wenwu*
           [2005], front cover.)   74

Fig. 4.5   Bronze vessels unearthed from the tomb of Lady
           Hao. (From Institute of Archaeology, CASS, *Yinxu
           Fu Hao mu* [Beijing: Wenwu chubanshe, 1980], pls.
           1, 2.1, 3, 6, 7.)   76

Fig. 4.6   Styles of bronze décor from Anyang, identified by
           Max Loehr. (Images assembled by the author based
           on bronzes in the Asian Society, New York; Max
           Loehr, *Ritual Vessels of Bronze Age China* [New York:
           Asian Society, 1968], pp. 23, 33, 45, 57, 87.)   77

Fig. 4.7   *Ding*-cauldron cast for "Mother Wu" (h. 1.33 cm,
           w. 110 cm). (From *Zhongguo da baike quanshu*
           [Beijing: Zhongguo da baike quanshu chubanshe,
           1986], p. 20.)   79

Fig 4.8   Correlation of Anyang periodization.   80

Fig. 4.9   Location of the Huanbei Shang City. (From *Chinese
           Archaeology* 4 [2004], 2.)   81

Fig. 4.10 Palace foundation F1 in the Huanbei Shang City.
           (From *Chinese Archaeology* 4 [2004], 24.)   82

Fig. 4.11 House foundation no. 14 and pottery jars from it, in
           Taixi, an alcoholic beverage production center in

	southern Hebei, possible supplier to Anyang. (From Hebei sheng wenwu yanjiusuo, *Gaocheng Taixi Shang dai yizhi* [Beijing: Wenwu chubanshe, 1985], p. 31.)	85
Fig. 4.12	Bronzes found in Xingan, Jiangxi. (From *Wenwu* [1991], pls. 1.1, 2.1.)	87
Fig. 4.13	The discoveries at Sanxingdui, Sichuan. Left, site map of Sanxingdui city; right, bronze human statue. (From Zhongguo wenwu jiaoliu fuwu zhongxin *et al.*, *Zhongguo wemwu jinghua* [Beijing: Wenwu chubanshe, 1990], pl. 30; map reworked from Robert Bagley [ed.], *Ancient Sichuan: Treasures from a Lost Civilization* [Seattle: Seattle Art Museum, 2001], p. 24.)	88
Fig. 5.1	Example of a turtle plastron with divination records (HJ: 06834). (From Institute of History, CASS, *Jiaguwen heji* [Shanghai: Zhonhua shuju, 1978–83], #06834.)	94
Fig. 5.2	Inscribed turtle plastrons unearthed at Huayuanzhuang-east, 1991. (From Institute of Archaeology, CASS, *Yinxu Huayuanzhuang dongdi jiagu* [Kunming: Yunnan renmin chubanshe, 2003], p. 40.)	97
Fig. 5.3	Example of consecutive records of royal sacrifice. (From Institute of History, CASS, *Jiaguwen heji*, #22779.)	101
Fig. 5.4	Shang king asking about the "Four Lands." (From Institute of History, CASS, *Jiaguwen heji*, #36975.)	108
Fig. 6.1	Bronzes and oracle bone from Nianzipo. (From Institute of Archaeology, *Nan Binzhou-Nianzipo* [Beijing: Shijie tushu chuban gongsi, 2007], pls. 3, 4, 5, 6.2.)	115
Fig. 6.2	Examples of late pre-dynastic bronzes and pottery. (From *Kaogu xuebao* 3 [1991], pp. 272, 273.)	116
Fig 6.3	Example of a Zhou oracle-bone inscription from Zhouyuan. (Photograph provided by Cao Wei.)	119
Fig. 6.4	The Li *gui* and its inscription recording the Zhou conquest. (Image from *Zhongguo meishu quanji: Gongyi meishu bian: Qingtongqi 1* [Beijing: Wenwu chabanshe, 1985], p. 122; inscription from *Wenwu* 8 [1977], fig. 2.)	121
Fig. 6.5	An early Western Zhou *you*-vessel (Photograph ©2013 Museum of Fine Arts, Boston.)	125

Fig. 6.6   Stylistic evolution of Western Zhou bronze vessels.
            (From Shaanxi sheng kaogu yanjiusuo *et al.*, *Shaanxi
            chutu Shang Zhou qingtongqi*, vol. 2 [Beijing: Wenwu
            chubanshe, 1979], pp. 3, 5, 13, 15, 21, 33, 36; vol. 3,
            pl. 8, pp. 32, 16, 118, 129; vol. 4, p. 82.)   126
Fig. 6.7   Standard burial pottery sets from Zhangjiapo.
            (Reworked based on *Kaogu xuebao* 4 [1980], 459,
            484, 485.)   128
Fig. 6.8   The Yihou Ze *gui*-tureen (Image from *Zhongguo
            meishu quanji: Gongyi meishu bian: Qingtongqi 1*,
            p. 167.)   131
Fig. 6.9   Tomb no. 1193 at Liulihe and the Ke *lei* from it.
            (From *Kaogu* 1 [1990], 22, 25.)   133
Fig. 6.10   Bone sculpture from Zhouyuan. (From *Wenwu* 1
            [1986], 47.)   136
Fig. 6.11   The Xiaochen Lai *gui*-tureen and its inscriptions on
            the eastern campaign. (From Rong Geng, *Shanzhai
            yiqi tulu* [Beijing: Yanjing daxue, 1936], pl. 70.)   137
Fig. 7.1   Configuration of the Zhou ancestral temple system.   146
Fig. 7.2   Organization of the Western Zhou central
            government: mid Western Zhou period.   148
Fig. 7.3   The Douyou *ding*-cauldron and its inscription which
            records Zhou combat with the Xianyun at four
            locations along the Jing River to the north of the
            Zhou capital. (From Li Feng, *Landscape and Power
            in Early China: The Crisis and Fall of the Western Zhou,
            1045–771 BC* [Cambridge: Cambridge University
            Press, 2006], p. 148.)   151
Fig. 7.4   Conditions of existence of the Zhou regional states.   156
Fig. 8.1   Iron objects from burial pit no. 44 from Xiadu
            of Yan, Hebei Province. (From *Kaogu* 4 [1975],
            pls. 4–5.)   170
Fig. 8.2   Covenant tablet 156: 20 from Houma. (From
            Shanxi sheng wenwu gongzuo weiyuanhui, *Houma
            mengshu* [Beijing: Wenwu chubanshe, 1976], pp.
            141, 267.)   179
Fig. 9.1   The long wall of Qin in Guyuan, Ningxia
            Autonomous Region. (Photograph by the author.)   186
Fig. 9.2   Territory-based states in comparison to settlement-
            based states in Fig. 7.4.   187
Fig. 9.3   Battle scene engraved on a bronze *jian*-basin from
            Shanbiaozhen, northern Henan. (Courtesy of the

Institute of History and Philology, Academia
Sinica.)   198

Fig. 9.4   A crossbow. (Reworked from Wang Zhenhua,
Shang Zhou qingtong bingqi [Taipei: Guyuege, 1993],
p. 295.)   200

Fig. 9.5   Bronze *zun*-container and *pan*-basin from the tomb
of Marquis Yi. (From *Zhongguo meishu quanji:
Gongyi meishu bian: Qingtongqi II* [Beijing: Wenwu
chubanshe, 1985], p. 64.)   204

Fig. 9.6   Bronze tiger from the tomb of the king of
Zhongshan. (From Zhongguo wenwu jiaoliu fuwu
zhongxin *et al.*, *Zhongguo wemwu jinghua* [Beijing:
Wenwu chubanshe, 1990], pl. 68.)   205

Fig. 11.1   *Ding*-vessel cast by an early Qin duke, possibly Duke
Xiang (*r.* 777–766 BC). (Image provided by Zhou
Ya.)   230

Fig. 11.2   The excavation of tomb no. 1 in Fengxiang, possibly
the grave of Duke Jing of Qin (576–537 BC).
(Photographs provided by Jiao Nanfeng.)   233

Fig. 11.3   Terracotta statue of a civil/legal officer recently
found in pit K0006 near the burial mound of the
First Emperor of Qin. (Photograph provided by Jiao
Nanfeng.)   238

Fig. 11.4   Standard volume measurer commissioned by Shang
Yang. (From Guojia jiliang zongju [ed.], *Zhongguo
gudai dulianggheng tuji* [Beijing: Wenwu chubanshe,
1981], pl. 81.)   240

Fig. 11.5   A modern portrait of Ying Zheng as the First
Emperor of Qin. (From www.chinapage.
comemperor.html.)   243

Fig. 11.6   The "Straight Road" of Qin in Fuxian, northern
Shaanxi (arrow: excavation trenches, 2007).
(Photograph provided by Huang Xiaofen.)   248

Fig. 11.7   The Lishan complex. (From Ann Delroy [ed.], *Two
Emperors: China's Ancient Origins* [Brunswick East,
Victoria, Australia: Praxis Exhibitions, 2002], p. 46).   252

Fig. 11.8   The underground city of the First Emperor. (From
Delroy [ed.], *Two Emperors*, p. 47.)   253

Fig. 11.9   Bronze crane from the underground river
constructed for the First Emperor, to the north of
the main burial mound. (Photograph provided by
Cao Wei.)   254

Fig. 11.10 The terracotta army of the First Emperor, pit no. 1.
            (Photograph provided by Cao Wei.)   255
Fig. 12.1   The imperial city Chang'an. (From Wang
            Zhongshu, *Han Civilization* [New Haven: Yale
            University Press, 1982], fig. 2.)   261
Fig. 12.2   Bronze objects from the Ordos region, 400–200 BC.
            (From Tian Guangjin and Guo Suxin, *E'erduosi shi
            qingtongqi* [Beijing: Wenwu chubanshe, 1986], pls.
            12, 15.)   268
Fig. 12.3   The Han–Xiongnu war depicted in a Han pictorial
            carving, Xiaotangshan, Shandong Province. (From
            Édouard Chavannes, *Mission archéologique dans la
            Chine septentrionale* [Paris: Leroux, 1909], pl. 50.)   272
Fig. 12.4   Wang Mang's architectural structures in Chang'an.
            (From Wang Zhongshu, *Han Civilization*, fig. 30.)   278
Fig. 13.1   Strips of Han law from Zhangjiashan. (From *Wenwu*
            1 [1985], pl. 1.)   290
Fig. 13.2   Population decline in the Han Empire from AD 2 to
            AD 140. (From Hans Bielenstein, "The Census of
            China: During the Period 2–742 AD," *Bulletin of the
            Museum of Far Eastern Antiquities* [Stockholm] 19
            [1947], pls. 2, 3.)   296
Fig. 14.1   Fragment of the Xiping stone classics found in
            Luoyang. (From *Kaogu xuebao* 2 [1981], 187.)   314
Fig. 14.2   The jade funeral garment of the king of Zhongshan
            in Mancheng. (From Zhongguo wenwu jiaoliu fuwu
            zhongxin *et al.*, *Zhongguo wemwu jinghua* [Beijing:
            Wenwu chubanshe, 1990], pl. 88.)   319
Fig. 14.3   Lacquer wares and painting from the tombs at
            Mawangdui, Changshan. (From Fu Juyou and
            Chen Songchang (eds.), *Mawangdui Han mu wenwu*
            [Changsha: Hunan chubanshe, 1992], pp. 19, 53,
            54.)   321
Fig. 14.4   The Wu Liang shrine: "Assassination of the First
            Emperor." (From Rong Geng, *Han Wu Liang si
            huaxiang lu* [Beijing: Yanjing daxue Kaogu xueshe,
            1936], pp. 11–12.)   323

Maps

Map 2.1   Major Neolithic archaeological sites in China   *page* 16
Map 3.1   Distribution of Erlitou culture sites   44
Map 3.2   Erligang and contemporary or nearly contemporary
          Bronze Age societies   62
Map 4.1   The external world of late Shang   84
Map 6.1   Location of the pre-dynastic Zhou cultural sites and
          the Zhou conquest campaign of 1045 BC   114
Map 6.2   The Zhou central area: royal domain   122
Map 6.3   Distribution of the Zhou major regional states   130
Map 8.1   Major states of the Spring and Autumn period   164
Map 9.1   The Warring States period   184
Map 11.1 Route of early Qin migration   232
Map 11.2 The Qin Empire   247
Map 12.1 The Han Empire in 195 BC   262
Map 12.2 The Han Empire in 108 BC   264
Map 12.3 The northern zone and the Xiongnu Empire   266
Map 12.4 The Central Asian city–states   270
Map 12.5 Han campaigns against the Xiongnu Empire   274

Preface

When Cambridge University Press's commissioning editor, Marigold Acland, appeared in my office in spring 2006, it was clear to me that our common goal was to produce a book that could offer a first lesson about Early China to the advanced undergraduate and graduate students and any non-specialist readers. It immediately came to mind that the monumental volume *The Cambridge History of Ancient China: From the Origins of Civilization to 221 BC* (edited by Michael Loewe and Edward L. Shaughnessy; Cambridge, 1999) can serve as a rich introduction to Early China. However, it was also understood that the volume's intimidating size and the essentially sinological nature of its presentation leave an immediate need for a future book that could better meet the needs of students beginning to study this critical period of Chinese civilization.

The present book certainly is not a summary of *The Cambridge History of Ancient China*, nor does it intend to show any resemblance to the latter work. Instead, it offers a reinterpretation of the process of formation of Chinese civilization from the beginning of farming life in China to AD 220, the end of the Han Dynasty, informed by many important new archaeological discoveries and the advances they have brought to the field over the past ten years. It would be adventurous if not considerably risky for anyone to try to write a general account of such a long period (in contrast to the short period in which one usually conducts his or her own research), thus exposing oneself to potential criticisms by scholars who have had much longer experience in certain periods or subject areas covered by the book. While this would seem inevitable, for no individual writer can be specialized in all periods, this is still a risk worth taking because a single-author book has the advantage of achieving a higher level of comprehension of the grand trends of development in a civilization. Such trends are observable only over a long span of time based on one's deep understanding of the logic of history, a level that is often difficult to reach by a collaborative work by multiple authors who are informed by different theoretical frameworks and who often insist on opposing views. Therefore, the present book promises to be a consistent account (at least within the book) of early Chinese civilization, although it cannot and should not be the only account of it.

As a historian of China, I have always believed that the best way to understand China's history is to study it as a part of the common human experience in a comparative framework. Over the millennia of early human experience, there have been a number of critical moments, each understood as the result of a social and cultural process, and each has had a major impact on the course of human history: the beginning of agricultural way of life, the formation of regionally based social organization, the chiefdom, the emergence of urban culture, the rise of the state, the emergence of bureaucracy and bureaucratic administration, and the formation of empire. These processes have been widely attested across the globe and discussed in depth by anthropologists and historians alike. The present book takes the social development in Early China towards more massive and more complex organizations as its main line of presentation and explores political and cultural institutions that supported this development. It does so not for the purpose of fitting the Chinese data into a global theory of social development, but to use social theories to help highlight the meaning of great changes in Early China, and to achieve a coherent understanding of the trajectory of early Chinese civilization.

Such a book will fit well, I hope, into Cambridge's new series titled *New Approaches to Asian History*, which promises to introduce to students some of the epoch-making events and developments that have happened in the history of Asia, from its border with Europe to the far Pacific coast, on the collective merit of recent scholarship. The book covers some essential historical facts or events as necessary to clarify the general outline of the history of Early China for non-specialist readers, and scholars who endorse the ultra-skeptical view that nothing is knowable in history, particularly in Early China, cannot avoid finding themselves disappointed. But the author believes that although we will continue to debate about many things that we study, there are basic historical processes in Early China on which most scholars with objective judgment can agree and which can be made the basis for further intellectual inquiry. However, this book is not a simple narrative of the rise and fall of kingdoms and empires, which is in fact impossible to narrate for a long period in Early China due to the absence of reliable written records. Instead, it strikes a balance between a general introduction and a review of our current evidence for Early China, and, as such, it says as much about how history should be viewed as what it really was. For this reason, the discussion within each chapter is arranged around subject topics to allow for consideration of different interpretations as meaningful in highlighting the salient features as well as problems of each period. While discussing the general trends in early Chinese history, it is also hoped that the book will serve as a general introduction to the current scholarship on Early China.

The selection of topics for discussion in this book has been influenced by the content of my course "History of Ancient China to the End of Han" which I have taught many times at Columbia University. Therefore, I would like to first and foremost thank the students who have participated in the course and raised thoughtful questions which have certainly helped enrich the contents of this book. Particularly in the past two years when the manuscript was circulated to the class, students have carefully read and helped me assess the level of difficulty of its presentation as a textbook. One student, Robert Alexander Woodend, deserves special thanks for his help with proofreading a large part of the manuscript prior to its final submission. In a more subtle but definitely sure sense, the book has been nourished enormously by presentations and discussions at the Columbia Early China Seminar, and I am grateful to all members of the seminar for their contributions that have profoundly helped expand the vision of this book. I owe special debt of gratitude to Marigold Acland, a debt that was only deepened by the fact that the book was not able to meet the target for publication before her recent retirement; but at least now with some delay I can fulfill my promise to her. I thank too the anonymous readers appointed by Cambridge University Press who carefully examined the book and offered constructive suggestions to improve it. My thanks are due further to the many friends including Cao Wei, Jiao Nanfeng, Zhang Jianlin, Zhou Ya, Huang Xiaofen, Fang Hui, Liu Li, Chen Xingcan, and Chen Chao-jung who have provided me with new images to be used in the book or helped acquire permissions. The author and publisher also acknowledge the following sources of copyright material and are grateful to the institutions for the permissions they granted. Among them, the Institute of Archaeology, Chinese Academy of Social Sciences, deserves special thanks for generously permitting the use of multiple images it published. Other institutions include the Institute of History and Philology, Academia Sinica (Figs. 1.3 and 9.3), Museum of Fine Arts, Boston (Fig. 6.4), Bloomsbury Publishing, London (Figs. 3.1 and 3.4), Yale University Press (Figs. 2.1, 4.2, 12.1, and 12.4), and the National Museum of China, Beijing (Figs. 3.6 and 4.12). While every effort has been made, it has not always been possible to identify the sources of all material used, or to trace all copyright holders. If any omissions are brought to our notice, we will be happy to include the appropriate acknowledgements on reprinting. Finally, I would also like to thank Lucy Rhymer for her willingness to pick up the responsibility for this book and to oversee its final production.

Chronology of Early China

Early farming communities
Pre-Yangshao   6500–5000 BC
Yangshao Period   5000–3000 BC

Early complex societies
Longshan Period   3000–2000 BC

Early settlement-based states
Erlitou State (Xia Dynasty?)   1900–1555 BC
Shang Dynasty   1554–1046 BC
Zhou Dynasty   1045–256 BC
Western Zhou   1045–771 BC
Eastern Zhou   770–256 BC
Spring and Autumn Period   770–481 BC

Territorial states
Warring States Period   480–221 BC

Early empires
Qin Dynasty   221–207 BC
Han Dynasty   206 BC – AD 220
Western Han   206 BC – AD 8
(New Dynasty)   AD 9–24
Eastern Han   AD 25–220

Collapse of early empire

Map

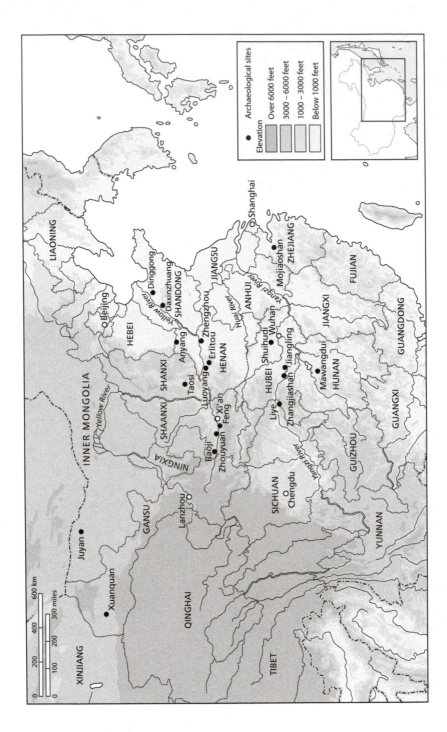

1 Introduction: Early China and its natural and cultural demarcations

"Early China" refers to a long period from the beginning of human history in East Asia to the end of the Eastern Han Dynasty in AD 220, a date that is often, though imprecisely, used to mark China's entry into the Buddhist Era. As the initial period that gave the Chinese civilization much of its foundation, Early China has always served as the gateway to China, by offering a series of essential lessons in government, social practice, art, religion, and philosophical thought, necessary for students of all periods of Chinese history. But in a more general sense, if history is the best way to teach about a culture in which people live, it is perfectly natural that knowledge of Early China can provide what is often the most fundamental explanation of aspects of the social life in modern China and of its underlying values. As a field of research, Early China Studies is one of the areas that have most dramatically benefited from the advancement in modern academia, particularly in the discipline of archaeology which has been renewing daily our understanding of China's distant past. It is also a field that has seen occasional interplay between politics and scholarship, and that has been much shaped by different national or international traditions.

To begin our journey into this distant past, below I will first introduce the natural and temporal settings of Early China as necessary for understanding the social and cultural developments soon to be discussed in this book. For the same purpose, the chapter will then turn to a brief discussion of the process by which Early China Studies has emerged as a modern academic field, and the state of the field will alert the reader to the need not only to see the past, but also to understand the different ways in which it was seen and interpreted.

A Geographical China: Natural Environment

Geographers of China often tend to analyze China's topography in four massive steps: the Qinghai–Tibetan Plateau with an average elevation of 4,000 m above sea level is known as the "Roof of the World." The high

1

plateau combines the territories of the modern Qinghai Province and the Tibet Autonomous Region, taking up about a quarter of the total area of the People's Republic of China (see map of China, p. xxii). The second step extends north and east from the edges of the Qinghai–Tibetan Plateau and it consists of multiple ranges of mountains and high plateaus such as the Loess Plateau and Inner Mongolia, rising to an average height of 1,000–2,000 m above sea level. The third step is formed by floodplains such as the North China Plain, the Manchurian Plain in northeastern China, and the Yangzi Delta in the south, interspersed by hilly grounds generally ranging between 500 and 1,000 m in elevation. The fourth step is the continent itself, extending into the seas beyond the east and south coasts of China.

Even when we are talking only about the areas that can be considered as part of Early China, back in a time when "China" as a nation was still in her infancy, we find that more cultural developments had taken place in the valleys and strips of plains that are surrounded by the mountains and plateaus on the second step mentioned above, or on the transitional belts along the major mountain ranges, but not at the centers of the floodplains located in the east.[1] The reason for this development was simply ecological, given the fact that in the second millennium BC most of the eastern China plains were still covered by marshes and lakes,[2] and the coastline in some sections was at least 150 km inland from today's seashores. The pre-Qin texts record the names of more than forty marshes or lakes on the North China Plain, most of which had dried out after the third century AD. In fact, for millennia the North China Plain was continuously caught in the process of sedimentation by the Yellow River which carried on its way east huge quantities of earth from the topographical second step. The natural environment, particularly landforms and climatic change doubtless had a very major impact on the early development of human society and culture. On the other hand, human subsistence activities could also transform the surface of the earth and cause modifications to the environment in very significant ways, as most dramatically shown by the expansion of the industrial societies in the modern era.

Over the past thirty years, Chinese paleoclimatologists have made significant progress through fieldwork in understanding long-term climate

---

[1] We find analogies of this development in other world regions. For instance, in Mesopotamia early sedentary cultures began in north Iraq and then moved southeastwards to occupy the lower reaches of Tigris and Euphrates close to the Persian Gulf only during the Samara Culture period, dating to c. 5500–4800 BC.

[2] Even in the historical period, it was recorded that the Yellow River had changed its course some twenty-six times.

changes in China across multiple ecological zones (Fig. 1.1).[3] By correlating data from different locations, the researchers were able to isolate a number of periods of important change in the temperature fluctuations over some 11,000 years. As the world was moving out from the last Glacial Age at the end of the Pleistocene Epoch in about 11,700 BP,[4] the temperature in North China climbed up to a level of 3–4 °C higher than the average temperature of the present years, and the precipitation was 40% (150 mm per annum) more than today's. This meant very abundant rainfall and a large number of lakes and marshes in most areas of North China up to perhaps the edges of the Qinghai–Tibetan Plateau, and China as a whole enjoyed very warm and humid weather and thick vegetation prior to the beginning of the agricultural way of life. This high temperature (the long lower curves in Fig. 1.1) continued from 8000 BP to 5000 BP with wide fluctuations in the later millennia until the arrival of the third millennium BP when the temperature suddenly dropped down to below the present-day level.[5] In historical chronology this drop corresponded with the end of the Shang Dynasty (1554–1046 BC) and the early Western Zhou (1045–771 BC) period. But even during most of the Shang Dynasty, the temperature in North China was still about 2 °C higher than today's. After the sudden drop around the beginning of the third millennium BP, temperature rose again for a period of time, but in the most recent 1,500 years, as we move out from Early China, the temperature in North China was mostly considerably colder than it is today.

South China was relatively less affected by the climate changes discussed above. But the south is more mountainous than the north, being divided by the major mountain ranges into largely three independent zones along the Yangzi River: the Sichuan Basin, the middle Yangzi lakes and marshes, and the lower Yangzi Delta. The recent drop in temperature close to the middle of the first millennium AD had also caused some major lakes in South China to shrink and dry up. For instance, in pre-Qin times, a large stretch of the middle Yangzi plain of some 120 km from present-day Wuhan westwards was under the water of

---

[3] The basic method is to drill hundreds of soil samples from riverbeds and lake floors. By analyzing the pollen samples and the various types of ancient plants represented by them, it is possible to reconstruct the outline of long-term temperature fluctuations of a region.

[4] BP (before present) is used in geology for long spans of time, whereas BC (before Christ) is used by historians and archaeologists to represent time in more recent millennia. The Pleistocene Epoch is the geological age in the Earth's history that began in 2,588,000 BP and ended in 11,700 BP, to be followed by the Holocene Epoch (the recent epoch).

[5] See Shi Yafeng and Kong Zhaozheng, et al., "Mid-Holocene Climates and Environments in China," Global and Planetary Change 7 (1993), 222.

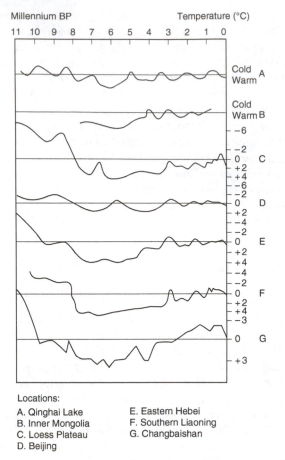

Millennium BP   Temperature (°C)

Locations:
A. Qinghai Lake   E. Eastern Hebei
B. Inner Mongolia   F. Southern Liaoning
C. Loess Plateau   G. Changbaishan
D. Beijing

Fig. 1.1 Temperature fluctuation in China, 11,000 BP to present.

the famous Yunmeng Marsh, known also by its nickname of the "Great Marsh" in historical records. But after the third century AD, most of this marsh had gradually dried up and had long been transformed into agrarian fields surrounding urban centers.

Seafaring along the eastern China coast was certainly possible in Early China as indicated by early cultural contacts widely stretching across the coastal regions from the north to the south. This is also evidenced by the cultural connection in archaeology between the southeast Mainland and the island of Taiwan inhabited by the various groups of the Austronesian-language-speaking people who had further connections to the Pacific Islanders.[6] In the southwest, through the rainforests of present-day Yunnan, cultural contacts with the South Asian subcontinent were established in the late Bronze Age and were expanded under the Qin and Han Empires. In the northwest, there were many oases leading the way west out of China. Although the exchange of material goods and ideas over these oases or broadly across the northern steppe might have begun by the early Bronze Age if not earlier, China's geographic isolation from the inner Asian continent was not completely broken until the first century BC. Even after the discovery of the road into Central Asia in the second century BC by the early Chinese explorers, the trip along the emerging "Silk Road" was known to have been very difficult.

Early China and the Grand Historical Trend

Why "Early China"? Are there compelling reasons for treating Early China as a large and separate phase in Chinese history? As mentioned above the Early China period ends at the fall of the Eastern Han Dynasty in AD 220.[7] There are three general reasons to treat this long period as an integrated field of research and teaching in Chinese history. First, in this early phase civilization, though modified inevitably by interregional influences, evolved on essentially indigenous East Asian ideas, and the development of social and political institutions can be seen as largely an internal process of this subcontinent. However, the expansion of the Han Empire into Central Asia in the first century BC brought China into sustained contact with other major world civilizations, most importantly Middle Eastern and Indian, and the subsequent introduction of Buddhism to China gave Chinese civilization a totally different dimension, a drastic beginning of a new era. In world history, this shift paralleled the transition from the Classical to the Christian West. Second, there is a common source base offered by archaeology. Even for the later part of the period

---

[6] "Austronesian" is a language family widely distributed throughout the Pacific and the Southeast Asian islands and peninsulas as far west as Madagascar. On the linguistic divisions of Early China, see E. G. Pulleyblank, "The Chinese and Their Neighbors in Prehistorical and Early Historical Times," in David N. Keightley (ed.), *The Origins of Chinese Civilization* (Berkeley: University of California Press, 1983), pp. 411–466.

[7] A clear temporal demarcation of "Early China" is found in the editorial remarks of the inaugural issue of the journal of *Early China*, by David N. Keightley, who explained the goal of the journal as: "*Early China* is a newsletter devoted to the dissemination of information and the testing of new ideas in the fields of pre-historic, Shang, Chou [Zhou], and Han China."

when substantial information has become available from the received texts, documents (particularly legal statutes unearthed from underground) still constitute the most critical basis for our inquiry. Third, particularly because of the nature of sources, many being created before the unification of the Chinese writing system around 221 BC, the study of Early China is deeply indebted to the methodological support of paleography which deals with various forms of archaic scripts and inscriptions.

Although everything that dates before the end of the Eastern Han falls reasonably within the confines of Early China, by convention we choose to begin with the emergence of early farming communities in China in about the seventh millennium BC,[8] particularly in the lands reached by the Yellow and Yangzi Rivers. Over the next two millennia in the greater part of eastern China these original farming societies had developed into large-scale cultural complexes with regional characteristics. During the late fourth millennium BC, early complex societies began to emerge in a number of regions which were each organized into a settlement hierarchy, headed by a large political center that was often surrounded by rammed earth walls.[9] This stage was followed, first in limited areas in North and South China, by intense social development into early states, or state-level societies. In North China, these early states are best known from archaeology and history to have been ruled by the dynastic houses such as that of Shang (1554–1046 BC) and of Western Zhou (1045–771 BC). Therefore, they can be called the early "royal states." The collapse of the Western Zhou state in 771 BC and the lack of a true central authority thereafter opened ways to fierce inter-state warfare that continued over the next five hundred years until the Qin unification of China in 221 BC, thus giving China her first empire. Finally, after the consolidation of the imperial bureaucratic system under the Western Han Empire (206 BC – AD 8), the period ended with the collapse of the Eastern Han Empire (AD 25–220).

Therefore, in Early China we observe the rise and fall of social organizations at different levels and scales, and it is the focus of this book to trace and explain the development of society from the early farming villages to states and then to empires. If we take a proportional view of the whole of Chinese history, Early China would have been the longest period and the

---

[8] The development of human society and particularly the human body in the preceding Paleolithic period was shaped more by natural than cultural processes, to be dealt most effectively in the domain of science based on global contexts. Therefore, it is not tied to the cultural–geographical mass that we call "Early China."

[9] In its anthropological definition, the term "complex society" denotes a society that had at least two and often more strata, and a centrally directed decision-making process, centering on the power of the chief.

one that saw the most dramatic social changes and political developments. This was also a long process during which cultural traits originally developed in regional contexts were gradually modified and merged to characterize what can be called the distinctive Chinese civilization.

Rediscovering China's Antiquity

Although the concept of "Early China" was formed relatively recently, the study of the period has had a much longer history in both China and the West. It is commonly held that three major discoveries at the turn of the twentieth century opened new windows to China's past and contributed directly to the rise of modern historiography in China: first, the discovery in 1899 of inscriptions carved on oracle bones and shells of the Shang Dynasty in Anyang in northern Henan, second, the discovery in 1900 of a secret inventory of medieval manuscripts totaling some 50,000 items in a Buddhist cave in Dunhuang on the edge of the desert in western Gansu Province, and third, the disposal in 1909 and the subsequent reclamation of the Ming and Qing Dynasty archival documents from the imperial palace in Beijing. These are very important cultural events that had multiple implications for modern Chinese history and for the world beyond it.

Although the last two discoveries fall outside of the confines of Early China, the British explorer Aurel Stein, on his way to Dunhuang, excavated some 700 bamboo strips with writing on them from a desert fortress (which has recently been re-excavated), a discovery that was to lead to a long series of findings of administrative documents from the Western Han Empire in and out of the region. The strips from Dunhuang were subsequently studied and published, since Stein was unable to study them himself, by Édouard Chavannes (1865–1918) (Fig. 1.2a), a French scholar in Beijing and the reputed founding father of Western sinology. Chavannes by this time had just published his translation of the most important historical text from ancient China, the *Grand Scribe's Records* (Shiji), written by Sima Qian in the first century BC. When Chavannes's book on the Dunhuang strips was brought to China, it was reproduced and further annotated by prominent Chinese scholars in new editions.

The Dunhuang manuscripts, combined with the historical texts that Chavannes knew well, provided an important context in which a generation of early French sinologists was trained with a clear focus on philology and historical linguistics, an interest that was certainly not restricted to the Han Chinese language, given the fact that nearly ten languages are represented in the Dunhuang materials. But gradually the French interest

(a)   (b)

Fig. 1.2 Pioneers of early sinology: (a) Édouard Chavannes, (b) Wang
Guowei.

was expanded to various fields of history and religious studies, and in the
hands of the Swedish sinologist Bernhard Karlgren the research scope of
early sinology was further expanded to include the study of material
objects, particularly the bronze vessels and their inscriptions.[10]

In China itself, the discovery of oracle bones, which were by and large
handled by the Chinese dealers, had led to their collection and subsequent
study and publication by scholars who also worked on Shang and Western
Zhou Dynasty bronze inscriptions recorded in the native antiquarian
tradition since the Song Dynasty (AD 960–1279). In particular the
scholar Wang Guowei (1877–1927) (Fig. 1.2b), Professor at Tsinghua
University after years of exile in Japan after the fall of the Qing Dynasty to
which he owed his loyalty, produced a long series of essays that address
religious and cultural institutions of the early royal states Shang and
Western Zhou. Wang's works set the fundamental tone of research for

---

[10] For the early history of Western sinology, consult: D. Honey, *Incense at the Altar:
Pioneering Sinologists and the Development of Classical Chinese Philology* (New Haven:
American Oriental Society, 2001), pp. 1–40; H. Franke, "In Search of China: Some
General Remarks on the History of European Sinology," in *Europe Studies China: Papers
from an International Conference on the History of European Sinology* (London: Han-Shan
Tang Books, 1992), pp. 11–23.

Fig. 1.3 Excavators at Anyang wearing bronze helmets freshly excavated from the Shang royal tomb no. 1004; photograph taken in 1935 during the twelfth excavation. In the middle, playing the role of a Shang King, is Shi Zhangru, senior archaeologist in the Academia Sinica; to his left (behind) is Xia Nai who went on to serve as the Director of the Institute of Archaeology in Beijing from 1962 to 1982. Shi holds a long bronze knife on his arm; the man on the right, Wang Xiang, has a cat sleeping on his arm.

modern historical studies of Early China which was based largely on excavated paleographical materials. The identification of the oracle-bone inscriptions as the divination records of the late Shang royal court led to the excavation of the Shang capital in Anyang in northern Henan in 1928, a notable beginning of Chinese archaeology. Until Japan's full-scale invasion of North China began in July 1937, the Academia Sinica in Nanjing planned and executed fifteen large-scale excavations in Anyang, uncovering both the royal palace zone and the cemetery of Shang kings, yielding huge quantities of materials including of course more oracle bones (Fig. 1.3). As the excavation there was resumed after the war and has continued to the present day, Anyang archaeology has played a central role in our understanding of the Shang Dynasty, and of early Chinese civilization in general.

However, modern Chinese historiography had many different roots, and it was never a homogeneous tradition. While Wang was pursuing a research method that aimed to re-establish China's antiquity on the basis of corroboration of excavated data with the transmitted historical records, a new trend of essentially textual scholarship argued for the total rejection of the traditional view of history. The deepening frustration with China's political reality since the late nineteenth century had come to a head in the May Fourth Movement in 1919. The reflection of this political–cultural current in historical studies was the so-called "Doubting Antiquity" movement led by Gu Jiegang (1893–1980), a young graduate from Beijing University who began in 1921 to formulate his own theory of Chinese history. To Gu, the received textual tradition about China's antiquity was the piling up of layered fabrications produced in the later periods, because quite obviously texts dated later, particularly from the Han Dynasty, often have more to say than early texts about their contemporary time. Although these sources can be used to study the intellectual mentality of the Warring States to Han times, they are ultimately invalid as sources for early history.[11] In the words of Gu's spiritual mentor Hu Shih, China's history has to be cut short by at least two thousand years, to start only with the Eastern Zhou period (770–256 BC).

The revolutionary role of Gu and his colleagues in undermining the authority of the received tradition should not be underestimated – by doing so they had taken traditional Chinese historiography along the very first step towards modernization. However, as serious scholarship the "Doubting Antiquity" movement was weakened by a number of logical problems. Not only did Gu and his followers conduct research almost entirely neglecting the already promising solid progress that had been made by scholars like Wang Guowei, in most cases the persuasiveness of their argument for the late fabrication of a certain tradition depended entirely on the *non-existence* of relevant records in the earlier period, which was itself an argument that cannot be proven. When such proof does turn up through archaeology as in many cases where texts were judged later forgeries by Gu and his followers, they are bound to be on the losing side.[12] But in a more general sense, the "Doubting Antiquity"

---

[11] Gu publicized the theory in his autobiography in the first issue of *Gushibian* (Debating Ancient History) in 1927. Seven issues of the journal had been published before 1941, standing as the central literature of the "Doubting Antiquity" movement. For an English literature on Gu Jiegang, see L. A. Schneider, *Ku Chieh-kang and China's New History: Nationalism and the Quest for Alternative Tradations* (Berkeley: University of California Press, 1971).

[12] The principle by which Gu and his followers operated is also undermined by another logic – the earlier we move up in time, the fewer sources have survived to the modern days.

scholarship simplified the study of history to the study of the dates of texts, and this resulted in a very narrow view of history. As essentially a textual scholarship, it failed to respond to the changes in the Early China field that on the whole turned to rely more and more on contemporaneous paleographical and archaeological materials. Because of these problems, the "Doubting Antiquity" movement has been largely sidelined by mainstream historiography both in the Mainland and on Taiwan after the 1950s, which has adopted a more positive attitude towards transmitted historical records.

Crossing the sea eastwards to Japan, the "Doubting Antiquity" position was anticipated in works by scholars like Shiratori Kurakichi (1865–1942) who, operating in a completely different intellectual context, spent much of his life attempting to disprove the actual existence of the legendary emperors down to the founder of the reputed Xia Dynasty. However, a parallel development took place particularly in the areas of oracle bone and bronze studies where Japan soon produced her first generation of scholars at a time when such scholarship was also in the formative stage in China. Given Japan's strong tradition of Chinese textual scholarship, encouraged further by visits by eminent Chinese scholars since the early twentieth century, Japan has been one of the birthplaces of modern sinology outside China. In particularly Guo Moruo (1892–1978), the most ingenious modern scholar of bronze inscriptions and a leading Marxist historian of Early China, completed most of his research work while taking refuge in Japan after the Nationalists–Communist split in 1928.

It is true that since the 1930s both Chinese and Japanese traditions of historical scholarship have been heavily influenced by Marxist social theories. But particularly because of the unofficial position of Marxism in Japan after the war, Japanese scholars, while using certain Marxist concepts for social analysis, were able to break away from the confines of Historical Materialism and the Marxist periodization of history, popularly and politically endorsed in China. This allowed Japanese scholars to generate new research paradigms and to explore new topics in the Early China field. As a result, Japanese sinology was able to maintain its high standards through the 1950s to the early 1970s, while in China scholarly rigor had completely given way to political zeal. In general, it can be said that Japanese scholarship has the advantage of balancing detailed evidential research with broad theoretical perspectives, and this played no small

---

Given the impressive number of new texts discovered in Warring States tombs over the past three decades, one is only left to wonder just how much had vanished in history before the Qin unification of China in 221 BC.

role in the production by Japanese scholars of some of the finest works in the socioeconomic history of Early China.

The Recent Development of a North American Tradition of Early China Studies

Herrlee G. Creel (1905–94), a native of Chicago who had just earned a Ph.D. in Chinese philosophy, and studied Chinese with Berthold Laufer (1874–1934) at the Field Museum of Natural History in Chicago, arrived in China in 1931 with the purpose of furthering his understanding of China's early past. Creel had gone to China at a time when there were only a very few intellectuals in North America who had a serious scholarly interest in Early China. While in China Creel maintained close contacts with pioneering scholars in the Academia Sinica and made a number of tours to observe the excavation that was taking place in Anyang. Back in the United States in 1936 as a professor at the University of Chicago, Creel soon published his book, *The Birth of China*,[13] which offered a suitable new introduction to Early Chinese civilization for a Western audience who had so far been reading solely the French scholarship. Chicago in this period also served as the focus for visits by distinguished scholars from China, whose interests complemented those of the university's own faculty in the early period of Chinese history.[14] By the end of the 1950s, with a few more scholars whose interests fell in periods before the end of Han taking up teaching posts in major universities, a rudimental curriculum for the study of Early China was established in North America. However, it was in the hands of the students of these early scholars that Early China became an established academic field defined by its own scholarly organization, which has published the journal *Early China* since 1975. In the words of David N. Keightley, respected founder of the journal and the first true American specialist of the Shang oracle-bone inscriptions: "If modern China is to be understood in sympathy and in depth its ancient history cannot be ignored. The study of early China has a legitimate place in modern curriculums; we must ensure that its value is appreciated."[15]

However, with relatively weak roots (compared to the situation in Europe and Japan) in past scholarship except in such fields as art history

---

[13] See H. G. Creel, *The Birth of China: A Survey of the Formative Period of Chinese Civilization* (New York: Frederick Ungar, 1937).

[14] Among these visitors the most significant were Dong Zuobin, a leading scholar of Shang oracle-bone inscriptions, and Chen Mengjia, a young and ingenious scholar of bronzes and bronze inscriptions.

[15] *Early China* 2 (1976), i.

and philology inherited from European sinology, North American scholars of Early China came under the very strong influence of the "Doubting Antiquity" movement originating in China. Not only was Gu's autobiography translated into English almost immediately after its publication in China, a monographic study of Gu's life and scholarship by Laurence A. Schneider was published just a few years before the journal of *Early China* was founded, making Gu the best-known modern Chinese historian in America.[16] Against this special background, North American scholarship on Early China not only grew in its youth in near isolation from China as China was closed to the Western world after 1950; it has also taken the path of debating with China, particularly in the past twenty years, on a number of major issues such as the historicity of the Xia Dynasty, or broadly about the process by which Chinese civilization was formed and China had become a nation.

At the bottom of the debate is a fundamental difference with regard to the value of the transmitted textual information about China's antiquity. While the "Doubting Antiquity" agenda continues to shape the essential intellectual attitude of many in the field in North America, in China and Taiwan the scholarly traditions have grown farther and farther apart from that lineage. While blessed by the spirit of criticism which in many cases rescued North American scholars from falling into the trap of traditional historiography, few have been really aware of the problems of logic that handicapped the "Doubting Antiquity" school and of the resultant loss of research opportunities. However, it is fair to say that scholars who hold the view of ultra-skepticism so thoroughly as to totally deny the value of the received textual tradition for understanding China's early past are few, while the majority of Early China scholars continue to employ traditional textual records in their study of early Chinese civilization. In better situations, the transmitted textual records would be used in conjunction with excavated paleographical or material data to achieve a more balanced, and less partial, understanding of antiquity.

There has always been the question of whether the sinological traditions described above, those of China, Japan, and the West (European and American), are three distinctive domains of scholarship, or if they can be regarded as one coherent intellectual enterprise. This is a very hard question. But perhaps the arrival of the new millennium has made both the question and the possible answers to it less important if not irrelevant as the tendency towards globalization is affecting all areas of human life. The digitalization of both textual and epigraphic sources and the

---

[16] See Schneider, *Ku Chieh-kang and China's New History.*

electronic publication of new materials have made it possible for scholars outside China to respond to new discoveries almost as quickly as do most scholars in China. The growing wealth of China has offered more Chinese scholars opportunities to study in Western universities and for more Western students to study in China; as a result, the younger generations of scholars will become more familiar with different scholarly traditions and be more receptive to different views. The study of Early China was the product of international effort from the beginning, and it will continue to see higher levels of international collaboration in the future.

SELECTED READING

Honey, David, *Incense at the Altar: Pioneering Sinologists and the Development of Classical Chinese Philology* (New Haven: American Oriental Society, 2001).

Franke, Herbert, "In Search of China: Some General Remarks on the History of European Sinology," in *Europe Studies China: Papers from an International Conference on the History of European Sinology* (London: Han-Shan Tang Books, 1992), pp. 11–23.

Schneider, Laurence A., *Ku Chieh-kang and China's New History: Nationalism and the Quest for Alternative Traditions* (Berkeley: University of California Press, 1971).

Dirlik, Arif, *Revolution and History: The Origins of Marxist Historiography in China, 1919–1937* (Berkeley: University of California Press, 1978).

Creel, Herrlee G., *The Birth of China: A Survey of the Formative Period of Chinese Civilization* (New York: Frederick Ungar, 1937).

2 The development of complex society in China

When the Swedish geologist Johan Gunnar Andersson (1874–1960) discovered the Yangshao culture in western Henan in 1921 (Map 2.1), he did not fail to suppose a connection over a few millennia between this early Neolithic culture and the cultures known to have been those of the Zhou and Han, but he was also quick to trace the origin of the Yangshao culture far to the West, pointing to western Asia.[1] In our time that no longer favors diffusionist agendas,[2] Neolithic cultures worldwide are more often than not regarded to have been products of particular regions and to be explained by regional environmental and ecological differences, rather than having a common origin. Regional cultures are related to one another through mutual influence or stimulation, and cultures in different regions have passed through similar stages of social development along a line of increasing complexity. Therefore, in the contemporary study of Neolithic cultures, "geographical regions" play a very important role in our understanding of the human past.

Theories of Neolithic Cultural Development in China

The early cultural development of China has been traditionally considered as a process of continuing expansion of civilization from the so-called "Central Plain" (or North China Plain), roughly corresponding to

[1] See Johan Gunnar Andersson, *Children of the Yellow Earth: Studies in Prehistoric China* (New York: Macmillan, 1934), pp. 224–225. Andersson, a pioneer of the study of Neolithic cultures in China, was affiliated to the National Geological Survey, having been hired by the Chinese government in 1914. Neolithic cultures worldwide differ from one another vastly, but they share some common features: the use of polished stone tools, the technology to manufacture pottery wares, subsistence dependent on agriculture and the domestication of animals, and the sedentary way of communal life.

[2] "Diffusionism" is an anthropological theory popular in the nineteenth and early twentieth centuries. It holds that all world cultures ultimately originated from one or at most a limited number of culture centers. Similarities between cultures are regarded as the result of diffusion of traits from one society to another, and cultural relations are viewed in terms of cultural genealogy.

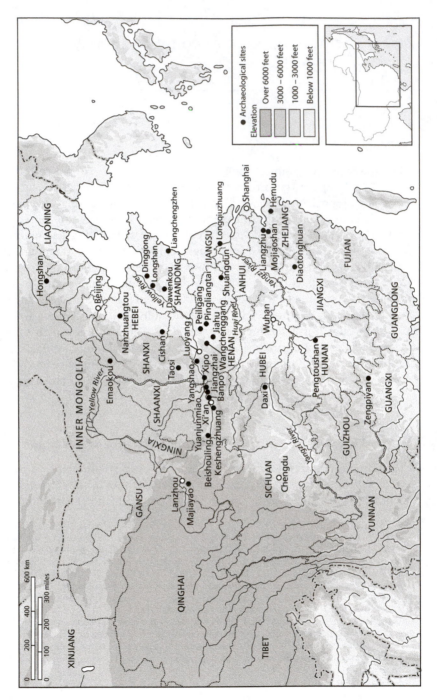

Map 2.1 Major Neolithic archaeological sites in China.

present-day Henan Province on the middle and lower reaches of the Yellow River, inhabited by a core Chinese population, to the peripheral regions that were known to have been lands occupied by the various groups of "barbarians." This view was of course inherited in the traditional historiography of China which represented the worldview of the unitary political states based for the greater part of Chinese history on North China. When Andersson discovered the Yangshao culture, its location in western Henan seemingly lent support to this theory, although Andersson gave the culture an origin farther in the west.

In the 1930s, two sites of the Neolithic Longshan culture on the Shandong Peninsula were excavated which yielded finely made black or gray pottery wares, in contrast to the red–brown-surfaced pottery of the Yangshao culture, often colorfully painted with patterns representing plants or fish. This prompted archaeologists to popularize a bipolar paradigm of cultural development in Early China: it was argued that the Yangshao culture represented the culture of the Chinese nation in the distant past, which was located in the slightly western part of North China, and the Longshan culture represented the "barbarian" culture in the east coastal region. However, later work soon proved that this version of a Neolithic world divided into two halves was merely a reflection of the lack of knowledge in the early stage of Chinese archaeology about cultural developments in other regions. Breaking away from this bipolar paradigm, a new and much more complicated picture of Neolithic cultures gradually emerged from the 1970s onwards as the result of full-scale archaeological work in China and the application of scientific methods of dating. In this new picture, the Yangshao and Longshan cultures are best seen as representatives of two large stages of development of the Neolithic cultures of various types in different regions of North China. In South China, a series of advanced Neolithic cultures contemporary to these two stages have also been identified and intensively studied to reveal their relations to each other and to their neighboring cultures in the north.

This new "multi-region" model of Neolithic cultural development in China was described in a lengthy article published in 1981 co-authored by the senior archaeologist Su Binqi and his younger colleague Yin Weizhang in the Institute of Archaeology. Known as the theory of "Regional Systems and Cultural Types," it divided China proper into six regions: the middle Yellow River, Shandong and eastern coastal region, Hubei and the middle Yangzi, the lower Yangzi Delta, central southern China and the south coast, and the north region along the Great Wall. The analysis emphasizes continuity of cultural traditions within each region, viewed as a gigantic and proto-independent sociocultural system posed in a distinctive environmental setting, and with distinctions between regions. Importantly in this new model, the Central Plain, the cradle of Chinese civilization in traditional historiography, has become just one among the several others that are considered equally important to the development of civilization in China.[3] It has been said, mostly by Su's disciples, that this was his most important contribution to archaeological theory. However, taking it more succinctly the new theory does little more than synthesize what had already been revealed by the extensive archaeological work in China. But it did provide a powerful analytical tool for explaining Neolithic cultural development in China, and it has been widely accepted since its publication.

It is interesting that this "multi-region" theory was developed in complete isolation from Western academia, but it shows a strong resemblance to the "multilinear" model of social development as the cornerstone of the Neo-evolutionist theory popular since the early 1960s.[4] Perhaps because of this theoretical orientation, the "multi-region" theory has also won some acceptance in the West. Developing from it, the late Professor K. C. Chang of Harvard University proposed his theory of the "Chinese Interaction Sphere" in 1986. In Chang's model, the regions not only played the role of hotbeds for independent cultural development, but also provided the reasons for it. According to this theory, the regions, while maintaining their unique cultural traditions through much of the Neolithic period, had in fact stimulated each other to grow in complexity and to move on to higher stages of social development (Fig. 2.1).[5] Although hardline critics may criticize Chang for the use of the term "Chinese" in this early period, few scholars have seriously wanted to reject his theory.

However, what the "multi-region" theory or the improved "Chinese Interaction Sphere" theory cannot explain is the question why, given that the Central Plain was only one among the many equally important regions in Neolithic China, early states emerged first in the Central Plain and continued to grow and prosper there afterwards, but not in other regions. This is certainly a major interpretive problem. Moreover, the "multi-region" paradigm has provided a limiting power which typified, if not

---

[3] For a discussion of this regionalist paradigm in Chinese archaeology, see L. von Falkenhausen, "The Regionalist Paradigm in Chinese Archaeology," in Philip L. Kohl and Clare Fawcett (eds.), *Nationalism, Politics and the Practice of Archaeology* (Cambridge: Cambridge University Press, 1995), pp. 198–217.

[4] "Neo-evolutionism" is a social theory that was developed in American anthropology in the 1960s. Neo-evolutionist theories accept the essential idea of evolution of Charles Darwin, but they allow different tracks of evolution, called "multilinear evolution" in the words of Julian Steward (1955), and reject the idea of universal social progress. For a first reading, see Julian H. Steward, *Theory of Culture Change: The Methodology of Multilinear Evolution* (Urbana: University of Illinois Press, 1972; first edn. 1955).

[5] K. C. Chang, *The Archaeology of Ancient China*, 4th edn. (New Haven: Yale University Press, 1986) p. 234.

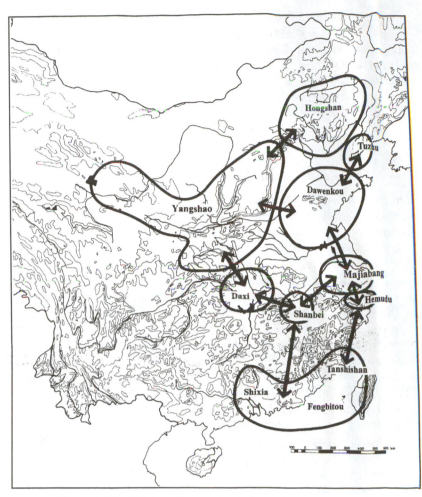

Fig. 2.1 The "Chinese Interaction Spheres."

simplified, the practice of Chinese archaeology into the sole pursuit of cultural chronology and genealogy. Therefore, since the 1990s there have been some important new trends among archaeologists in China to rethink the previous framework of Neolithic cultural development and to break the stranglehold of the regionalist theory in favor of new research paradigms. In an article published in 1998, Professor Yan Wenming of Beijing University argues that, although most regions in China show comparable cultural developments, the Central Plain region for the greater part of the Neolithic period was often if not always at a higher stage in social development. The Central Plain constantly generated and radiated new cultural elements to other regions while taking in stimuli from the latter peripheral regions. This advantageous position of the north in cultural development led to its arrival at civilization earlier than all other regions.[6] However, what still needs to be explained is what really gave the Central Plain such an advantage in cultural development.

Theories of Social Development

The above theories dealt strictly with Neolithic cultural development within China and with the roles different regions had played in the process of the formation of Chinese civilization. What they have left out is the question of how and by what standard social developments in China can be measured. For a long time, particularly during the early decades of the People's Republic of China, archaeologists in China had been strongly motivated to see social progress in Neolithic China in terms of a transition from a matrilineal society to patrilineal society according to Marxist theory. Thus there was a major split between the old Marxist theories that guided Neolithic studies in China and the research paradigms developed in the West since the 1960s, a gap that the Chinese archaeologists have struggled hard to bridge since the breakdown of the ideological confines in the 1980s. This trend continued through the 1990s as these latter theories were continuously brought to China by Western colleagues along with new methods of archaeological fieldwork. Although it came as no surprise that some senior archaeologists were still not ready to give up the old Marxist framework they were so used to, younger generations of scholars felt free to use new Western concepts and vocabulary in their research. As these new Western theories become more and more relevant to Chinese archaeology, it is necessary to offer a brief coverage of the ground here.

In the Western world, the old evolutionist theory of social development put all existing societies from modern Europe to the Asia–Pacific region on a single evolutionary tree. This met a strong challenge in the 1930s–1940s from the so-called "Cultural Particularism" of Franz Boas (1858–1942), who opposed the rule of universal progress and the evolution of society from lower to higher levels. The Marxist theory about matrilineal and patrilineal societies arose from the same idea of universal progress. From

---

[6] On this new trend, see the summary by Xingcan Chen, "Archaeological Discoveries in the People's Republic of China and Their Contribution to the Understanding of Chinese History," *Bulletin of the History of Archaeology* 19.2 (2009), 4–13.

...er, as the West became more and more confident a...
...asing living standards brought by advances in technol...
...t view was revived. This "Neo-evolutionism" emphasiz...
...advancement as the foundation for social progress and
...logical factors as the ultimate cause of cultural change. Its
"m... ar evolution" also allows the possibility of deviations from the
main line of evolution. This theoretical reorientation taking place mainly in
American anthropology gave rise to a Neo-evolutionist scheme of social
development, described in the works of Elman Service and Marshall
Sahlins as: band – tribe – chiefdom – state.[7] Despite some recent critical
reflections, this theory remains important to anthropologists and archaeologists alike worldwide who strive to understand social development in a
comparative framework.

The tribal organization in its most typical form, in Sahlins's interpretation, can also be described as the "segmentary lineage system" which means
a lineage with a shared ancestor but internally divided into many segments
which stand equal to each other; there is also a correspondence between the
genealogical distance of the segments and the geographical distance in
the location of the segments.[8] The "chiefdom" is a critical invention by the
Neo-evolutionists who regarded it a social organization significantly higher
than the segmentary lineage system. In chiefdoms a process of centralized
decision-making already took place, so did regional control, associated with
which was a certain degree of social stratification. The chief's power is
limited in comparison to that of a king as he exercises it through negotiation
and by example, not by coercive means. The further development of power
concentration would lead a society to reach the level of a state.

However, to archaeologists such political processes as decision-making
are simply not as immediately detectable in most contexts as they are to
anthropologists who deal with societies that still operate; therefore, there is
considerable difficulty in applying the above theory of social development
to material remains, especially with regard to a distinction between chiefdom and state. The concept of "complex society" was thus invented by
archaeologists to study material cultures in terms of the degree of complexity
without having to fit them into either the "chiefdom" or "state" model at the
beginning of their research. In Norman Yoffee's description, a "complex

[7] Marshall D. Sahlins, "Political Power and the Economy in Primitive Society," in
G. E. Dole and R. L. Carneiro (eds.), *Essays in the Science of Culture in Honor of Leslie
A. White* (New York: Crowell, 1960), pp. 390–415; Marshall D. Sahlins and Elman
R. Service (eds.), *Evolution and Culture* (Ann Arbor: University of Michigan Press,
1960); E. R. Service, *Primitive Social Organization* (New York: Random House, 1962).
[8] See Marshall D. Sahlins, "The Segmentary Lineage: An Organization of Predatory
Expansion," *American Anthropologist* 63.2 (1961), 322–345.

ty" is qualified by the following relatively loose criteria: (1) a cult. n subsystems performing diverse functions with relative autonomy; (2) e development of centrality; (3) social inequality leading to hierarchy in erms of health and social status; (4) increased number of occupational roles such as ruler, administrator, clerks, soldiers.[9] It is apparent that "complex society" encompasses a complex array of societies at very different levels of social development, but it does not fail to be the first stepping-stone in understanding social changes across millennia of history.

Early Farming Communities

As discussed in Chapter 1, the transition to Neolithic life in China was achieved under much more favorable climatic conditions when the average annual temperature in North China was 3–4 °C higher than the present-day temperature and the lakes on average were some 4.5 m above today's level. Interestingly in China the three critical inventions that made Neolithic life possible – agriculture, the manufacture of pottery ware, and sedentary life – seem to have taken place in more or less the same period of time, being different from some other regions such as Mesopotamia where agriculture and sedentary life appeared around 10,000 BP, predating pottery-making by some two millennia.

It is now widely accepted that farming began in North China roughly concomitant with the rise of the Cishan–Peiligang culture in eastern Henan and southern Hebei with sites dated mostly between 6500 and 5000 BC.[10] Earlier signs of Neolithic culture were found in 1987 at a site in Hebei Province which yielded a few primitive pottery shards mixed with stone tools; the carbon-14 samples derived from the site have been dated to 10,815–9,700 BP, being the earliest of Neolithic culture in North China.[11] Possibly even earlier, at Emaokou in northern Shanxi, a stone-tool workshop site was found, dating probably to the transition from the Paleolithic to the Neolithic period; it yielded regularly shaped stone hoes and sickles,

---

[9] Norman Yoffee, *Myths of the Archaic State: Evolution of the Earliest Cities, States, and Civilization* (Cambridge: Cambridge University Press, 2005), p, 16.

[10] In archaeology, the name of a non-literate culture is usually derived from the site where its remains were first identified. But sometimes variations do occur when a culture is renamed after its most representative, and usually most prominent site.

[11] This is the Nanzhuangtou site in Hebei. The carbon-14 dating method was developed by Willard F. Libby in 1946 at the University of Chicago. Carbon-14 is one of the carbon isotopes. It exists in all living organisms at an even level and decreases at a constant rate (half of the amount of the radioisotope at any given time will be lost in the succeeding 5,730 years) after the organism dies. By measuring the amount of carbon-14 that still remains, the age of the organism can be determined. Carbon-14 dating was introduced to China in the 1960s, and is now widely used in Chinese archaeology.

Fig. 2.2 Peiligang and Jiahu: 1, cooking vessel; 2, stone sickle blade; 3, three-legged bowl; 4, stone quern and roller; 5, oracle shell; 6, rice impression on clay.

indicating the possibility of agriculture at that time. But scholars have not agreed on how to fit the assemblage into the general chain of evolution before the coming of a firmly established agricultural economy.

The settlements of the Cishan–Peiligang culture are normally small, measuring about 1–2 ha, never exceeding 6 ha, with features such as simple subterranean dwelling structures and storage pits. Pottery types are simple and three-legged bowls and jars are common, fired at a relatively high temperature; surface treatments are rare but may feature loose cord impressions (Fig. 2.2). At the Cishan site in Hebei, 80 of the 120 ash pits yielded remains of grain and the charcoal samples were determined to have been millet. At the Peiligang site in Henan, charcoal samples of millet were also excavated. By now, some twenty sites contemporary with Cishan–Peiligang have been identified in the Yellow River regions from Shaanxi in the west to Shandong in the east, many being considered "fountainheads" of the "regional" cultures that prospered thereafter according to the "multi-region" theory, and many have yielded charcoal grain samples. These findings suggest that the Cishan–Peiligang culture represents a widely existing first stage of cultural development in the Yellow

River valley. They also suggest that farming and sedentary life had already become widespread in North China in the seventh to sixth millennia BC and that millet was the staple crop under cultivation by early communities of village-dwellers. A recently reported site is Jiahu in southern Henan, measuring 5.5 ha and belonging to the millet-farming Cishan–Peiligang culture. However, in a chunk of burnt earth, impressions of ten grains of rice were discovered (Fig. 2.2), securely dated to 6500–5500 BC. The discovery revealed an alternative food strategy available to the Cishan–Peiligang communities, but it also raises the question about the region where rice was first domesticated. At the same site, archaeologists also discovered the earliest tortoiseshell most likely used for divination purposes, inscribed with two isolated graphs.

It had been thought for a long time that rice was domesticated and cultivated first in South China, centering on certain sites located near Hangzhou Bay, dating around 5000 BC (roughly contemporary to the Yangshao culture in the north), and easily predating South Asia, the other center for rice cultivation in the ancient world, by at least 2,000 years. It took at least the same length of time for the rice agriculture that originated in South China to reach the Korean Peninsula in the north and Southeast Asia in the south. However, recent discoveries have pushed the date of rice domestication far back by at least two millennia, pointing to the inland basins along the Yangzi River. In two early Neolithic sites in Hunan Province, carbon-14 dated to 7500–6100 BC, charcoal remains of rice have been found either in pottery bodies, or in a large quantity of as many as 15,000 grains in a section of a moat surrounding what was probably the earliest defense wall in China.[12] Further research has even detected a transitional stage from an economy possibly dependent on the gathering of wild rice to an economy based on the production of domesticated rice – at the site of Diaotonghuan in Jiangxi Province, wild rice was gathered in the early period and domesticated rice was found in the later period, thus fixing this epic-making moment in human history at around 10,000 BC.

In recent years, archaeologists have also made efforts to understand the process by which pottery-making technology was invented in China. In the excavation of the cave site at Zengpiyan in Guangxi, archaeologists were able to define a sequence of strata in which early pottery remains were identified. From the period I stratum, dated to 12,000–11,000 BP, were found a few coarsely made and thick shards, fired at a low temperature. From period II, dated to 11,000–10,000 BP (c. 9100–8000 BC) pottery shards were found that were much better made, their surfaces

[12] Gray W. Crawford, "East Asian Plant Domestication," in Miriam T. Stark (ed.), *Archaeology of Asia* (Malden: Blackwell, 2006), pp. 83–84.

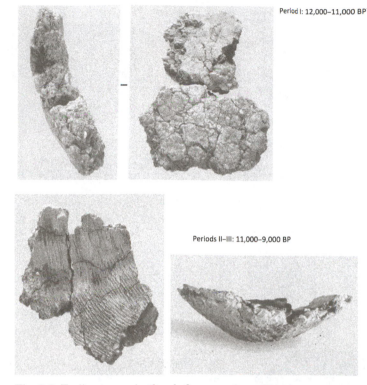

Period I: 12,000–11,000 BP

Periods II–III: 11,000–9,000 BP

Fig. 2.3 Earliest ceramic shards from southern China.

decorated with patterns, and fired at a higher temperature (Fig. 2.3). Although the subsistence pattern of the Zengpiyan society was likely to have been based on fishing and gathering, the findings offer good lessons as to how pottery-making was developed from its infancy, perhaps in a stage even earlier than in North China.

Yangshao Society: Segmentary Lineages?

We have no true data that would help us understand the community life in the Cishan–Peiligang culture or its contemporaneous cultures in North and South China. This of course may reflect the limit of archaeological fieldwork, but it can also be surmised that although sedentary life was widely established in North China, the size of human communities was still rather small and the period of site occupation was relatively short,

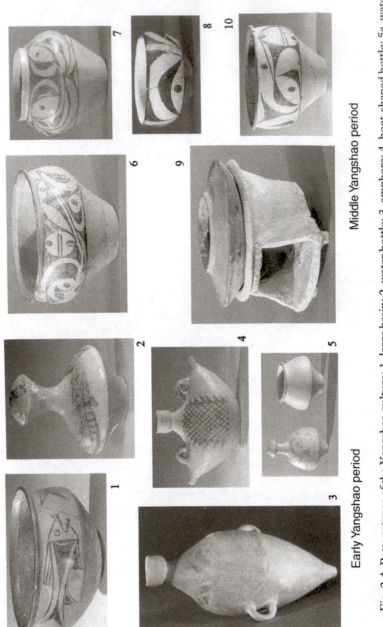

Early Yangshao period

Middle Yangshao period

Fig. 2.4 Pottery types of the Yangshao culture: 1, large basin; 2, water bottle; 3, amphora; 4, boat-shaped bottle; 5a, water bottle; 5b, storage jar; 6, large basin; 7, wide-mouthed jar; 8, small serving bowl; 9, cooking pot on a stove; 10, large basin.

ᵒording to certainly seas⸱

are widely distribu⸱
⸱ar the territorial jun⸱
⸱ao realm, cultures roug⸱
⸱n culture in Shandong, t⸱
⸱n the south, and the Hongshan⸱
⸱research has not only identified a
⸱larger Yangshao realm, but has also
⸱ses of evolution, making a total length of
⸱gshao Era. Pottery typology became much
⸱ngshao period consisting of various types of
⸱ge jars, water bottles, and food-serving bowls
⸱rly pottery wares in the latter two categories were
⸱ beautiful patterns, although the preference for such
⸱ed over time. For instance, the various forms of fish
⸱favored by the early Yangshao communities gave way to
⸱abstract, streamlined, and geometric patterns popular among
⸱ddle Yangshao people, and by the late period, monochromic
⸱on returned to favor with the Yangshao people.

There have been a number of large-scale excavations carried out on Yangshao sites, but nowhere has a Yangshao village come closer to being completely exposed than at Jiangzhai, located about 20 km to the east of Xi'an at the middle of the Wei River valley in Shaanxi Province.

The site has five periods of occupation covering the entire Yangshao period with the latest phase extending into the next Longshan period. The initial early Yangshao stage occupation is the best preserved stratum of all. It includes a large settlement of some 200,000 m^2 surrounded by a complete circular moat, outside which are located three contemporaneous cemeteries. The entire village is centered on an open court where remains of two animal pens were excavated indicating the domestication of animals in the Jiangzhai community. Surrounding the central square, five clusters of house remains were excavated, forming the basic structure of the village. Each cluster is composed of a main house, several smaller houses, numerous storage pits, and pottery kilns, and sometimes also burials of infants (Fig. 2.5). Most houses were subterranean with floors lower than ground level on which were found remains of hearths and raised bed surfaces.

The Jiangzhai site offers a holistic view of the social organization of a Yangshao village. A widely acknowledged view – based on Marxist theory of social development – claims that Jiangzhai represents typical matrilineal

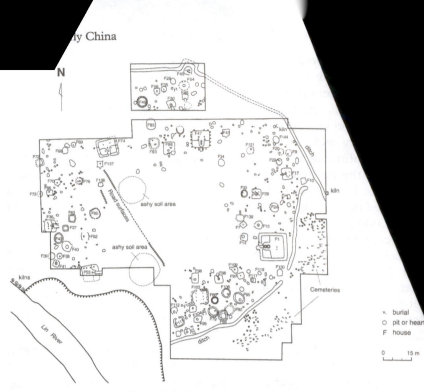

Fig. 2.5 The Jiangzhai village.

society practicing something like the "Punaluan marriage" described by Louis Henry Morgan (1818–81) for native Americans.[13] It is thus said that the five clusters of houses represent five clans, middle houses represent the families, and small houses which also have basic household functions such as a hearth and domestic implements were dwellings of the families' daughters and their husbands who are members of the neighboring clans. The three cemeteries were the burial grounds of members of three clans living in the village, and the total population of Jiangzhai was estimated at around some 500 people. A similar interpretation was also applied to the Yuanjunmiao cemetery, located in the east part of the Wei River valley, where a total of fifty-one tombs were

[13] The "Punaluan marriage" was a form of marriage in which several brothers of a group were the husbands of each other's wives belonging to another group, and several sisters were the wives of each other's husbands. This marriage relationship was described by Morgan for Iroquois of upstate New York, but it was also practiced by Hawaiians in the late nineteenth century. See Louis Henry Morgan, *Ancient Society* (Palo Alto: New York Labor News, 1978), pp. 424–452.

excavated in the 1950s, dating also to the early Yangshao phase. The cemetery was considered to have belonged to a single tribe, which was composed of two clans each using one of the two sub-cemeteries. And each tomb pit represents the collective burial of a single kin family, reflecting the similar social structure at Jiangzhai. The society of the Yuanjunmiao cemetery was also considered matrilineal, because children buried in the cemetery were all girls.

The argument of the Yangshao being matrilineal society was controversial from the beginning. Anthropologists have shown that matrilineal society was by no means common in human history, and in China, the evidence deduced to support its identification in archaeological records was far from convincing. Today, although the view is still reiterated by some eminent scholars, the majority of Chinese archaeologists no longer see it as indisputable.[14] Alternatively, a later analysis suggests that in Jiangzhai the small and medium houses were both individual socioeconomic units, and the large houses were public spaces for the entire village; therefore, there is no evidence for matrilineal control of the small houses by medium-size houses. The analysis shows that the early Yangshao occupation in Jiangzhai can be further divided into three phases and that the same centrifugal layout of the houses was constant in all three. Thus, the Jiangzhai community is considered to have run a close parallel to the "segmentary lineage system" described by Marshall Sahlins.[15]

Recent archaeology has also shed new light on the social integration beyond the village level during the late Yangshao phase. From the early 1990s, sites in the area called Zhudingyuan in western Henan, the core of the Yangshao culture, have come under intensive archaeological research. The fieldwork has revealed a major concentration of settlements – in an area of roughly 350 km^2 as many as thirty-five late Yangshao settlements have been identified. The most important is the Xipo site where a number of extra large houses were discovered, with the largest, F106: 240, measuring 16 × 15 m. Outside the Xipo village, tombs of unusually large size and rich furnishing were excavated. Although we need to wait for future excavations to reveal the overall settlement structure of the site and the region, information available so far has already changed our understanding of the level of social development in the later centuries of the Yangshao era. Concentration of wealth within the community and social integration at the regional level

---

[14] The "matrilineal" view of Yangshao society has been emphasized recently by Zhang Zhongpei in K. C. Chang and Xu Pingfang (eds.), *The Formation of Chinese Civilization: An Archaeological Perspective* (New Haven: Yale University Press, 2005), pp. 71–72, 68.

[15] Yun Kuen Lee, "Configuring Space: Structure and Agency in Yangshao Society," paper delivered at the Columbia Early China Seminar, 2002.

had evidently taken place, and the relationship of economic, if not political, dominance of smaller villages by their stronger neighbors seems to have already occurred. To analyze the new picture of the Yangzhao society will need new theoretical tools, and it has been proposed that the late Yangshao society might have already come to resemble an early form of "chiefdom,"[16] thus higher than the "segmentary lineage system" in developmental stage. Certainly, this question is to be decided by future excavation.

The Longshan "Town" Culture

Around 3000 BC, societies in North China entered a new stage of development, the so-called "Longshan millennium" which lasted for over 1,000 years during which black or gray pottery with various impressed or incised patterns was manufactured and widely used. Different from the preceding Yangshao period, the Longshan cultures are currently analyzed under provincial names such as "Shandong Longshan culture" or "Henan Longshan culture," which are certainly not accurate, but reflect further regional differentiation in the late Neolithic period. Social integration within relatively smaller regional units, a tendency that had already appeared in the late Yangshao period, was intensified, leading to the emergence of settlement networks with clearly definable hierarchies. Located at the hubs of the regional settlement networks are large population centers characterized by a new archaeological feature – the rammed earth wall – which indicates a social system that was significantly more complex than that of the Yangshao village.[17] More than ten such fortified Longshan "towns" had been identified in Henan, Shandong, and Shanxi before the end of the twentieth century.[18] An early discovered example was the walled site at Pingliangtai in Henan Province, where a square wall enclosed an area of some 34,000 m^2 at the center of the site that extends farther beyond the wall enclosure over a slightly raised mound. Access to the central citadel was controlled at two gates, on the south and the north. The area of the walled enclosure at Pingliangtai is comparable to that of the Jiangzhai village. But while the moat at Jiangzhai encircled the entire residential area of the village, at Pingliangtai the wall only protected the core functions of the site, occupied perhaps by the elite group, leaving the ordinary dwelling areas outside it unprotected.[19]

---

[16] Li Liu, *The Chinese Neolithic: Trajectories to Early States* (Cambridge: Cambridge University Press, 2004), pp. 189–191.

[17] In fact, defensive walls had already appeared during the late Yangshao period; *ibid.*, p. 94.

[18] Anne Underhill, "Variation in Settlements during the Longshan period of North China," *Asian Perspectives* 33.2 (1994), 200.

[19] Chang, *The Archaeology of Ancient China*, p. 266.

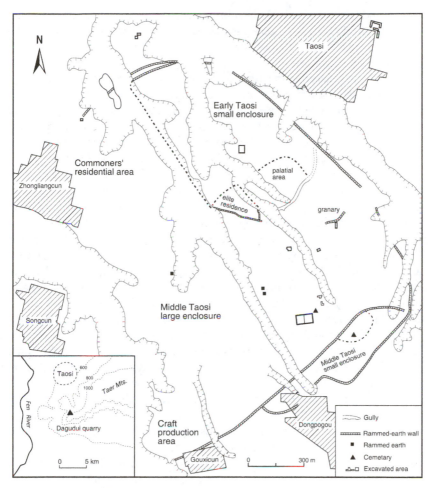

Fig. 2.6 Taosi town of the Longshan period.

Or perhaps the wall was intended as demarcation between the two orders of the population of the Pingliangtai society.

So far the largest town of the Longshan period to have been found is at Taosi in Shanxi Province, the outer wall enclosure covering an area of 2,800,000 m^2 (Fig. 2.6). In fact, the Taosi site, dated to 2600–2000 BC and belonging to the so-called Shanxi Longshan culture, shows a sequence of constructions over a span of some 500 years. In the early Taosi stage, a smaller wall enclosure was constructed at the northeastern corner of the site, in which were found large rammed palatial foundations indicating elite functions of the site. In the middle Taosi stage, we see a clear extension of elite control over the entire site and the population for which the outer wall was constructed, providing an administrative boundary for the entire Taosi community. When the elite quarter in the inner wall enclosure was still under occupation, large concentrations of commoners' residential structures such as caves or semi-subterranean dwellings were constructed in the northwestern part of the site between the two walls. A large cemetery containing both elite and commoners' tombs was excavated in the southern part of the outer wall area. Elite control is also seen in the location of a granary area, possibly protected by another wall enclosure, close to the palatial zone in the inner circle. But most importantly, double layers of wall were constructed in the south, forming a separate enclosure in which is found one of the world's oldest solar observatories, marking the intellectual center of the Taosi community (Box 2.1).

There is also evidence that Taosi in its late stage might have been destroyed by force during the political turmoil caused possibly by people based on another large site located to the south.[20] However, during the hundreds of years when Taosi was prosperous, it must have been a major cultural and economic center in the lower Fen River valley in southern Shanxi. It exhibits beyond any reasonable doubt features of a social system that was sufficiently complex with a stratified population that was divided into at least two classes. The development of functional roles such as astrologers and administrators, and a possible centralized administration within the city, are all evident in Taosi, if not beyond it.

Burial remains also tell of the ongoing process of social differentiation in Taosi. Over 1,000 tombs have been excavated in Taosi, clearly belonging to three classes. The great tombs measure 3 × 2 m or more, are furnished with wooden coffins, and are buried with an inventory that can easily exceed 100 items including beautifully painted wooden vessels, jades, and skeletons of pigs. The occupants of the medium tombs are buried with a wooden coffin, pottery wares, and jades, totaling twenty to thirty items. The small tombs are very narrow pits of 0.5 m wide with no wooden coffin and no burial goods at all, but they make up 90% of the burials in Taosi. If we take this as the direct reflection of distribution of wealth in the Taosi community, then more than 90% of the wealth in Taosi would have been concentrated in the hands of the top 10% of the population, higher in comparison to the concentration of wealth in many modern industrialized nations (the figure for the United States was 69.8% in 2007). Doubtless Taosi was a highly stratified society.

---

[20] Liu, *The Chinese Neolithic*, pp. 103–112.

Box 2.1 The Taosi Solar Observatory

This is one of the most astonishing archaeological discoveries of the new century. Excavated in 2003 and located in the small enclosure attached to the southeastern wall of the Taosi city, this circular building was originally shaped in three steps, and the platform at each level is demarcated by a wall constructed with rammed earth, the outmost wall being located some 25 m from the center of the compound. The innermost or central platform has a radius of 12.25 m and the wall of its circumference continues for about 25 m. An array of eleven solid square pillars was constructed along this thin wall, leaving ten narrow slits between them (later, two more pillars were found at the north end of the line, making a total of thirteen pillars and twelve slits). Since these solid pillars are deeply inserted into the platform, the excavators suggest that they might have served merely as bases to support stone pillars that topped them. The sightlines going through the twelve slits lead back to a single observation spot at the center of the platform (Fig. 2.7).

Stratigraphic evidence suggests that the building was constructed and used for perhaps a few centuries during the middle period of Taosi before its destruction around 2100 BC. On-site experiments that took place in the years following the discovery leave little doubt that the platform was used for solar observation between the two solstitial extremes in any given year, and it is one of the oldest astronomical observatories in the world confirmed by archaeology. The astronomical historian David W. Pankenier suggests that the structure could be used to determine sections on a horizontal calendar that could have yielded an approximation of the length of the solar year to within a week. Thus, the Taosi astronomers were concerned with correlations between the lunar months and the solar year and this eventually gave rise to a lunar–solar combined calendar with the intercalary thirteenth month inserted in the regular year circles, a system that was definitely in use in China by the thirteenth century BC, proven for the late Shang by oracle-bone studies. More importantly, Pankenier further suggests that the Taosi astronomical observatory provided a context in which a writing system would likely be needed for keeping the calendar starting with signs invented to identify sections of time or celestial bodies.[21]

---

[21] See David W. Pankenier, "Getting 'Right' with Heaven and the Origins of Writing in China," in F. Li and D. P. Branner (eds.), *Writing and Literacy in Early China: Studies from the*

Fig. 2.7 Solar observatory discovered in the walled town in Taosi, Shanxi, 2003.

Moreover, we know that the process of social stratification was simultaneously going on in other regions in China. The Liangzhu culture in the Yangzi Delta, roughly contemporary with the Longshan cultures in the north, was remarkable for its production of jades. A large mound tomb found in Sidun in Jiangsu contains more than fifty beautifully crafted jade objects; such tombs containing large numbers of jade objects were also found in a number of sites near Hangzhou Bay in Zhejiang Province. These are clearly elite burials that are usually segregated from the commoners' tombs in the regional society. In 2007, a Liangzhu city centering on Mojiaoshan protected by walls even slightly larger than Taosi was discovered in the district of Hangzhou, and it became clear that some of the previously known rich burials possibly belonged to elite members who lived in this large city. The discovery suggests that contemporary with the Longshan culture in the north, South China had been undergoing a similar process of social transformation leading to higher levels of social complexity. However, in South China this process was suddenly interrupted around 2000 BC when the Liangzhu culture mysteriously disappeared from the surface of the Earth.

Columbia Early China Seminar (Seattle: University of Washington Press, 2011), pp. 19–50, especially, p. 27. In another study, Pankenier emphasizes the use of the platform for ritual activities, perhaps ritualized worship of the rising sun, and advises avoidance of the English term "observatory" due to its modern scientific connotations, see David W. Pankenier, Liu Ciyuan, and Salvo De Meis, "The Xiangfen Taosi Site: A Chinese Neolithic 'Observatory'?"

Furthermore, recent archaeological discoveries suggest that the social life of the Longshan millennium towns was not only redirected by the new political dynamics that emerged among its population, but, perhaps related to the rise of the social elites, was enriched by a number of new technological and cultural inventions. Among these new advancements, the most important ones are high-quality pottery-making, metallurgy, and possibly, early "writing."

High-quality pottery-making

For the Longshan people, pottery wares were not merely utensils for their everyday life; on the contrary, a certain type of pottery-making technology was developed clearly with the purpose to facilitate elite life in the Longshan towns, particularly in the Shandong region on the east coast. This is the so-called egg-shell pottery reputed for their extremely thin body-wall – each piece is an artwork emerging from a very delicate process of crafting that required professional skills. They are often found in large town sites with wall enclosures and were apparently luxury items for elite use, possibly associated with ritual or religious activities of the elites (Fig. 2.8.1–2).

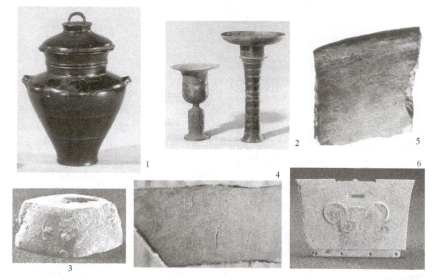

Fig. 2.8 The Longshan and Liangzhu town culture: 1–2, egg-shell pottery from the Shandong Longshan culture; 3, Copper bell from Taosi; 4, inscribed shard from Dinggong, Shandong Province, Longshan culture; 5, inscribed shard from Longqiu, Jiangsu Province, Liangzhu culture; 6, jade ornament, Liangzhu culture.

Metallurgy

Recent archaeology has shown beyond doubt that metal objects were in use across a large geographic area during the Longshan millennium in North China. In the world context, the earliest use of copper ore dates to 9000 BC in Anatolia, almost as old as the Neolithic pottery in the region; from 7000 BC small copper objects like pins and drills began to be made in Mesopotamia. Between 4500 and 3000 BC residents of lower Mesopotamia manufactured a considerable number of tools and weapons in copper. In China, small metal objects dating from the beginning of the fourth millennium have been found in the wide geographical area from Gansu and Qinghai in the west to Shandong in the east, and a few sites belonging to the Longshan culture in Henan have also yielded copper ores and debris, suggesting that metal objects were locally manufactured. So far the most important discovery is a copper bell found in a middle-size tomb in the outer wall enclosure in Taosi in 1983 (Fig. 2.8.3). The metallurgical composition of the bell was determined to be of 97.86% copper, 1.5% lead, and 0.16% zinc – it is almost purely a copper object. But most importantly it was cast in a holistic process by using clay molds, a method that was to become the mainstream bronze manufacturing technology thereafter in China, but underdeveloped in the West.

Early writing

For a long time scholars have been fascinated by the numerous marks engraved on Neolithic pottery from as early as the Cishan–Peiligang period. Although not a few have tried to seek the origin of the Chinese writing system in these Neolithic marks, such attempts ultimately failed to establish the basic fact that they were representations of language, or were used to form any system of notation, the minimum requirement for "writing."[22] However, in the past fifteen years, archaeology has turned out a new type of materials. On a pottery shard found in the walled town of Dinggong in Shandong, eleven graphs were incised in five rows to form a continuous "reading." Another shard was found at Longqiu in Jiangsu, belonging to the Liangzhu culture, which carries graphs arranged in two rows: on the right are four graphs each depicting a distinctive type of creature, seemingly buffalo, snake, bird, and something else; on the left

---

[22] William G. Boltz, *The Origin and Early Development of the Chinese Writing System* (New Haven: American Oriental Society, 1994), p. 36.

side are four abstract graphs each leading a creature on the right (Fig. 2.8.5). These graphs apparently exhibit a higher level of communication than the isolated marks on the Yangshao pottery. On each of the two shards the graphs form an internally related sequence of ideas that can only be connected through language. Therefore, the majority opinion has been that these are early forms of writing in China, although they are not necessarily ancestral to the system that we call "Chinese writing." Despite the fact that they are of unknown linguistic affiliation and are after all unreadable, their appearance suggests that in some of the Longshan millennium towns at least a high culture was already in place to serve the spiritual and administrative needs of the Longshan/Liangzhu elites.

The Question of Longshan "Chiefdom"

The above discussion has highlighted the dramatic social changes that took place during the Longshan millennium. The question is: where should we place these changes in the chain of social development also observed in other regions of the world? Or are the Neo-evolutionist theories mentioned earlier in this chapter applicable to China? There has been a trend among archaeologists in China to redefine the Longshan societies as "archaic states." It was earlier suggested that the settlements belonging to the Longshan period in Shandong constituted three levels, and that the walled towns were centers of the "archaic states" with centralized political power. Similarly, the senior archaeologist Zhang Zhongpei proposed in 2005 that the Liangzhu culture in southern China had also entered the stage of civilization characterized by the political power of the state. The alternative view is held, mainly by scholars in the West, that Longshan society exhibits features of a "chiefdom."[23]

The high level of social complexity viewed in the archaeological records of the Longshan period (and the Liangzhu culture in the south) in fact poses a major problem to the theory of social development originally formulated by anthropologists. Recent anthropological literature tries to redefine the boundary between "chiefdom" and "state." It has been suggested that, in addition to the difference in exercising power as noted above, the organization of chiefdoms was normally based on kinship structure, but that of the state was not necessarily so. Chiefs lacking internally specialized enforcement machinery avoid delegating central authority and rely on the local power of sub-chiefs, while kings systematize and segment their power

[23] Underhill, "Variation in Settlements," 197–228; Liu, *The Chinese Neolithic*, p. 191. Li Liu further defined the Longshan society as "complex chiefdom" society in contrast to the late Yangshao culture which she considers as "simple chiefdom" society.

Box 2.2   Lajia: A Neolithic Village Ravaged by Earthquake 4,000 Years Ago

In summer 2000, archaeologists who were excavating the residential site called Lajia, located on the plateau to the north of the upper Yellow River some 190 km to the southeast of Xining, capital of Qinghai Province, were stunned at what they saw gradually emerging from the ground (Fig. 2.9). In a subterranean dwelling pit (F4) of 3.81 × 2.95 × 3.55 m, they first encountered the skeleton of a young woman (age 28–30), kneeling on her left leg and leaning on the east wall, an unusual situation for a dwelling site. Below her chest were found the remains of 1–2-year-old infant with his/her two little arms around the waist of the mother. The young mother was apparently pressed down by a huge weight from above as she tried to support her body with her left arm on the floor in order to protect the child. To the west part of the pit, two clusters of skeletons were found. Another younger mother (age 35–40) was surrounded by three teenagers and one child under 10, who died together in the southwest corner of the pit. To their north, four other children, all under 13 and the youngest aged only about 3, held each other in a group, and died while struggling for their lives. Some of the bodies were heavily twisted by an unknown force. In addition, an older male of 40–45 was found lying close to the entrance to the dwelling and another of 15–17 was found crouching and dead on the top of the central stove.

This was the first find of such a scene of disastrous death in Chinese archaeology. Continuing fieldwork on the site helped by geologists identified the subterranean pit as the base of a loess cave and determined that the cause for its collapse was a major earthquake, although the village might also have been subsequently invaded by floods. The damage was extensive in the village that was formed by both dwelling caves and dozens of house foundations located in its east part. For some reason, children probably belonging to different families were gathered in cave F4 which then became their common grave when the earthquake hit the ground. Because of the special moment of the collapse, some details of the village life have been preserved – it is above all astonishing that when archaeologists turned over a pottery bowl left on the floor, they discovered the earliest noodle in China! The initial laboratory work suggested that the noodle was made of starches derived from millet, but subsequent studies suggest that it must have been made of flours of wheat. Pottery typology identifies the village with the Neolithic Qijia

Box 2.2 (cont.)

culture in its late phase, dating around 4000 BP, thus likely slightly later than the astronomical observatory in Taosi.

An additional discovery in Lajia was an earth-built sacrificial platform located in the open square of the village. At the center of the earth platform was found the luxury burial of perhaps the priest of the village, yielding as many as fifteen beautifully made jade objects.

Fig. 2.9 The earthquake site in Lajia and the earliest noodle in China.

so as to undermine local authority.[24] Furthermore, there has also been the opinion among some anthropologists that chiefdom societies were "dead end" in the evolution of society, and they simply did not have the potential to develop into state-level societies.

There is considerable ambiguity in the definition of "chiefdom," and anthropologists will doubtless continue to face difficulties in refining their theories to match the archaeological reality. It is nevertheless acceptable to call the Longshan societies "chiefdoms." The theoretical problems notwithstanding, the evidence analyzed in this chapter suggests that the Longshan societies were clearly at a higher stage of social development than the relatively equalitarian societies of the Yangshao culture. If "chiefdom" is the inevitable form of social organization developed out of the "segmentary lineage system" which seems to relate well to the Yangshan societies, then "chiefdom" would seem to be a reasonable term to highlight the organizational complexity of the Longshan societies, before the rise of the state (Box 2.2).

SELECTED READING

Fiskesjö, Magnus, and Chen Xingcan, *China Before China: John Gunnar Andersson, Ding Wenjiang, and the Discovery of China's Prehistory*, Museum of Far Eastern Antiquities Monograph 15 (Stockholm: Östasiatiska museet, 2004).

Falkenhausen, Lothar von, "The Regionalist Paradigm in Chinese Archaeology," in Philip L. Kohl and Clare Fawcett (eds.), *Nationalism, Politics, and the Practice of Archaeology* (Cambridge: Cambridge University Press, 1995).

Chen, Xingcan, "Archaeological Discoveries in the People's Republic of China and Their Contribution to the Understanding of Chinese History," *Bulletin of the History of Archaeology* 19.2 (2009), 4–13.

Chang, K. C., and Xu Pingfang (eds.), *The Formation of Chinese Civilization: An Archaeological Perspective* (New Haven: Yale University Press, 2005).

Crawford, Gray W., "East Asian Plant Domestication," in Miriam T. Stark (ed.), *Archaeology of Asia* (Malden: Blackwell, 2006), pp. 77–95.

Chang, K. C., *The Archaeology of Ancient China*, 4th edn. (New Haven: Yale University Press, 1986).

Liu, Li, *The Chinese Neolithic: Trajectories to Early States* (Cambridge: Cambridge University Press, 2004).

Underhill, Anne, "Variation in Settlements during the Longshan Period of North China," *Asian Perspectives* 33.2 (1994), 197–228.

[24] Yoffee, *Myths of the Archaic State*, pp. 23–25.

3   Erlitou and Erligang: early state expansion

What the "multi-region" model of Neolithic cultural development cannot explain is how state-level society arose first not from other regional traditions but from the heartland of the Yangshao culture and its successors the Longshan cultures in Henan and Shanxi. However, the line of development in this large region leading to the rise of state was by no means very straight. The power of the Taosi "chiefdom" waned after a few hundred years of prominence and whoever remained to live in the Taosi community seem to have come under domination by another nearby political center. Archaeologists have much to do to understand this process of competition among the pre-state polities and the resultant regional integration in the middle reaches of the Yellow River and other regions in the contemporary time-frame. However, at the beginning of the second millennium BC, one society had risen to a level of power that was far above the limit of other "chiefdom"-level societies in western Henan and southern Shanxi. The Erlitou state or culture occupied a critical position in the formation of state and civilization in North China. It opened a new era that was marked by royal authority, urban civilization, larger political organization, and a strong coercive military presence.

The "State" and "State Formation"

Unlike the term "chiefdom" which is essentially an anthropological construct, the term "state" has a long history in the Western intellectual tradition,[1] and is the one modern term to which different disciplines attach different meanings. In political science which conceives the meaning of "state" in legal–political terms, the "state" is defined as the embodiment

---

[1] In medieval political philosophy, the term originally designated the condition or standing of the community, peoples, or the prince, very similar to its modern American use in such terms as the "State of the Union." However, after the fifteenth century, the meaning of "state" gradually evolved into one that referred to the apparatus of government or the bearer of sovereign power from which the term's most common modern application as a form of social–political organization descended.

of "sovereignty," hence there is the notion of the modern "Nation State" which identifies the present unit of the "nation" as the bearer of such sovereignty. For political economists, the "state" is an institution equipped with coercive powers, standing in opposition to the individual citizens, and is supposedly the representation of public and collective interest versus individual or private interest. But in a sociological view, which is also the view of most social historians, the "state" is a human organization with multiple qualifications including territory, unified political order, law and coercive power to enforce it, and sovereignty. Finally, in an anthropological sense, the "state" is a type of society or a "stage" in social development, being different from and more massive and complex than the "chiefdom" society, therefore, validating the concept of "state-level society."

A society certainly does not have to be organized in such a way as a state; there are other social organizations such as tribes or chiefdoms which, according to the non-evolutionist view, may never develop into state or state-level societies. Therefore, there is the question of why did the state arise? Why did some societies develop into states, while others did not? And how, or what trajectories did they take to develop into states? This is the issue of "state formation" and there have been numerous explanations about this process. For some scholars, the state was the inevitable result of the internal struggle of a society and it was invented as a means to compromise or contain such internal conflicts. For others, the state arose as the response to a more massive and constant external threat, cast either by natural force or by another society, and it emerged as the means to unite the society's members in their common interests to cope with such external threat. This latter view has become particularly popular in recent years in the explanation of the rise of the nomadic empires in the northern steppe regions. For still others, for instance the late Professor K. C. Chang, the state arose as the end-product of the long process of the internal tendency of a society to better manage its resources to reorganize and centralize its ritual system. These are all important theoretical dimensions that we should take into account in studying the rise of the state in Early China.

The Erlitou Culture and the "Erlitou State"

Most scholars agree now that after the beginning of the second millennium BC, something that can be properly called a "state" had indeed arisen in China, particularly in western Henan, to the south of the Taosi chiefdom. The time-frame for this new development has been fixed, based on the scientific dating of numerous carbon-14 samples from sites of the relevant culture, and by recent calibrations, to 1900–1600 BC. To provide a comparative dating in global contexts, this period overlaps the time of the Babylonians and of King Hammurabi in Mesopotamia; in Egypt, this is the time of the Middle Kingdom, before the Hyksos Invasion from the delta. In the New Continent, this is the time immediately preceding the emergence of the Olmecs. In other words, the "state" had already had a history of more than a millennium in Egypt, and slightly shorter in Mesopotamia, but it was a new phenomenon in China.

In autumn 1959, a team of archaeologists was sent to western Henan by the Institute of Archaeology, Chinese Academy of Sciences (Beijing), on confidence gained recently from archaeological substantiation of the historically known Shang Dynasty, to search for the possible ruins of the Xia Dynasty described in the same historical tradition as having ruled before the Shang Dynasty. By this time, pottery and bronze types earlier than those from Anyang had already surfaced at some sites in central and northern Henan, and of course sites with the similar cultural contents (earlier than Anyang) were the targets of their search. Among the more than ten sites turned up by the search, Erlitou, located about 20 km to the east of the modern city Luoyang, was the most prominent. By the close of the field-work season, the archaeological team had managed to test-excavate a small area of the site, and the rich deposits from the site confirmed the existence of a new culture that was subsequently named the "Erlitou Culture." Since that time Erlitou has gained international fame as a center for the study of the rise of states and civilization in China, but clear understanding of the organization of the site has been achieved only through careful archaeological fieldwork in the past fifteen years. It should also be noted that by now our knowledge of the Erlitou culture has extended far beyond the Erlitou site itself, confirming a large region of distribution of sites that have the same cultural contents as far as eastern Henan, several sites in the Fen River valley in southern Shanxi, and the upper Huai River valley in southern Henan (Map 3.1). The confirmation of this cultural realm has suggested that the Erlitou site was located at the center of a settlement system, and doubtless at the top of a settlement hierarchy.

The central site of Erlitou is located to the south of the Luo River (Fig. 3.1), stretching over 2.5 km E–W and 2 km N–S. It covers an area of 5,000,000 m^2 (500 ha), at least twice as large as Taosi, and much larger than other Longshan centers in North China. At the center of this immense site is located the palatial complex surrounded by a wall that forms a rectangle, in which as many as eleven earth building platforms have been excavated or identified for excavation later. The most outstanding structures are Foundations nos. 1 and 2, each forming a self-enclosed compound surrounded by a wall. Foundation no. 1 was excavated in 1960, measuring 108 m E–W and 100 m N–S, and raised about 1–2 m above the

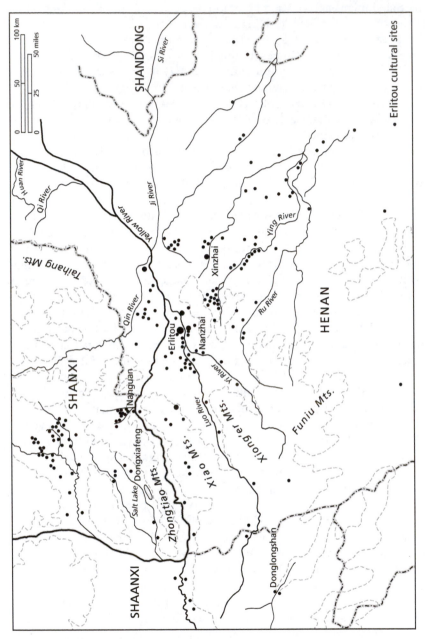

Map 3.1 Distribution of Erlitou culture sites.

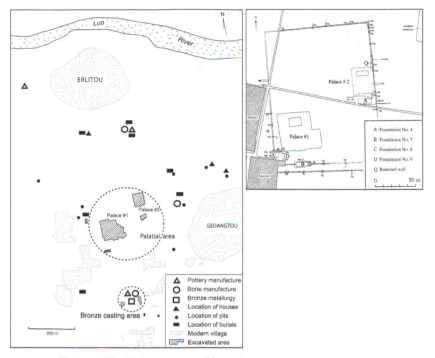

Fig. 3.1 The Erlitou site and its palace zone.

original ground. The entire surface of the platform is surrounded by roofed hallways constructed along its edges. At its center north, a second step of platform was built, and the locations of postholes on its surface suggest a rectangular architectural layout. Foundation no. 2 is located along the east wall of the palatial zone and has an area slightly smaller than but structurally similar to Foundation no. 1. Outside the palatial zone, three sections of road were found, forming a part of the road system traversing the central area of the Erlitou site.[2] Significantly, in the southern gateway to the palace, tracks of vehicles were discovered, providing the earliest example of the use of wheeled wagons in China.

Tombs excavated within the site are mostly small, leaving the possibility that the elites of Erlitou society might have been buried at certain selected locations away from the site. Only on Foundation no. 2 in the corridor behind the main hall was a large tomb (5.2 × 4.25 m) excavated, but it had been completely looted a long time ago. However, from one of the

---

[2] R. Thorp, *China in the Early Bronze Age: Shang Civilization* (Philadelphia: University of Pennsylvania Press, 2006), pp. 21–61.

Fig. 3.2 Bronze vessels and turquoise objects from Erlitou: 1, *jue*-drinking cups; 2, *ding*-cauldron; 3, *jia*-heating pitcher; 4, dragon-shape object decorated with turquoise (70.2 cm), possibly a hand-cane symbolizing political power; 5, bronze plaque inlaid with turquoise; 6, *jue*-drinking cup.

middle-size tombs, a 70.2-cm long dragon-shape object decorated with turquoise was discovered (Fig. 3.2.4). Within the site, numerous pits of various functions were excavated, and in one of these structures located just outside the south wall of the palace, a large quantity of turquoise pieces were discovered, identifying the location of a workshop that might have produced many of the turquoise objects found on the site.

Bronze vessels are among the most outstanding objects from Erlitou; they suggest that metallurgy in China had achieved a major stage of advancement at the beginning of the second millennium BC. And the Erlitou culture can be described as the first Bronze Age culture in China. Here, bronze was no longer used only to make small items, but was also used to manufacture vessels of considerably larger size at a much higher degree of technological complexity and sophistication – in a process that is called by scholars "sectional mold casting."[3] To date some fifteen

---

[3] "Sectional mold casting" requires the making of a clay model of the intended bronze. Then, soft clay will be applied to it to produce an impression of the bronze's outer surface and cut into sections in order to be removed from the model. When baked dry, the sectional molds will be reassembled around a casting core, usually acquired by reducing the dimension of the model. Molten bronze would be poured into the hollows between the

pieces of bronze vessels have been unearthed at Erlitou, in addition to a greater number of bronze weapons and implements. Vessel types included *jue*-cups, *jia*-heating vessels, and *ding*-cauldrons, all central to the bronze inventory of the Shang Dynasty (*c.* 1554–1046 BC) which clearly owed its source to the Erlitou bronze culture. The workshop for bronze production has been located at the center south of the Erlitou site where clay molds and copper debris were unearthed in large numbers. Besides bronze objects, jades and other luxury items were also important elite objects produced and utilized in Erlitou.

However, bronzes are more than just luxury goods; they have multiple social and political meanings. Since the Luoyang Plain yields no natural copper deposits, it has been recently suggested that the copper ores used by the Erlitou elites to cast bronze vessels and weapons were probably quarried in the Zhongtiao Mountains of southern Shanxi, an area that probably also provided the source of salt needed by the Erlitou population. The maintenance of a stable source-supply and transportation over a distance of hundreds of kilometers involved a level of organizational power only state-level societies could afford to have. The immense and complex building compounds at Erlitou suggest that the Erlitou leadership did possess such organizational power over a population that was estimated to have ranged somewhere from 18,000 to 30,000 people at the central site. It has further been suggested that organizing the bronze industry and distributing its products to the local elites for ritual and political purposes might have been among the most important functions of the Erlitou state.[4]

The proposition of an "Erlitou State" has been widely accepted by scholars because the material evidence is compelling by comparison to that for other early states in world contexts. Due to the lack of contemporaneous written evidence from the Erlitou site or from any other site associated with the Erlitou culture, it can hardly be determined whether Erlitou was a "royal state" or a state of some other kind. Within some three centuries, Erlitou was doubtless the political and cultural center of the middle Yellow River region, far surpassing any other contemporary sites both in size and in the level of cultural development. Recent archaeological research has also confirmed the continuation in pottery typology from the late Longshan culture in Henan to the Erlitou culture, and even a transitional phase between the two longer cultural periods has been

---

core and the molds to form the bronze. This method of casting is highly developed in Bronze Age China as its technological mainstream, but it was underdeveloped in the West where wax molds were used.

[4] Li Liu and Chen Xingcan, *State Formation in Early China* (London: Duckworth, 2003), pp. 57–84.

identified at a site near modern Zhengzhou. This certainly lends weight to the general understanding that the transition to state-level society was likely the result of accumulated social and cultural changes that took place in the world of the Longshan people particularly in the adjacent regions of Shaanxi, Shanxi, and Henan Provinces. However, the Erlitou culture apparently also received heavy influence from the late Neolithic cultures of the east coastal regions especially the Longshan culture in Shandong, which might have offered the Erlitou elites typological standards for the vessels they cast in bronze.

State Formation in Early Historical Traditions and the Debate about the Xia Dynasty

The process of the formation of states in China has also been told in the received historical tradition, though in a more subtle way hidden behind a series of legends that anticipated the founding of the Xia Dynasty. This tradition, most systematically presented in *The Grand Scribe's Records* written by Sima Qian (*c.* 145–86 BC) in the Western Han Dynasty, first describes a period in which a series of five legendary emperors including the Yellow Emperor and Emperors Zhuanxu, Ku, Yao, and Shun ruled China in their capacity of elected leader.[5] They represented a time when the world was governed by virtue, but not by force, and political leadership was conceived in terms of personal charisma helped by mythical energy. This idea of the "Five Emperors" did not come into existence until the fifth century BC, and modern scholars see the mythical tradition of succession through abdication as the ideological support of the political agenda of the late Spring and Autumn or early Warring States period ministers who frequently attempted the overthrow of their state rulers. However, the tradition also distantly echoes the social and political conditions before the rise of the state in China, known also from other world contexts, where regional leaders competed with each other for political supremacy. At the time of Emperor Shun, the last in the series, there were horrible floods overflowing the North China Plain, causing a great many deaths. Thus the emperor summoned the chief of a major tribe unit whose name was Yu, or "Great Yu," to carry out irrigation works to overcome the floods. Yu then traveled throughout China, cleaning up the rivers and dredging canals; hence the floods of the rivers were guided to enter the eastern sea. Yu won great respect among the people and henceforth became the leader of all China after the death of Shun. However, when

---

[5] See Sima Qian, *The Grand Scribe's Records*, vol. 1, *The Basic Annals of Pre-Han China*, edited by William H. Nienhauser Jr. (Bloomington: Indiana University Press, 1994), pp. 1–40.

Yu died, the power did not pass on to a new elected leader like Yu himself, but was taken likely by force by Yu's own son, Qi, who then founded the Xia Dynasty. In the way this story is told in the tradition, the accession of Qi is described as the breakdown of the tradition of elected leadership and the establishment of a royal state in China to be ruled by a hereditary house. After Qi, the Xia house's dynastic rule continued over sixteen generations until the last Xia king, Jie, who was overthrown by the Shang Dynasty. For one time early in the Xia Dynasty, the rule of the Xia house was usurped by a tribe from eastern China led by the Greater Archer Yi.[6] But after the latter was murdered by his advisor, the Xia Dynasty was restored by King Zhong Kang and was to continue for another 200 years.

The earliest references to Yu and the Xia Dynasty are found in Western Zhou (1045–771 BC) texts, in the chapters that are parts of the transmitted Book of Documents, and in some of the poems in the Book of Poetry.[7] The Western Zhou date of this tradition is confirmed by the discovery in 2003 of a bronze vessel cast during the mid Western Zhou, the Bingong xu, whose inscriptions tell stories of Yu in close parallel to the received tradition ascribed to him (Box 3.1; Fig. 3.3). The earliest complete list of the Xia kings is found in the Bamboo Annals, securely dated to the early third century BC. In fact, this list was buried in a tomb until being rediscovered in AD 280 and was unknown to the Han Dynasty historian Sima Qian who in his book offers a reign-by-reign independent account of the Xia Dynasty in the same order of the Xia kings as is given by the Bamboo Annals.[8] In other words, from the Western Zhou to the Han Dynasty there had been a consistent tradition regarding the historicity of the Xia Dynasty. One would further hope, if

---

[6] The story of Greater Archer Yi is itself fascinating, and probably originated in the east coastal region. There, facing the crisis of all ten suns coming out altogether in the sky, it was Yi who, using his vermilion bow, shot down nine of the suns, thus saving humankind from total destruction by the solar conflagration. See Anne M. Birrell, Chinese Mythology: An Introduction (Baltimore: Johns Hopkins University Press, 1993), pp. 77–79.

[7] The Book of Documents and Book of Poetry are the core texts transmitted through the millennia of Confucian tradition. To give a quick summary here, the former is a collection of some twenty-eight government documents from the Zhou Dynasty, and is regarded as the embodiment of Western Zhou values and manifestation of a model government; the latter is an anthology of 305 poems. Both texts seem to have existed at the latest by the time of Confucius (551–479 BC) and both include a substantial part of works composed during the Western Zhou period. The two texts will be discussed in more detail in Chapter 7.

[8] The Bamboo Annals is a text originally written on bamboo strips, discovered in the Western Jin Dynasty (AD 265–316) in a tomb in northern Henan, belonging to a Warring States period (480–221 BC) king. Though a Warring States period text, the chronicle goes back to the beginning of history. For issues regarding the transmission of early Chinese texts, see relevant chapters in Michael Loewe (ed.), Early Chinese Texts: A Bibliographical Guide (Berkeley: Institute of East Asian Studies, University of California, Berkeley, 1993).

Box 3.1   The Bingong *Xu* and the Memory of History

This rare bronze can be dated to the mid Western Zhou period (*c.* 950–850 BC) by its typological and decorative features, being one of the earliest examples of a *xu* square tureen. Although it was acquired in the antique market in Hong Kong, the technological features shown by the vessel guarantee its authenticity. When the vessel was brought back to Beijing and cleaned in early 2003, its emergent inscription took everyone by surprise by offering a lengthy commemoration of the virtues of Great Yu, the legendary founder of the Xia Dynasty, paralleling much of the received tradition about his revered rule (Fig. 3.3).

Although this inscription cannot be taken as evidence of the historicity of the Xia Dynasty, it is a concrete piece of evidence that certain beliefs about the rule of Great Yu already existed and were perhaps widespread during the Western Zhou period. More importantly, the inscription shows how, in Zhou mentality, the earliest history of the state and civilization was crystallized in the role of such cultural heroes like Yu whose superior virtue continued to live on and provided the foundation for the current kingship of Zhou. With regard to the latter point, the inscription unusually goes beyond the horizon of the religious–intellectual system of the Zhou which, as shown by numerous inscriptions from the period, was framed largely on the reverence for Zhou's own ancestors.

Heaven commanded Yu to spread out the soil, and to cross the mountains and dredge the streams.

Thus, he (Yu) cut off the trees to open land for plantation, taxed the subjugated people, and oversaw virtues.

He made himself the partner [of Heaven] and rejoiced in the people, being [their] father and mother, and gave birth to our kingship.

He showered himself with nothing but virtue, and the people also loved the bright virtue – [he] worried about all under Heaven.

[He] used his illuminating goodness to expand and strengthen the fine virtue, and to strengthen fully those who were not diligent.

[He] was filial, friendly, open, and bright; [he] was constant and even in loving sacrifice, having no ugly heart.

[He] loved virtue and promoted marriage, which was also in harmony with Heaven and to be respectful to the deities.

[He] again used fortune and wealth, to forever live (?) in peace.

Bin Gong proclaims: "May the people use this virtue! No regret!"

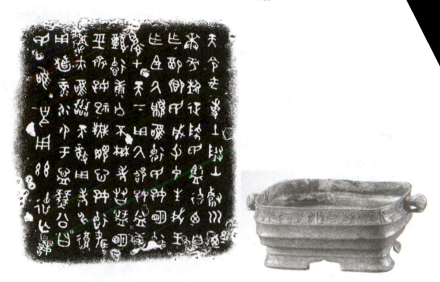

Fig. 3.3 The Bingong *xu* and its inscription.

the Xia Dynasty ever existed, we would find references to it in the written sources of the Shang Dynasty that comes even closer to the Xia time. But this is not true and the Shang oracle-bone inscriptions say nothing about a Xia Dynasty the Shang had conquered. However, the strength of this evidence to negate the historicity of the Xia Dynasty is itself weakened by the bare fact that the Shang oracle-bone inscriptions are divinatory records that are narrowly concerned with powers that still affected the Shang state; therefore, they show no historical curiosity at all about an enemy power that exited in the distant past and no longer affected the life of the Shang king.

It is intriguing, and indeed natural, for any scholar to want to see whether there is a link between the two processes: the development of state-level society evident in the archaeological data, and the establishment of a dynastic royal state as learned from the transmitted historical tradition. Chronological studies of early Chinese history certainly project the three to four centuries before Shang back onto the Xia Dynasty, depending on the dates of the Shang Dynasty (c. 1554–1046 BC). This suggests a time-frame into which the range of carbon-14 dates of the Erlitou culture (c. 1900–1600 BC) mentioned above fall perfectly. In fact, in several sites the deposit of the Erlitou culture overrides the strata of the Longshan culture, and in other sites it is intruded or overlapped by Shang strata. Moreover, the ancient sources also indicate that the various centers asso-ciated with activities of the Xia kings, based on historical–geographical

...udies, were located largely in the same region as the sites that belong to the Erlitou culture – western Henan and southern Shanxi.[9] In short, the evidence places the Erlitou culture into the same time period and space in which the Xia Dynasty described by the received tradition is supposed to have been the rule.

To many scholars in China and still some in the West, this temporal and spatial coincidence provides a suitable base for identifying the Erlitou culture as the material culture of the Xia Dynasty and the Erlitou site as the Xia royal capital. In fact, there were not a few studies published in China in the past thirty years that took the identification of the so-called "Xia Culture" as their basic research assumption. However, this identification of the Erlitou culture with the Xia Dynasty would appear to lack any ground to other scholars; some have written strong rejections against the identification, in effect continuing a scholarly debate that has its origins in the "Doubting Antiquity" movement (see Chapter 1). The strongest point against the identification has been the complete lack of any *written evidence* from the Erlitou site or any other sites of the Erlitou culture that may be connected to the historical records about Xia. In the absence of such clear written evidence there is no way to link Erlitou to Xia. Except for a few, this latter view has been widely shared among scholars in the West.

Therefore, the issue is not only intriguing, but can be academically and politically contentious.[10] It is, however, our intellectual responsibility to disassociate scholarly discussions from any politically toned claims or accusations which are invariably based on ideology, not evidence. On the other hand, we need to be realistic about the current condition of the evidence and be aware of the full range of possible interpretations. First, there is no way at present, lacking written evidence from Erlitou or other culturally affiliated sites, to determine that Erlitou was indeed the capital of Xia. Before such evidence is brought to light and a direct link, rather than logical reasoning, can be established, the question will remain open. On the other hand, our current evidence has not proved that Erlitou was not Xia by, perhaps, identifying Erlitou with another polity that existed in the relevant time period and space. If one wants to make a strong argument that Erlitou was not Xia, then the only evidence that he/she can draw on is that there is no evidence that it was Xia. The point regarding contemporaneous written evidence is well taken, but it is itself

[9] K. C. Chang, *The Archaeology of Ancient China*, 4th edn. (New Haven: Yale University Press, 1986), p. 319.
[10] For a summary of the recent debate about the Erlitou–Xia relation, see Li Liu, "Academic Freedom, Political Correctness, and Early Civilisation in Chinese Archaeology: The Debate on Xia–Erlitou Relations," *Antiquity* 83 (2009), 831–843.

ultimately an assumption that Xia, if it existed, did have a writing system and did produce the needed records; there is no evidence for this either.

Since no solid ground can be gained from proving or disproving the Erlitou–Xia relation, it would seem inevitable that we return to the basic facts in archaeology and take a general consensus as the starting point – that is, Erlitou was a state-level society that possessed a level of power and wealth unrivaled by any other societies in its contemporary time context in the middle and lower reaches of the Yellow River. It is quite probable, from the perspective of anthropological study of other regions in the world, for such a society to have left deep impressions on the cultural memory of the people who thereafter continued to live in North China. There is also the possibility that the Erlitou people never called themselves "Xia," a term that could have been bestowed on them by their enemies and passed down into the Western Zhou dynasty, and this can make the "Erlitou–Xia" debate lose its focus. But the transmitted historical records, if we do not take them at face value and are not trapped by the superficial "Erlitou–Xia" debate, seem to transmit a true historical moment well known in anthropological literature – the transition from the pre-state society of free-standing chiefdoms to the state. The Erlitou state before Shang happened to have dominated at this particular moment a region to which the historical records ascribe the transition to the state. In the end, it is not the spatial or temporal overlap, but the parallel historical and archaeological processes in their shared time and space that offer us a meaningful piece of understanding of the possible relationship between Erlitou and the received tradition about the first royal dynasty in China – pending the name "Xia."

Certainly there is the possibility that Erlitou was not the capital of Xia but was the center of another state-level society which the received tradition did not record or failed to preserve. But then the question is: what is this Bronze Age state that archaeology has pulled out in front of us? Until archaeological research turns up another Bronze Age society with comparable power and wealth in the middle Yellow River region before Shang, the possibility that Erlitou was associated with activities of the early state transmitted in the name of "Xia," though it cannot be substantiated, cannot be ruled out either.

The Founding of the Shang Dynasty and Early Shang Migrations

The city of Erlitou had fallen in the later sixteenth century BC. Recent systematic carbon-14 dating has fixed the end of the last period of the cultural deposit in Erlitou at around 1530 BC, which comes very close to

1554 BC as the first year of the Shang Dynasty previously suggested by historians.[11] With the founding of the Shang Dynasty, we enter into a historical period when North China was ruled by a royal dynasty whose outline history, most typified in the list of the Shang kings (Fig. 3.4), is testified by the excavated written records in a close match with the received tradition on Shang royal genealogy. In the Shang case, though this list was reconstructed on the basis of the divination records from the late part of the dynasty (see Chapter 4), there seems little doubt that it manifests rules and stipulations that go back to the early centuries of Shang.

However, the narrative account of the origins of the Shang people by Sima Qian in *The Grand Scribe's Records* has a clear mythical element. According to this account, the genitorial ancestor of the Shang people was named Qi, who was born because his mother swallowed an egg laid by a blackbird (swallow) – the "blackbird" myth is celebrated in a poem in the *Book of Poetry*. The early Shang people are reported as being engaged substantially in trading activities, but because they lived in an area frequently threatened by floods, probably on the eastern plain, the Shang people had moved their capital some eight times contemporary with the Xia Dynasty to their west. One of the trading trips took Wang Hai, six generations after Qi, to a polity of a greedy chief probably in present-day northern Henan where he was treacherously murdered and his fortune stolen. His nephew, Shang Jia, avenged his death by conquering that polity.

Shang Jia happened to be the first pre-dynastic ancestor to whom the late Shang kings made frequent sacrificial offerings (Fig. 3.4, P1). He must have been critically important to the Shang people's rise as a state and power, although further information on this had been lost. After five more generations, the Shang eventually grew into a major power under the leadership of Tang, known as Da Yi in the oracle-bone inscriptions (Fig. 3.4, K1). Tang, from his capital in a place called "Bo" and helped by his eastern allies, thus conquered the Xia Dynasty and founded the Shang Dynasty around 1554 BC. However, even after the founding of the Shang Dynasty, for various natural or political reasons as the tradition says, the Shang people continued to relocate their political center five times in different places including most importantly Zhong Ding's (K9) capital at Ao, Jian Jia's (K11) capital at Xiang, and finally Pan Geng's (K18) capital at Yin, which is present-day Anyang.

[11] David W. Pankenier, "Astronomical Dates in Shang and Western Zhou," *Early China* 7 (1981–2), 3–37. David Keightley now also accepts 1554 BC as the first year of the Shang dynasty; see David N. Keightley, "The Shang: China's First Historical Dynasty," in Michael Loewe and Edward L. Shaughnessy (eds.), *The Cambridge History of Ancient China: From the Origins of Civilization to 221 BC* (Cambridge: Cambridge University Press, 1999), p. 248.

Fig. 3.3 The Bingong *xu* and its inscription.

the Xia Dynasty ever existed, we would find references to it in the written
sources of the Shang Dynasty that comes even closer to the Xia time. But
this is not true and the Shang oracle-bone inscriptions say nothing about a
Xia Dynasty the Shang had conquered. However, the strength of this
evidence to negate the historicity of the Xia Dynasty is itself weakened by
the bare fact that the Shang oracle-bone inscriptions are divinatory records
that are narrowly concerned with powers that still affected the Shang state;
therefore, they show no historical curiosity at all about an enemy power that
exited in the distant past and no longer affected the life of the Shang king.

It is intriguing, and indeed natural, for any scholar to want to see whether
there is a link between the two processes: the development of state-level
society evident in the archaeological data, and the establishment of a
dynastic royal state as learned from the transmitted historical tradition.
Chronological studies of early Chinese history certainly project the three
to four centuries before Shang back onto the Xia Dynasty, depending
on the dates of the Shang Dynasty (*c.* 1554–1046 BC). This suggests a
time-frame into which the range of carbon-14 dates of the Erlitou culture
(*c.* 1900–1600 BC) mentioned above fall perfectly. In fact, in several sites
the deposit of the Erlitou culture overrides the strata of the Longshan
culture, and in other sites it is intruded or overlapped by Shang strata.
Moreover, the ancient sources also indicate that the various centers associated with activities of the Xia kings, based on historical–geographical

studies, were located largely in the same region as the sites that belong to the Erlitou culture – western Henan and southern Shanxi.[9] In short, the evidence places the Erlitou culture into the same time period and space in which the Xia Dynasty described by the received tradition is supposed to have been the rule.

To many scholars in China and still some in the West, this temporal and spatial coincidence provides a suitable base for identifying the Erlitou culture as the material culture of the Xia Dynasty and the Erlitou site as the Xia royal capital. In fact, there were not a few studies published in China in the past thirty years that took the identification of the so-called "Xia Culture" as their basic research assumption. However, this identification of the Erlitou culture with the Xia Dynasty would appear to lack any ground to other scholars; some have written strong rejections against the identification, in effect continuing a scholarly debate that has its origins in the "Doubting Antiquity" movement (see Chapter 1). The strongest point against the identification has been the complete lack of any *written evidence* from the Erlitou site or any other sites of the Erlitou culture that may be connected to the historical records about Xia. In the absence of such clear written evidence there is no way to link Erlitou to Xia. Except for a few, this latter view has been widely shared among scholars in the West.

Therefore, the issue is not only intriguing, but can be academically and politically contentious.[10] It is, however, our intellectual responsibility to disassociate scholarly discussions from any politically toned claims or accusations which are invariably based on ideology, not evidence. On the other hand, we need to be realistic about the current condition of the evidence and be aware of the full range of possible interpretations. First, there is no way at present, lacking written evidence from Erlitou or other culturally affiliated sites, to determine that Erlitou was indeed the capital of Xia. Before such evidence is brought to light and a direct link, rather than logical reasoning, can be established, the question will remain open. On the other hand, our current evidence has not proved that Erlitou was not Xia by, perhaps, identifying Erlitou with another polity that existed in the relevant time period and space. If one wants to make a strong argument that Erlitou was not Xia, then the only evidence that he/she can draw on is that there is no evidence that it was Xia. The point regarding contemporaneous written evidence is well taken, but it is itself

---

[9] K. C. Chang, *The Archaeology of Ancient China*, 4th edn. (New Haven: Yale University Press, 1986), p. 319.

[10] For a summary of the recent debate about the Erlitou–Xia relation, see Li Liu, "Academic Freedom, Political Correctness, and Early Civilisation in Chinese Archaeology: The Debate on Xia–Erlitou Relations," *Antiquity* 83 (2009), 831–843.

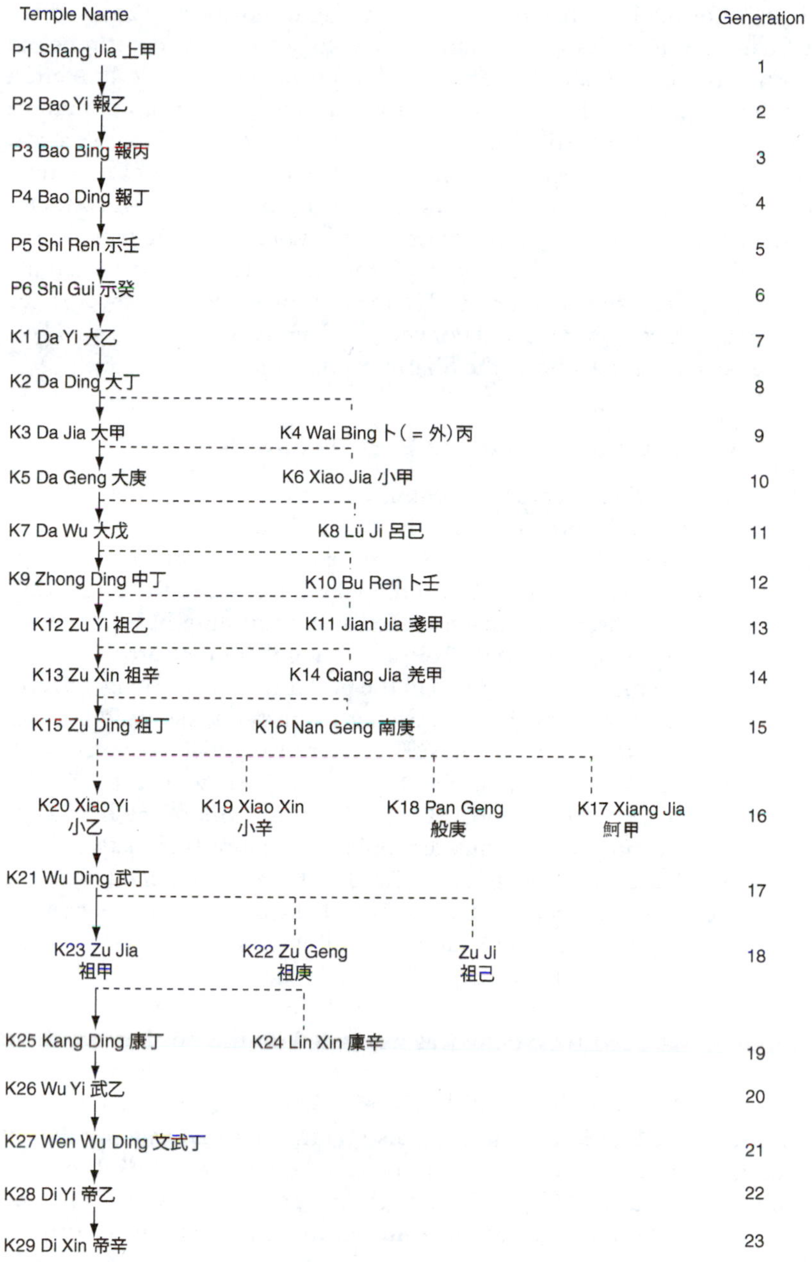

Temple Name   Generation

P1 Shang Jia 上甲   1

P2 Bao Yi 報乙   2

P3 Bao Bing 報丙   3

P4 Bao Ding 報丁   4

P5 Shi Ren 示壬   5

P6 Shi Gui 示癸   6

K1 Da Yi 大乙   7

K2 Da Ding 大丁   8

K3 Da Jia 大甲   K4 Wai Bing 卜（＝外）丙   9

K5 Da Geng 大庚   K6 Xiao Jia 小甲   10

K7 Da Wu 大戊   K8 Lü Ji 呂己   11

K9 Zhong Ding 中丁   K10 Bu Ren 卜壬   12

K12 Zu Yi 祖乙   K11 Jian Jia 戔甲   13

K13 Zu Xin 祖辛   K14 Qiang Jia 羌甲   14

K15 Zu Ding 祖丁   K16 Nan Geng 南庚   15

K20 Xiao Yi   K19 Xiao Xin   K18 Pan Geng   K17 Xiang Jia   16
小乙   小辛   般庚   阿甲

K21 Wu Ding 武丁   17

K23 Zu Jia   K22 Zu Geng   Zu Ji   18
祖甲   祖庚   祖己

K25 Kang Ding 康丁   K24 Lin Xin 廩辛   19

K26 Wu Yi 武乙   20

K27 Wen Wu Ding 文武丁   21

K28 Di Yi 帝乙   22

K29 Di Xin 帝辛   23

Fig. 3.4 The Shang king list.

Except for the last Shang capital in Anyang in northern Henan where the Shang oracle bones were found, archaeology has yet to determine the locations of other Shang centers. In addition to the possible limitation of archaeological work, there is perhaps also the issue of interpretative meaning of the so-called "moves of capital" in the traditional records. Very likely, some of the Shang kings might have at some point of time constructed more than one base and frequently traveled between them. Some of these centers might have been very minor and only temporarily occupied by the Shang king, and therefore they are hard to determine during field archaeological survey. There is strong evidence, however, for two Shang centers, both located not very far from Erlitou, which are likely to have been counted among the Shang capitals mentioned above.

Urban Civilization of the Early Bronze Age

In the archaeological records, concomitant with the fall of Erlitou, there arose two large-scale urban centers in the middle Yellow River region, Yanshi, only 5 km from Erlitou and located on the north bank of the Luo River, and Zhengzhou located some 90 km further to the east. While archaeological research has shown undoubted continuity in terms of the typological progression of pottery from Erlitou to these new urban centers, the relocation of the political centers in the post-Erlitou era and its possible connections to the founding of the Shang Dynasty in the middle of the sixteenth century BC have puzzled scholars for nearly half a century.

The city in Yanshi was a major archaeological discovery in the 1980s. In particular, its proximity to Erlitou on the south bank of the Luo River naturally raised questions about the political relationship between the two cities. Continuing research in the 1990s has confirmed that the construction of the city wall at Yanshi can be divided into two phases. In the initial phase (Period I), a rectangular wall-enclosure of 1100 × 740 m was built centering on building group no. 1, identified as the "Central Palace Zone," which was itself surrounded by a thinner wall about 20 m wide. During Period II, the city was expanded on the northeast with an additional wall constructed to protect this new area, and the whole city thus measured 1200 m E–W and 1700 m N–S. This history of continuous construction in Yanshi is confirmed also by the fact that in a number of building compounds architectural remains belonging to two subsequent periods were excavated (Fig. 3.5). The central palace zone was connected by ditches to the moat which surrounded the outer city wall, forming the drainage system of the city. About 100 m to the west and indeed near the southwest corner of the city was located another group of fifteen rectangular building foundations, considered by the excavators to have

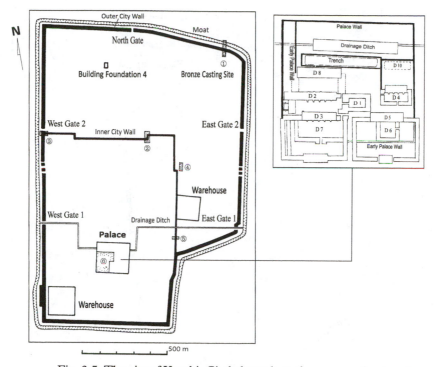

Fig. 3.5 The city of Yanshi. Circled numbers show excavation trenches 1996–8; inset shows palace foundations D1–D8 and D10.

functioned as the main warehouse of the city. A number of other foundations were discovered in the north half of the outer city, possibly serving as religious centers, and remains of a bronze casting foundry have been located at its northeastern corner. Recent carbon-14 dating has dated Period I (the initial construction phase) to 1605–1490 BC and Period III to 1425–1365 BC. This suggests that the whole city in Yanshi was probably under occupation for some 250 years, postdating the fall of Erlitou, during which it was the most prominent political and cultural center on the Luoyang plain, but might not be the most impressive in North China.

The Shang city in Zhengzhou was discovered in the early 1950s. The wall, which still stands above ground today, runs about 1700 m N–S and 1870 m E–W, having a total area of 3,179,000 m^2 (317.9 ha), being much larger than the city in Yanshi. While this wall-enclosure has been known for forty years, new research conducted in the 1990s has made it perfectly clear that the wall only encircled the core area of what was once the great metropolis in Zhengzhou. A section of the outer wall was found to the

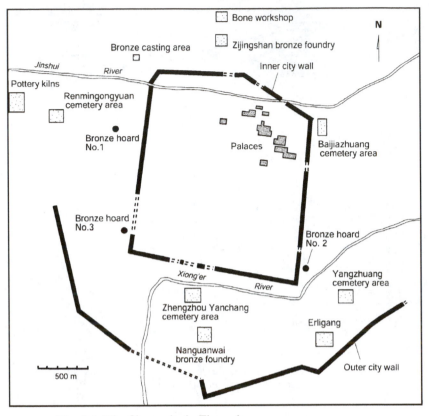

Fig. 3.6 The Shang city in Zhengzhou.

south, running for some 5,000 m, which if complete, would have encircled an area of some 2,000 ha (Fig. 3.6). In other words, the entire area of the Zhengzhou city was nearly ten times larger than the city in Yanshi. Located about 500 m to the south of the inner city was the famous site called Erligang, excavated in 1953, where the material culture of the period was first identified, giving rise to the term "Erligang culture" which, based on stratigraphic evidence, was further divided into two phases – the Upper Erligang Phase and the Lower Erligang Phase during which the inner city in Zhengzhou was constructed.[12]

However, the quality of archaeological data from the inner city of Zhengzhou is not as good as those from Yanshi due largely to the difficulty involving fieldwork in the area now buried under the modern city.

[12] K. C. Chang, *Shang Civilization* (New Haven: Yale University Press, 1980), pp. 263–283.

Fig. 3.7 Bronze vessel from Zhengzhou.

Between the two wall circles, numerous settlements, burials, and workshops have been found. These include more than twenty elite tombs that contain sets of bronze vessels, in addition to hundreds of tombs that contain only pottery. These tombs suggest that, in comparison to Erlitou, burying bronze vessels and weapons was now rather a common practice in relatively large tombs. However, bronzes in Zhengzhou were frequently also excavated from specially prepared storage pits or caches which have yielded some of the masterpieces of the Zhengzhou bronze industry. The most important are a cache discovered at Duling in 1974 and another in the Nanshuncheng Street in 1996 (Fig. 3.7). Bronzes from these pits are considerably heavier and technically more advanced, suggesting that the bronze industry at Zhengzhou had advanced to a higher level of development than at Erlitou. This is best indicated by the introduction of square vessels of large magnitude which are technologically more difficult to produce.[13]

Based on the dates of fifteen carbon-14 samples, the Lower Erligang Phase can now be placed with considerable accuracy at between 1580 and 1415 BC. In other words, the construction of the inner city of Zhengzhou began at about the same time as the inner city of Yanshi, and thereafter the

[13] Thorp, *China in the Early Bronze Age*, pp. 85–99.

two centers separated by 90 km coexisted for some 200 years covering the early part of the Shang Dynasty, by historical chronology. Although only three pieces of inscribed oracle bones have been found in Zhengzhou, which failed to link the immense city to the Shang Dynasty through contemporary written evidence,[14] the great continuity in the material culture and the writing system from Zhengzhou to the late Shang capital Anyang certainly offers grounds for scholars to consider the historical contexts woven behind the construction of this urban center prior to Anyang. To some it was the ruin of capital Bo, the political center of Shang since its founding king, Tang (K1); to others, it was the second Shang capital Ao, constructed by the ninth king, Zhong Ding, who ruled during the middle Shang period.[15] In recent years, the gap has been significantly narrowed and it looks more plausible now to associate the middle Shang period with another important site that is later than Zhengzhou (see Chapter 4), leaving the early Shang as the only time-frame in which the Zhengzhou Shang city can fit. But its historical name still cannot be properly determined.

Compared to Zhengzhou, the city in Yanshi was apparently a minor or secondary center. In view of the cultural complexity of Yanshi and its geographical proximity to Erlitou, many consider it as a stronghold for the Shang state that centered on Zhengzhou, believing that the population on the Luoyang plain was mainly Xia, whom the Shang state had recently subjugated and who were in need of being kept under close watch. While the question has to remain open at present particularly when it comes to the issue of Xia, the transition from Erlitou to Yanshi in the archaeological records must have corresponded to a major political change that happened on the Luoyang plain and served to factually integrate the region with the larger geopolitical entity of the Shang state to the east. A recent important archaeo-astronomical study reveals that the difference between the orientation of building foundations in Erlitou some 6–10 degrees west of north and that in the Yanshi city where buildings were oriented about 7 degrees to the east of north, must have been the result of using different stellar features to align architectures on the true north. The latter orientation (east of north) seen in Yanshi was followed by buildings in all Shang sites including Zhengzhou and Anyang, and was very much identified with the Shang culture.[16] This suggests strongly that the transition from

[14] The oracle-bone inscriptions from Zhengzhou have been recently examined in Ken-ichi Takashima, "Literacy to the South and the East of Anyang in Shang China: Zhengzhou and Daxinzhuang," in Li Feng and David Branner (eds.), *Writing and Literacy in Early China* (Seattle: University of Washington Press, 2011), pp. 141–172.

[15] Chang, *Shang Civilization*, pp. 271–272.

[16] David W. Pankenier, "A Brief History of Beiji (Northern Culmen): With an Excursion on the Origins of the Character Di," *Journal of American Oriental Society* **124.2** (2004), 211–236.

Erlitou to Yanshi/Zhengzhou, despite continuities in pottery typology, might have corresponded with a fundamental change in the political–cosmological culture of North China, possibly related to the establishment of a new dynastic rule, if not to the collapse of an old political regime.

Erligang Expansion: Political Landscape Learned from Material Cultures

In the three centuries before Shang, Erlitou was the only society in China so far as we know that enjoyed a developed bronze industry; beyond the Erlitou metropolis, social life remained essentially similar to that of the previous Longshan period. This phenomenon has encouraged some scholars to propose that the fundamental function of the early state in China was to centralize the production of the bronze vessels and to control their distribution to the local elites.[17] However, this situation had changed dramatically during the Erligang period that ended the single-center monopoly of the use (and perhaps also production) of bronze vessels. Bronze vessels began to be found at a distance from Zhengzhou, in such sites like Yuanqu in southern Shanxi and Panlongcheng in central Hubei in the middle Yangzi region. The manufacturing of bronze vessels was carried out, beyond Zhengzhou, evidently also in such regional centers like Yanshi and Yuanqu.

Archaeological discoveries suggest that this process of spreading of the bronze technology previously developed at Erlitou was actually embedded in a much larger process of the cultural expansion from central and western Henan to regions far beyond (Map 3.2). Standard Erligang types of pottery have been found in several sites in the Wei River valley in the west. In the north, the same pottery inventory has been identified in central and southern Hebei; in the south, the sites associated with the walled city of Panlongcheng offer an indisputable presentation of the Erligang culture in the middle Yangzi region. Evidently, an extensive process of cultural homogenization was taking place during the Erligang centuries that gave birth to a gigantic geo-cultural unity that had never been achieved under any Neolithic culture before, and was no longer maintained after the Erligang period. Of course, we cannot tell to what extent the cultural expansion we see in archaeology was underscored or affected by the political expansion of the Erligang Shang state, for the relationship between material culture and political entity can never be straightforward. Usually the expansion of a political system can take on two forms: through enlargement of the system itself or through replication of the system to

[17] Liu and Chen, *State Formation in Early China*, pp. 133–137.

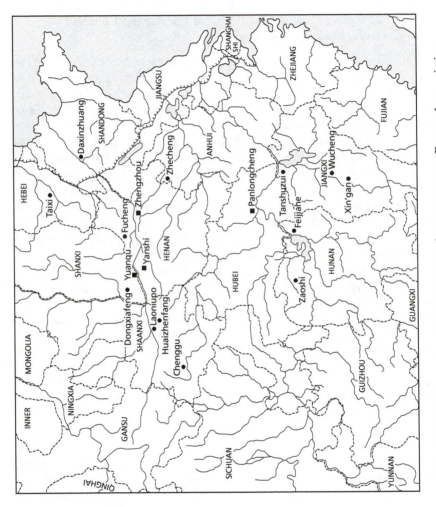

Map 3.2 Erligang and contemporary or nearly contemporary Bronze Age societies.

produce competing autonomous units of various degrees. The expansion of the Erligang Shang state could have taken both routes.

Some of the regional centers such as Panlongcheng might have indeed had a direct political relation with the Erligang state based on Zhengzhou, some 500 km away in the north. The walled site is located on a small hilltop near the north bank of the Yangzi River in Hubei Province. The wall-enclosure, measuring 290 × 260 m, was excavated in the 1970s. In its center north was found a rectangular building foundation as the main structure on the site. Outside the wall circle, at several locales, tombs of large size were excavated, yielding bronze vessels and weapons identical to those from Zhengzhou. Not only these bronze vessels but also the pottery types found in the district of Panlongcheng match closely those found in Zhengzhou. This high degree of uniformity suggests strongly that the site of Panlongcheng might have been an outpost of the Erligang Shang state. More importantly, Panlongcheng was located at the south end of the ancient road from the north through the Nanyang Basin and reaching the north bank of the Yangzi River to the east of the ancient Yunmeng Marsh, at a key point to cross the Yangzi south into Hunan and Jiangxi Provinces. The recent discovery of a copper-mining site in Tongling in Jiangxi Province suggests that Panlongcheng might have suitably located at the key point of transportation of copper from the middle Yangzi region to the north (Box 3.2).

Box 3.2   Mining in Early China

Over the past half century, archaeologists have made important progress in understanding the technological system that supported the bronze industry of the Shang and Western Zhou states as well as other Bronze Age societies in China. Modern geological surveys suggest that the richest concentration of copper deposits in China lie in the mountains along the south bank of the Yangzi River in present-day Hubei, Hunan, and Jiangxi Provinces. In 1973–5, an important ancient mining site was discovered on the mountain slopes called Tonglushan to the west of Daye City, located some 40 km from the bank of the Yangzi River in Hubei Province. Ancient mining activities on Tonglushan can be divided between open-surface quarrying and underground mining; underground mining was carried out through horizontal tunnels densely integrated with vertical shafts supported by wooden structures. Five large clusters of tunnels were cleared, yielding a large number of wooden and bronze tools and carrying baskets, as well as pottery vessels once used for meals by the ancient miners. In the areas surrounding the mines were scattered multiple smelting sites

Box 3.2 (cont.)

where tonnes of debris and remains of furnaces were found, suggesting that copper ores were locally smelted and transported out of the
region in the form of copper ingots (also found at the sites). Two
wooden samples from mining site XI are determined by carbon-14
dating to 3140 ± 80 and 2750 ± 70 BP, falling in a period contemporaneous with the Western Zhou.

The ancient mining area called Tongling is located in Ruichang in
Jiangxi Province, some 50 km to the southeast of Daye City, and was
excavated in 1989–92. Multiple ancient mines were discovered in the
area and the excavation suggests that they adhered to the same practice
of using wooden frames to stabilize the underground tunnels and the
straight shafts. Similarly in these tunnels were found a large number of
bronze tools and wooden equipment and bamboo baskets used for
transporting the ores. Interestingly in the same contexts were also
found pottery vessels that match very closely those types found in
Panlongcheng, belonging to the Upper Erligang and the middle
Shang culture in the north (Fig. 3.8). Other types of pottery found in
the mines date as late as the Warring States period. More than twenty
carbon samples have been extracted from the mines and dated to 3330
±60–2365 ± 75 BP, supporting the dates established on the basis of
pottery typology. They suggest that the local copper deposit continued
to be exploited from a time contemporaneous with middle Shang in
the north to the Warring States period. At the earliest stage, whether
the mining activities were managed by the local communities of the
Wucheng culture in Jiangxi or by certain Shang elites in close communication with Panlongcheng is still open to question, but there seems
little doubt that the region was among the major sources of copper that
supported the prosperity of bronze industry centered on Zhengzhou
and Anyang.

It is also true that under Erligang influence, in regions more distant
from the Yanshi–Zhengzhou axis, a number of bronze cultures gradually
developed that were almost certainly politically independent and culturally differentiated from Erligang. These include the Wucheng culture in
northern Jiangxi which evidently arose in prominence as a response to
the Erligang-associated political and economic activities in the middle
Yangzi region. In the east, a Bronze Age center was located near modern
Jinan in northwestern Shandong. In the west, another regional center of

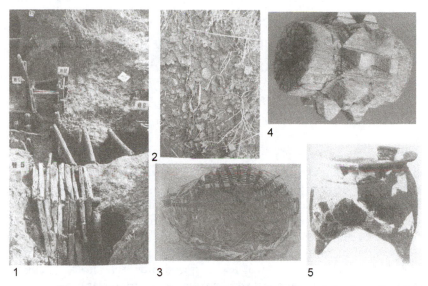

Fig. 3.8 Mining remains found in Tongling, Jiangxi: 1, view of ancient mine shafts; 2, layer of copper debris from on-site smelting; 3, basket; 4, wooden windlass; 5, a Shang-style pottery *li*-tripod.

bronze culture was found near Xi'an in central Shaanxi. These regional bronze cultural centers arose more or less simultaneously towards the end of the Erligang period and prospered in a time contemporary with the middle Shang period in central and northern Henan. It is well possible that at least some of these sites were centers of the newly rising state-level societies that subsequently competed with the Shang in the remaining centuries of the Shang Dynasty.

SELECTED READING

Liu, Li, and Chen Xingcan, *State Formation in Early China* (London: Duckworth, 2003).

Liu, Li, "Academic Freedom, Political Correctness, and Early Civilisation in Chinese Archaeology: The Debate on Xia–Erlitou Relations," *Antiquity* **83** (2009), 831–843.

Chang, K. C., *The Archaeology of Ancient China*, 4th edn. (New Haven: Yale University Press, 1986).

Shang Civilization (New Haven: Yale University Press, 1980).

Thorp, Robert, *China in the Early Bronze Age: Shang Civilization* (Philadelphia: University of Pennsylvania Press, 2006).

Nienhauser, William H. Jr. (ed.), *The Grand Scribe's Records*, vol. 1, *The Basic Annals of Pre-Han China* (Bloomington: Indiana University Press, 1994).

Anyang and beyond: Shang
and contemporary Bronze Age cultures

If we were to point to an archaeological site that over the course of more
than half a century has unceasingly offered sources of inspiration to
researches in various disciplines in understanding the essentials of early
Chinese civilization, it has to be Anyang. This immense Shang metropolis
of some 24 km^2 extending along the Huan River in northern Henan was
not only the "cradle of Chinese archaeology," but has also served as a firm
base for the joint operation of text-inspired inquiries into the political
history of the royal Shang state and studies that aim to clarify the characteristics of its material culture. Even since the beginning of the new
century, Anyang has continued to offer a number of astonishing new
discoveries that have significantly deepened our knowledge about the
Shang state and civilization. As Anyang has just celebrated the eightieth
anniversary of its discovery in 1928, its newly granted status as a "World
Heritage Site" is indeed very richly deserved.[1]

Discovering the Late Shang Dynasty

Beijing's winter was cold in the years that witnessed the crumbling of the
once glorious Manchu Empire when famine and malaria could easily take
control over the streets of the imperial capital. Towards the end of 1899,
Wang Yirong, President of the Imperial University, was terribly sick. His
servant turned up what were known as the "dragon bones" among other
prescribed ingredients in two bags which he brought back from a drugstore in the commercial street of southern Beijing.[2] Already well known
for his learning in traditional "Studies of Bronze and Stone Inscriptions,"[3]

---

[1] See UNESCO *World Heritage List*, "Yin Xu" (Ruins of the Shang) (ref. 1114); see http://
whc.unesco.org/en/list/1114.

[2] There are discrepancies in the accounts of the discovery of the oracle-bone inscriptions.
Another source says that the bones were brought from northern Henan directly to Wang's
residence in Beijing by a certain Merchant Chen from Shandong.

[3] "Studies of Bronze and Stone Inscriptions" (*Jinshixue*) is a native Chinese scholarship
developed first in the Northern Song dynasty (AD 960–1279) when scholars began to

Wang immediately noticed that there were archaic forms of writing on these bones; therefore he sent his servant back to the drugstore and purchased the remaining several hundred pieces at a high price. After about eight months when the allied Western armies invaded Beijing, the fleeing Manchu court appointed Wang to command the remaining Qing troops to defend the capital. This was mission impossible! After foreign soldiers broke his line of resistance and entered the city, Wang saw no hope for the imperial city to survive the onslaught and thus committed suicide to preserve his loyalty to the emperor and his people. The inscribed bones numbering some 300 pieces were handed by his son to Wang's friend, the famous scholar Liu E, who was himself banished to Central Asia upon the return of the Empress Dowager to the capital. However, the collection was able to go into print in 1903, the very first publication of oracle-bone inscriptions ever.

While the discovery of the ancient bones with writing soon became known in intellectual circles particularly in Beijing and Tianjin, it took about ten years for scholars to understand the historical significance of the bones as remains from the Shang Dynasty. By 1911, the end of the Qing Dynasty, some 2,000 newly collected oracle bones were published by Luo Zhenyu, the ultra-famous scholar collector in China, and they greatly enriched the contents of these rare divinatory inscriptions. In a series of essays published between 1915 and 1920, Wang Guowei, the other pioneer of oracle-bone scholarship, based on examining a number of sacrificial tables recorded on the bones, successfully reconstructed a list of Shang kings extending as far back as the pre-conquest Shang ancestors. When he compared this list with the Shang royal genealogy recorded by Sima Qian in his *Grand Scribe's Records*, he found only the ancestor Bao Ding (pre-dynastic P4 after Shang Jia) (Fig. 3.4 above) was switched in his position in the transmitted source (in the *Grand Scribe's Records*, he is the first ancestor immediately after Shang Jia). Another mistake is the place of Zu Yi (King 12) who was a son of Zhong Ding (King 9), but was mistaken in the latter source as a son of Jian Jia (King 11). Despite these mistakes, the information given by Sima Qian is proven to have been largely accurate with regard to Shang royal genealogy.

As for the provenance of the oracle bones, it was eventually tracked down to a place called "Anyang" in northern Henan, which is a middle-size

collect and study inscriptions on stone steles and bronze vessels as a way to interpret institutions of the ancient time. The Song Dynasty was responsible for the publication of some twenty such works. The Qing Dynasty saw the resurgence of this scholarship in the seventeenth to eighteenth centuries. It was regarded as one of the roots of archaeology in the pre-modern world. See K. C. Chang, *The Archaeology of Ancient China*, 4th edn. (New Haven: Yale University Press, 1986), pp. 4–13; Bruce G. Trigger, *A History of Archaeological Thought* (Cambridge: Cambridge University Press, 1989), pp. 42–43.

Fig. 4.1 Anyang or the "Ruins of Yin."

city today. This came as no surprise as there is strong evidence in the Han Dynasty sources that explicitly identifies Anyang with the capital of the eighteenth Shang king, Pan Geng. As late as the Han Dynasty, the area on the south bank of the Huan River near Anyang was still called the "Ruin of Yin" (Fig. 4.1). Further studies of the oracle-bone inscriptions confirm that they were indeed divination records of the Shang kings from Wu Ding (King 21) to the end of the Shang Dynasty. The records of the first three kings after the move including Pan Geng himself have not been identified among the current corpus of oracle-bone inscriptions, and there has been the question of whether these earlier kings were buried in Anyang. But this question has now been answered to everyone's satisfaction by an important archaeological discovery made in the new century (see below). Tradition says that after King Pan Geng's historical move, doubtless to present-day Anyang, for 273 years the Shang never relocated their capital again until the fall of the dynasty. But the second half of the statement, however, does not seem to be precisely true.

The Late Shang Metropolis: Royal Life and Economic Power

With a rudimentary background already learned from the oracle bones and the historical records about the site, from 1928 until the breakout of the Sino-Japanese war in 1937, fifteen large-scale excavations were planned and executed in Anyang by the Institute of History and Philology, Academia Sinica. With a series of important reports published prior to and during the war, Anyang soon became an internationally known archaeological site. From 1949, the Institute of Archaeology, Chinese Academy of Social Sciences, took over the excavation of Anyang, and continued to turn out important discoveries over the next fifty years. With the additional excavation of two large tombs in the royal cemetery and the finding of two large storage pits filled with oracle bones, one being published only recently, and the numerous bronzes and other types of artifacts, we now know a fair amount about this immense site and its material wealth – the center of the Shang civilization. The total area of the Anyang site is estimated at 24 km^2 (or 2,400 ha) which is at least 45 times bigger than any second-level settlement and perhaps 200 times bigger than the small villages that existed at the same time on the North China plain.

The center of this huge city complex is located right below the bend of the Huan River flowing southeast along the edges of the Shang royal palace zone (Fig. 4.2). The name Huan (river) was in use already during the Shang Dynasty, the same graph appearing on both the Shang oracle bones and bronze vessels. The palace zone is protected on its south and west by a deep moat 1,800 m long, though no wall was found along it. Because of its better condition of preservation in comparison to the city core of Zhengzhou, we have a much clearer picture of the internal organization of the palace zone located on gently rising ground over-looking the Huan River. The entire palace complex is composed of as many as fifty-three large-scale building foundations, divided by the archaeologists into three clusters, and the function of each cluster can be determined with some confidence. Cluster B, located at the center and composed of twenty-one foundations, was apparently the focus of the entire zone. It was centered on two large foundations in the early construction period, and an 85-m-long later foundation (B8) was super-posed on the early ones. Numerous small burial pits were found under the buildings or surrounding the compound particularly to its west, suggesting perhaps the ritual/religious function of at least some of the buildings in this cluster. It is very likely that these buildings once hosted the activities of the Shang kings and the divinatory officials of the Shang state. Cluster C is located close to the southwest corner of Cluster B and is dominated by the main foundation C1, which is surrounded by smaller strips of buildings and by a large number of sacrificial pits. The excavators considered Cluster C to have been temples constructed later than Cluster B, perhaps some time towards the end of the Shang

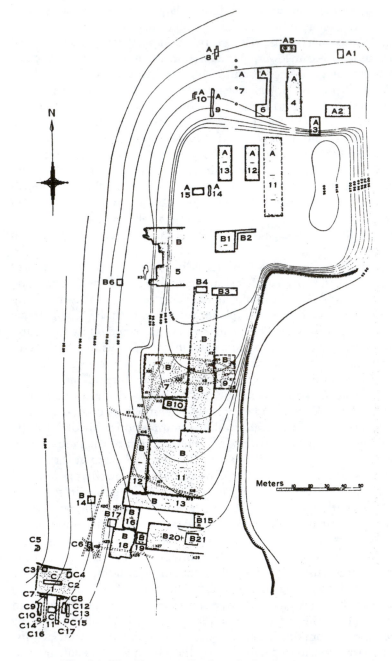

Fig. 4.2 The Shang royal palaces in Anyang.

dynasty. Cluster A, located to the north of Cluster B, is composed of fifteen buildings, mostly oriented north–south with doors open to the east. Very few sacrificial pits were found in this area; therefore, the excavators consider it to have been the living quarters of the Shang king and his family.[4]

All wooden structures were constructed on tamped earth platforms. It is clear that the process of construction was accompanied by ritual killings and sacrificial activities which continued even after the completion of the building project. Walls were also built by tamping earth up with wood columns as the interior supporting structure and their surface was carefully treated.

Crossing the Huan River north is the large area referred to as Xibeigang, where the Shang royal cemetery was located (Fig. 4.3). In this open area surrounded today by a wall that demarcates this onsite museum, a total of thirteen large tombs were found and divided in two groups.

The western group comprises seven tombs with four long ramps and another unfinished huge pit. Separated by some 200 m, the eastern group comprises one tomb with four ramps and four others with one or two ramps. Taking tomb no. 1001 as an example, the tomb pit is about 10 × 10 m with a wooden chamber originally constructed at the bottom of the pit; in each corner of the chamber a human guard with a bronze dagger was buried. Human skeletons were also found at the bottom of the ramps and in the layers of the earth that filled in the huge pit. Certainly human sacrifice was an important character of Shang civilization and an integral part of Shang burial practice. In that regard, the most astonishing demonstration of this point is the sacrificial pits located in the vast areas surrounding the large tombs in the east group. To date, more than 2,500 sacrificial pits have been found of which about 1,500 have been excavated, yielding ten to fifteen skeletons (with heads or without) in each pit. There is no doubt that these are the remains of the sacrificial humans said in the Shang oracle-bone inscriptions to have been offered to the deceased Shang kings buried in the huge tombs. At least 30,000 human victims were offered in this way in the religious sacrificial activities that took place in the royal cemetery.

The cultural and religious meaning of the burial remains in Xibeigang has been well understood by scholars. But since so little has been excavated from the royal tombs themselves (due to looting

---

[4] K. C. Chang, *Shang Civilization* (New Haven: Yale University Press, 1980), pp. 90–99.

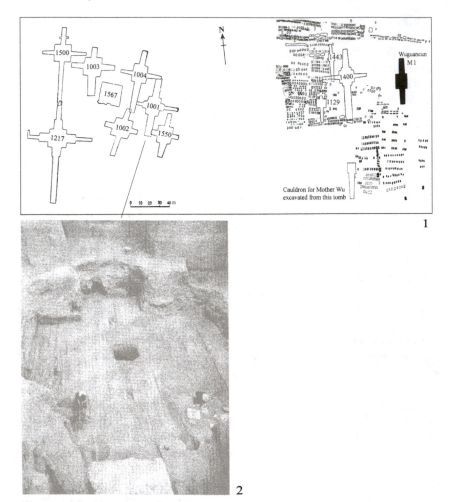

Fig. 4.3 1, Plan of the Shang royal cemetery; 2, royal tomb no. 1001.

which seems to have taken place soon after the fall of Anyang), there is disagreement with regard to the identification of the tombs with particular Shang kings. There are two essential points on which scholars differ from each other. The first point is whether only tombs with four ramps (eight in total) belonged to the Shang kings, or whether the royal burials also included pits with only two ramps (three in total). The second point is whether all twelve Shang kings were buried in Xibeigang, or whether some of them might have been absent from the

royal cemetery.[5] Based on new knowledge of the pottery sequence accumulated over thirty years, in 1981 members of the Anyang Archaeological
Team rejected the possibility that the first three kings, Pan Geng, Xiao
Xin, and Xiao Yi, who also ruled from Anyang, were buried in the royal
cemetery in Xibeigang. This leaves only the eight tombs with four ramps
which they identified with the eight Shang kings from Wu Ding (King 21,
in tomb no. 1001) to Di Yi (King 28, in no. 1003), leaving the unfinished
no. 1567 to be the tomb of the last king, Di Xin.[6] Recent archaeological
discoveries in Anyang suggest that the absence of the first three kings from
the cemetery in Xibeigang is very probable, since another Shang center,
which is chronologically earlier than the building foundations in the palace
zone and the royal tombs already known, indeed was also located in the
Anyang region (see below).

The Huan River, given the relatively warmer climate during late Shang,
must have been more abundant in water then today, providing an important
lifeline through the Shang metropolis. The oracle-bone inscriptions record
Shang kings making repeated offerings to the deity of the Huan River. The
river also offered a suitable resort for the Shang king and his attendants to
carry out various kinds of ritual activities and entertainments, as vividly shown
by the recently discovered bronze turtle, the Zuoce Ban *yuan* (Box 4.1).
Recent archaeological fieldwork has revealed a large pond, located on the
western edge of the royal palaces and connecting to the Huan River, and this
might have provided a convenient location for the Shang king to board a boat
for tours on the Huan River. On the two banks of the river were numerous
smaller residential sites such as those excavated in a number of locations
crossing the river to the east. On the west bank, the areas close to the palace
zone, as recent archaeological discoveries show, might have been taken up by
blocks of elite residences, including the palaces of the Shang royal princes.
Further south is an area called Miaopu where archaeologists have located the
remains of a large-scale bronze-casting foundry. Tombs of middle or small
sizes have been found in numerous locations in Anyang, but the largest

---

[5] For instance, in 1975, Virginia Kane first proposed to identify all eleven tombs with either
two or four ramps with the eleven Shang kings from Pan Geng (King 18) to Di Yi (King
28), leaving the unfinished tomb no. 1567 to have been prepared for the last king, Di Xin,
who was killed by the invading Zhou army. See Virginia Kane, "A Re-examination of Anyang Archaeology," *Ars Orientalis* **10** (1975), 103–106, 108–110. K. C. Chang, while
agreeing on the basic point that both tombs with two ramps and those with four are royal
tombs, regarded the two zones of the cemetery as having contained the burials of the
alternative generations of Shang kings starting with Pan Geng (west zone: generations 1, 3,
5, 7; east zone: generations 2, 4, 6). See Chang, *Shang Civilization*, pp. 187–188.
[6] To be more specific, in this system: 1001 (Wu Ding) → 1550 (Zu Geng) → 1400 (Zu Jia)
→ 1004 (Ling Xin) →1002 (Kang Ding) → 1500 (Wu Yi) → 1217 (Wen Ding) → 1003
(Di Yi) → 1567 (Ding Xin).

Box 4.1   Zuoce Ban's Turtle: An Example of an Inscribed Shang Bronze

Bronzes began to be inscribed in the early phase of Anyang. However, only a handful of inscriptions on bronzes from the entire Anyang period (mostly from its later half) offer a narrative context, while the majority is composed of single-graph marks that are considered to be family emblems. This bronze was cast in the shape of a turtle measuring 21.4 cm from the head to the tail, with four arrows standing on its back and side. Along the central line on the plastron thirty-three characters were cast in four columns (Fig. 4.4). The content of the inscription explains well the origin of the bronze turtle, situating it in the historical context and geographical environment of Anyang:

On the *bingshen* day (#33), the Shang king floated the Huan River in a boat and captured a turtle. As it happened, the king shot four arrows and none of them had missed the target. Coming up on the bank and returning to the royal palace, the king decided to offer the turtle to Zuoce (Document Maker) Ban who was very likely to have been in the king's entourage. The king verbally commanded Ban to cast the story onto a bronze to be treasured. Apparently, not only did Ban cast a bronze with an inscription to commemorate the royal award, but actually cast a bronze turtle with four arrows shot on it. The archery ritual performed from a boat continued to serve as a royal game during the Western Zhou period.

Fig. 4.4 Zuoce Ban's turtle.

concentration of such burials seems to have been located in the so-called "Western Zone" of Anyang, the broad area to the west of the palace zone.

The beginning of the twenty-first century has brought important new discoveries that shed light on the level of complexity of the economic life in Anyang with particular regard to craft production. In 2003–4 a large cluster of bronze-casting facilities was uncovered in an area of 380 × 100 m to the north of Xiaomintun on the western periphery of Anyang, yielding as many as 70,000 pieces of molds and about 100 clay models of bronze vessels and numerous other types of objects. This is the largest bronze-casting site ever found dating to the Shang Dynasty, and it provides important new information about the organization, production process, and technology of bronze manufacture in Anyang, which await further analysis. Shortly afterwards, in 2006, about 34,000 kg of processed bones were excavated from a 10-m-wide trench that was a part of an immense bone workshop estimated to have had a total area of 17,600 m^2, located to the north of Miaopu in the southern part of Anyang. Included are bones from predominantly large bovines (and some from pigs) that were there cleaned, cut, and made into various types of implements. A recent analysis has estimated the output of the bone factory to have been 77 bone artifacts per day, with a total of more than 4 million items over the 150 years when the workshop was in operation. The high figure raises the possibility that the workshop produced not only items for use by the local Anyang elites, but perhaps also artifacts traded in markets beyond Anyang.[7]

The Tomb of Lady Hao and Advance in Bronze Casting

In 1975, a spectacular discovery was made in Anyang – the excavation of the tomb of Lady Hao – which nicely alleviated the disappointment of archaeologists at having found so little in the royal tombs in Xibeigang. Although not a royal tomb itself and therefore much smaller in that regard, the occupant of the tomb is believed to have been the politically most active wife of the most powerful Shang king in Anyang, Wu Ding (King 21). Oracle-bone inscriptions from the reign of the king offer plenty of information about this royal lady. King Wu Ding once divined that Lady Hao would give birth to a royal prince; he also divined for her good fortune on a military campaign along with a famous Shang captain. Another inscription records her mission to recruit, perhaps, soldiers in a locality away from Anyang. Other records have Lady Hao herself leading an army of more than 10,000 soldiers on campaign against the Qiang

[7] See Roderick B. Campbell, Zhipeng Li, Yuling He, and Yuan Jing, "Consumption, Exchange and Production at the Great Settlement Shang: Bone-Working at Tiesanlu, Anyang," *Antiquity* 85 (2011), 1279–1297.

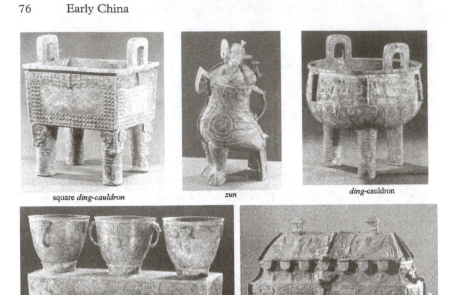

square *ding-cauldron*

zun

ding-cauldron

Joint-body *yan* -steamer

square *yi*-vessel

Fig. 4.5 Bronze vessels unearthed from the tomb of Lady Hao.

people to the west of Shang. Lady Hao was doubtless the most accomplished royal woman in the entire Anyang period.

Her tomb (no. 5) was not in Xibeigang, but about 150 m to the west of Cluster C in the western part of the royal palace zone, evidently suggesting her special status and close relationship to the reigning king, certainly Wu Ding, who must have wanted to keep her spirit in close reach. Above the tomb pit was the foundation of her temple, and it was actually this very earth foundation that kept the hands of the tomb robbers away from her tomb. Nearly 2,000 artifacts were unearthed from this tomb, including, most importantly, as many as 468 bronze vessels and weapons (Fig. 4.5) and 755 beautiful jade items, making it the richest tomb ever excavated in Anyang.[8] Certainly, one can only imagine how much could have been found in any of the huge royal tombs if they had not been looted. Some of the bronzes on which Lady Hao is referred to as "Mother Xin" were likely cast by her son while others were probably used by herself on various ritual

---

[8] On the discovery of Lady Hao's tomb, see Elizabeth Childs-Johnson, "Excavation of Tomb No. 5 at Yinxu, Anyang," *Chinese Sociology and Anthropology* 15.3 (1983), 3–125.

Fig. 4.6 Styles of bronze décor from Anyang, identified by Max Loehr.

and religious occasions before they were buried with her. They represent the highest level of bronze manufacturing during the late Shang Dynasty.

Bronzes from the Anyang period used to be famously divided by the art historian Max Loehr into five different styles, each representing a stage in the evolution of bronze art from simpler to more complex (Fig. 4.6).[9] Styles I and II, the two earliest types, are single-layer broad bands and thin linear patterns that were popular largely in the Erligang to the early Anyang period. However, the discovery of the tomb of Lady Hao suggests that the most elaborate style V, representing the latest stage in Loehr's evolutionary model, already dominated the decorative pattern on bronzes cast for/by Lay Hao in the early Anyang period. In other words, Max Loehr's analysis is methodologically simply unsound as the chronological sequence of bronzes in Anyang; instead, it is valuable only as a system of stylistic classification.[10] It seems likely that the choice from among styles III–V for use on bronzes depended entirely on the preference of the artists and their patrons, mediated also by considerations of the economic

[9] Max Loehr, "Bronze Styles of the Anyang Period," *Archives of Chinese Art Society of America* **7** (1953), 42–53.
[10] Robert Thorp, "The Archaeology of Style at Anyang: Tomb 5 in Context," *Archives of Asian Art* **41** (1988), 47–69.

resources they would have liked to commit to achieving a certain aesthetic standard. On the other hand, standards for dating can be better based on analyses of changes in vessel shape and their grouping in funeral contexts as demonstrated already by numerous archaeological studies.

In general, it can be said that high-quality bronzes from Anyang such as those for Lady Hao are products of an industry that was technically more advanced than that in the previous Erligang period. For instance, Lady Hao's bronzes exhibit a clear preference for a square vessel body as seen in the various types of food and wine vessels; they are more difficult to manufacture than vessels with a round body. Another important advancement was the casting of bronzes in various types of three-dimensional animals or birds such as the owl *zun* from the tomb of Lady Hao or the so-called "Man-Eating Tiger" in the Cernuschi Museum in Paris. The production of such beautiful pieces required not only high aesthetic standards, but also skills to execute high-precision work. Apparently, artisans in the royal workshop of Anyang were able to handle large-scale casting, and the masterpiece of such extraordinary dimension is the square *ding* cauldron cast for "Mother Wu" (Fig. 4.7). This huge cauldron, discovered in 1939 and now back on exhibition in the onsite museum of Anyang, measures 1.33 m high and weighs 875 kg, being the largest bronze vessel ever known to the world. It has been estimated, in view of the relatively small size of furnaces used in the royal workshop in Anyang, that in order to cast a huge bronze like this, more than 1,000 artisans must have had to work at the same time in a well-organized production line, excluding those who might have shaped its clay model and had molds taken from it in a piece-mold production process.

The Discovery of Middle Shang

Standards for dating in Anyang have been worked out mainly in two ways: archaeological and historical. In the archaeological method, an interruption in the occupation of a site under excavation often offers the initial recognition of the overall trend of typological transition from the lower (earlier) stratum to the upper (later) stratum. This was exactly the case in the excavation of the residential site near the Dasikong village in 1959, to the east of the Huan River, where Anyang archaeologists were first able to isolate two large periods of occupation shown by stratigraphy. Then, the typological sequence usually needs to be refined by comparing and correlating types from underground structural units such as houses and storage pits to produce a seriation of types as foundation for further temporal periodization. In the case of Dasikong village, the site was subsequently divided into four consecutive periods. A large cemetery that was continuously used for burial over a long span of time can also provide an ideal

Fig. 4.7 *Ding*-cauldron cast for "Mother Wu" (h. 133 cm, w. 110 cm).

situation for such operation. In Anyang, the largest concentration of tombs is the area to the west of the palace zone and south of the Huan River, where pottery types from more than 1,000 tombs excavated between 1969 and 1977 have been divided into three consecutive periods. The historical method represented by the work of Dong Zuobin on the oracle-bone inscriptions depends on the identification of the so-called "diviner groups" in relation to the reigning Shang kings.[11] This enabled Dong to divide the oracle-bone inscriptions from Anyang into five periods. In addition, bronze vessels from Anyang have been separately

[11] A "diviner group" is a group of names identified as diviners who usually pose the charge in the inscriptions on the same shell or bone. The significance of the role of the diviners is discussed in detail in Chapter 5.

Shang kings	Settlement (Dasikong)	Burial pottery (Western Zone)	Burial bronzes	Oracle bone
Pan Geng (King 18)				
Xiao Xin (King 19)	I		I	
Xiao Yi (King 20)				
Wu Ding (King 21)				I
Zu Geng (King 22)	II	II		II
Zu Jia (King 23)				
Lin Xin (King 24)			II	III
Kang Ding (King 25)				
Wu Yi (King 26)	III	III		IV
Wen Ding (King 27)				
Di Yi (King 28)	IV	IV	III	V
Di Xin (King 29)				
	Anyang team		Zhang 1979	Dong 1943

Fig. 4.8 Correlation of Anyang periodization.

analyzed by Zhang Changshou who grouped them into three large periods. Based further on the co-occurrences of the oracle bones with pottery types in the actual context of excavation and the dating of the bronzes, the three systems can be linked to one another (Fig. 4.8).

This widely accepted scheme of periodization has enabled scholars to systematically analyze various types of materials from various locations in Anyang with a level of precision that was not possible at other sites; it has also sometimes been used as a standard for the comparative dating of sites beyond Anyang. As far as its use in Anyang is concerned, the periodization also exposed a thorny problem that had long puzzled archaeologists – a chronological gap between the oracle bones that appeared suddenly in large quantity in the reign of King Wu Ding (King 21), and the archaeological remains from Anyang that can be dated earlier than him, to a time roughly corresponding with Pan Geng, Xiao Xin, and Xiao Yi (Kings 18–20), the three kings of the first generation of the Shang royal house at Anyang. In other words, while

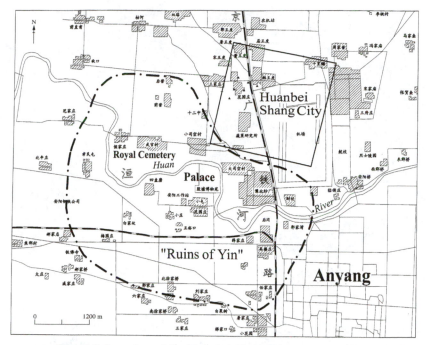

Fig. 4.9 Location of the Huanbei Shang City.

archaeological research had identified remains of Shang occupation under
the three early kings (Period I), their records of divination are missing from
the current corpus of oracle bones and shells.

But this question has now been satisfactorily answered. In 1997, the
Institute of Archaeology (Chinese Academy of Social Sciences) and the
University of Minnesota organized a joint regional survey in the large area
to the north of the Huan River, and east of the royal cemetery in Xibeigang.
The team soon identified a high concentration of Shang cultural remains of
Period I in the area near the Anyang airport. When the team carried out test
coring two years later, to everyone's surprise, they came across the base of a
long wall 10–20 m wide, and by the end of 1999 all four sides of the wall
have been confirmed and a new city of Shang date has been discovered.[12]
This new city, referred to as the "Huanbei Shang City" and located on the
periphery of the previously known Anyang, is impressively large, measuring
2,150 m E–W and 2,200 m N–S, oriented 13 degrees to the east of north
(Fig. 4.9). In subsequent years, archaeologists have surveyed the inner area

[12] Anyang Work Team of the Institute of Archaeology, CASS, "Survey and Text Excavation
of the Huanbei Shang City in Anyang," *Chinese Archaeology* 4 (2004), 1–28.

Fig. 4.10 Palace foundation F1 in the Huanbei Shang City.

of the city, and found a group of twenty-nine building foundations located along the central axis of the city square. In 2001, building foundation F1 was excavated, showing structural differences from the known building in the palace zone to the south of the Huan River (Fig. 4.10). More importantly, the excavation also recovered pottery remains from refuse pits filled probably when F1 was still in use. These pottery types date even slightly earlier than the initial Period I in Anyang.

Thus it turned out that this new city was indeed the Shang center in Anyang before the palaces to the south of the Huan River were constructed. As the pottery sequence continues uninterruptedly from the north to the south of the river, placing the new city safely before the time of King Wu Ding, it is highly possible that oracle bones from the reigns of the first three kings in Anyang are buried somewhere in this newly discovered city. And this, in any event, has inevitably led scholars to rethink the overall development of the Shang culture. In 1999, Tang Jigen, the main excavator of the Huanbei Shang City, proposed to define a "Middle Shang" period based on the current archaeological evidence. Working from Anyang, Tang further confirmed the existence of the "Middle Shang" stage in a dozen other sites on the North China Plain. Since the Huanbei Shang City provides a clear and uninterrupted transition between the early Shang center in Zhengzhou and the late Shang center to the south of the Huan River in Anyang, the suggestion of a "Middle Shang" period has been generally accepted among scholars.

The Regional Network

Anyang was certainly not isolated from the world in which it was situated and the Shang king certainly had powers going beyond the royal capital. However, with little written evidence from other sites, it is hard to determine the extent of the political network of the Shang state. At the methodological level, this question about the extent of Shang's political control is fundamentally related to the question of how power relations in the Shang state were constructed and how royal control was achieved. As will be discussed later, the Shang state was itself an elusive congregation of communities that were in various degrees of relationship to the political Shang state, loosely bound together by the hegemonic power of the Shang king (see Chapter 5). Archaeologically, however, Anyang, with its paramount power, was located at the center of a widely connected settlement network of secondary and even minor sites that had shared the same material entity – the "Shang culture" – although settlements that shared this archaeological culture might not necessarily all be part of the Shang state, which was a political relationship that cannot be directly projected from material evidence.

Archaeologists have uncovered some of these secondary settlement centers such as the one located in Taixi in southern Hebei, some 200 km to the north of Anyang. Shang cultural remains were found in an area of 100,000 m^2 (about 10 ha) centering on three earth mounds raised above the plain (Map 4.1). On one of the mounds, archaeologists excavated fourteen houses, in which were found a large number of pottery jars (some with thick layers of dry yeast), filter-shaped pottery, and a large number of small jars containing various sorts of fruit remains (Fig. 4.11). The evidence suggests strongly that the Taixi community was engaged in the production of alcoholic beverages and might have been one of the production centers that supplied alcohol for consumption in early Anyang. Another recently discovered site is Daxinzhuang in Shandong, located about 240 km to the east of Anyang, having a time-span from the Upper Erligang period to late Anyang. Most importantly, some fourteen pieces of inscribed oracle shells were found here, making them very important evidence for literacy outside of Anyang.[13]

---

[13] Oriental Archaeology Research Center of Shandong University *et al.*, "Inscribed Oracle Bones of the Shang Period Unearthed from the Daxinzhuang Site in Jinan City," *Chinese Archaeology* 4 (2004), 29–33.

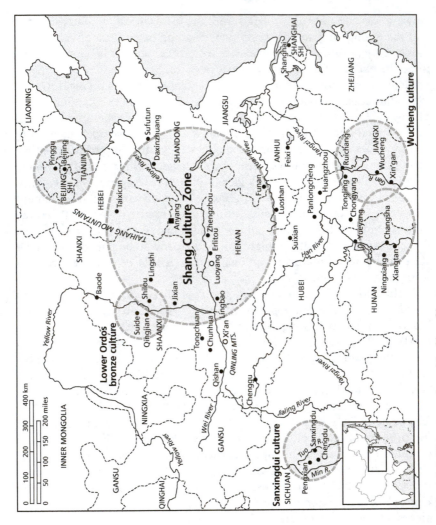

Map. 4.1 The external world of late Shang.

Fig. 4.11 House foundation no. 14 and pottery jars from it, in Taixi, an alcoholic beverage production center in southern Hebei, possible supplier to Anyang.

The above are only two examples of what might have been largely lying beyond the reach of the archaeologists as the regional centers that were connected to the royal capital at Anyang. In more frequent cases, it was the tombs yielding bronze vessels and weapons that identified elite activities in the regions. There is a great deal of sharing of the same material "Shang culture" between these regional centers and Anyang, and some of them might have indeed been occupied by Shang elites who had migrated there from Anyang or Zhengzhou, hence forming local branches of the Shang people. Others might have been strongholds of autonomous groups of local elites who might or might not have submitted to the authority of the Shang king, hence taking part in the political Shang state, or perhaps traded or collaborated on occasions with the Shang. While the political relationships between the various local groups and the Shang elites in Anyang could have been constructed at several levels, they were all integral parts of the geopolitical network in North China over which the Shang state extended its control. The question is of course the extent to which the Shang state could do so, an ability that might have changed from time to time.

Independent Bronze Cultures in the External World of Shang

In the centuries when Shang was the dominant power in the Yellow River region with its capital in Anyang, we see the rise of a number of Bronze Age societies with evidently local characteristics in regions lying very possibly beyond the reach of the Shang state, particularly in South China. However, these independent bronze cultures were evidently in contact with the Shang culture in North China. There seems little question that they, embracing elements originally introduced from the early bronze culture in the north, had risen as the direct or indirect response to the continuing expansion of the Erligang culture from the north.

In 1989, an astonishing discovery was made in Dayangzhou in Jiangxi Province where as many as 1,900 artifacts including 480 bronze vessels and weapons were found in the sands of a river bed. The bronzes were apparently based on models borrowed from the north. But cultural hybridization is evident in the fact that the bronzes were often shaped in distorted proportions or show strong local features in the use of dense decorative patterns, particularly the three-dimensional tigers sometimes superposed on the handles of many vessels (Fig. 4.12). They were apparently a collection of bronzes produced over a long stretch of time that paralleled the Upper Erligang to the late Anyang period in the north. The accompanying pottery wares identify the site with the local Wucheng culture, known since the 1970s. The Wucheng culture is a good example of a regional bronze culture that was developed under the influence of the Erligang culture; in this particular case, it is very likely that the initial stimulus for the rise of the Wucheng culture was somehow generated by possible Shang activities to exploit copper deposits in the middle Yangzi region, if not specifically at Tongling, only about 180 km to the north of Wucheng.[14]

Crossing the high Qinling Mountains south from the Wei River valley in Shaanxi Province, or crossing the Wushan Mountains west from the middle Yangzi region, there lies the Sichuan Basin. During the late 1980s, Sichuan archaeology made the national news headlines in China because of the discovery of two sacrificial pits at Sanxingdui on the Chengdu Plain. The complete city wall enclosure, located about 30 km to the east of Chengdu, would have measured more than 1,600 m on the west and east sides and 2,000 m on the south side, probably a little shorter on the north side – just about the same size as the inner city in Zhengzhou. The pits in Sanxingdui are located in the south part of the city (Fig. 4.13),

---

[14] See Robert Thorp, *China in the Early Bronze Age: Shang Civilization* (Philadelphia: University of Pennsylvania Press, 2006), pp. 107–116.

Fig. 4.12 Bronzes found in Xingan, Jiangxi.

and stratigraphical evidence suggests that both pits were dug at a time roughly contemporary to the late Shang in Anyang.

The artifacts from each pit make a very impressive list. Roughly speaking, there are hundreds of bronzes and jades, hundreds of elephant tusks, along with a complete life-size human bronze statue. It is clear that the artifacts were buried after purposely burning – some bronzes were actually partly melted because of the heat. Thus it was suggested that these two pits were made for sacrificial purposes after perhaps a major ceremony taking place on the site. The human statue from pit no. 1 is perhaps the only complete life-size bronze human statue in the entire Bronze Age in China. It is 172 cm tall, just the height of a medium-size Chinese male, standing on a square base cast into a single piece with the statue. The whole piece is covered with detailed décor imitating the actual robe of a man. The figure was clearly holding something, perhaps an elephant tusk, as already suggested by some scholars. But this is perhaps not the only statue that once stood on the site of Sanxingdui; the dozens of bronze heads buried in the two pits were originally all parts of complete statues, the bodies of which were likely to have been made of wood. The exaggeration of the eyes is another outstanding feature of Sanxingdui, probably having something to do with the local religious beliefs. Another characteristic item is the bronze tree from pit no. 2, measuring 396 cm high. This image of a tree in bronze is distantly echoed by the bronze money trees found in the Sichuan region dating to the Han Dynasty (206 BC–AD 220). Clearly,

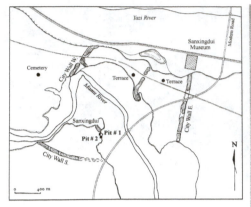

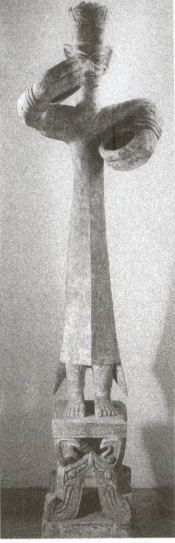

Fig. 4.13 The discoveries at Sanxingdui, Sichuan. Left, site map of Sanxingdui; right, bronze human statue, h. 262 cm including the base.

Sanxingdui had a cultural and religious system that was significantly different from that of the Shang in the north. On the other hand, contact with the north and the middle Yangzi region to the east is indicated by the appearance of a group of bronze vessels from the two pits, clearly modeled on Shang types, though they might have been locally produced.

Back to North China, in the regions of northern Shanxi and Shaanxi, archaeologists have long noted the existence of a Bronze Age society along the two banks of the Yellow River. This region, more often called the "Lower Ordos," features high loess plateaus and deep villages lying in a semi-arid climate. By the end of the 1980s, more than ten groups of bronzes had been found in this region, all likely to have been from elite tombs belonging to this Bronze Age society. Most bronzes from these groups are similar to bronzes found in the central areas of Shang, and at least some might have been imported or looted from the Shang region. But there are also distinctive local designs, particularly in the types of *hu* (jar) and *gui* (tureen), and more in bronze weapons such as swords and knives with integrally cast hilts shaped as horse, snake, or other animals. It is also interesting to note that locally designed vessels were often paired up in burial contexts with pieces possibly imported from Shang. More importantly, archaeologists have found a wall enclosure constructed with stone slabs on a cliff in Qingjian County, indicating the location of a political center of this local bronze culture.

Due particularly to their geographical proximity to Shang as sufficiently shown by the high degree of Shang influence in its material remains, the Lower Ordos bronze culture must have been in very close contact with the Shang through the Fen River valley in southern Shanxi. Indeed, there are good reasons to believe that at least some groups affiliated with this bronze culture were probably at war with the Shang, but this situation can be better clarified with reference to the Shang oracle-bone inscriptions.

SELECTED READING

Chang, K. C., *Shang Civilization* (New Haven: Yale University Press, 1980), pp. 69–136.
Thorp, Robert, "The Archaeology of Style at Anyang: Tomb 5 in Context," *Archives of Asian Art* **41** (1988), 47–69.
Thorp, Robert, *China in the Early Bronze Age: Shang Civilization* (Philadelphia: University of Pennsylvania Press, 2006), pp. 117–171.
Bagley, Robert (ed.), *Ancient Sichuan: Treasures from a Lost Civilization* (Princeton: Princeton University Press, 2001).
Bagley, Robert, "Shang Archaeology," in Michael Loewe and Edward L. Shaughnessy (eds.), *The Cambridge History of Ancient China: From the Origins of Civilization to 221 BC* (Cambridge: Cambridge University Press, 1999), pp. 124–231.
Anyang Work Team of the Institute of Archaeology, Chinese Academy of Social Sciences, "Survey and Test Excavation of the Huanbei Shang City in Anyang," *Chinese Archaeology* **4** (2004), 1–28.
Oriental Archaeology Research Center of Shandong University *et al.*, "Inscribed Oracle Bones of the Shang Period Unearthed from the Daxinzhuang Site in Jinan City," *Chinese Archaeology* **4** (2004), 29–33.

5   Cracking the secret bones: literacy and society in late Shang

With the arrival of the late Shang with its political center relocated to the south of the Huan River in Anyang, the study of Early China has gained another footing – contemporary written evidence. We are now able to understand the past not only through the material remains it has left behind and to a limited degree through the retrospective documentation produced by later generations, but also through the eyes of the protagonists of history. The perspectives offered by such written evidence, though not without bias (as is true for all records which are the products of the human mind), are unparalleled in the sense that they are both the eyewitness record of the time they speak about, and also the least ambiguous presentation of events and institutions that are usually not directly evident in the material remains. In the case of the Shang oracle-bone inscriptions, particularly because they were the divination records of the Shang kings, they offer especially rich information about the concerns and activities of the king and the operation of the Shang royal court. But there are other areas in which we can only expect that they remain silent.

Writing and Social Contexts

For a very long time, the oracle-bone inscriptions from Anyang were regarded as the earliest system of writing in China. While this assumption has been challenged by the recent finding of possible writing forms on Neolithic pottery shards (Chapter 2), it nevertheless remains true that a precursor stage of the oracle-bone inscriptions has not yet been uncovered. Therefore, the perceived "sudden" emergence of the oracle-bone inscriptions raises a number of important questions. The first question is about the developmental history of the oracle-bone scripts. The majority position holds that because the oracle-bone scripts are a fully functioning system of writing, it must have taken centuries for writing to have reached this point of maturity. This view is widely held by most Chinese and Japanese scholars and by many in the West. The opposing position is that, as is true for any system of writing, the oracle-bone scripts are governed by strictly formational rules. As soon as such rules are invented and the principle of writing is learned, the whole system can be generated according to these rules in a relatively short period of time, perhaps over a few generations.[1] While future archaeological discovery can probably bring this debate to a close, the recent discovery of multiple graphs written on the pottery jars from a site dated to the middle Shang period,[2] most likely a sacrificial center located near the south bank of the Yellow River to the north of Zhengzhou, has at least brought to light the fact that writing was actually in use in the pre-Anyang period.

The more fundamental question is about the social contexts of writing. Because of the "sudden" appearance of the oracle-bone inscriptions as divination records that emerged from religious contexts, a strong view has been that writing at its initial stage performed mainly religious roles in China, in contrast, for instance, to the economic roles of writing in Mesopotamia or perhaps political roles in Egypt. From this perspective, it can even be argued that the need to convey messages to the spirits might have provided the first cause of the rise of writing in China. Moreover, it has been suggested by some that even the bronze inscriptions of the Western Zhou period, cast on the so-called "ritual vessels," were actually messages addressed to the ancestral spirits, and this further strengthens the religious role of writing in China.[3] However, in recent years, scholars have attempted to achieve new and fuller understanding of the social roles of writing in Early China. David Keightley has argued that during the late Shang a considerable amount of writing would not have been focused primarily on ritual and cult, and that a culture so capable of producing self-referential inscriptions on bones, bronzes, or ceramics must have been able to produce other types of writings referring to events that happened independently of the act and object of inscription.[4] The latter point was discussed more fully by Robert Bagley who has suggested a number of contexts in which the writing might have been employed in later Shang

---

[1] See William G. Boltz, *The Origin and Early Development of the Chinese Writing System* (New Haven: American Oriental Society, 1994), pp. 38–41. In a recent study, Boltz argued further that the existence of certain graphs that were each used to write two different words, a phenomenon that is called "polyphony," indicates that the oracle-bone scripts, though appearing as a mature system of writing, were still not far from their origin. See William G. Boltz, "Literacy and the Emergence of Writing in China," in Li Feng and David Branner (eds.), *Writing and Literacy in Early China: Studies from the Columbia Early China Seminar* (Seattle: University of Washington Press, 2011), pp. 51–84.

[2] This is the Xiaoshuangqiao site excavated in 1990.

[3] Lothar von Falkenhausen, "Issues in Western Zhou Studies: A Review Article," *Early China* **18** (1993), 146–147, 167.

[4] See David Keightley, "Marks and Labels: Early Writing in Neolithic and Shang China," in Miriam T. Stark (ed.), *Archaeology of Asia* (Malden: Blackwell, 2006), pp. 184–185.

such as communication between Anyang and the outlying cites of Shang, listing of people and goods, recording trade, royal campaigns, and hunting, and certainly family genealogy.[5] Although there is a complete lack of evidence for writing related to these activities during late Shang, it has been sufficiently demonstrated that the bronze inscriptions of the Western Zhou time do offer a good number of references to written documents used in administrative, commercial, and other social contexts independent of religious purpose.[6] Therefore, it is safe to say that despite their huge numbers, the oracle-bone inscriptions offer only a limited view of Shang society, a large part of which is still absent from the written records we have.

The language reflected by the oracle bones, hence the languages spoken by at least the elite population in Anyang, was characteristically Sinitic;[7] that is, an archaic form of single-syllabic languages that is spoken today in its various regional dialectic forms in modern China. The scripts used on the oracle bones represent an important early stage of development of the Chinese writing system, exhibiting morphological principles that can be observed in the modern forms of Chinese characters. On the oracle bones, the graphs were hand-carved and display a higher level of freedom in writing than the inscriptions on Shang and Western Zhou bronzes. It is not unusual for anyone who is familiar with modern traditional Chinese characters to make out the meaning of a few graphs in the Shang oracle-bone inscriptions, but informed reading and comprehension of the contents of oracle-bone records demands considerable professional training. It has been recently argued that during the Shang, the learning of writing seems to have taken place within the context of individual workshops that served the Shang king for the purpose of producing and preserving the divinatory records.[8]

Royal and Non-Royal Divinatory Traditions

The materials that were used for divination were of two kinds: (1) animal shoulder blades (scapulae), mostly from cattle, with some water buffalo;

[5] See Robert Bagley, "Anyang Writing and the Origin of the Chinese Writing System," in Stephen D. Houston (ed.), *The First Writing* (Cambridge: Cambridge University Press, 2004), pp. 190–249.

[6] Li Feng, "Literacy and the Social Contexts of Writing in the Western Zhou," in *Writing and Literacy in Early China*, pp. 271–301.

[7] See Edwin G. Pulleyblank, "The Chinese and Their Neighbors in Prehistoric and Early Historic Times," in David Keightley (ed.), *The Origins of Chinese Civilization* (Berkeley: University of California Press, 1983), pp. 411–466.

[8] See Adam Smith, "The Evidence for Scribal Training at Anyang," in *Writing and Literacy in Early China*, pp. 173–205.

(2) turtle shell (plastron), which was the material used for the major divinations. The use of both types of materials for divinatory purpose goes back far in history with bones accounting for most of the case during the Longshan period; the earliest divinatory use of turtle shells is found in Jiahu, dating back to the pre-Yangshao period (*c.* 6500–5500 BC). While there are good reasons to suppose that the shoulder blades of cattle used by the royal diviners were drawn from local sources, studies have shown that a large proportion of the turtle shells found in Anyang might have been imported from the far-outlying regions in the south.[9] Before these materials could be used for divination, they were carefully prepared. In the case of cattle shoulder blades, the round joint was cut off and the long spine on the back of the bone was trimmed. In the case of plastrons, of which only the flat bottom shell is usable, the bridges connecting the top shell were carefully cut off. In both cases, oval holes intercepted on one side by a round hole would be carved out on the back of the bone or shell, making them ready for divination.

In the process of actual divination, a diviner would first pose a charge, or a question that makes clear the subject to be divined about. After this, a metal stick would be heated in fire to a high degree; when the metal stick touched the joint of the oval and round holes smoke would rise and the heat would necessarily produce a crack in the shape of the Chinese character *bu* ⼘ ("to divine") on the front of the bone or shell (Fig. 5.1). Then, in the case of royal divination, it was the king who would examine the crack and make the relevant prognostication. Afterwards, inscriptions would be carved onto the surface of the bone or plastron in places near the relevant cracks. Very often, the charges were posed in two ways – positive and negative – as the inscriptions that record the charges were placed on the opposing sides of the plastron, a phenomenon rarely appearing on the bones. It is also common that multiple pairs of charges could be posed (sometimes three or four times) with regard to a single matter, and the sequence of the charges can be well established by examining the date records in inscriptions that repeat the same content of divination. These facts became well known after the discovery of the renowned four largely complete plastrons in Anyang in 1929. Thus, a divination inscription in its fully stated form would include four parts: preface, charge, prognostication, and verification.

[9] David Keightley, *Sources of Shang History: The Oracle-Bone Inscriptions of Bronze Age China* (Berkeley: University of California Press, 1978), pp. 12.

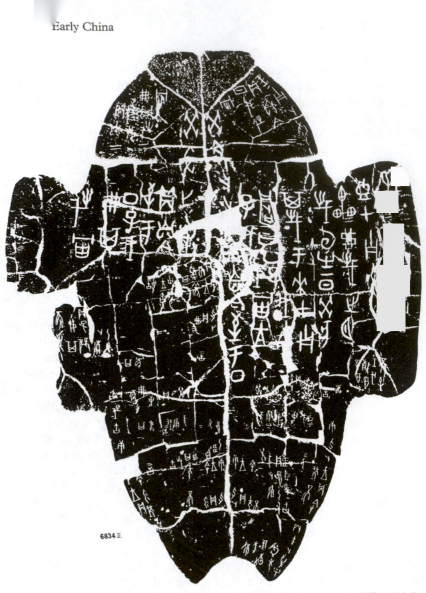

6834 正

Fig. 5.1 Example of a turtle plastron with divination records (HJ: 06834).

Example 1 (HJ: 00902):

1. Crack-making on the *jimao* day (#16), Que divined: "Will it rain?" The king prognosticated: "If it will rain, it will be on a *ren* day." On the *renwu* day (#19), it really did rain.
2. Crack-making on the *jimao* day (#16), Que divined: "Will it not rain?"

Example 2 (HJ: 06834, large characters) (Fig. 5.1):

1. Crack-making on the *guichou* day (#50), Zheng divined: "From today to the *dingsi* day (#54), will we harm Zhou?" The king prognosticated and said: "Down to the *dingsi* day (#54), we will not harm (them); on the coming *jiazi* day (#1) we will harm (them)." On the eleventh day, *guihai* (#60), our chariots did not harm (them); in the *dou* period between that evening and *jiazi* (#1), we really harmed (them).

2. Crack-making on the *guichou* day (#50), Zheng divined: "From today to the *dingsi* day (#54), will we not harm Zhou?"

Example 3 (HJ: 00641):

1. Crack-making on the *guiyou* day (#10), Huan divined: "Will the servitors be captured?" The king prognosticated and said: "If they will be captured, it will be on a *jia* day or a *yi* day." On the *jiaxu* day (#11), the servitors crossed (the river) in boats, and went to Zou. They were not reported. After ten and five days, on the *dinghai* day (#24), they were shackled. Twelfth month.

2. Crack-making on the *guiyou* day (#10), Huan divined: "Will the servitors not be captured?"

In the first case, the king's prognosticated date was proven by the rain on the *renwu* day (#19).[10] In the second case, the Shang chariots really did harm the enemy polity Zhou on the *jiazi* day (#1) as predicted by the king. In the third case, however, the runaway servitors were caught on neither a *jia* nor a *yi* day as the king predicated, but were captured on the *dinghai* day (#24), which in fact disproved the king's prognostication. There is always the question about how the Shang king examined the crack and on what basis he made certain decisions, but this remains unknown. Inscriptions that were equipped with verifications are quite rare, and the decision to engrave such verified cases of divination on the shell or bone must have had special political and religious meanings; or certain specific matters may have been more important than others to the Shang king and the Shang state. In fact, the majority of the inscriptions do not even record the king's prognostication (the rate is 1.2% for the Bin-group diviners), leaving virtually most of the charges unanswered on the

---

[10] The Shang used the combination of two series of terms to record dates. The first is called "Heavenly Stems" today and included ten: *jia, yi, bing, ding, wu, ji, geng, xin, ren, gui*. The Shang kings also used these ten terms in their names (see below). The second series is called "Earthly Branches" and included twelve: *zi, chou, yin, mao, chen, si, wu, wei, shen, you, xu, hai*. When combined, any two-character number repeats every 60 days; therefore, the system is referred to as the "Sixty-Day Circle." Here, #19 means the nineteenth day from the beginning of the circle at *jiazi* (#1), and it is the *renwu* day.

bones or shells.[11] Keightley takes this as an indication of the purpose of the inscriptions being simply a means to record the divinatory ritual itself that had taken place. However, there are certainly other possibilities. For instance, the king might have preferred his orally expressed prognostications not to be put into written form in order to avoid the possibility that he might be proven wrong, or perhaps the king preferred to keep the decision to himself, not even pronouncing it to the diviners. It was also suggested earlier, by Keightley himself and others, that the divinatory charges on Shang oracle bones and shells might not be questions after all (they should not be rendered as question sentences with "?" marks), but were straightforward statements which purport to command what may happen in the future. If so, there would be no need for prognostication since it is already expressed by the statements as "wishes." However, there are prognostications on some bones and shells. In short, there are many aspects of the divinatory process that scholars, even with numerous divinatory records at hand, still do not fully understand.

There is a total of some 133,092 pieces of oracle bones or shells available in various collections in or outside China, and nearly a half of them belonged to King Wu Ding, the most powerful Shang king in Anyang. The key to the dating of oracle-bone inscriptions is the name of the diviners; there are some 120 such names recorded on the bones and shells. By checking the occurrences of the names that appear on the same shells, indicating that these diviners had served the Shang king in more or less the same period, Dong Zuobin was able to divide them into five groups. Then, by looking into the temple names of the Shang kings mentioned in the inscriptions, he established dates for the five groups of diviners and the inscriptions engraved in their respective times (Fig. 4.8). With minor revisions of the date of some diviner groups originally proposed by Dong, the five-period scheme has been proven largely accurate in subsequent archaeological excavations and is generally accepted among scholars. This offered a solid ground for the study of Shang history in general as it enabled scholars to date with confidence the sources they use to study a variety of topics within the range of one or two kings.

However, for a long time scholars have suspected that among the existing corpus of oracle-bone inscriptions, there may have been some that were not the records of Shang royal divination, but were records of similar practices by other elites in the Shang capital. This point has now become crystal clear because of the discovery in 1991 (fully published in 2003) of some 1,583 pieces of oracle shells and bones to the east of

---

[11] Keightley, "Marks and Labels: Early Writing in Neolithic and Shang China," pp. 193–194.

Fig. 5.2 Inscribed turtle plastrons unearthed at Huayuanzhuang-east, 1991.

Huayuanzhuang, south of the palace zone in Anyang (Fig. 5.2). This was the second major discovery of inscribed oracle bones since the founding of the People's Republic of China, the first being the discovery in 1973 of some 5,000 pieces of royal oracle shells within the palace zone. Stratigraphic evidence suggests that the new shells from Huayuanzhuang-east were buried in the late phase of Period I of Anyang according to the periodization of the archaeological remains. But in contrast to the royal divinations, the protagonist, the person who makes frequent prognostication on the Huayuanzhuang-east oracle shells, was a certain "Prince" (*zi*); based on the early date of the pit and the mention of certain names which also appear on the royal divinatory bones and shells, most scholars consider this person to have been a brother of Wu Ding (King 21).

Thus, the Huayuanzhuang-east oracle bones in fact represent a divinatory tradition outside the mainstream practice by the royal diviners. Fourteen of these non-royal diviners appear on the bones and shells produced for the prince who actually also plays the role of a diviner himself on as many as twenty-six shells – something that the Shang king would never do. In a number of ways, the Huayuanzhuang-east oracle bones are distinctive. For instance, in many charges after the day number and before the character that means "to divine" (*bu*), terms such as "late afternoon" (*ze*) and "evening" (*xi*) would appear to further specify the time of divination within a day; this is not a feature in royal divination. Second, while on the royal bones and shells the inscriptions are placed side by side with the relevant cracks reading downwards, on the Huanyuanzhuang-east shells their layout was quite irregular, and in the majority of the cases, the inscription goes around the relevant crack. Third, the use of the term "used" or "not used" at the end of the divinatory record is very common in Huayuanzhuang-east; this usage is certainly not found on the royal bones and shells from the palace zone. Despite these differences, the ancestors to whom sacrifices are recorded to have been offered are identical to those recorded on the royal divinatory bones.

The importance of the Huayuanzhuang-east oracle bones lies in the fact that they opened a new window for us to look into the complexity of the culture of divination in Anyang. They suggest that the non-royal divinatory practices in Anyang did not have to adhere to the standards and conventions established by the royal diviners serving in the late Shang palace. In this regard, it is above all significant that the Huayuanzhuang-east divinatory shells represent a distinctive tradition at a location that was only about 300 m from the palace zone where the royal divinatory agencies were located and carried out divination on a far larger scale. Thus, the distinctive textual and linguistic features discussed above can only help to highlight the fact that divination was a highly secret proceeding. It is very possible that the diviners responsible for these records on the Huayuanzhuang-east shells might not have ever been exposed to the standards for texts and vocabulary employed in the Shang royal divinatory institution.

The level of variability in the culture of divination increases when we move beyond Anyang, to Zhengzhou in the south or to the Shandong region in the east. The former city during the late Shang was probably occupied by a branch of the Shang people, while the latter region was home to a number of Shang allies. In both regions, local characteristics are identified in the inscriptions on bones and shells.[12] However, particularly in the Shaanxi region farther to the west, the local Zhou tradition of divination contemporary to Anyang was dramatically different from the Shang practice both in terms of the selection and preparation of bones, and of the language and calligraphy which the local diviners used to engrave the divinatory records (see Chapter 6). Certainly the Shang

---

[12] For a recent analysis of the oracle bones from Zhengzhou and the Daxinzhuang site in Shandong, see Ken-ichi Takashima, "Literacy to the South and the East of Anyang in Shang China: Zhengzhou and Daxinzhuang," in *Writing and Literacy in Early China*, pp. 141–172.

were not the only people who employed this sacred art to determine what may happen in the future. Studying this divinatory culture or cultures can offer us an important path to understand the religious and political institutions in Bronze Age China.

Shang Religion and Shang Royal Sacrifices

The most important topic addressed in the oracle-bone inscriptions was royal sacrifice, and this was closely related to the religious beliefs of the Shang people who actually had a very complex pantheon. For the Shang, the supreme deity was "High God" (*Shangdi* or *di*). There is considerable disagreement regarding the nature of the Shang God. While some scholars believe that this High God can be identified with the founding ancestor of the Shang people, possibly the legendary Qi, others think that he comes quite close to the notion of God in the Judeo-Christian tradition. There are also scholars who think that the High God was at a stage of transition from an ancestral deity to the supreme and ultimate divine power. In the oracle-bone inscriptions, the Shang people seem to have been basically positive about the High God who had power over both natural and human phenomena. The High God is always the *being* whom the Shang kings asked for rainfall, for good harvest, and for protection in military campaigns. But there were also occasions that the Shang appeared uncertain about the will of the High God; there was the worry on behalf of the Shang king that the High God might send down some disasters. However, one thing is clear – there were never sacrificial offerings made to the High God, which implies that there was a fundamental difference between the Shang ancestors and the High God in Shang religion. In recent decades, however, scholars have come increasingly to the realization of the celestial basis for the concept of High God in Shang oracle-bone inscriptions. Two recent studies in particular have identified the High God with the celestial Northern Pole, the hollow and most secret area in the sky around which all stellar constellations revolve, thus drawing a direct connection between Shang religion and Shang cosmology.[13] While this theory of the celestial origin of the concept of High God (*di*) seems to have been well grounded,

---

[13] In an article published in 2004, David Pankenier demonstrated that even the oracle bone form *di* 帝 was derived from the stellar formation including the Kochab, Thuban, and others situated around the Northern Pole which the Shang people used to locate the real north due to the lack of a particular star at the pole. See David W. Pankenier, "A Brief History of Beiji (Northern Culmen), with an Excursus on the Origin of the Character Di," *Journal of the American Oriental Society*, 124.2 (2004), 229–235. In the second study, published in 2007, Sarah Allan argues that the deity *di* on the oracle bones has a status much higher than the ancestral deities whom she identified with the ten suns; therefore, in

by the end of the Shang dynasty, at least two Shang kings had come to assume this sacred title as Di Yi (King 28) and Di Xin (King 29).

Much less controversial are the various natural deities that frequently received sacrificial offerings from the Shang king. Most frequently mentioned on the bones and shells are the deities of Earth, River (Yellow River to the east of Anyang), and Mountain (the Taihang Mountain to the west of Anyang). To these three most important natural deities, the set of sacrificial offerings, including cattle, sheep, and pig, was offered together with the performance of the wood-burning ritual. There were also numerous minor deities related to particular locales. Thus, to the Shang, the landscape was not merely the location of the natural features, it was inhabited by the spirits, and the successful operation of the Shang state and the good fortune of the royal court would need to be ensured by enlisting their cooperation. Of particular interest is the cult of winds, which must have had tremendous impact on Shang agriculture. The Shang associated winds with particular directions and gave a name to each of the four directional winds. Thus the Shang king frequently made offerings to the four winds and asked them for a good harvest.[14]

However, the most regularly maintained cult was that of the Shang royal ancestors, to whom five different types of sacrifices (*yi, ji, zai, xie, yong* – all used in their verbal form in the oracle-bone inscriptions) were offered on scheduled times throughout the year. Scholars disagree on the meaning of the five terms and thus on the content of the actual offerings, but it is likely that most of them are combinations of the offering of material goods such as wine, animals, and humans, and the performance of music and/or dance in different ways. The offerings begin with the pre-dynastic ancestor Shang Jia (P1; see Fig. 3.4 above), the first of the Shang ancestors to have been named after one of the ten Heavenly Stems. As names of days, the ten stems also formed a Shang week. In a descending order, each of the five types of offerings was subsequently applied to ancestors on the Shang king list, and any ancestor received offerings made to him only on the day that is identified with his name. Thus, in the oracle-bone inscriptions, a record relating to the use of a five-type sacrifice can read like this:

Example 1 (HJ: 22779) (Fig. 5.3):

1. Crack-making on the *bingyin* day (#3), the [king] divined: "[On the next day, *dingmao*], when the king [hosts Da Ding (King 2) and performs the *zai* sacrifice (type 3), will there be no harm]?"

the cosmology of the Shang people, High God (*di*) could only be identified with the Northern Pole. See Sarah Allan, "On the Identity of Shang Di and the Origin of the Concept of a Celestial Mandate," *Early China* 31 (2007), 1–46.

[14] For a discussion on this point, see Aihe Wang, *Cosmology and Political Culture in Early China* (Cambridge: Cambridge University Press, 2000), pp. 28–37.

Fig. 5.3 Example of consecutive records of royal sacrifice (HJ: 22779).

2. Crack-making on the *guiyou* day (#10), the king divined:
   "On the next day, *jiaxu* (#11), when the king hosts Da Jia
   (King 3) and performs the *zai* sacrifice (type 3), will there be
   no harm?"

3. Crack-making on the *dinghai* day (#24), the king divined: "On
   the next day, *wuzi* (#25), when the king hosts Da Wu (King 7)
   and performs the *zai* sacrifice (type 3), will there be no harm?"

4. Crack-making on the *jiachen* day (#41), the king divined: "On
   the next day, *yisi* (#42), when the king hosts Zu Yi (King 12)
   and performs the *zai* sacrifice (type 3), will there be no harm?"

5. Crack-making on the [*gengxu* day] (#47), the king [divined:
   "On the next day], *xinhai* (#48), when the [king] hosts Zu Xin
   (King 13) and performs the [*zai* sacrifice] (type 3), will there
   be no harm?"

These are consecutive records of offering the *zai*-type sacrifice over a period of forty-four days, arranged on the same piece of bone from bottom up, to five ancestors on the king list, all in the main line, that is, direct ancestors of the king. In the sacrificial table constructed by the oracle-bone scholars, these kings were arranged across five weeks based on the circulation of the ten stems in royal genealogy. Certainly the *zai* sacrifice would continue to be applied to next generations of ancestors and each ancestor after receiving the *zai* sacrifice would continue to receive other types of sacrifice. When all sacrifices were subsequently applied to all ancestors, they just made one year. Therefore, the Shang people called one year "a sacrificial cycle." The important point here is: this is the most important religious and political activity of the Shang king and the necessary way to maintain his power. In some other cases, however, the king also made irregular sacrifices to certain ancestors when the ancestors are detected to have caused the king misfortunes such as toothache or shoulder pain. The king's duty to maintain such sacrifices, whether routine or irregular, to the deceased ancestors would in turn ensure the good fortune of the Shang state and the well-being of the king himself and his family. Not only did the reigning king derive his power from his connection to the royal ancestral line and maintain it through continuing the offering of sacrifice, in fact the entire Shang state rested on the maintenance of the royal sacrifice.

What did the Shang king actually offer to his ancestors? The most common offerings were wine and meat, including three types of livestock, cattle, sheep, and pigs, which constituted a set of standard offering. However, on not rare occasions, war prisoners by the name "Qiang," a people located to the west of Shang, were also among the offerings to the ancestors. A typical luxury record goes like this:

> Examples (HJ: 00301):
>
> Offering to Da Ding, Da Jia, Zu Yi (three deceased kings) hundred cups of wine, hundred Qiang prisoners, and three hundred cattle, three hundred sheep, and three hundred pigs.

> Example (HJ: 00295):
>
> Offer three hundred Qiang prisoners to (father) Ding.

In the first record, 100 cups of wine, 100 Qiang prisoners, 300 cattle, 300 sheep, and 300 pigs were collectively offered to the three ancestors Da Ding, Da Jia, and Zu Yi. In the second case, Father Ding alone was to receive 300 Qiang prisoners. Since no massive burials of such domesticated animals killed for sacrificial purposes have been found in Anyang, it is likely that after the ritual offering, their meat was distributed among the Shang elites for consumption. Then, their bones were probably recycled to the bone workshops excavated by the archaeologists in Anyang (Chapter 4). Certainly, human victims did not go through this process of distribution for consumption for the value of their flesh; instead, they ended up in grouped earth pits specially prepared for their burials. More than 2,000 such sacrificial pits containing the skeletons of human victims have been found in Xibeigang around the royal tombs to the north of the Huan River.

The Shang Royal Lineage

The study of the oracle-bone inscriptions offers us an important chance to look into the ruling apparatus of the Shang state, particularly about the ways in which the Shang kings came to power, the core institution in an ancient state or kingdom. In this regard, the Shang had unique rules which regulated royal succession. Based on information from the oracle-bone inscriptions, it is possible for us to clarify how these rules were established and maintained, and were subject to changes over time. The rule of primogeniture, which was followed by most Chinese dynasties thereafter, was gradually established as the result of these changes. In order to understand this process, we need to take a closer look at the Shang king list (Fig 3.4).

Before the founding of the Shang dynasty, it seems likely that the Shang had followed a simple scheme of succession, or at least the ancestors were remembered as have come in a line of direct succession as we know them through the dynastic records of divination, also transmitted in Sima Qian's *The Grand Scribe's Records*. For six generations from Shang Jia to Shi Gui, it was always a son who succeeded his father who undoubtedly also had other sons; but the point is that only one son in a single generation had the chance to succeed to the royal throne. However, a new rule was adopted after Tang (or Da Yi, King 1) established the Shang Dynasty that the royal throne began to be passed among the brothers in the same generation. And when the youngest royal brother died, the throne was then given back to the oldest son of the oldest brother and was passed among his sons as the next generation of Shang kings. The reason for this interesting pattern of succession is not transmitted in the historical record, but since its beginning was associated with the founding of the Shang dynasty, it might be a reasonable explanation that the rule was created to ensure that the royal throne would always be passed onto an adult, important for the political consolidation of the Shang state.

For about twelve generations from Da Ding (King 2) to Lin Xin (King 24), this rule seems to have been essentially observed. But a careful look at the king list will identify three places where the number of kings counts backwards: (1) the generation of Jian Jia (King 11) and Zu Yi (King 12);

(2) the generation of Xiang Jia (King 17) to Xiao Yi (King 20); (3) the two generations from Zu Geng (King 22) to Kang Ding (King 25). These are clearly times when the normative rule of succession established at the beginning of the dynasty was interrupted. That is, Zu Yi (King 12) as the younger brother of his generation refused to give the throne back to his older brother Jian Jia's son, but passed it onto his own son, Zu Xin (King 13), who became the next king. The same was true with King Wu Ding (King 21) who directly succeeded his father Xiao Yi (King 20) who was the youngest of his generation. Interestingly, these two cases of irregular succession corresponded well with two major political changes in Shang history: Zu Yi is said to have transferred the Shang capital from Xiang, where his elder brother Jian Jia ruled, to Xing in the north; Wu Ding was the most powerful king in late Shang and the new archaeological evidence suggests that he was probably responsible for the move of the Shang capital from the Huanbei Shang City to the south of the Huan River. Wu Ding was also the sole king of his generation (which meant that he passed this power directly on to his own sons), and this had not happened in the previous eight generations.

The normative rule of a younger brother succeeding his elder brother to become king was restored after Wu Ding, but in each of the next two generations the younger brother, once he was the king, refused to return the throne to his elder brother's family, again resulting in the order of the kings counting backward in the list. When Wu Yi (King 26) became the king, he did exactly what Wu Ding had done by simply refusing to give his throne to his younger brothers and passing it directly down his own family line. The next two kings all did the same. Thus, by the end of the Shang dynasty, the new rule (in fact, the pre-dynastic rule) that allowed a father to be succeeded directly by his son was firmly established.

Because of the complex situation in royal succession described above, in Shang ancestral worship a clear distinction was drawn between the main-line kings, whose son/sons became king, and the collateral kings, whose offspring fell off the king list soon after them. The two groups of kings were accorded different ritual offerings in the Shang system. For instance, only the main-line ancestors had their consorts worshipped side-by-side with them, not the collateral kings. But, as will be discussed below, the kingship might still come back to these collateral families later through the female line; that is, through marriages of their female members with the main-line kings.

For a very long time, scholars have wondered how the Shang kings acquired their names – the ten Heavenly Stems. The arguments have largely proceeded along the line that the Shang kings were given these names according to the designation of actual days (using also the ten Heavenly Stems) on which they were born, or that they were assigned a name corresponding to the days on which they died. The first position was further elaborated by Sarah Allan who sees the Shang as a people who, in the absence of historical accounts, largely conceived their own past in mythological terms. In her view, the Shang ruling lineage was in a totemic relationship with the ten suns as the Shang kings were considered to have been born of the ten suns. When a Shang king was born, he was assigned a stem name according to the date of his "birth ritual" (not the actual day on which he was born); this ritual thus classified him with a particular sun of which he was metaphorically born (the same word *ri* means both sun and day).[15]

Another theory proposed by K. C. Chang seems to account even better for the various phenomena that we observe in the oracle-bone inscriptions and archaeology. Chang started by looking into the distribution of the ten Heavenly Stems on the Shang king list and detected a number of regularities. For instance, the names "Ding" and "Yi" never appear in the same generation, but in alternate generations, and none of them appears in two consecutive generations. "Jia," appearing in the same generation as "Yi," never appears in the same generation as "Ding" or "Bing." "Geng" and "Xin" could go with either group. From this, Chang proposed to divide the Shang kings into two groups:

Yi-group	Ding-group
Yi	*Ding*
Jia	*Bing*
Wu	*Ren*
Ji	

This analysis offered a new basis for understanding the internal organization of the Shang royal lineage. It was hypothesized that the Shang royal lineage was actually organized into ten different branches, each bearing a unique stem name as its branch name. The ten royal branches were further united into two exogamous groups (Yi and Ding) that alternately occupied the throne of the Shang king. Chang gave some anthropological examples to show that some peoples in the South Asia, Pacific Region, and Africa had practiced such a system of "circulating succession." He further explained that when a king from the Yi-group married a woman from one of the branches belonging to the Ding-group, the son or sons born of the marriage would be raised up in their mother's branch; therefore, they would be considered members of their mother's Ding-group, not their father's. When a king died, he would be posthumously referred to by the stem name of his branch which would give him a position in the

---

[15] Sarah Allan, *The Shape of Turtle: Myth, Art and Cosmos in Early China* (Albany: State University of New York Press, 1991), pp. 25, 54–56.

Shang royal sacrificial table to receive offerings from subsequent kings. In such a way, the kingship constantly shifted between the two large groups of the Shang ruling elites.[16] As mentioned in Chapter 4, Chang further used this theory to explain the division of the Shang royal tombs into two large zones in Xibeigang, located to the north of the Huan River.

The Underdevelopment of the Shang Government

As far as the Shang royal government is concerned, Chang described it as essentially a gathering of not clearly differentiated roles filled by shamanistic officers in service of the king who was himself the "head shaman." As such, bureaucracy was out of the question, and the Shang king ruled with his shamanistic power to communicate with the various deities relying on the assistance of the various animals whose images are depicted on the king's bronze vessels. While differing on the issue of "shamanism," the other authority on Shang in the West, David Keightley, agrees with the point that religious officials played a very central role and indeed formed the main body of the Shang royal government. It seems very likely that Shang governance depended essentially on the personal rule of the Shang king, who was assisted by a large group of diviners who were little more than his personal attendants. In recent years, Keightley has begun to bring the same approach he introduced to the study of Shang religion to the realm of actual governance,[17] suggesting that although the Shang government remained centered on religious officers, the actual management of royal divination involving a large number of professional diviners indeed exhibited features of an "incipient bureaucracy."[18] However, this position is in fact very ambiguous, and there is a genuine question of whether religious institution, though important as the foundation of the Shang government, can be directly transferred into the institution of governance.

The late Shang bronze inscriptions actually mention the roles of secretarial officials such as "Document Maker" and the role of "Superintendent" who was possibly a palace official. On the other hand, the oracle-bone inscriptions offer such terms as "many officers," "many horses," "many

---

[16] K.C. Chang, *Shang Civilization* (New Haven: Yale University Press, 1980), pp. 158–209.

[17] Keightley's early view is that although the Shang royal ancestral worship was essentially religious, it exhibited certain "bureaucratic logic" as the institution was maintained routinely and the ancestors promoted according to rules. See David Keightley, "The Religious Commitment: Shang Theology and the Genesis of Chinese Political Culture," *History of Religions* 17.3–4 (1978), 214–220.

[18] David Keightley, "The Shang," in Michael Loewe and Edward L. Shaughnessy (eds.), *The Cambridge History of Ancient China: From the Origins of Civilization to 221 BC* (Cambridge: Cambridge University Press, 1999), pp. 286–288.

captains," and so on, and these terms have been taken by some scholars as "official titles." However, they are most likely to have described functions or status of certain groups of people, and there is no way to determine any superior–subordinate relations among the people referred to by these terms. The oracle-bone inscriptions also suggest that although the Shang king divined about a very wide range of topics that concerned him, and many of the divinations could have actually taken place in respect to the actual management of the Shang state in specific ways, yet the Shang king showed very little if any interest in the establishment of administrative offices. This situation certainly cannot be explained only by the bias of oracle-bone records, but most likely reflects the rudimental nature of the Shang government.

It is very likely that, therefore, except for roles like "Document Maker" and "Superintendent" which appeared towards the end of Anyang, specific administrative offices had not been differentiated and a bureaucratic structure of the government had not emerged during the late Shang. It is above all possible that the diviners had occasionally also handled administrative matters that were brought to the royal court and helped the Shang king make decisions about them as the administrative functions of the Shang government had not been clearly separated from its religious roles. Indeed, one may observe that this rudimentary level of development of the Shang royal government might have well suited the peripatetic nature of the Shang king and the royal court, described recently by David Keightley.[19]

Late Shang as a Religion-Focused Hegemonic State

Beyond Anyang, the Shang state was essentially conceived in terms of the "Four Lands" (situ) – the eastern land, western land, southern land, and northern land – that were located around the "Central Shang." The term frequently appears in the oracle-bone inscriptions in the context where the Shang king divined about good harvest that these lands will receive:

> Example (HJ: 36975) (Fig. 5.4):
> Crack-making on the yici day (#42), the king personally divined, asking: "This year will (our) Shang receive good harvest?" Having read the crack, the king said: Auspicious. [Then asking:] "Will the eastern land receive harvest? Will the southern land receive harvest? Will the western land receive harvest? Will the northern land receive harvest?"

---

[19] David Keightley, *The Ancestral Landscape: Time, Space, and Community in Late Shang China* (ca., *1200–1045 B.C*) (Berkeley: Institute of East Asian Studies, 2000), p. 58.

Fig. 5.4 Shang king asking about the "Four Lands" (HJ: 36975).

There were frequent communications between these regional lands and the Shang capital, and the oracle-bone inscriptions offer records that the Shang king divined about military actions taken to secure settlements in these lands when they were under foreign attacks by the various enemies. The leaders of the "Four Lands" are referred to in the inscriptions as the "Archer-Lord" (*hou*) and sometimes "Prince" (*zi*), the latter being most likely leaders of groups of the Shang people who lived near Anyang. The Archer-Lords were most likely to have been leaders of the autonomous local groups who might or might not be ethnic Shang. The political relationship between the Shang royal court at Anyang and the various local groups that recognized the supremacy of the Shang king was one of negotiation that demanded the Shang king's continuous display of military might through royal hunting or punitive campaigns. As a matter of fact, the Shang kings particularly in the late Anyang period spent many days every year on hunting trips away from the capital. These hunting trips were important for bringing the various local groups into service of the Shang state and were an essential part of the Shang state's political strategy.[20] In this way, the power that the Shang king possessed to bring these local groups into submission can be better characterized as "hegemonic" than "legitimate," because it had no other source except for the Shang king's military might. No political relationship higher (or more permanent) than that level can be confirmed with the current evidence, and consequently beyond the royal center at Anyang there was little government that was originated from or integrated with the royal Shang government. Thus, the geographic perimeter of the Shang state, if any, could indeed be very elusive and changed dramatically over time, extending very far when a Shang king's power was strong enough to bring distant local groups into submission to the Shang state and their leaders to accept the title "Archer-Lord," but shrinking quickly when a king's power diminished. In other words, the Shang state was conceived in terms of the relationship between the Shang king and the various local leaders. For one time, probably during the long reign of Wu Ding (King 21) during early Anyang, the oracle-bone inscriptions suggest that the network of relationships of the late Shang state had probably reached regions as far as the Fen River valley and possibly even the Wei River valley in the west and the western periphery of Shandong in the east as groups likely located in these regions were periodically called on by the Shang kings for coordinated military operations.[21] But this height of Shang power seems to have passed soon after Wu Ding, and for the greater part of the late Shang, the king's activity seems to have been confined to central and northern Henan along the middle course of the Yellow River. The various pro-Shang groups might have shared a common cultural background, which is recognizable in archaeology as the "Shang culture," although groups that shared the "Shang culture" might not necessarily all be members of the Shang state, which was after all a political relationship accessible for the most part only through the written records. There was no permanent membership in the Shang state as there was no permanent enemy of it.

On the other hand, the oracle-bone inscriptions record frequent Shang military campaigns against the so-called Fang enemies located even

---

[20] On the Shang king's hunting practice, see Magnus Fiskesjö, "Rising from Blood-Stained Fields: Royal Hunting and State Formation in Shang China," *Bulletin of the Museum of Far Eastern Antiquities* **73** (2001), 48–192.

[21] See David Keightley, "The Late Shang State: When, Where, and What?" in *The Origins of Chinese Civilization* (Berkeley: University of California Press, 1983), pp. 540–543.

farther in western Shanxi, northern Shaanxi, northern Hebei, and western Shandong.[22] Some of these Fang entities might have from time to time allied themselves with the Shang and their leaders hence held the title "Elder of the Fang" (*Fangbo*), such as is the case of the leader of the pre-dynastic Zhou people, but on the whole they remained hostile to the Shang. There is good evidence that these foreign polities mentioned in the oracle-bone inscriptions can be identified with those regional bronze cultures situated in the periphery of the Shang cultural realm, mentioned in Chapter 4. For instance, the Gui Fang and possibly also Gong Fang were probably groups that shared the Bronze Age culture distributed in northern Shanxi and Shaanxi, in the "Lower Ordos" region, which was in close contact with the Shang bronze culture. Recent archaeological discoveries in Shandong have also provided hard evidence that the Ren Fang (Polity of People) frequently appearing in the late Anyang inscriptions as target of Shang military campaigns can be suitably located, as scholars who studied oracle bones suggested decades ago, in southwestern Shandong to northern Jiangsu. The Qiang Fang, the most important source of war prisoners that the Shang frequently used as human sacrifice, were likely to have been located to the west of Shang's west land, probably in western Shaanxi and eastern Gansu in the upper Yellow River region. The Hu Fang (Polity of Tiger), there is good reason to suggest, might have been located in the region to the south of the Yangzi River, in present-day Jiangxi and Hunan, where a developed regional bronze culture, the Wucheng culture, existed contemporaneously with late Shang in the north.

These various Fang polities formed the external world with which the Shang were in close contact and against which the Shang king planned his military campaigns. Warfare was the most frequent relationship between these outlying independent Fang polities and the Shang. Some of these polities might well have developed a state-level society, while others might have been at the chiefdom level of development. There were still foreign polities located in regions that the Shang might have never reached, for instance, Sanxingdui on the Chengdu Plain which was most likely the center of a state-level polity. Studies have shown that at least a large proportion of the copper that the Shang used to cast bronzes in Anyang might have come from as far as Sichuan, if not farther, but there is no direct evidence in the oracle-bone inscriptions of communication between Anyang and the polity centering on Sanxingdui.

---

[22] Keightley, *The Ancestral Landscape*, pp. 66–67.

SELECTED READING

Keightley, David. "The Shang," in Michael Loewe and Edward L. Shaughnessy (eds.), *The Cambridge History of Ancient China: From the Origins of Civilization to 221 BC* (Cambridge: Cambridge University Press, 1999), pp. 286–288.

Sources of Shang History: The Oracle-Bone Inscriptions of Bronze Age China (Berkeley: University of California Press, 1978).

"Marks and Labels: Early Writing in Neolithic and Shang China," in Miriam T. Stark (ed.), *Archaeology of Asia* (Malden: Blackwell, 2006), pp. 177–202.

The Ancestral Landscape: Time, Space, and Community in Late Shang China (ca., 1200–1045 BC) (Berkeley: Institute of East Asian Studies, 2000).

Bagley, Robert, "Anyang Writing and the Origin of the Chinese Writing System," in Stephen D. Houston (ed.), *The First Writing* (Cambridge: Cambridge University Press, 2004), pp. 190–249.

Chang, K. C., *Shang Civilization* (New Haven: Yale University Press, 1980).

Allan, Sarah, *The Shape of the Turtle: Myth, Art, and Cosmos in Early China* (Albany: State University of New York, 1991).

6   Inscribed history: the Western Zhou state and its bronze vessels

The Zhou Dynasty occupies a special position in the cultural and political history of China, being held in high esteem as the paradigm of political perfection and social harmony in the long Confucian tradition.[1] In some way the reputation was well earned because there was no another civilization (such as that of the Shang) that separated the Zhou Dynasty from the well-documented early imperial times; on the contrary, the Zhou Dynasty created a social and cultural context in which, particularly because of the decline of the Zhou royal order, the embryo of the imperial system grew, and in which all the founding figures of Chinese philosophy lived. On the other hand, the Zhou Dynasty can be seen as a period in which the value of literary culture had been fully explored and appreciated, thus allowing us the opportunity to analyze its political and social institutions in a more coherent way than is possible for the Shang Dynasty on the basis of the contemporary written evidence. It was also a period during which the key to bureaucratic administration was discovered and the concept of the state had become differentiated from that of the royalty.

The Search for Pre-Dynastic Zhou

The question of whether there were a people called by the name "Zhou" before the Zhou conquest of Shang would seem quite super-fluous if not contradictory. However, in the 1970s–1980s studies of the various "pre-" or "proto-" dynastic cultures of the regimes that once ruled a large part of China, e.g. Shang, Zhou, and Qin, formed an important stream in Chinese archaeology. Underlying these studies was the methodological assumption that the prehistory of a dynasty

---

[1] The high prestige of the Zhou Dynasty can be seen in the fact that the word "Zhou" was subsequently used as the dynastic title of five regimes in Chinese history: Northern Zhou (AD 557–581, founded by Yuwen Jue), Wu Zhou (AD 690–705, founded by Wu Zetian), Later Zhou (AD 951–960, founded by Guo Wei), Great Zhou (AD 1354–1367, founded by Zhang Shicheng), Wu Zhou (AD 1674–1681, founded by Wu Sangui).

can be sought in the archaeological records and, by virtue of its identification with a material culture, the origin of that prehistory can be
traced farther back to a time that was beyond what the often ambiguous
textual records purport to tell.

The Zhou case provided an ideal platform for this operation. The
Zhou are mentioned frequently in the Shang oracle-bone inscriptions
of Wu Ding (King 21) period in Anyang, and the received genealogy of
the Zhou royal house goes back to at least the end of the Xia Dynasty
when the Zhou ancestor Buku allegedly quit his office in the corrupted
Xia regime and went to live among the barbarians. Not only that, the
received records suggest that for most part of their early history the Zhou
people lived in a place called Bin, presumably to the west of the Shang
kingdom (Map 6.1). While there has been no dispute in the past 2,000
years regarding the location of Bin in the upper Jing River valley in
Shaanxi, a few modern scholars have proposed that the Fen River valley
in southern Shanxi was home to the Zhou people based primarily on the
phonetic similarity between "Bin" and the name of the "Fen" River in
archaic Chinese. Although this second location conveniently places
Zhou in the immediate neighborhood of Shang, it has been collaborated
by virtually no archaeological sites that can be surely dated to the pre-
dynastic Zhou time and still show strong connections to the dynastic
Zhou culture.

In the Shaanxi region, however, mainly along the Wei River and Jing
River valleys, archaeologists have excavated a large number of sites with
deposits dating from the pre-dynastic Zhou period (contemporary with
late Shang). There has been a considerable disagreement among scholars with regard to their identification with the historical Zhou people,
complicated by debates about the date and periodization of a number of
sites. Out of this complication, the site of Nianzipo (early stratum) in
the upper Jing River valley seems to have been commonly accepted as
belonging to an earlier stage of development than most sites found on
the Wei River plain. This date is not only based on careful pottery
typology, but has also been confirmed by the apparently archaic styles
of bronze vessels found in the site, comparable to the earliest types of
bronzes found in Anyang (Fig. 6.1). Further support to the early date of
Nianzipo was provided by Carbon-14 dating that safely placed the site
before the end of the thirteenth century BC, roughly two centuries
before the founding of the Western Zhou Dynasty. In a number of
ways the Nianzipo pottery assemblage displays features that continued
thereafter to characterize later pre-dynastic and even dynastic Zhou
cultures in the Wei River valley; particularly features in the way
oracle bones were prepared for divination at Nianzipo show strong

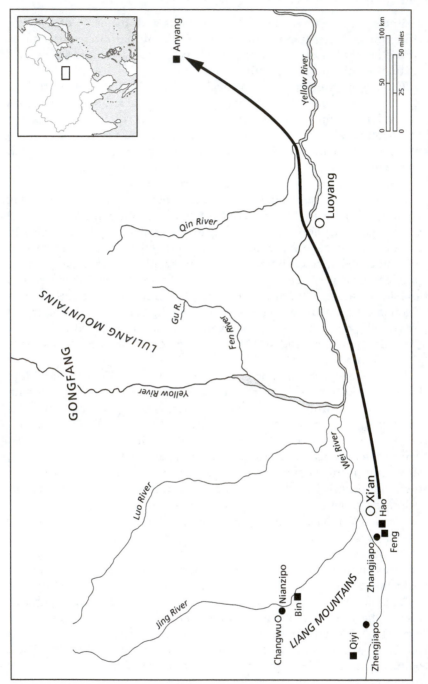

Map 6.1 Location of the pre-dynastic Zhou cultural sites and the Zhou conquest campaign of 1045 BC.

Fig. 6.1 Bronzes and oracle bone from Nianzipo: 1, 2, *ding*-cauldrons; 3, *pou*-wine container; 4, oracle bone.

connections to Zhou divinatory practice but not to the Shang tradition. Incidentally, the site is located in the upper Jing River valley, and this fact lends some support to the historically documented Zhou activities in the upper Jing River region, although Nianzipo might not be the site of Bin.

It is obvious that pre-dynastic sites located in the Wei River valley, usually later in date than the early stratum of Nianzipo in the north, show a typical mixture of cultural elements that can be analyzed under three pottery production traditions (Fig. 6.2): (A) elements probably developed in the Shaanxi region, typical for the joint-lobed *li*-tripod and broad-shouldered jars; (B) elements that had their origins in regions to the northwest, as

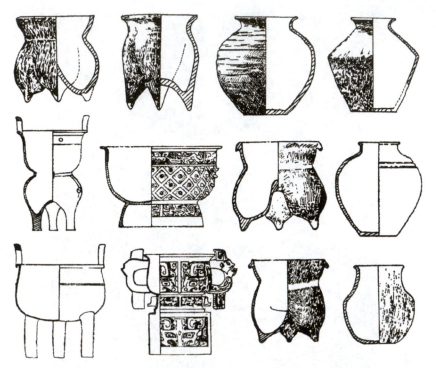

Fig. 6.2 Examples of late pre-dynastic bronzes and pottery. Bronze types include *yan*-steamer, *gui*-tureen, and *ding*-cauldron; pottery types include *li*-tripod and *guan*-jar.

representative in the divided-lobed *li*-tripod;[2] (C) elements such as *gui*-tureen and *dou*-high plate that were clearly identified with the Shang cultural tradition in the east. These elements are variously assembled at different locations along a wide spectrum and, except for a few sites that display nearly purely B or C type elements, in most cases it is difficult to determine whether the site was occupied by a Zhou or non-Zhou population. In fact, recent analyses show that even the dynastic Zhou material culture was no less a body of mixed elements than the pre-dynastic Zhou culture. The inconclusiveness of the search for a pre-dynastic Zhou cultural identity indeed reflects the silent and ambiguous nature of the archaeological record, something that urges the archaeologists to rethink their working assumptions.

---

[2] For a discussion of pre-dynastic pottery types from the Wei River valley, see Jessica Rawson, "Western Zhou archaeology," in Michael Loewe and Edward L. Shaughnessy (eds.), *The Cambridge History of Ancient China: From the Origins of Civilization to 221 BC* (Cambridge: Cambridge University Press, 1999) pp. 375–385.

On the other hand, the archaeological picture may still reflect at least a part of the social reality – a population of highly mixed origins might have inhibited the Wei River plain in a broad network of cultural and political exchange with the outlying regions in the century before the Zhou conquest of Shang. Therefore, pending the material identity of the Zhou people, the archaeological works have indeed contributed to clarify the cultural context from which the Zhou people rose to power. By the time represented by these late pre-dynastic sites mentioned above, there is no doubt that the center of the Zhou people was already relocated in the west part of the Wei River valley following their historical migration under the Ancient Duke sometime in the later twelfth century BC. In other words, it can be said that the material culture with which the Zhou people can be identified and which gradually became the dominant tradition in North China after their conquest of Shang was indeed formed by elements already present in the various sites in the west part of the Wei River valley contemporary with the late Anyang period. However, the specific identification of sites with the Zhou people or other ethnic groups can always be debated.

Zhou literary tradition in fact documents Zhou's activities in the northwest indicating that a military campaign had taken them to the upper Jing River region following an incident of diplomatic interference in the territorial dispute between two small polities in the time of King Wen (Cultural King), grandson of the Ancient Duke. Zhou's relation with the mighty Shang kingdom in the east was even more celebrated in the *Book of Poetry* as King Wen's mother was a Shang princess and his wife was also from the east. This close tie with Shang is vividly demonstrated by records in the oracle-bone inscriptions produced by the Zhou themselves, found in the pre-dynastic Zhou capital, Qiyi (present-day Zhouyuan) (Box 6.1). Surprisingly, the inscriptions on these bones and shells suggest that in addition to their own ancestors, the pre-dynastic Zhou house literally worshipped the Shang ancestors, including the most recently deceased Shang kings. The inscriptions offer an unequivocal sense that the Zhou, after establishing themselves as a regional power in the Wei River valley, had at least for some time to accept the political reality that Shang was the superpower in North China.

The Zhou Conquests of Shang

Late in the fifth month of 1059 BC, the five major planets of the solar system (Jupiter, Saturn, Mars, Venus, and Mercury) gathered in a narrow area measuring only about 7° by 2° in declination in the northwestern sky visible from the Zhou capital at the foothills of the Qi Mountains. Modern science has confirmed this date of the planetary conjunction which happened in the 32nd year of the late Shang king according to the written records, transmitted

Box 6.1   The Zhou Oracle Bones

Although the Shang are better known for their oracle-bone inscriptions, the Zhou were doubtless also practitioners of oracle-bone divination. Since the 1950s, a number of sites in eastern China have yielded pieces of inscribed bones from strata or structures of Zhou cultural content. However, the number of pieces from these sites was very small and their inscriptional contents hard to contextualize. A much larger corpus of oracle bones from Zhou cultural contexts includes some 293 inscribed fragments from two pits (H11 and H31) that were dug into a building foundation excavated in 1977 in the pre-dynastic Zhou capital in Zhouyuan. Since the discovery, both the date of the bones and the date of the building structure in which they were found have been in serious debate. Roughly speaking, a large portion of these materials were produced before the Zhou conquest of Shang in 1045 BC; in other words, they were contemporary with the reign of the last Shang king in Anyang. The rest were produced in the early decades of the Western Zhou dynasty.

Topics covered by these inscriptional fragments are of a wide range, but those that can be better contextualized include divinatory records about ritual sacrifices offered to the deceased Shang ancestors and kings including Tang, Wu Ding (King 21), Wen Ding (King 27), and Di Yi (King 28). This has led some scholars to argue that the bones were produced by Shang diviners and brought to the Zhou capital after the conquest. But from their material features to the styles of writing and calligraphy the bones are so different from the oracle bones in Anyang that there can be little doubt that they were produced in a cultural environment that was of Zhou (Fig. 6.3). Other topics mentioned in the Zhouyuan oracle bones include sacrifice to King Wen, royal hunting trips, reports to Heaven, etc. It is also interesting that three pieces mention the state of Chu and two of them clearly report on the visit of the Chu leader to the Zhou center.

Another corpus of some 600 inscribed bones has been discovered since 2003 at the Zhougongmiao site, located 18 km to the west of Zhouyuan. These new oracle-bone inscriptions are doubtless much more numerous and richer in content, mentioning the names of a list of important figures in early Zhou history including King Wen and his father Ji Li, the Duke of Shao, the Duke of Bi, brothers of King Wu, and most importantly the Duke of Zhou who was likely to have been the protagonist of the divinatory activities behind many of the inscribed bones. However, the new oracle bones from Zhougongmiao remain largely unpublished at present.

Box 6.1 (cont.)

Example:

On the *guisi* day (#30), sacrifice was offered at the temple of the Cultured and Marshal Di Yi (Shang king). Divining: "Will the king (of Zhou) offer *shao*-sacrifice to Cheng Tang (Shang founder)? . . . exorcism and worship . . . Will [he] not offer three sheep and pigs? It is appropriate."

in the Zhou literary tradition as a Red Crow that perched on the Zhou altar to the soil. This very rare astronomical phenomenon that occurred only every 516 years was likely to have been taken as the sign of Heaven's Mandate to Zhou and occasioned King Wen's declaration of kingship, hence officially breaking away from the Shang regime.[3] More importantly, this belief in King Wen's receipt of Heaven's Mandate has made the ideological foundation of

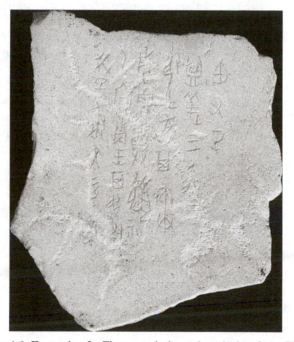

Fig. 6.3 Example of a Zhou oracle-bone inscription from Zhouyuan.

---

[3] See David W. Pankenier, "The Cosmo-Political Background of Heaven's Mandate," *Early China* **20** (1995), 121–176.

the Zhou state and was continuously celebrated in the Zhou inscriptions throughout the entire Western Zhou period.

It seems likely that in the ten or so years of King Wen's rule as king, the Zhou had managed to eliminate most of the pro-Shang communities located in the Wei River valley, thus achieving Zhou's regional hegemony over the western periphery of Shang. It was even possible that in the east the Zhou forces attacked some polities located in southern Shanxi and thus not far from the Shang center. Symbolizing the growth of Zhou power, a new capital, Feng, was constructed on the west bank of the Feng River occupying the central position on the Wei River plain, shortly before King Wen passed away in 1049 BC.

At the death of King Wen, the Zhou leadership must have been quite impatient to begin a final combat with the Shang who at about this time had embarked on a number of major military campaigns in the Shandong region against the Ren Fang and perhaps also some other indigenous polities in the Shandong region. Combining information in the received texts and that which can be learned from the bronze inscriptions, modern scholars have recovered some important details about this epic-making campaign. In the middle of the twelfth month of 1046 BC, after the completion of the three years' mourning for his father, King Wu (the Marshal King) set out on a campaign to the east and arrived with the Zhou troops at Muye (wild of shepherd) on the southern outskirts of the Shang capital Anyang by the middle of the first month of 1045 BC.[4] The Zhou were joined by their variously allied tribes and communities from the western lands, in confronting an enemy that was reported to have largely outnumbered the invaders. The battle was apparently very bloody. It began on the morning of the *jiazi* day (#1) and continued into the following night, leading to a complete victory for the Zhou by the next sunrise, as suggested by the inscription on the Li *gui*, discovered in Shaanxi in 1978 (Fig. 6.4). The last Shang king retreated to his palace and set himself on fire together with his beloved concubines.

Li *gui* (JC: 4231):

King Wu campaigned against Shang. It was the morning of the *jiazi* day (#1). Jupiter was upright, and we defeated [them] at the dusk [of the day]. By the dawn, we had occupied Shang. On the *xinwei* day (#8), the king was at Jian Garrison and he rewarded official Li with metal. [Li] herewith makes [for] Duke Zhan [this] treasured sacrificial vessel.

---

[4] See Edward Shaughnessy, "'New' Evidence on the Zhou Conquest," *Early China* 6 (1981–2), 66–67.

Fig. 6.4 The Li *gui* (h. 28 cm, diam. 22.0 cm) and its inscription recording the Zhou conquest.

This historic battle which inaugurated the foundation of the Western Zhou dynasty was a major confrontation between the union of tribes and communities that inhabited the mountains and valleys in western China and the Shang and pro-Shang peoples of the eastern plains. Without fully understanding the long-term impact of this confrontation, King Wu adopted a temporary occupation policy by stationing two of his brothers near the Shang capital, and the conquered Shang people were placed under Wugeng, a son of the last Shang king, as their nominal ruler. The main body of the Zhou army returned west with the king. When King Wu died in 1043 BC, only two years after the conquest, and when the Duke of Zhou became the de facto leader at the Zhou court, his two older brothers, joined by Wugeng and his former Shang subjects on the eastern plains, rose in a total rebellion against the Zhou court in the west. It took another three years for the Zhou to regain control over the east but this had also led the Zhou to push further to regions like northern Hebei and western Shandong in pursuing Shang remnants and eliminating possible future rebels. In the south, the Zhou troops might have reached the area to the north of the Huai River.

The post-Western Zhou literature tends to exaggerate how young King Cheng was when this happened, in order to promote the role of the Duke of Zhou as the real founder of Zhou's political order through his tireless effort in this difficult period. The bronze inscriptions

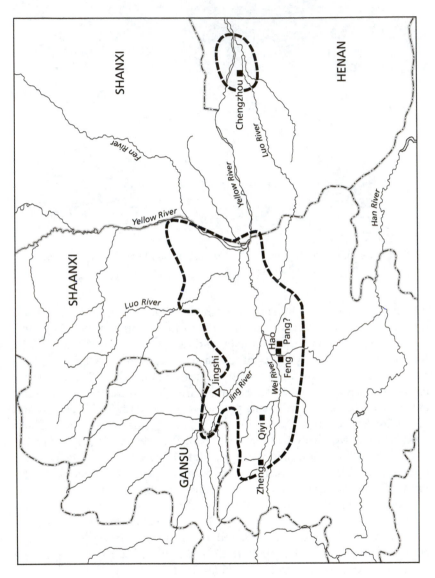

Map 6.2 The Zhou central area: royal domain.

suggest that King Cheng was in fact leading military campaigns in the east. However, there is no doubt that the Duke of Zhou and Duke of Shao, another brother of the deceased King Wu, both played prominent roles in consolidating Zhou control over the eastern regions. The Duke of Zhou is recorded in the inscription as having conquered former Shang allies located in the Shandong region including most importantly Yan and Bogu. The Duke of Shao (known as the Grand Protector), whose important role in the Zhou court even outlasted that of the Duke of Zhou, is credited with having pacified five local rulers in the east who were presumably loyal to the Shang regime.[5] Much of what we can say about the Western Zhou state was the result of the second conquest, rather than the first conquest under King Wu.

The Royal City Network and the Material Culture of Zhou

In contrast to the late Shang state whose political and religious energy was focused on a single major city – Anyang, Zhou royal power rested on a network that linked multiple royal centers located on the Wei River plain. These cities included first of all the pre-dynastic capital Qiyi (referred to as "Zhou" in the inscriptions) which continued to prosper during the entire Western Zhou period (1045–771 BC). The capital Feng, on the west bank of the Feng River, was constructed under King Wen, and the capital Hao on the east bank of the river, was constructed under King Wu and is referred to in the bronze inscriptions as the "Ancestral Zhou" (Zongzhou). Even though scholars past and present have raised doubts about the identification of some of these cities with the Zhou royal centers mentioned in the bronze inscriptions, there has been a general consensus about their status and locations. Beside the above three cities, the bronzes' inscriptions also frequently mention the capital Pang, located somewhere to the southeast of Hao, and Zheng, located to the west of Qiyi. It is very possible that these five cities are collectively mentioned in the inscriptions as the "Five Cities" that formed the top level of the Zhou local administration (Map 6.2). In the east, a new city, Chengzhou near present-day Luoyang, was constructed soon after the Zhou conquest and had since the day of its foundation served as the administrative center of the Western Zhou state on the eastern plain. It is significant that we find the Zhou king

---

[5] For a discussion of the historical development in the early years of the Western Zhou, see Edward Shaughnessy, "The Role of Grand Protector Shi in the consolidation of the Zhou Conquest," *Ars Orientalis* **19** (1989), 51–77.

frequently appearing in any one of these cities (Zheng during the middle Western Zhou) where he met with officials, announced appointments, and held state ritual and banquet.

Although the sociopolitical functions of the these cities might have been slightly different from one another, for instance, Qiyi (Zhou) might have been where all the royal ancestral temples were located, they had achieved a comparable level of complexity and all served as bases for the Zhou. Perhaps because of their special political status as royal centers, the Zhou court frequently appointed officials with overall responsibilities in all five cities. These responsibilities ranged from religious services to local security; during the late Western Zhou, we know of an official who was given responsibility for controlling the farming populations that resided in the five cities. The inscriptions show clearly that these responsibilities were categorically different from the regular responsibilities charged to officials belonging to a specific city.[6]

It is understandable that the major cities are also the concentrations of archaeological works. So far the sites of three cities, Feng, Hao, and Qiyi, have been confirmed by archaeology, while the locations of Pang and Zheng are still being sought. Archaeologists have uncovered a large number of palace and temple foundations at the three central sites under investigation along with a huge quantity of artifacts either from their residential areas or from the associated cemeteries of the three cities. Each category of the materials constitutes an independent area of intensive research to determine their specific dates and explore their cultural meanings, but perhaps a highlight of their main features can help clarify the material characteristics of the Zhou civilization as manifested at these central sites. The bronze culture of the early Western Zhou inherited the solemn and mysterious nature of Shang bronzes, with its characteristic use of various types of animal masks. On high-quality vessels, the Zhou craftsmen were able to create a more elaborate appearance of the bronzes by frequently using high-rising flanges and even raised projections of pendants that were cast in advance and were inserted into the molds when the body of the vessel was cast (Fig. 6.5). Overall, the profile of the early Western Zhou bronzes incorporated more curved lines, which made them look more graceful and better proportioned when compared to Shang bronzes. Almost all types of bronzes fashioned in the late Shang survived into the early Western Zhou, but the centrality of such wine vessels as *jia*-pitchers, and *gu*- and *jue*-cups seems to have been lost, giving way to a new emphasis on the set of food-serving vessels including *ding*-cauldron and *gui*-tureen. Even within the same type of bronzes, for instance, the

---

[6] See Li Feng, *Bureaucracy and the State in Early China: Governing the Western Zhou (1045–771 BC)* (Cambridge: Cambridge University Press, 2008), pp. 165–170.

Fig. 6.5 An early Western Zhou *you*-vessel (h. 35.5 cm, w. 22.8 cm).

gui-tureen built on a high square base (such as the Li *gui*) was doubtless a Zhou invention. Although the early Western Zhou craftsmen in the foundries located at the central sites operated largely within a production tradition heavily influenced by Shang practice, by the middle phase of the early Western Zhou they had created an assemblage of styles that are fully distinguishable from their Shang predecessors (Fig. 6.6).

Fig. 6.6 Stylistic evolution of Western Zhou bronze vessels: 1 and 7, *zun*-pitchers; 2 and 6, *you*-jars; 3, *gong*-wine container; 4, square *yi*-vessel; 5, *gui*-tureen; 8 and 12, *ding*-cauldrons; 9, *hu*-wine jug; 10, *he*-water pot; 11, *fu*-grain box. 1–4, early Western Zhou, 5–8, mid-Western Zhou, 9–12, late Western Zhou.

From the early phase of the mid Western Zhou, significant new changes were introduced to Zhou bronze culture. The mysterious feature that once dominated Shang bronze art and also characterized early Western Zhou bronzes began to disappear – very few bronzes still bear animal masks and display complex surface structure created by the use of flanges and pendants. Instead, the craftsmen seem to have shifted their interests to more detailed plain depiction of the preferred images. This trend led to the creation of various types of bird, often portrayed with exaggerated feathers that became the most salient feature of mid-Western Zhou bronzes. At the same time the set of wine vessels began to disappear completely from burials in the Wei River valley, although some remained in use for a longer time in the regional centers outside of Shaanxi. This gave rise to groups of burial bronzes that consisted almost entirely of food containers supplemented often by a set of water vessels used for hand-washing. These two changes put an end to the long-lasting bronze production tradition of the Shang. However, almost immediately after the reign of King Mu, Zhou bronze art began to take another new turn – the various bird patterns began to dissolve structurally and evolved gradually into different types of abstract pattern of geometric formation. These new geometric patterns were often executed in bold lines as single-layer reliefs and could be freely replicated in four directions, thus leaving no image as the visual focus of the decorated bronzed surface.[7] This new trend of artistic expression seems to have fully taken root before the arrival of the late Western Zhou period and continued to dominate the bronze art of China until the late Spring and Autumn period.

In contrast to the Zhou bronze culture in which new standards developed in the central area could win early acceptance across a large geographic space in the Western Zhou state, the pottery culture of the Western Zhou remained essentially local. Although the Wei River pottery traditions in pre-dynastic time already adopted certain types such as *gui*-tureen and *dou*-high plate from the Shang culture, the high frequency of the appearance of the set of "*li*-tripod + *guan*-jar" in burials suggests a ceramic culture that was fundamentally different from that of the Shang. In fact, through the entire early Western Zhou period, the pottery assemblage in the eastern plains continued to follow the Shang tradition, while in the Zhou central sites in the Wei River valley the pottery culture seems to have gone through a long process of adaptation and modification of the types of different cultural origins. For instance, all three types of pottery *li*-tripod that were present at the various pre-dynastic sites had made their ways into the pottery assemblage found in the Zhou capitals Feng and Hao (Fig. 6.7). During the mid Western Zhou period burial pottery types seem to have undergone a process of standardization and simplification at central sites such as Feng and Hao. As the range of typological changes at a single site was significantly narrowed down, inter-site variation in the use of standard burial pottery sets gradually became evident in the Wei River valley. For instance, by the late Western Zhou period, distinctions in the production and use of pottery types can even be seen between the Zhouyuan area to the west and the Feng–Hao area at the center of the Wei River valley.

[7] See Lothar von Falkenhausen, "Late Western Zhou Taste," *Études chinoises* **18** (1999), 143–178. For a more detailed discussion of the typological and decorative progression of Western Zhou bronzes, see Jessica Rawson, *Western Zhou Ritual Bronzes from the Arthur M. Sackler Collections* (Washington, DC: Arthur M. Sackler Foundation, 1990), pp. 15–125.

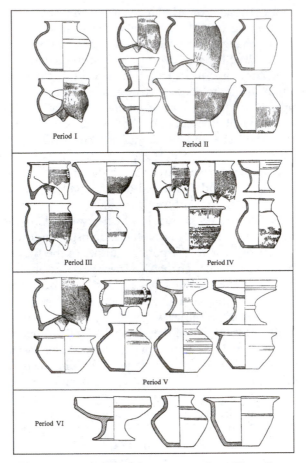

Fig. 6.7 Standard burial pottery sets from Zhangjiapo.

"Fengjian," not "Feudalism"

For a long time, the political system of the Western Zhou state has been analyzed within the theoretical framework in which historians of the West analyzed medieval European feudalism.[8] In this framework, the Western Zhou state was regarded as a cluster of proto-independent political entities loosely bound together by contracted obligations between the vassals and the Zhou king. The Zhou king, in such relations,

---

[8] Most typical of the view is Herrlee Creel, *The Origins of Statecraft in China*, vol. 1, *The Western Chou Empire* (Chicago: University of Chicago Press, 1970), pp. 317–387.

had little power beyond the small area of his own domain. The Zhou royal government, on the other hand, was staffed with hereditary officials who were little more than the king's personal servants. Recent analyses have shown that this is an inaccurate characterization of the Western Zhou system. A number of newly discovered inscriptions show that even in the last reigns of the period, the Zhou king was still able to command regional forces to conduct warfare far away from the Wei River valley. There was clearly a state structure at work that was fully recognized by the regional elements and, to a higher degree, by the Zhou king and the royal officials. The failure of "Western Zhou feudalism" is due at the fundamental level to the collapse of "feudalism" as a valid sociopolitical model in global context when its legitimacy in European historiography has been seriously challenged since the 1970s. Today, very few scholars still think that "feudalism" was a proper way to describe what had been a much more complicated situation in medieval Europe.[9]

The system that characterized the Western Zhou state was referred to retrospectively by Warring States politicians as "Fengjian" (literally, to define borders and to establish states), but the two characters that formed the term both had their origins in the Western Zhou bronze inscriptions, and were used in contexts clearly related to the founding of the regional states. A number of inscriptions record circumstances of the founding of the regional states, but most fully in the inscription of the Yihou Ze *gui*-tureen, discovered in the 1950s (Fig. 6.8).

Yihou Ze *gui* (JC: 4320):

It was the fourth month; the time was the *dingwei* day (#44). [The king] observed the map of King Wu and King Cheng's campaigns against Shang, and thereupon inspected the map of the eastern states. The king stood in the ancestral temple of Yi, facing south. The king commanded Ruler of Yu, Ze, and said: "Transfer and be the ruler (*hou*) at Yi. [I] award you X-fragrant wine of one *yu*-jar, and award *zan*-jade, one red-lacquered bow and one hundred red-lacquered arrows; ten black bows and one thousand black arrows. [I] award you land, the *zhen*-fields of which are three hundred and [...]; the [..] of which are one hundred and [...]; the residential settlements of which are thirty-five; and the [...] of which are one hundred and forty. [I] award you [...] and seven clans of the king's men at Yi, and award the seven Elders (*bo*) of Zheng whose X-retainers are [...] and fifty men. [I] award you commoners of Yi six hundred and [...] six men." Yihou Ze extols the king's beneficence, making [for] Yugong, Father Ding, [this] sacrificial vessel.

Thus, a regional state received everything from the Zhou king that is needed to form a local polity in defense of the Zhou capital, of which particularly

[9] Li Feng, "'Feudalism' and Western Zhou China: A Criticism," *Harvard Journal of Asiatic Studies* **63**.1 (2003), 115–144.

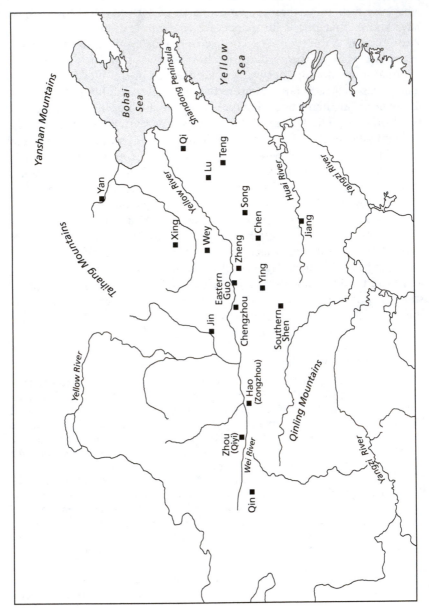

Map 6.3 Distribution of the Zhou major regional states.

Fig. 6.8 The Yihou Ze *gui*-tureen.

noteworthy is the granting of people either from the possession of the king's or as state property. No bronze inscription gives the total number of regional states founded by Zhou, but a list in the Warring States period texts names twenty-six states which were founded either by brothers of King Wu, or by sons of King Wu and the Duke of Zhou. This genealogical relationship between the Zhou king and the regional rulers can be confirmed with inscriptions with regard to a number of prominent states such as Wey, Jin, Lu, and Yan; thus through the "Fengjian" practice, the house of Zhou actually established its kin branches all over eastern China. Furthermore, the regional states were not randomly distributed (Map 6.3); they were either established in former Shang strongholds or were located at key points in the main transportation lines in eastern China near places of potential threat. They formed a network that could effectively defend the Zhou kingdom.

The establishment of the regional states was first of all considered necessary based on the grant strategy of the Western Zhou state. Once established, the regional rulers enjoyed full rights to decide matters of administration within their respective states, and the inscriptions show that the Zhou king accorded the regional rulers a level of courtesy and hospitality much higher than what a royal official serving at the central court could expect to have. There is no evidence that the central court had ever attempted to interfere in the domestic affairs of the regional states, except in matters of succession to regional rulership that could well concern the interests of the Zhou king. The latter situation could bring a regional state into sharp conflict with the Zhou king and could have needed to be settled by means of civil war, as was once perhaps the case with respect to the state of Qi in Shandong during the short reign of King Yi. However, the regional states were not independent kingdoms but were active participants in the political life of the Western Zhou state. The early Western Zhou inscriptions suggest that, if not a rule, it must have been quite frequent for the regional rulers, especially newly established ones, to pay visits to the Zhou king in his capital in the Wei River valley. Moreover, the bronze inscriptions also show that the Zhou king stationed royal inspectors in the regional states, a practice that continued through the entire Western Zhou period. Thus the Zhou system was one that was designed to achieve political control over the whole population in the area perceived as Zhou "territory" through the delegation of administrative authority to its regionally based agents. Clearly, the Zhou king regarded the security of the whole of the Western Zhou state as his responsibility and would when necessary call out the service of the regional rulers in coordinated military actions to defend it. The regional rulers not only enjoyed a high degree of administrative autonomy, but also had obligations to the Western Zhou state.[10]

However, it is also true that with the passing of time, the ties between the Zhou king and the regional rulers tended naturally to be weakened as the position of the latter on the genealogical tree became more and more remote from the Zhou king. As the regional rulers sank their roots deeper into the local society in their respective regions, they inevitably provided a centrifugal force that contributed significantly to the eventual weakening of the Western Zhou state.[11]

Discovering the Regional Zhou States

In the 1980s and 1990s, the regional states were the focus of Western Zhou archaeology. By the turn of the new century, archaeologists had exposed fully or partially the cultural remains of about nine regional states including Wey, Ying, Guo (Henan), Lu, Qi, Teng (Shandong), Xing (Hebei), Yan (Beijing), Jin (Shanxi), and Qin (Gansu), all dating to the Western Zhou period. The most systematically explored sites are those of

---

[10] On the status and role of the regional states, see Li, *Bureaucracy and the State in Early China*, pp. 235–270.

[11] On the weakening of the Western Zhou, see Li Feng, *Landscape and Power in Early China: The Crisis and Fall of the Western Zhou, 1045–771 BC* (Cambridge: Cambridge University Press, 2005), pp. 110–121.

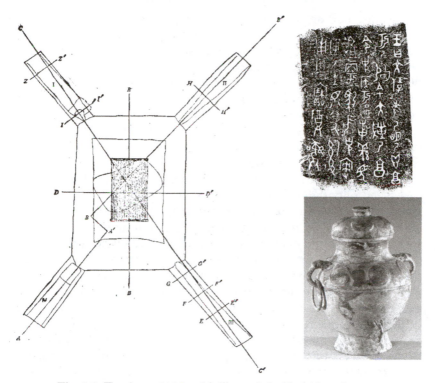

Fig. 6.9 Tomb no. 1193 at Liulihe and the Ke *lei* from it.

Jin and Yan. The center of Jin, founded by a son of King Wu, was located in the lower Fen River valley in southern Shanxi where archaeologists had been excavating residential sites and cemeteries since the early 1980s. A major burial ground was discovered in 1992 to the south of the Beizhao village where nine rulers of Jin with their spouses were buried in three rows, dating from the early Western Zhou to the early Spring and Autumn period. Most recently, a large pit situated in the south section of the burial ground was excavated, offering a dramatic scene of forty-eight chariots together with one hundred and five horses that accompanied the Jin rulers to the afterlife. The state of Yan, founded by a son of the Duke of Shao, was located at Liulihe to the south of Beijing where not only a cemetery consisting of tombs of different ranks has been discovered, but also, not far from the cemetery, the walled city of the state. Most importantly, two bronze vessels whose inscriptions record the initial granting of the Yan state by the Zhou king have been excavated from a large tomb (no. 1193) that was apparently the burial of the first Yan ruler (Fig. 6.9). These discoveries not only confirmed the geographical locations of these regional states known previously from the received texts and the inscriptions, but offered important new insights into the formation and characteristics of their material culture. Most importantly, the archaeological discovery of the regional states in the Western Zhou period offers us new ideas about the roots of the regional cultures during the Eastern Zhou period.

In general, the elite culture in the regional states, located at varying distances from the Zhou capitals in the Wei River valley, show a remarkable degree of consistency with their metropolitan counterparts in terms of the design of the decorative patterns of their bronzes. Diachronically, the regional bronzes seem to have followed the same trend of development shown in the metropolitan bronzes, a phenomenon that has led scholars to suggest a close communication necessary for the timely adoption of new patterns developed in the central area to the regional sites. In fact, this phenomenon in the material culture of the regional states can be explained by the visits of the regional rulers and their officials to the Zhou capitals, frequently documented in the bronze inscriptions during the early and early–mid Western Zhou, many being found in the regional centers. There are minor differences between bronzes from different regions which need further study to clarify them, but the differences were not really significant until the arrival of the later Western Zhou when some regional centers continued to use types no longer in use in the Wei River valley; other regional centers began to create new types of bronzes possibly based on the local pottery. However, material culture represented by the more practically useful items such as ceramics shows very different trends tying strongly to local traditions. For instance, the pottery assemblages in regional centers like Xing and Yan show strong links to the pre-conquest Shang culture, not the Zhou manufacture tradition, which began to be introduced to these distant regions only gradually from the mid Western Zhou period. However, in the Fen River valley where the state of Jin was located, the pottery assemblage was essentially identical to that of the Wei River valley.

Therefore, the formation of the Western Zhou state, viewed from a purely archaeological perspective, can be seen as a process of installation of elements of the Zhou elite culture in the various regions with strong local traditions lying beyond the Wei River valley. And the eventual merging of the Zhou tradition with the various regional traditions since the beginning of the mid Western Zhou provided foundations for the regional cultures that prospered thereafter during the Eastern Zhou period.

The External World and the Great Early
Western Zhou Expansion

The Zhou were certainly not the only powerhouse in China. The preceding chapters have made clear that advanced Bronze Age societies existed in the Yangzi regions in the south and on the northern steppe during the late Shang, and their descendants continued to exist into the Western Zhou period. Through the establishment of the regional states, the Zhou were able to consolidate a geographical perimeter along the edges of the eastern plain. There is good evidence that the practice of granting states was revived on a number of occasions later in the dynasty in coping with changing situations on the borders; however, as an institutional practice, the process was largely completed within the reign of King Cheng, the second king after the conquest. By the middle period of King Kang, about fifty years after the conquest,[12] the Zhou periphery was firmly consolidated and became the new frontline for further military and cultural expansion, now conducted through the collaboration of the royal armies and the regional forces.

The bronze inscriptions indicate that two major expeditions were organized towards the end of the reign of King Kang to conquer a society located probably in the lower Ordos region, to the north of Zhou across the difficult terrain of northern Shaanxi and Shanxi. The enemies are identified as Gui Fang who were previously at war with the Shang people, according to the oracle-bone inscriptions from Anyang. The inscriptions record captures of as many as 13,081 people and 352 cattle, along with large numbers of wagons, sheep, and other war spoils. It is very possible that the campaigns were responsible for the collapse of this Bronze Age society that had been prosperous for some 200 years on the edge of the northern steppe. Moving westwards, typical Zhou burials with bronzes and pottery identical to Wei River styles have been found as far north as the south Ningxia plain. It is very possible that the Zhou troops were once active on the edges of the northern steppe, encountering the rising nomads or semi-nomadic societies farther north and northwest. Archaeological discoveries show that some groups that descended from northern cultures might have moved south, after the collapse of Ordos, to the centrally located areas of the Western Zhou, such as the polity of Peng whose cemetery has recently been found in Jiangxian in southern Shanxi.

---

[12] The recent discovery of bronze inscriptions shows that King Cheng ruled for at least twenty-eight years, following the regency of the Duke of Zhou which lasted seven years. King Kang, on the other hand, has been traditionally assigned a reign of somewhere between twenty-four and thirty years.

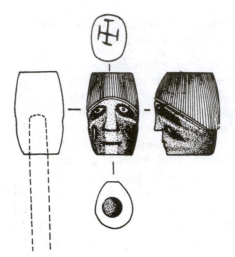

Fig. 6.10 Bone sculpture from Zhouyuan.

It is also possible that some foreigners might have arrived in Zhou from regions as far as Central Asia in the west, as vividly illustrated by the images of two small bone sculptures excavated in Zhouyuan whose Caucasoid features simply cannot be mistaken; the graph that means "shaman" (*wu*) on the top of one of the bone heads identifies him as a magician (Fig. 6.10).[13] This remote contact is also indicated by the frequent occurrence of carnelian and faience items in middle–late Western Zhou tombs whose origins were in India and West Asia.[14]

However, the main direction of Zhou expansion during the early period seems to have been the eastern Shandong peninsula against the local inhabitants referred to by the Zhou as the "Eastern Barbarians" (Dongyi). The inscriptions suggest that this took place mainly in the reign of King Kang and continued into early King Zhao when a series of campaigns were launched into this far eastern region. One campaign was fought by the royal Eight Armies with its base in the former Shang capital area that had reached seashores in the east where the soldiers captured substantial amounts of seashells, a type of currency used in the Western Zhou state (Fig. 6.11):

Xiaochen Lai *gui* (JC: 4238)

---

[13] For a study of this interesting finding, see Victor Mair, "Old Sinitic *M^{y}ag, Persian Maguš, and English 'Magician'", *Early China* 15 (1990), 27–47.

[14] Jessica Rawson, "Carnelian Beads, Animal Figures and Exotic Vessels: Traces of Contact between the Chinese States and Inner Asia, ca. 1000–650 BC," in Mayke Wagner and Wang Wei (eds.), *Archäologie in China*, vol. 1, *Bridging Eurasia* (Berlin: Deutsches Archäologisches Institut, 2010), pp. 5–12.

Fig. 6.11 The Xiaochen Lai *gui*-tureen (h. 24.5 cm, diam. 20.0 cm) and its inscriptions on the eastern campaign.

Alas! The Dongyi greatly rebelled and Bo Maofu led the Eight Armies of Yin to attack the Dongyi. It was the eleventh month when [he] dispatched troops from Ke Garrison, along Eastern XX to attack the sea coastal areas. When he returned to Mu Garrison, Bo Maofu received the king's command to award the troops cowries that he led them to attack and captured from Wuyu. Xiaochen Lai was acknowledged his merits, and was awarded cowries, with which [he] makes the treasured sacrificial vessel.

Some inscriptions also record that the Zhou king personally led campaigns in the region, assisted by the rulers of the regional states in western Shandong. It is impossible to demarcate accurately the areas affected by Zhou's military advances, but information from the inscriptions shows beyond doubt that the campaigns were aimed at conquering the hilly regions in the eastern Shandong Peninsula, traditionally known as the heartland of the "Eastern Barbarians." Archaeological surveys in areas along the north shore of the eastern peninsula, particularly cases of inscribed bronzes found in the region and showing political connections to the Zhou central court, offer good support for possible Zhou activities in eastern Shandong.

Zhou's relationship with the southeast during the early period, particularly the Yangzi Delta, has been a historical debate. However, there is no solid evidence for Zhou political contact with the Yangzi Delta around the Tai Lake, the heartland of the later state of Wu whose royal ancestry was traced back to the Zhou royal house in traditional historiography; but this seems more likely to have been a far-fetched connection created to legitimate Wu's hegemony in the early fifth century BC in a world that was still dominated by the ideal of Zhou. However, substantial contacts with the Huai River region are suggested by a series of wars between the Zhou and the so-called "Huai Barbarians" (indigenous people of the Huai region) documented in many inscriptions dating to the early mid-Western Zhou period. A recently dis-covered inscription indicates that contacts with the Huai River region might have begun much earlier, as the Duke of Zhou was credited for having organized extensive campaigns to attack the southern states. But there is no mention of war with the "Huai Barbarians" in any inscription after King Cheng until the beginning of the mid Western Zhou.

Warfare is the subject most frequently recorded in the inscriptions during the early Western Zhou, and this fully indicates the importance of war to the mind of the Zhou elites in the first century of the dynasty. However, later in the reign of King Zhao, the Zhou embarked on a plan to conquer the middle Yangzi region. The region, as mentioned in Chapter 5, had a much longer history of bronze culture and possibly also of state building than eastern Shandong and raised a much more formidable resistance to the Zhou. When a second campaign was launched by King Zhao in his nineteenth year, aiming most likely at the polity called "Hu Fang," the Zhou were totally defeated. Not only the royal Six Armies, representing nearly a half of Zhou's military formation, had vanished in the Han River, but King Zhao himself was killed during the campaign. Certainly no individual had ever cast a bronze to celebrate this disastrous end of the reign of King Zhao, but there are enough inscriptions that can help us reconstruct the developments lead-ing to the eventual defeat of the king.

Despite his ultimate failure, King Zhao is celebrated in Zhou inscrip-tions as the king who had broadly opened land to the south. In 1980, archaeologists excavated a cemetery at Huangpi to the east of the Han River and north of the Yangzi River. Tombs in that cemetery were filled with Zhou cultural contents including inscribed bronzes that show close links to individuals in the Zhou central courts. Thus, although further expansion to the south was curbed by the strong resistance of the indig-enous peoples, the reign of King Zhao might have indeed been an impor-tant period of Zhou expansion into the middle Yangzi region.

SELECTED READING

Rawson, Jessica, "Western Zhou archaeology," in Michael Loewe and Edward L. Shaughnessy (eds.), *The Cambridge History of Ancient China: From the Origins of Civilization to 221 BC* (Cambridge: Cambridge University Press, 1999), pp. 352–449.

Shaughnessy, Edward L., "Western Zhou History," in Michael Loewe and Edward L. Shaughnessy (eds.), *The Cambridge History of Ancient China: From the Origins of Civilization to 221 BC* (Cambridge: Cambridge University Press, 1999), pp. 292–351.

Hsu, Cho-yun, and Katheryn Linduff, *Western Chou Civilization* (New Haven: Yale University Press, 1988).

Li, Feng, *Landscape and Power in Early China: The Crisis, and Fall of the Western Zhou, 1045–771 BC* (Cambridge: Cambridge University Press, 2005).

"'Feudalism' and Western Zhou China: A Criticism," *Harvard Journal of Asiatic Studies* 63.1 (2003), 115–144.

The Western Zhou dynasty saw the rise of a core part of classical literature
that has been passed down to our days. On the other hand, there are
literally thousands of bronze vessels with inscriptions whose number has
been steadily growing over the past half century due to archaeological
excavations and uncontrolled looting by tomb robbers. Unlike the Shang
oracle-bone inscriptions whose number is very limited outside of Anyang,
inscribed bronzes have been found all over North China and a part of
South China from cemeteries or residential sites of the Zhou or non-Zhou
elites. This makes the Western Zhou one of the most important periods
for the spreading of literacy in Chinese history. Also different from the
Shang divinatory records that are often fragmentary and almost always
inconsequential, a core group of several hundred Western Zhou bronze
inscriptions are remarkably lengthy. It is true that a large number of
inscribed bronzes were used in the religious context of ancestral worship;
however, the historical events they record are almost always unrelated to
the ancestral ritual in which their material bronzes were used. Instead,
they record a wide range of topics such as military merit, official performance, royal orders, marriage, lineage genealogy, economic deals, diplomatic exchange, legal treaties, and so on. Certainly, the actual use of
bronzes in Western Zhou society was not confined to the religious scene
either. The improvement in the quality of the written evidence available to
us allows for a much better, or more consistent, understanding of the
political and ritual institutions as well as social conditions of the Western
Zhou than of Shang.

Clans and Lineages: The Social Organization
of the Zhou Elites

The Zhou were the first people in China to introduce the institution of clan
names (*xìng*; or later, "surname") as the hallmark of the system of lineage.
As clans were themselves kin groups bound together by a common ancestry, clan names usually were related to the maternal origins of the clan's

the other hand, were recent an
economic entities of the Zhou el
smaller units and usually were rela
s. By convention, as fully evident in the bro
Zhou elites were referred to by their lineag
en usually carried their clan names as part of their
s. The bronze inscriptions also suggest that the use of
of female names was based on the principle of marital
nder the common practice of polygamy among the Zhou
been suggested by scholars that the introduction of clan
t have been necessitated by the need to regulate marriage
ps among the various ethnic groups in the Zhou common-
If this is true, the invention of clan names might well have been
d to the nature of the pre-dynastic Zhou polity as a congregation of
erous ethnic groups in the Wei River valley and the adjacent regions
at jointly helped the Zhou achieve their conquest of Shang (see
Chapter 6). The Zhou royal clan, for instance, was named Ji, and through
the entire Western Zhou period, more than half of the twelve Zhou kings
took as their primary wives ladies from the Jiang clan which seems to have
had an origin in the farther west, possibly related to the ancient Qiang
people. Certainly, Ji clan members founded the largest number of lineages
in the royal domains and the overwhelming majority of regional states in
the east. Besides Ji and Jiang, there were about ten other intermarrying
clans frequently mentioned in the bronze inscriptions, and the actual
number of clans in the Western Zhou period must have been very large.

However, clans were not social solidarities; lineages were. As essential
social units, the history of some of the prestigious lineages of the Zhou
elites goes back to the pre-dynastic time when they first split off the royal
lineage that was continued by the succession of the Zhou kings. Lineages
were basic social units that held land estates and people, and competed
with each other for political power and economic interests in Zhou society. The bronze inscriptions suggest that land was held in the form of
settlements (called *yi* in the inscriptions) – natural villages that have a
residential core surrounded by fields; most lineages had multiple small
settlements under their control where their farmers lived and activities of
subsistence were carried out. Under the practice of primogeniture, only
the eldest son in each generation had the chance to become the head of the
lineage, while other sons formed their individual families and worshipped

---

[1] For a recent discussion of the role of lineage system in the formation of the Zhou state, see
Edwin Pulleyblank, "Ji and Jiang: the Role of Exogamic Clans in the Organization of the
Zhou Polity," *Early China* 25 (2000), 1–27.

Overlapping page fragment (partially visible, left margin):
ions also
r estates
n, most
where
vated
into
age
the
of
d

...nmon ancestral temple of the lineage. The inscrip... that while the lineage centers and the greater part of th... ...located in the rural areas across the fertile Wei River pla... ...minent lineages also held residences in the Zhou royal center... ...ronzes cast by the lineage members have frequently been exc... (Chapter 6). As time passed, such lineage branches could develop... new lineages. Another factor that might have contributed to lin... segmentation was the frequent sale or exchange of land between... aristocratic lineages which had inevitably led to the fragmentation... lineage properties; settlements located far from the lineage center tend... to be transferred into bases of new lineage segments.[2]

Later Confucian texts describe the process of lineage segmentation in the way that in every five generations, minor sons of a lineage would be required to move away and found a new lineage, so the lineage's growing population could be kept at a manageable level.[3] Naturally, there is a distinction between the primary lineage and derivative ones, and the minor lineages by their position on the genealogical tree were required to obey the primary lineage. The bronze inscriptions do not confirm the practice of a strict "five-generation" rule, but they offer sufficient evidence that the distinction between the primary and minor lineages indeed existed in the Western Zhou. There is also evidence that the primary lineage represented its minor lineages in cases of legal disputes that were brought for settlement at the Zhou court. Thus, genealogical relationships underlay the basic logic of social relationships during the Western Zhou.

This genealogical rule, conceived of not so much as a basis for relationships between the individuals as for lineages, was also applicable to the royal lineage. In a way, the "Fengjian" institution by which many regional states were established during the early Western Zhou can be seen as the process of segmentation of the royal lineage. Throughout the Western Zhou, minor sons of the Zhou king continued to receive estates in the royal domain in Shaanxi, thus founding new lineages, or, in a few cases, to

[2] This process of lineage segmentation can be best seen in the case of the Jing lineage, located in the west part of the Wei River valley. During the mid Western Zhou, the Jing lineage had already been divided between the lineage's two older brothers called "Jingbo" and "Jingshu," terms that by then came to designate the two sub-lineages. Because the "Jingshu" sub-lineage held residences in the city of Zheng and the Zhou capital Feng, by the end of the mid Western Zhou, it was further divided into two branches – "Jingshu of Zheng" and "Jingshu of Feng" – terms that were used by the members of their respective branches.

[3] For a recent discussion of this rule in Confucian ritual texts and its relevance to Zhou lineage system, see Lothar von Falkenhausen, *Chinese Society in the Age of Confucius (1000–250 BC): The Archaeological Evidence* (Los Angeles: Cotsen Institute of Archaeology, 2006), pp. 64–70.

be established as rulers of the new regional states. Because of th,
tions on the royal genealogical tree, they were required to obey the
lineage in the Zhou capital as the primary lineage.

Ideology and Religion

For a long time, the Shang–Zhou transition has been taken by historians
as one of the "revolutions" in Chinese history. With respect to the
ideological foundation of this revolution, the Zhou were credited with
the invention of the concept of "Heaven's Mandate," as opposed to the
concept of the "High God" of the Shang people. This theory of an
ideological opposition between Shang and Zhou has been modified by
recent studies with regard to the nature of "Heaven" (*tian*) in the Shang
dynasty.[4] Due to the lack of extensive records of royal divination as in the
Shang case, we do not understand Zhou religion in the way we do that of
Shang. Nevertheless, "Heaven" as an anthropomorphic deity, the ultimate power of the universe, seems surely to have been a Zhou discovery.
Modern scholars have further provided an astronomical base for the rise
of this concept – the conjunction of the five major planets in the solar
system in 1059 BC which was clearly visible from the Zhou capital and
that was evidently taken by the Zhou people as a sign of Heaven's
Mandate and left a deep psychological impact on the Zhou people (see
Chapter 6).[5] This event prompted the declaration of kingship by King
Wen, the sole recipient of Heaven's Mandate acknowledged in the
bronze inscriptions during the early Western Zhou period.

Thus, the Zhou conquest was not merely a military campaign, but also
an ideological or even psychological war. We read in chapters of the *Book
of Documents* that the last Shang king was denounced as a tyrant who was
vicious and paranoid; his officials were indulgent and alcoholic and
deserved a total destruction, and the Zhou had the inevitable responsibility to exercise Heaven's punishment. The Zhou state, although an
old polity, had a new mission, as so stated the *Book of Poetry*. This new
mission was not only to overthrow an evil Shang regime, but to create a

---

[4] The theory was originally proposed by Herrlee Creel, and followed by many others; see
Creel, *The Origins of Statecraft in China*, vol. 1, *The Western Chou Empire* (Chicago:
University of Chicago Press, 1970), pp. 81–100; Cho-yun Hsu and Katheryn Linduff,
Western Chou Civilization (New Haven: Yale University Press, 1988), pp. 101–111. In his
study of the concept of "Heaven," Robert Eno points out the possibility that "Heaven" as a
sky-god already existed in Shang, but it was ultimately different from High God in Shang
ideology. See Robert Eno, *The Confucian Creation of Heaven* (Albany: State University of
New York Press, 1990), pp. 181–189.

[5] See David W. Pankenier, "The Cosmo-Political Background of Heaven's Mandate," *Early
China* 20 (1995), 121–176.

eople," and those who dared to oppose this great enterprise would ...their due penalty. From this concept of Heaven's Mandate, it was ...ner theorized, probably by the Duke of Zhou, that the Shang once ...emselves hosted Heaven's Mandate when their sage kings ruled the kingdom, as did the Xia Dynasty before it was conquered by the Shang. Thus the subjugated Shang should have no blame for the Zhou because their own kings and ministers caused the removal of Heaven's Mandate from them.

Through the entire Western Zhou period, the bronze inscriptions continued to celebrate the divine origin of the Zhou conquest, and as such the Zhou state born from the conquest was seen as an institution to fulfill the will of Heaven. Since the mandate could be granted only once by Heaven, particularly to King Wen, no subsequent Zhou kings could again claim the status as the recipient of the mandate. Instead, their legitimacy as king rested first of all on their genealogical link to King Wen, and it was also strengthened by their commitment to virtuous conduct following the good example of the founding kings, thus helping host Heaven's Mandate in Zhou. On the other hand, the theory of history of the transmission of Heaven's Mandate from Xia to Shang and to Zhou actually called the future of the Zhou regime into question. Thus, Heaven's Mandate was not only a source of legitimacy, but also a source of great anxiety that one day it might be void if the Zhou kings did not conduct themselves in a responsible way. Therefore, in Zhou literature, particularly from the late part of the dynasty, there is constant fear that this may happen some day.[6]

The concept of High God or God (di) and his relationship to Heaven is a point of hot debate with regard to Zhou cosmology and religion. The predynastic Zhou oracle-bone inscriptions from Zhouyuan suggest that the Zhou had apparently adopted the concept of High God from the Shang. As mentioned in Chapter 5, God by origin was probably the celestial pivot (North Pole). No matter what attitude the Zhou had towards God, it seems evident that after the conquest the concept of God went through significant reworking by Zhou elites to suit their own political purposes. On the one hand, God lost his omnipresent power over both human and natural worlds, a power that was taken over by Heaven. On the other hand, the Zhou seemed to have forged their own genealogical relations going back directly to God (as in the poem "The Birth of People" in the *Book of Poetry*), thus transforming High God into their own guardian. Later Zhou tradition further put the Zhou in a more advantageous position by having Zhou's

---

[6] On this point, see Eno, *The Confucian Creation of Heaven*, pp. 23–27.

female ancestor Jiang Yuan as the primary wife of the legendary Di Ku and the Shang female ancestor as his secondary wife, an arrangement that shows clear influence from the Zhou practice of primogeniture. Thus, in Zhou sources, although Heaven represented the ultimate universal order, following the dynastic decline, it was increasingly described as a source of calamities, death, and destruction; in sharp contrast, God (*di*) appears as a patron of the Zhou king and protector of the Zhou people, and never appears as a source of misfortune. The coexistence of Heaven and God is an important feature of Zhou religion.

God was not only the guardian of the Zhou people, but he also hosted the deceased Zhou kings who would rise to the court of God after they physically faded away from the secular world. The former kings, while accompanying God in his court, occasionally descended to their temples during worships honoring them in the secular world ruled by their offspring. Thus, ancestral worship formed the foundation of the Zhou state and it tied the Zhou king and the various regional rulers of royal descent together in a political and religious "commonwealth." Because sessions taking place in the ancestral temples are frequently but briefly recorded in the bronze inscriptions, scholars have made efforts to recover the system of Zhou temples. Although there are questions that are likely to remain unknown in the near future, careful analysis of the information at hand offers an outline of the organization of the royal temples, composed of essentially two large clusters. The first cluster, called the "Grand Temple" or the "Temple of Zhou" (because it was located in Zhou, or Qiyi), was probably constructed in the pre-dynastic period with the Grand King (or Ancient Duke) occupying the central temple, to which the temples of King Ji, King Wen, King Wu, and King Cheng were subsequently added, forming a group of five temples. After the conquest, this temple cluster was replicated in all major royal cities as well as in the central settlements of the regional states, forming a common ancestral cult among the Zhou elites (Fig. 7.1). The second cluster was called "Kang Temple," beginning with the temple for King Kang (sixth king from the ancestral Grand King) as the central focus, to which the temples of four later kings including King Zhao, King Mu, King Yi, and King Li were added.[7]

---

[7] For a new consideration of the Zhou temple system, see Martin Kern, "Bronze Inscriptions, the *Shijing* and the *Shangshu*: The Evolution of the Ancestral Sacrifice during the Western Zhou," in John Lagerwey and Marc Kalinowski (eds.), *Early Chinese Religion*, Part 1, *Shang through Han (1250 BC–220 AD)* (Leiden: Brill, 2009), pp. 156–164. Kern notes that the new rearrangement of Zhou temples may have played an important role in the so-called "Mid-Western Zhou reform." On the Kang Temple and its importance for the study to Western Zhou bronzes, see Edward L. Shaughnessy, *Sources of Western History: Inscribed Bronze Vessels* (Berkeley: University of California Press, 1991), pp. 199–201.

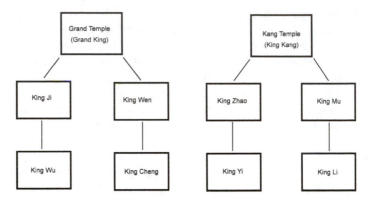

Fig. 7.1 Configuration of the Zhou ancestral temple system.

Although we do not know if the three kings between King Mu and King Yi and the two kings after Li should have constituted a different order, or if they would have been worshipped together after all, the inscriptions clearly mention the five temples headed by Kang Temple as a cluster, and they were invariably located in one place – Zhou (Qiyi). This five-temple group arrangement might have been the original model that gave rise to the "five-generation rule" that was transmitted in the later Confucian texts.

It has to be noted that ancestral worship was not the monopoly of the royal house aimed at the royal ancestors, but was universally practiced by the Zhou elites focusing on the lineage temples located in the numerous lineage centers far away from the royal capitals. In fact, the overwhelming majority of sacrificial bronzes that we have today were cast for use in the context of lineage sacrifice, whereas only a fraction were commissioned by the Zhou king. It has been suggested recently that the lineages (not limited to those that split off from the royal genealogy, but including also their marriage partners, usually non-Ji-surnamed lineages) were connected to the royal house through their "nexus ancestors" who had in time past served either King Wen or King Wu, and whose initial connection to the Zhou royal house determined the social status of their descendant lineages. These initial moments of service or alliance with the royal house needed to be instantiated through ritual ceremonies that motivated the casting of numerous sacrificial vessels dedicated to the lineage ancestors.[8] In other

---

[8] See Nick Vogt, "Between Kin and King: Social Aspects of Western Zhou Ritual" (Ph.D. dissertation: Columbia University, 2012), pp. 35–48, 67.

words, the reverence and continuing remembrance of the "nexus ances-tors" formed the essential logic that underlay both the ancestral worship carried out in the lineage temples and the religious ceremonies that took place in the royal compounds also involving the participation of lineage members. These religious practices played a critical role in creating and maintaining social order in Western Zhou society.

The Bureaucratization of the Royal Government

Quite different from the Shang government that was likely to have cen-tered on the role of the royal diviners, the Zhou central government from the beginning of the dynasty was centered on the role of the executive officials such as the Supervisor of Land, Supervisor of Construction, and Supervisor of Horses who were further organized into a general bureau of administration named "Ministry" (*qingshiliao*). Whether the Shang insti-tution of royal divination already displayed principles of a proto-bureaucracy, as argued by Keightley, is open to question; even if it did, it was not in any substantial way. But there can be no doubt that a bureaucracy that was set up for actual administrative purposes certainly did not exist in Shang. In the Zhou case, the administrative officials were further assisted by a large number of Scribes and Document Makers who produced and kept written records in the government. Only the office of Document Maker can be traced back to the Shang dynasty, while all others are likely Zhou inventions. This suggests that with their historical conquest, the Zhou might have introduced a new approach to the issue of governance through the refinement of civil administration in order to support the military, combined with a colonization operation in a much larger geographical space than that of Shang. This government worked in an oligarchical way through most of the early Western Zhou as the power of policy-making rested in the hands of one or sometimes two dukes who were uncles or brothers of the reigning Zhou king, and who evidently had the Ministry under their control. It was this government guided by strong-willed dukes that managed the state affairs through the period of great early Western Zhou expansion.

By the mid Western Zhou, the Zhou central government was clearly undergoing a process of bureaucratization. This is seen first in the com-partmentalization of the Zhou central government, resulting in three parallel structural divisions (Fig. 7.2). The Ministry was further expanded to embrace multiple officials serving at the position of each of the Three Supervisors. Mentioned as its counterpart in the inscriptions is the Grand Secretariat, the major secretarial body of the Zhou government headed by the Grand Scribes assisted by many minor scribes. The management of

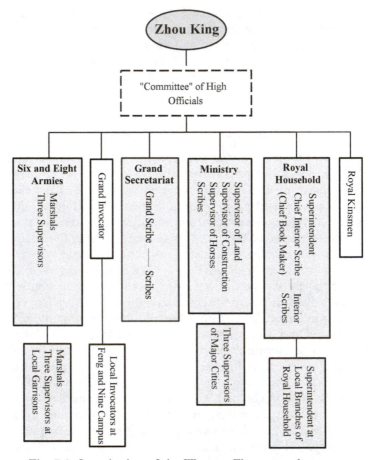

Fig. 7.2 Organization of the Western Zhou central government: mid Western Zhou period.

the Royal Household and its local branches had developed into a separate system of administration headed by the Superintendents. A parallel development was the separation of the interior scribe body from the Grand Secretariat; this secretarial body headed by the Chief Interior Scribe was located in the inner court of the Zhou king and assisted him in various matters brought to the king. Another major development lay in the military system; during the mid Western Zhou both the Eight Armies and Six Armies had developed into a huge system of administration employing officials who managed properties and land attached to the military. Above this structure was a group of five to six high officials who, appearing in a fixed order, acted together as decision-makers and as judges in legal matters, suggesting the expansion of impersonal rule.[9]

Importantly, the procedure of appointing officials had also become bureaucratized, giving rise to a new type of inscriptions – the "appointment inscriptions." Some 100 inscriptions constantly record official appointments that took place in the various facilities of the Zhou king or in building compounds under the authority of individual officials. In this ritual hosted almost exclusively by the Zhou king, the written command of the king was pronounced by the Interior Scribe to the candidates who were normally led to the courtyard and introduced to the king by an official in a superior position. Then, the appointee received the royal command which he brought home and subsequently transferred onto bronzes. The entire process was highly regularized both in terms of the officials involved and of the way in which each party acted. And the very fact that the numerous inscriptions (the ones we have are probably a fraction of what had been produced during the mid to late Western Zhou) were cast to commemorate royal appointments suggests strongly the high social value the Zhou elites placed on government service (Box 7.1); before the mid Western Zhou many inscriptions were cast to commemorate military exploits or the receipt of royal gifts, and none of them were cast to record the actual procedure of royal appointment.[10]

Bureaucratic features are manifest also in the process of selection of officials for government service. While traditional textual records tend to describe the Western Zhou as a period of hereditary offices, the bronze inscriptions instead describe a much more complex situation where although hereditary appointments were made by the Zhou king, he had considerable freedom to manipulate the system by appointing officials with no documented family history of government service or by assigning them to offices different from what had been held by their fathers or grandfathers. This tendency corresponded well with another practice in the Zhou government – promotion. Further analysis of the inscriptions suggests that younger elites were usually appointed assistants to senior officials, and then after some years of service were promoted to offices of full capacity. The current evidence shows that although family background was impor-

[9] See Li Feng, *Bureaucracy and the State in Early China: Governing the Western Zhou (1045–771 BC)* (Cambridge: Cambridge University Press, 2008), pp. 42–95.

[10] For a recent discussion of the official appointment ritual, see *ibid.*, pp. 103–114.

Box 7.1   Example of an Appointment Inscription: The Song *Ding*

This long text of 149 characters was cast on at least three hemispheric *ding*-cauldrons that formed a part of an original set, stylistically similar to but slightly later than the Duoyou *ding* (Fig. 7.3). The text offers one of the most detailed descriptions of the appointment ritual that took place in this case in King Zhao's temple that was a part of the Kang Temple complex. The caster Song is identified as Scribe Song in another shorter inscription that was cast on at least two *ding*-cauldrons and five *gui*-tureens.

It was the third year, fifth month, after the dying brightness, the *jiaxu* day (#11). The king was in the Zhao Temple of the Kang Temple in Zhou. At dawn, the king entered the grand chamber and assumed his position. Superintendent Hong accompanied Song to his right, entering the gate and standing in the center of the courtyard. The Chief (Interior Scribe) received the document of royal command, and the king called out to Scribe Guosheng to command Song with the written document. The king said: "Song! [I] command you to take office in charge of the storage of twenty households in Chengzhou, and to inspect and supervise the newly constructed storage house, using palace attendants. [I] award you a black jacket with brocaded hem, red knee pads, a scarlet semi-circlet, a jingle-bell pennant, and a bridle with bit and cheek-pieces with which to serve!" Song bowed with his head touching the ground, received the bamboo document of royal command, hung it [on his body], and came out [of the courtyard]. He then returned and brought in a jade tablet. Song dares in response to extol the Son of Heaven's illustriously fine beneficence, herewith making [for] my august deceased father Gongshu and august mother Gong Si [this] treasured sacrificial *ding*-vessel, which will be used to pursue filial piety, to pray for peaceful harmony, pure blessings, pervading wealth, and eternal mandate. May Song for ten thousand years enjoy abundant longevity, and serve the Son of Heaven, with no end. [May Song's] sons' sons and grandsons' grandsons treasure and use [it]!

---

tant, personal qualification might have also been an important consideration for government appointment, and the system was set up, at latest by the mid Western Zhou period, with the expectation that good performance of officials was a credential that would lead them up to the higher levels on the bureaucratic ladder.[11]

---

[11] *Ibid.*, pp. 190–234.

Fig. 7.3 The Douyou *ding*-cauldron and its inscription which records Zhou combat with the Xianyun at four locations along the Jing River to the north of the Zhou capital.

While the bureaucratic tendency continued to develop in the late Western Zhou, the whole process of bureaucratization of the Zhou government seems not to have been a response to the military expansion that took place mainly during the early Western Zhou, but was a natural process of internal reorganization that took place after the end of the great expansion and was intensified even more following the dynastic decline. This pattern of development of bureaucracy had many parallels in the ancient world. It should also be noted, however, that the sway of bureaucratization did not seem to have affected the regional governments which, even during the early Spring and Autumn period, remained largely personal and unbureaucratic.

The Mid Western Zhou Transition

Historians, art historians, and archaeologists have each taken a different approach to the changes that occurred during the mid Western Zhou period. Earlier, archaeologists observed a major change in burial bronzes in Western Zhou elite tombs where the assemblage of wine vessels popular during the early Western Zhou gradually gave way to a new set of bronze vessels composed almost exclusively of food vessels during the mid Western Zhou. Working mainly on bronze objects, art historians further hypothesized that the changes that occurred during the mid Western Zhou might have been the result of some kind of "Ritual Reform" or "Ritual Revolution."[12] These changes are quite obvious and important in reshaping a bronze art tradition that had its roots in Shang. By the closing of the mid Western Zhou period, Zhou bronze art had acquired a totally new image (see Chapter 6). However, the critical missing piece of information is whether these changes in bronze art were related to systematic changes implemented by an agent (or agents) in Zhou's political ritual system, or they were simply a change of "fashion" that gradually took hold among the Zhou craftsmen and was accepted by Zhou elites. Until what actually happened in the Zhou ritual system can be demonstrated, the "Reform" theory has to remain hypothetical.

A recent systematic study of the ritual tradition and ritual practice in the Western Zhou offers the first step towards recovering this missing ground which might have conditioned at least in part the changes in bronze art.

---

[12] See Jessica Rawson, "Western Zhou Archaeology," in Michael Loewe and Edward L. Shaughnessy (eds.), *The Cambridge History of Ancient China: From the Origins of Civilization to 221 BC* (Cambridge: Cambridge University Press, 1999), pp. 414–434. See also Lothar von Falkenhausen, "Late Western Zhou Taste," *Études chinoises* **18** (1999), 155–164.

According to this analysis, the mid Western Zhou saw a move from the practice that combined many ritual techniques inherited from the Shang, rituals that centered on the Zhou king and enrolled members of the various lineages, to a ritual system that was intended to create and implement internal differentiation among the Zhou elites. This new trend enabled the Zhou king to continue to distribute prestige to the elites in a time after the early Western Zhou expansion when war had ceased to be a sufficient source for the elite to win honor and prestige. Thus in effect the new system served to strengthen the power of the Zhou king and to maintain the solidarity of the Zhou elites. The time of this important change in Zhou ritual tradition has been pinned down to the end of the reign of King Mu which actually saw the peak of diversity of ritual techniques, many of which disappeared quickly thereafter.[13] The new standards and patterns observed on mid and late Western Zhou bronzes, relating more closely to the personal ranking and status of the elites, were reflections of the same trend.

In all, the closing of the great early Western Zhou expansion seems to have set the Western Zhou state and society on a different trend that was to develop in the next 100 years. The changes in government system and ritual practice are two aspects of a widely ranged sociopolitical transformation that took place during the mid Western Zhou period. In the history of the royal house, five Zhou kings came to rule for a total length of time that was shorter than three generations of an aristocratic family.[14] Possibly contributing to the short reigns was an incident of abnormal succession that happened for the first time since the beginning of the dynasty – King Xiao succeeded his nephew King Yih to become the eighth Zhou king. In foreign relations, the mid Western Zhou saw the first deep foreign invasion since the beginning of the dynasty – the invasion by groups of aboriginals from the Huai River region which posed a major threat to the security of Zhou's eastern capital in present-day Luoyang. Along with the weakening of royal power, the relationship between the Zhou central court and the regional states was also challenged by the ambition of some regional rulers such as that of Qi who was targeted by a royal campaign in the reign of King Yi. These are signs that the Zhou court was no longer able to keep its enemies beyond the border and regional rulers in line with royal interests. On a societal level, the most

---

[13] See Vogt, "Between Kin and King: Social Aspects of Western Zhou Ritual," pp. 316, 329–332.

[14] This is the Shan lineage whose bronzes were discovered in Meixian in 2003, including one, the Lai *pan*, which provide a complete family genealogy linked to the reigns of eleven Zhou kings.

important impact of the closing of the great expansion was the removal of opportunities to transfer population out of the Wei River valley to form new regional polities in an expanding territory. The bronze inscriptions suggest that the Zhou king was no longer able to grant the lineages large parcels of land, but had to hand out fields in a piecemeal fashion often located at a distance from one another. On the other hand, the lineages also traded land in such small pieces that they in turn accelerated the process of lineage fragmentation discussed above. This shift was itself an indication of intense competition for land resources when large areas of marginal land had been exhausted. Reports on disputes over land ownership or even incidences of robbery of land products were frequently filed at the Zhou court and recorded on bronzes by those who won the respective legal cases. The inscriptions offer us a vivid picture of tense competition over economic resources and social conflicts in the royal domain during the mid Western Zhou period. In short, the current evidence shows that the mid Western Zhou was an important period of sociopolitical transition.

The Nature of the Western Zhou State

As discussed in Chapter 6, the Western Zhou state has long been examined in the framework of "feudalism" which suggests a false comparison with medieval Europe; this has resulted in a chain of misunderstandings of the Western Zhou political system. Most importantly, the comparison misled previous scholars into believing that the relationship between the Zhou king and the various regional rulers was based on contracted reciprocity as in the lord–vassal relationship in Europe; it also misled scholars to interpret the nature of the Zhou regional states in terms of "feudal fiefs." But neither of these claims is true. It has been shown further that other sociopolitical models such as "city–state" and "territorial state" are also inadequate in characterizing the Western Zhou state.[15]

In order to capture the nature of the Western Zhou state and to highlight its comparative values, I have recently described it as a settlement-based state that was founded on delegatory rules. On the one hand, the current Zhou king ruled with a power that was understood in Zhou political philosophy as originating with King Wen, the dynasty's true founder as the recipient of the Mandate of Heaven. On the other hand, the Zhou king delegated his administrative power to the numerous regional rulers who acted as his local agents. In such a political system,

---

[15] See Li, *Bureaucracy and the State in Early China*, pp. 271–299.

the right of the regional rulers to decide policies over all domestic matters in their respective states was fully recognized by the Zhou king, but the regional rulers were not independent "sovereign" rulers. It was the kinship structure of the royal lineage that provided the main avenue along which the Zhou king delegated his political power – granting power to the regional states. Thus, the regional rulers were not only local agents of the Western Zhou king, but were also members (or marriage partners in cases of non-Ji-surnamed states) of the king's lineage bound together by a common ancestral cult. They owed allegiance to the Zhou king and participated in the larger Western Zhou state not merely because of their fear for the actual military might of the king which was also important, but on understanding of the source of their own power which commanded moral and legal obligations and the reverence for a common ancestor.

The fundamental mission of the Western Zhou state was to control the thousands of settlements (*yi*) scattered over the valleys and plains of North China. These settlements were organized into a huge web by the political power of the Western Zhou state and its numerous regional agents. This was the settlement-based state, and it was kin-ordered. That the Western Zhou state can be regarded as a huge layered network of settlements has two important implications in geopolitical terms: (1) The state did not exist as an integral geographic landmass demarcated by a linear border, but was marked by the very physical existence of the settlements under its control; (2) because the state existed as clusters of settlements by which it was defined, there were empty spaces within the state's perceived "territory" of authority. There were also overlaps in space between clusters of settlements that belonged to different regional states (Fig. 7.4). This condition of existence of the regional states provided an important starting point for a whole range of socioeconomic changes that occurred after the political power of the Western Zhou state waned (discussed in Chapter 8).

In the Zhou royal domain in central Shaanxi which was an independent zone in the Western Zhou administration, the spatial configuration of the state was a little different from the normal pattern of existence of the regional states in the east. Here, the royal cities such as the capitals Feng, Hao, and Qiyi served as focuses of political power and social integration. Around the royal centers were located the various lineage bases that were linked to the royal centers through the social and economic ties of the lineages. As shown by the inscriptions, each lineage center, usually located in the rural areas of the Wei River valley, was in turn surrounded by numerous smaller and affiliated settlements where activities of production of the lineage were carried out. It is likely that by the late Western Zhou some of the prominent lineages in the western part of Wei River valley such as the lineage of San had already developed internal layers in the

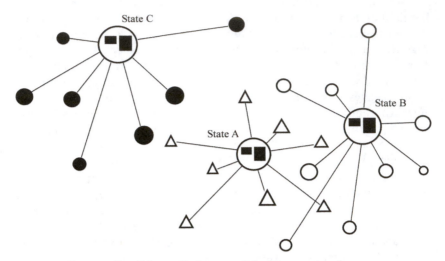

Fig. 7.4 Conditions of existence of the Zhou regional states.

organization of their settlements as well as a central administration that was created to control their settlements.

The Spreading of Literacy and the Creation of Classical Literature

The archaeological evidence suggests that the Western Zhou was a very crucial period in the expansion of literacy in China, or East Asia. A good indication of this process is the discovery of inscribed Western Zhou bronze vessels and weapons all over North China and a part of South China, posing a sharp contrast to the geographically limited existence of writing during the Shang period. The contrast shows that the culture of reading and writing was implanted widely in the numerous regional centers as the result of the migration of the Zhou elites from the Wei River plain to these remote areas, bringing along perhaps also their educated Shang subjects. However, literacy did not spread just over geographical space, but also extended across the various social realms of the Western Zhou. The bronze inscriptions show that writing played a crucial role in the administrative process of the Zhou government, and official appointments by the Zhou king were regularly delivered in writing. Apparently, the over 100 appointment inscriptions all derived their core information from such written letters which the candidates received in the royal court. The bronze inscriptions show further that writing presented on perishable materials was in wide circulation beyond the royal court, particularly in activities of significant economic consequences such as sale of goods or property; land registers and perhaps even contracts were also used by the aristocratic lineages in deals of transaction. Certainly we have cases that bronze vessels were cast to seal such deals, or simply to carry a copy of the original document of a territorial treaty.[16] In the military context, we also have cases where a scribe was asked to keep records on the misconduct of some disobedient soldiers during a campaign.[17]

Moreover, the inscriptions on bronzes are themselves testimony of a broad extent of literacy. Many of these bronzes were used in the ancestral temples and their metal texts witnessed by members of the respective lineages. Others were used in various social gatherings that took place in the family's domestic quarters where accounts of the virtue of the ancestors or the merits of the family's recent members cast on bronzes were cherished by their relatives and friends in the family's social circle. In both scenarios, the inscribed bronze vessels helped create a wide readership that was necessary for the maintenance and further expansion of literacy in Western Zhou society. Although literacy remained in the possession of the social elites whose number was small, a considerable number of people in that social group must have learned to read and appreciate the art of writing and calligraphy so as to make the manufacture of the large number of long texts meaningful at all.

In complete agreement with the situation of literacy we learn from the inscribed bronzes, some of the written works on perishable materials had apparently survived the fall of the Western Zhou and were then passed down to the age of Confucius. The most important are the *Book of Changes* (Yijing), and parts of the *Book of Documents* (Shangshu) and the *Book of Poetry* (Shijing). Since these texts have been transmitted mainly in the Confucian tradition, hence conveniently called the "Confucian Classics," they had enormous impact on Chinese civilization and beyond. However, it must be noted that at least a very large portion of the components of these texts were created some 300 years before Confucius was born, thus having nothing to do with Confucianism in origin.

---

[16] This is the case of the inscription on the famous Sanshi *pan*, cast by the San lineage after a conference to resolve its territorial dispute with the polity of Ze, both located in the western part of the Wei River valley in Shaanxi. During the conference, the original treaty was signed.

[17] For a recent discussion of the nature of literacy in the Western Zhou, see Li Feng, "Literacy and the Social Contexts of Writing in the Western Zhou," in Li Feng and David Branner (eds.), *Writing and Literacy in Early China: Studies from the Columbia Early China Seminar* (Seattle: University of Washington Press, 2011), pp. 271–301.

Book of Changes

The most "ancient" among the "Classics." Generally speaking, the book
is a collection of mutually unrelated clusters of divination records. Some
of these records were probably formed as early as the pre-dynastic Zhou
time based on sources similar to the oracle-bone inscriptions from
Zhouyuan. Each cluster is headed by a hexagram mark (similar forma-
tions also appear on late Shang to early Western Zhou bronzes) which is
explained by a hexagram statement. This statement is then followed by six
line statements, each tying to a line (or number) in the hexagram formation. It is likely that these statements were put together to form an
integrated work some time during the mid to late Western Zhou, and
the completed work was then used as a manual for actual divination. But
how it was or should be used in divination has remained a mystery for
more than 2,000 years. The newly discovered manuscript of the *Book of
Changes* in the Shanghai Museum suggests that by at the latest the fourth
century BC, the book had already taken a form very similar to what we
have received in modern times.[18] By the early Han Dynasty, the text had
already come to be accompanied by ten commentaries attributed to
Confucius. Additional commentaries on the texts were found in a Han
Dynasty tomb in 1973, dated to the mid first century BC.

Book of Documents

Strictly this is a collection of government documents from ancient times,
and it is regarded as the embodiment of Western Zhou values and the
manifestation of a model government, founded by King Wen and King
Wu, and consolidated by the Duke of Zhou. The earliest part of the book,
usually called the "Five Announcements," are authentic Western Zhou
works most likely to have been produced by scribes in the government
during the early decades of the dynasty, and all of them have something do
to with the Duke of Zhou. Whether these government documents ever
had a chance to be cast on bronze is unknown; perhaps not likely because
their contents are not directly tied to the life of the individual elite. But
similarities between them and the bronze inscriptions are clear at the level
of the archaic language. They contrast sharply with the language of the
latest parts in the book which purport to speak about earlier periods in
history – the Xia and Shang Dynasties – but which are retrospective
compositions of the Warring States period. Another cluster of about

---

[18] See Edward L. Shaughnessy, "A First Reading of the Shanghai Museum Bamboo-Strip
Manuscript of the *Zhou Yi*," *Early China* **30** (2005–6), 1–24.

seven chapters which purport to speak about the early Western Zhou were probably composed during the middle to late period of the dynasty. The question about when and how the various documents in the *Book of Documents* came to be associated with each other to form an integral book is still debated. The tradition credits Confucius with having selected these chapters and put them into a book, but this cannot be verified on the current evidence. However, since lines from its chapters are quoted frequently in Warring States texts under such names as "Xia Documents," "Shang Documents," or "Zhou Documents," divisions that still exist in the received edition, it is likely that by the late fourth century BC these chapters must have begun to be transmitted as parts of the whole textual entity, if not as three separate texts.

Book of Poetry

The oldest anthology of poetry in the world, an inventory of 305 poems divided into three sections: the "Odes" ("Major Odes" and "Minor Odes"), "Liturgies," and "State Airs." It is impossible to date precisely every single poem in the *Book of Poetry* as there is a great deal of uncertainty regarding the circumstances under which the poems were composed. However, most modern scholars agree on a rather broad span of time, 1000–600 BC, during which the poems were produced. Since Confucius (551–479 BC) is recorded as systematically commenting on these poems in the newly discovered Warring States period texts in the Shanghai Museum, an anthology similar to the present text was probably in circulation by the middle of the sixth century BC. The latest segment in the book is the "State Airs," a total of 160 poems most likely to have been collected from the various regional states in the seventh to fifth centuries BC. The "Odes" section is considerably earlier, though not every poem there is necessarily earlier than everything in the "State Airs." It is very likely that many poems in the "Minor Odes" expressing clear political sentiments were composed by individuals associated with the Zhou court from the late Western Zhou to the early years of the Spring and Autumn period, and their contents confirm historical events recorded in the late Western Zhou bronze inscriptions. The "Major Odes" includes some poems that could have been composed at a much earlier time, but others may be as late as the latest poems in the "Minor Odes." The Zhou "Liturgies," on the other hand, were songs sung at the ancestral temples in the Zhou capital. As such, some of the poems there might have been transmitted from a time as early as the Zhou conquest of Shang, but others might have been composed at a more recent time retrospectively extolling the virtues of the Zhou ancestors. Despite their discrepancies in time, the

305 poems offer us valuable perspectives on the society and culture of the Zhou dynasty from its beginning to the sixth century BC.[19]

The End of the Western Zhou

Through much of the ninth century and into the early eighth century BC, the Western Zhou state was troubled by a number of factors. In the southeast, groups from the Huai River region who had launched a major invasion in the time of King Mu continued to present a threat to Zhou's security in the following reigns. The unrest amounted to a total rebellion in the reign of King Li by various groups in the Huai River region and south Shandong, perhaps as a response to the rebellion of the ruler of E in northern Hubei, formerly responsible for Zhou's security in the middle Yangzi region. However, the new threat posed by a people called "Xianyun" from the northwestern highlands seems to have been more pressing and was very close to the Zhou home. From the late phase of the mid Western Zhou period, the Zhou elites had to go through a long series of battles with these invaders. Both the *Book of Poetry* and the bronze inscriptions such as the Duoyou *ding* offer firmly contextualized descriptions of this prolonged warfare, pointing to the Jing River valley as the main battleground, only a little more than 100 km from the Zhou capital (Fig. 7.3). Facing such a dangerous situation, the Zhou king could call on little help from the regional states that were far in the east and had by now gained considerable independence from royal court. On the other hand, the Zhou court was itself vexed by a number of policy debates that worked to dissolve the solidarity of the Zhou elites.

The end of the Western Zhou Dynasty in the eleventh year (771 BC) of the last Zhou king, You, has been famously told in the traditional literature in a very dramatic way. According to this account, King You had a favorite concubine named Bao Si. This young lady was of a mysterious nature and would never smile, nor would she even speak often. Somehow haunted by her power, King You tried hundreds of ways to please her but eventually failed to amuse her. One day, it happened that there was a false report that the northwestern barbarians had come to attack the Zhou capital. In a hurry King You went up the Lishan Mountain near the capital and lit beacon fires to summon the regional rulers from the east to come to his rescue. However, when the many rulers rushed into the royal capital area, they found no enemies at hand and thus caused huge chaos by crashing into each other's lines. Seeing this huge mess that happened under the mountains, Bao Si

---

[19] For further reading on the contents and textual history of the three texts, see relevant chapters in Michael Loewe (ed.), *Early Chinese Texts: A Bibliographical Guide* (Berkeley: Institute of East Asian Studies, University of California, 1993), pp. 216–228, 376–389, 415–423.

then burst out laughing! Having finally discovered a way to amuse his lady, King You thus lit beacon fires again and again until nobody came to his help any longer. A few years later when the barbarians really did attack the Zhou capital, King You failed to call on any help and was killed under the Lishan Mountain. The Western Zhou Dynasty thus came to a sudden end.

Recent critical analyses have shown that this account is essentially fictional. The problem that finally brought the Western Zhou Dynasty down had its origins in the generational transition from the long reign of King Xuan (827–781 BC) to that of King You. This was a fierce political struggle between the group of senior officials led by the "August Father" (Huangfu) who had served at prominent positions under King Xuan, and the newly rising King You and his party. The two parties openly split in 777 BC and this resulted in the former's departure from the capital to the east and the crown prince's exile in his mother's home state, Western Shen, most likely to have been located in the upper Jing River valley. Taking advantage of his temporary political victory, King You set out to reorganize the Zhou central government and then, after a few years, sent the royal army to attack Western Shen and demand the prince. This was a step taken to ensure the succession of another younger heir given birth by his favored concubine Bao Si. However, the royal army was defeated by the joint forces of two states on the northwest border, Western Shen and Zeng, which were helped by Zhou's traditional enemy, the Xianyuan. Subsequently, the allied forces from the northwest marched down the Jing River valley and captured the Zhou royal capital in the first month of 771 BC, killing the fleeing King You and his companions at the foot of the Lishan Mountain.[20] The Western Zhou Dynasty fell.

SELECTED READING

Li, Feng, *Bureaucracy and the State in Early China: Governing the Western Zhou (1045–771 BC)* (Cambridge: Cambridge University Press, 2008).
  Landscape and Power in Early China: The Crisis and Fall of the Western Zhou, 1045–771 BC (Cambridge: Cambridge University Press, 2005).
Hsu, Cho-yun, and Katheryn Linduff, *Western Chou Civilization* (New Haven: Yale University Press, 1988).
Shaughnessy, Edward L., *Sources of Western History: Inscribed Bronze Vessels* (Berkeley: University of California Press, 1991).
Loewe, Michael (ed.), *Early Chinese Texts: A Bibliographical Guide* (Berkeley: Institute of East Asian Studies, University of California, 1993).

[20] For a recent reinterpretation of the political dynamics in the fall of the Western Zhou, see Li Feng, *Landscape and Power in Early China: The Crisis and Fall of the Western Zhou, 1045–771 BC* (Cambridge: Cambridge University Press, 2005), 193–232.

8   Hegemons and warriors: social transformation of the Spring and Autumn period (770–481 BC)

Historical events that happened in the three centuries following the collapse of the Western Zhou state in 771 BC are chronicled in the *Spring and Autumn Annals* (and further detailed in the *Zuo Commentary*) which gave the period its epic name.[1] Whether Confucius' authorship of the book was true or false, he lived towards the end of the period, and indeed died only three years after the annals ended in 481 BC. He reflected upon the Western Zhou and before as the cultural past for his time. Therefore, the transition from the Western Zhou (1045–771 BC) to the Spring and Autumn period (770–481 BC) in which Confucius lived represented the fine line dividing "antiquity" and "post-antiquity" in the intellectual conceptualization of China's past in Early China.[2] The changes that occurred across this line were wide-ranging and fundamental, and, when taken together, had the consequences of totally reshaping the Yellow River society for a new era of great empires to come.

While previous scholarship has offered a valuable basis for analyzing these changes in different scholarly domains, the logical order in which the changes took place and the complex relationships between them have not been fully understood. This was due largely to the inaccurate understanding of the political and social systems of the late Western Zhou period as the starting point for all subsequent changes that took place in the Spring

[1] The *Spring and Autumn Annals* offers year-by-year brief accounts of historical events that happened in China between 722 BC and 481 BC, centering in the state of Lu, whose ducal reigns were used as the divisions of the records. There seems little doubt that the records were copied from the official chronicle of the state of Lu. The current *Spring and Autumn Annals* are sliced and attached to the beginning of the corresponding years in the *Zuo Commentary* (which actually runs down to 468 BC), composed one hundred years or more later in the Warring States period (480–221 BC), which gives detailed narratives to the events recorded in the annals. See Michael Loewe, *Early Chinese Texts: A Bibliographical Guide* (Berkeley: Institute of East Asian Studies, University of California, 1993), pp. 67–76.

[2] In the periodization scheme proposed by the Warring States philosopher Han Fei (380–233 BC), the Shang–Western Zhou period falls under his term "Recent Antiquity" which comes after the "High Antiquity" (the age of legendary emperors) and "Middle Antiquity" (the Xia Dynasty and the centuries before it). For Han Fei, see Chapter 10.

and Autumn period. Based on new knowledge acquired about the Western Zhou state in recent scholarship, discussed in Chapters 6 and 7, we can now reassess these changes and logically explain the origin of the social transition of the Spring and Autumn period.

The Institution of Hegemony: Geopolitics and the Balance of Power

The history of the Spring and Autumn period began with the relocation of the Zhou royal court, after its restoration by the new king, Ping (the formerly exiled Zhou prince), to Luoyang at the confluence of the Luo and Yi Rivers in western Henan in 770 BC. The move was the inevitable result of the collapse of Zhou defense in the west, particularly the loss of the upper Jing River valley, and it was also motivated by the new court's political struggle with another pretender king in the old Zhou capital region supported by the lineage of Western Guo which had by now established its new base near the narrow passes separating present-day Shaanxi and Henan. However, the relocation of the Wei River elites in the east, after they had hidden their treasured bronze vessels in hoards and caches in their home bases in the west, took on a much larger scale of movement that lasted for a much longer time. Followed further by the move of the various non-Zhou groups who had driven the Zhou elites out of the Wei River valley, the political transition to the Spring and Autumn period might have caused one of the major waves of population migration from the western highlands to the central and eastern plains in Chinese history.

Thus, the political and military conflicts that were soon to overtake China for as long as some five centuries found their initial impetus precisely in such newcomer states which tried hard to consolidate for themselves a foothold in the east. The state of Zheng, the most typical, was initially founded by a brother of King Xuan who received from the king one of the royal centers, Zheng, in the western part of the Wei River valley. Taking advantage of his long period of service as a minister in the Zhou court, stationed in the eastern capital Chengzhou, Duke Huan of Zheng gradually transferred his possessions for temporary relocation in the suburb of Chengzhou. After the fall of the Western Zhou, his son Duke Wu conquered the statelets Kuai and Eastern Guo by 767 BC, re-establishing Zheng in the territory of the two states (Map 8.1). This transition meant not only the evacuation of the state's properties from the endangered Wei River valley in the west, but also a stage through which an original elite lineage in the royal domain in the west acquired its membership in the class of the regional states in the east. In the next half

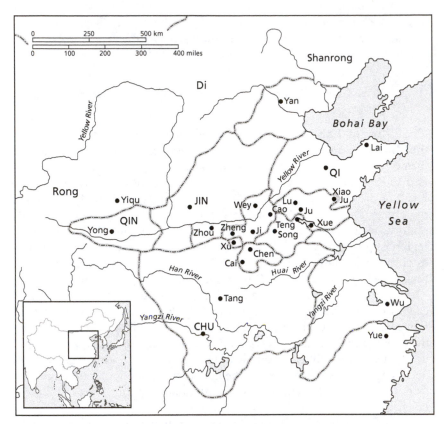

Map 8.1 Major states of the Spring and Autumn period

century, Zheng was politically and militarily the most active state in all of China. At first, it was Zheng's domestic strife that brought it into conflict with the older state Wey in northern Henan which supported the political rivals of its duke. Wey therefore called on the help of the states of Song and Chen which jointly attacked the eastern gate of Zheng in 719 BC; Zheng, on the other hand, expanded its alliance to include the larger and wealthier states Qi and Lu (after 715) in western Shandong to form a strong power axis. However, Zheng eventually waned both because of its internal instability and because of its vulnerable strategic location on the Central Plain, being exposed to attacks from all directions. This made it impossible for Zheng to sustain long-term domination.

Thus, in the long run the politics of the Spring and Autumn period were determined by the ambitions of the larger outlying states. Most of these states, located on the periphery of the Zhou world, protected by mountains and rivers, had their backs towards or even were located among the economically underdeveloped non-Zhou groups. They enjoyed the strategic advantage of being able to expand outwards and to absorb social and economic resources, among which most important was population, from the underdeveloped peripheral regions, needed for competition with their peers in the Central Plain.

The first peripheral state to have achieved this goal was Qi. Located in northwestern Shandong near Bohai Bay, Qi was traditionally known to have had a natural surplus of fish and salt that it could easily sell to the centrally located states. This point has acquired strong support by the recent archaeological discovery of salt fields in the Bohai Bay region.[3] By the middle of the sixth century BC Qi had annexed the states of Ji and Lai on the east coast and had effectively extended control over the greater part of the Shandong Peninsula. This meant that the previously active "Eastern Barbarians" in the Shang–Western Zhou period had now become the new citizens of Qi. In the event of 662 BC when the Northern Di tribesmen poured into the Central Plain from the north, destroying the states of Xing and Wey, it was only Qi that had the military power and political influence to form a "Chinese League": fortresses were built along the south bank of the Yellow River all the way to the royal capital in present-day Luoyang. Two years earlier, when the Rong people attacked the state of Yan near Beijing, Duke Huan of Qi responded by personally leading his army north to rescue Yan. In 656 BC, after successfully repelling the assault on Zheng by the southern state Chu, Duke Huan led the many rulers in a joint effort to attack Chu. In 651 BC, Duke Huan called on an interstate conference in Kuiqiu in eastern Henan which was attended by the rulers of six other regional states; even the Zhou king sent his representative to deliver to the duke sacrificial meat from King Wen and King Wu's temples, a sign of high royal favor, along with the royal sanction of Duke Huan's status as "Hegemon" (*Ba*), the provisional leader of the Chinese (or former Zhou) states in the face of a weakened royal power.

For a much longer time thereafter, the struggle for hegemony had taken place mainly between the powerful northern state Jin based on the Fen River valley and the emerging southern power Chu based on the middle Yangzi valley, both having conquered large portions of land in their respective regions by the late sixth century BC. Jin's hegemony began with Duke Wen who had defeated Chu in the battle of Chengpu in 632 BC

---

[3] This includes large areas of salt production sites dating back as early as the Shang Dynasty and as late as the Han Dynasty, under intensive archaeological research in the recent years.

and received royal sanction of his hegemon status at a conference that took place in the same year, and it lasted for another generation until the death of his son in 621 BC. Chu's hegemony was established by King Mu by defeating Jin in 597 BC and lasted until the resurgence of Jin power some twenty years later. For many decades, the minor Central Plain statelets that had suffered badly from the Jin–Chu conflict had tried to negotiate a peace treaty between the two superpowers, and this goal was eventually reached in 546 BC; the treaty ensured that there was no major war between them in the next three decades. However, both Jin and Chu were to see the decline of their own power and the rise of two new hegemonic states, Wu and Yue, in the Yangzi Delta in the southeast. The rulers of Wu and Yue, at the height of their powers, had each led an army north and hosted interstate conferences in the Central Plain.

The historical development outlined above is meaningful and worth serious study in a number of ways. Historical political scientists see this development as having taken place in a stable structure wherein the rise of powerful states one after another was encouraged by the uneven chances of growth and particularly chances of acquiring new peripheral territories, and their decline was then called in by the "mechanisms of balance of power and rising costs of expansion." This historical process was quite rare in China but is seen to have paralleled closely the historical development of early modern Europe.[4] For historians, the institution of hegemony provided a new structure of authority, a new form of political unification ensured by the overlordship of the hegemon.[5] As such, the role of the hegemon would have been more than his proven military strength and his influence to call other rulers to the inter-state conference; it was also the role which established and maintained social order in the absence of a legitimate ultimate power, the king.

While the political role of the hegemon was well understood in earlier scholarship, recent studies have paid particular attention to the institutional aspects of the role of hegemon. For instance, what had come out of the conference in Kuiqiu in 651 as agreements between Duke Huan of Qi and the other six regional rulers was not so much concerned with their military alliance; instead, there were broad principles aimed at promoting social norms concerning the domestic policies of allied states, and some even interfered in the household matters of the elite such as "exalt no

---

[4] See Victoria Hui's discussion in *War and State Formation in Ancient China and Early Modern Europe* (Cambridge: Cambridge University Press, 2005), pp. 55–64.

[5] See Cho-yun Hsu, "The Spring and Autumn Period," in Michael Loewe and Edward L. Shaughnessy, (eds.), *The Cambridge History of Ancient China: From the Origins of Civilization to 221 BC* (Cambridge: Cambridge University Press, 1999), pp. 556–557.

concubine to be the wife."[6] In another study, it was suggested that even the renowned "Five Ranks" traditionally attributed to the Western Zhou might indeed have been a by-product of the hegemon system, implemented in the Spring and Autumn period to regulate the relative statuses of the states and to determine the standards of tributes they were required to pay to the hegemon.[7] In a more general sense or perhaps on a larger scale of history, the Spring and Autumn period has revealed a situation where new powers rose from the periphery of an old civilization rather than from its center, drawing on experiences from the civilization and on new resources lying beyond it, a process that has many parallels in the history of the world past and present.

The Rise of *Xian*: Redefining the Administrative Framework

The key to understanding the social institutional changes in the Spring and Autumn period lies in the emergence of the "County" (*Xian*) system. The importance of the counties as the origin of the so-called "County-Commandery" system, the essential administrative infrastructure of the Chinese empires after Qin unification, has been fully recognized since the beginning of modern historiography,[8] and recent scholars have devoted numerous studies to revealing the historical details of this system. But their social impact has only been superficially understood. Warring States period texts, especially the *Zuo Commentary*, explicitly describe the county in the prominent states since the early Spring and Autumn period as a new type of geo-administrative unit essentially different from the traditional aristocratic lineage estates discussed in Chapter 7. The texts also make it clear that the counties were administered by the magistrates, called by various terms, who were appointed by the rulers of the states and were responsible directly to them in the central courts.

The Western Zhou bronze inscriptions suggest that the Zhou king appointed officials to take charge of certain rural areas in the royal domain in Wei River valley of Shaanxi during the tenth to early eighth centuries

---

[6] Cho-yun Hsu, "The Spring and Autumn Period," pp. 556–557.

[7] Although all five titles (*gong, hou, bo, zi,* and *nan,* often translated as duke, marquis, earl, viscount, and baron) had already appeared in the Western Zhou period, they did not form a system of ranking. During the Spring and Autumn period the five titles were combined to form the so-called "Five Ranks." See Li Feng, "Transmitting Antiquity: The Origin and Paradigmization of the 'Five Ranks'," in D. Kuhn *et al.* (eds.) *Perceptions of Antiquity in Chinese Civilization* (Heidelberg: Edition Forum, 2008) pp. 103–134.

[8] In the West, Herrlee Creel's article on the county as the origin of bureaucratic administration in China is well known. See Herrlee Creel, "The Beginning of Bureaucracy in China: The Origins of the *Hsien*," *Journal of Asian Studies* 22 (1964), 155–183.

BC, with general titles such as Supervisor of Land or Supervisor of Construction conferred on these local officials. The county shows no direct connection to the early royal administrative system of the Western Zhou, although the Zhou royal practice might have been well known to the regional rulers. The nature and political position of the county can be better explained by its history and geopolitical context. Between 740 and 690 BC, when King Wu of Chu conquered a small polity on Chu's western border,[9] he did not give it to his kinsmen as in the past, but appointed a magistrate to govern it directly for the king. Chu subsequently conquered a number of former Zhou regional states in the Nanyang Basin in southern Henan and converted each of them into a county.[10] Before these events took place in the south, the state of Qin, now relocated in the western part of the Wei River plain, created a number of counties in southeastern Gansu and eastern Shaanxi in 688–687 BC.[11] In the state of Jin, ministers were frequently given power over a number of counties in areas newly conquered during the seventh to sixth centuries BC. In short, early counties were all located in strategically important border areas, and indeed many of them incorporated land and population of the newly conquered territories. These were usually also areas where virgin lands were located, and the state was eager to open these new lands to exact taxes from a free labor force. The introduction of iron to China and the subsequent use of iron tools helped accelerate this process (Box 8.1).

The word for "county" is *Xian*, which is written in the inscriptions with the same graph that stands also for the word *Xuan*, meaning "to suspend" or "to hang." Therefore, the counties (*Xian*) were the "suspended" border areas of military importance for the states. In the old state model that continued to affect the status of land since the Western Zhou, newly conquered areas would be given as awards by the ruler to his sons or brothers to become their estates. Counties were those newly acquired/conquered areas in manageable units that were *suspended* from the traditional process of land redistribution by the state ruler to the nobility along a kinship structure. In other words, the counties were reserved land units put under direct control by the state and the ruler. In order to compete with other states, the state ruler needed these land units at his immediate disposal, governed by magistrates directly appointed by him, which could

---

[9] This was the polity called Quan, located in present-day Yicheng in northern Hubei, in the Han River valley.

[10] These were the states of Southern Shen, Xi, and Lü.

[11] These were the counties of Shanggui in eastern Gansu, and Du and Zheng in eastern Shaanxi.

Box 8.1   The Beginning of the Iron Age in China

Iron-working was the most revolutionary advance in technology, with far-reaching social and political impact in pre-imperial China. Although cold-working of iron had previously been possible, due to the extremely high melting temperature of iron (1538 °C), human societies learned to handle this material in its liquid form only after millennia of working with bronze. Similar to other regions in the world, the early history of iron in China was marked by the use of meteoric iron, the earliest piece being found at Taixi in Hebei Province from a mid-Shang culture context (*c.* 1300–1200 BC). The first evidence for iron-smelting technology was three bronze weapons with iron blades or handles found in the elite tombs of the state of Guo in Sanmenxia in western Henan, dating to *c.* 800–750 BC. There have been some 100 iron objects reported from eastern China dating before the end of the Spring and Autumn period (481 BC), and analysis shows that the technology of smelting and liquid-casting was already widespread by the beginning of the fifth century BC. But by and large, bronze still played a more important role in the social life of Spring and Autumn China.

During the Warring States period, although bronze was still used to cast vessels used for ritual and entertainment purposes, it was replaced by iron as the most widely available metal for casting weapons such as swords, halberds, and arrow-heads and agricultural tools such as axes, chisels, shovels, hammers, hoes, sickles, etc. Iron was also used to make helmet and chariot parts and horse harnesses. Even some vessel types were cast in iron such as those from the Chu state tombs in Changshan in Hunan and Jiangling in Hubei. There can be no doubt that in many states iron tools and weapons were mass-produced in workshops directly controlled by the government. Archaeologists have identified more than twenty iron production sites that can be fully or partly dated to the Warring States period, and many of them were located in the state capitals. Some of the state capitals, for instance, that of Yan in Yixian, Hebei Province, apparently had multiple iron production centers (Fig. 8.1), although these centers might have simultaneously engaged in the production of bronze, jade, and bone objects. From the single site no. 21 in the Yan capital in Yixian, as many as 1,678 iron tools, weapons, and other types of iron objects were unearthed, along with a large quantity of iron ingots, molds, and debris. The mass production and wide use of iron dramatically increased agricultural production in the many states and improved their killing capacity in war against each other.

Fig. 8.1 Iron objects from burial pit no. 44 from Xiadu of Yan, Hebei Province: 1, butt-end of a weapon; 2, hoe; 3 and 4, halberds; 5, short sword; 6, helmet.

provide him with ready-to-use tax revenue and manpower. A Chu county is said to have been able to provide troops equal to that of a small state, measured by 100 war chariots at minimum. Previous studies have also tried to pin down the relative numbers of counties in the major states by the fifth century BC, yielding about thirty for Chu, forty to fifty for Jin, and forty to fifty for Qin.[12] Apparently some of these figures might have been

---

[12] The Figure for Qin is not known for the fifth century, but it was forty-one after the reform of Shang Yang in the mid fourth century BC.

exaggerated, and even the verifiable counties could not all be the same in terms of their size and composition.

However, they shared certain features as a new type of social political organization, the most important being universal taxation and military service that were placed directly on the shoulders of individual farmers. The power of the traditional lineage, if it had survived the conquest and conversion to county, was kept to a minimum; in the county, the state had never before come so close to the farmers as farmers to the state. Some counties, particularly in Jin, might have been held by members of an official family for a few terms, but such an arrangement was rather rare, and the political situation of the period actually made it impossible for a county to be held by a family over many generations. The texts offer many examples where magistrates were transferred, dismissed, and even executed on order of the king for their misconduct. Even in such cases where a county was awarded to an official, it is more likely that the award was meant only as the gift of the tax quota available from the targeted county. This was very different from the hereditary estates the traditional aristocratic lineages received under the Western Zhou. In short, the invention and spreading of the county totally reshaped ancient Chinese society which had hitherto been based on the organization of the lineages that mediated between the state and the populace. In the social and political history of China, the emergence of the county was undoubtedly a milestone. It was the inter-state warfare following the fall of the Western Zhou that provided the initial impulse for the conversion of peripheral lands to counties and the reason for rulers to want to keep them as such.

Decline of the Lineage System and the Rise of the *Shi* Status

What has constantly eluded the focus of previous studies was the destructive impact the county might have had on the traditional lineage system. With the demise of royal power and the collapse of the Western Zhou state, a Zhou world, though continuing to exist culturally and ritually, had lost its point of moral support. Inter-state war was not the only war the Spring and Autumn period elites fought; more often, they had to fight wars immediately across their neighborhood. Thus, the stories we hear most often of the period, besides inter-state wars and diplomacy, are those of state rulers murdered by their ministers or ministers killed by their own domestic officials. Civil strife was a common feature of society, but it acquired a new character under the special social and political circumstances of the Spring and Autumn period. It was no longer the game of the upper class, but had come to involve more and more elements from the lower strata of the society.

The evidence for this upward movement in an age of the declining aristocracy was analyzed by Cho-yun Hsu nearly a half century ago. It was shown there that among the some 500 individuals that were politically active, the number of sons and brothers of the state rulers took up 53% of the total at the beginning of the Spring and Autumn period, but this proportion decreased to nearly no mention by the end of the period. This decline was accompanied by the rise of the ministerial families – usually unrelated to the state rulers by blood – which had established their dominance in most states by the middle of the Spring and Autumn period. Another steady growth appears in the number of the lower elites called *Shi* (see below) which had risen from no mention to taking up roughly 22% of the total at the end of the Spring and Autumn period. Overall, if we take the statistics 100 years into the following Warring States period (by mid fourth century BC), we can see that the number of individuals of obscure origins had grown by then to occupy 60–70% of the offices.[13] The analysis reflects well the profound social changes that were taking place in China during the eighth to fourth centuries BC. Furthermore, Barry B. Blakeley's regional analysis revealed the imbalance of this social transformation among the many states with the states of Song, Zheng, Lu, and Chu as the more conservative where the rulers and the collateral lineages remained relatively stronger, and the states of Jin, Qi, and Zhou as more progressive where the independent lineages (no kin relation to the ruler) achieved a much higher degree of dominance over the three centuries.[14] Blakeley also shows that, for instance in Qi, people of obscure origins were expanding their hold on offices at different levels, and even in conservative states like Lu and Chu their numbers increased gradually over time, although it seemed more common that they occupied lower offices.

To understand the nature of this historical process, we should take a closer look at the situation in the state of Jin, one of the more progressive states analyzed by Blakeley. The early struggle between Jin's ducal house and its minor branch at Quwu in the seventh century BC had led to the

---

[13] See Cho-yun Hsu, *Ancient China in Transition: An Analysis of Social Mobility, 722–222 BC* (Stanford: Stanford University Press, 1965), pp. 25–39.

[14] Barry B. Blakeley, *Functional Disparities in the Socio-Political Traditions of Spring and Autumn China* (Leiden: Brill, 1980), pp. 107–113.

elimination of most of the old collateral lineages of Jin. Shortly afterwards, the new collateral lineages founded by the sons of the victorious Duke Wu were extinguished by Duke Xian in 671 BC who further drove all of his own sons into exile to ensure the succession of the favored Duke Hui. After the return of Duke Wen of Jin in 636 BC and Jin's quick rise to hegemony, the political map of Jin was completely redrawn and it was the ministers who had previously accompanied the duke during his long exile who gained firm control of power and continued to struggle against each other over the next century. In 607 BC the ministerial Zhao family murdered Duke Ling and took actual control of the ducal house, eliminating some other influential families. At the beginning of the sixth century BC the fierce political struggle further buried a number of other ministerial families, leaving only six (Hann, Zhao, Wei, Fan, Zhonghang, and Zhi) which by 514 BC had together destroyed the Qi and Yangshe families and converted their lands into ten new counties. In 490, the Zhao family eliminated Fan and Zhonghang, and three decades later the Zhi family was destroyed by Hann, Zhao, and Wei, the only survivors of the struggle in Jin. The political struggle that overtook many states in the Spring and Autumn period was indeed a highly self-destructive process that cast fatal blows to the traditional lineage system as a whole.

The county's erosive role on the traditional lineage system in the context of domestic conflicts can be seen in two ways. First, the institution of counties, once invented as a result of inter-state warfare, provided a model ready to be used by the state ruler or the ministers, for the same economic and military advantage it could offer, to reorganize lands confiscated from their domestic enemies as in the incident of 514 BC in the state of Jin mentioned above. It is not impossible that acquiring such lucrative units was among the purposes of some of the domestic wars. Although this point is not clear in the records, it is nevertheless safe to say that as a result of the domestic conflict the county gradually made its way from the periphery to the interior of the states. Second, the counties were economic competitors of the lineages. In the counties, lineage tradition was weak and farmers, besides the taxation and military service they owed to the state, had no other obligations. Although the situation might have varied from state from state, we know that a number of states actually offered tax exemptions for opening peripheral virgin lands under administrative control by the counties. Thus, the counties might have provided a major attraction to farmers who would flee their original lineages both for the economic opportunities and for personal autonomy without obligations to the lineage heads. Studies of intellectual history show that the Spring and Autumn period rulers and ministers were seriously concerned about the dispersal of the people and searched for ways to return a mobile population to agricultural production.[15] The covenant tablets from Houma in Shanxi offer a particular category of inscriptions that prohibited the covenanters, most likely heads of the branches of the Zhao family, to take on land and people (see Box 8.2 below). Although scholars disagree on the purposes for which such terms were sworn,[16] the inscriptions seem to unveil the undeniable fact that a significant number of farmers with broken lineage ties were available and posed a social problem in the state of Jin.

The rise of the *Shi* status, variously defined as "officials," "warriors," and "stewards of noble households," must be understood in the context of the fierce political struggle and the profound socioeconomic changes described above. It has been noted in Chapter 7 that even in the Western Zhou the lower orders of the aristocracy did have a share of offices in the Zhou royal government; however, the members of the social group rising in the Spring and Autumn period with the self-identification of *Shi*, "Man of Service," distinguished themselves by the fact that their living came to depend solely on the service they were able to provide to the state or those in power, and no longer on the hereditary right of their lineages, if their lineage still existed. Confucius himself was a good example. His ancestral family derived its origin from the ducal lineage of Song, but caught in the conflicts with the Hua family that took power in 692 BC, his great-grandfather was forced to flee to the neighboring state Lu. Since then the Kong family descended to the status of *Shi* and Confucius' own father served as a warrior attached to the Zang family of Lu. Such was probably very common in the Spring and Autumn period. When the lineages had demised, with their land and people annexed by other lineages or incorporated into counties by the conquering states, it was their aristocratic heritage, most importantly education and warrior spirit, that they could rely on for their future, as the states and rulers were looking for talented and brave young men to serve in their governments. Certainly, there were also people rising to the status of *Shi* from perhaps the commoner class. Confucius is said to have included some of these people among his students such as his famous disciple Zengzi.[17] In an age of rapid political change, one's status as *Shi*, which originally implied a place in the lower order of the aristocracy, was no longer a social identity that could be simply assumed at birth or taken for granted,

---

[15] See Robin McNeal "Acquiring People: Social Organization, Mobilization, and Discourse on the Civil and Martial in Ancient China" (Ph.D. dissertation: University of Washington, 2000), pp. 78–107.

[16] See Susan Roosevelt Weld, "Covenant in Jin's Walled Cities: The Discoveries at Houma and Wenxian" (Ph.D. dissertation, Harvard University, 1990), pp. 401–405.

[17] Zengzi is said to have self-planted melons. Another student of Confucius, Min Zijian, is said to have helped his father push carts on the road.

but came under different views and was subject to serious debate and constant negotiation.[18]

Despite the possible differences in their origins and the ambiguity sometimes associated with their status, the *Shi* as a social group with a strong self-awareness did exist and played an increasing social role in the late Spring and Autumn period. It is generally agreed that this group placed themselves at the lowest level of the social elites, but their social standing was definitely higher than that of the commoners. However, as time went on many *Shi* actually succeeded in making their way to the higher levels of state power, and therefore, the concept of *Shi* had come gradually to designate people who shared with each other a common commitment to higher moral principles and a somewhat "inflated self-esteem" as intellectual and political leaders of the society.[19] As Mencius says, only the *Shi* can keep his good heart constant despite changing economic circumstances; the commoners will definitely lose it. By Mencius' time, the *Shi* were widely present and were active elements of the society. Most powerful political figures hosted a large number of *Shi* in their entourage if they were not themselves originally *Shi*, and the newly rising bureaucratic states offered ever increasing opportunities for the *Shi* to serve and demonstrate their talent.

Transition in Legal Thought: The Emergence of Political Contract

Another major change took place in legal practice and the legal system, leading to the emergence of codified law. However, this transition in the legal system must be understood in the broad historical context of the Spring and Autumn period. The bronze inscriptions show that the royal court of the Western Zhou took an active role in legal matters that were brought to its attention, and the high royal officials frequently gave verdicts in disputes that occurred between the aristocratic lineages. Disputes between members within the lineage fell completely to the autonomous judgment of the lineage head. But when disputes occurred between his lineage members or those of his sub-lineages and members of another lineage, the lineage head would have to stand in the court on behalf of his men. According to a previous assessment of the legal tradition of the

---

[18] This point has been fully demonstrated by Andrew Meyer in a recent paper. See Andrew Meyer, "The Baseness of Knights Truly Runs Deep: The Crisis and Negotiation of Aristocratic Status in the Warring States," paper presented to the Columbia University Early China Seminar on October 1, 2011.

[19] See Yuri Pines, *Envisioning Eternal Empire: Chinese Political Thought of the Warring States Era* (Honolulu: University of Hawaii Press, 2009), pp. 115–135.

Western Zhou period, law operated only in a legal system that was largely based on shared cultural tradition, value, and experience, and could always be validated by existing social–cultural norms and political legitimacy.[20]

However, the decline of the lineage system and the weakening of the power of the lineage head gradually served to eliminate the focal point of the traditional lineage-based legal system. In a general sense, the gradual disappearance of the lineages in many areas brought the state into direct contact with its new citizens. This is most significant in the county units, but even in the more centrally located settlements such as the state capitals, the recent urban and commercial expansion had created a new free citizen body – the so-called "townspeople" (*guoren*) – that needed the protection and control by a new legal system. The idea of having prohibitions written out and posted directly to the citizens, without mediation by the lineage heads according to their political needs, had gradually become accepted in many states. Although legal historians are justified to argue that through most of Chinese history statutes were written to protect the interests of the state by imposing rules on its citizens rather than defending the rights of the citizens, the codification of law was undeniably a significant milestone in the legal thought of Early China. It had the effect of recognizing the personal "autonomy" of the individual citizens who were now regarded by the state as being able to organize their own lives and be responsible for their own conduct without being a member of a lineage; certainly talented citizens could learn the tricks of the system and use them to protect their own interests.

Thus, we learn from the received textual sources that in 536 BC the famous minister Zi Chan ordered the casting of "Legal Statutes" on a huge bronze cauldron to regulate the conduct of the people in the state of Zheng; some twenty years later a certain individual named Deng Xi was punished for producing a new set of legal statutes on bamboo strips in the same state. In the hegemonic state Jin, between 577 and 531 BC, legal statutes were composed by the minister from the Fan family, and were cast on a cauldron by Zhao Yang in 514 BC. Even in the conservative state Chu in the south, the kings were said to have promulgated a number of statutes to prevent people from hiding from the government and soldiers from fleeing from battles. These were not isolated incidences, but show a general trend among the states that took on an active role to interfere directly in the lives of their citizens. However, in matters that concerned

---

[20] On this point, see Laura Skosey, *The Legal System and Legal Tradition of the Western Zhou (ca. 1045–771 BCE)* (Chicago: Department of East Asian Languages and Civilizations, University of Chicago, 1996), pp. 284–287.

members of the extant lineages, particularly ones founded recently by powerful ministers, this also led to a number of recorded debates as to whether such matters belonged to the legal jurisdiction of the lineage or that of the state.

Within the lineage, the weakening of the traditional social norms that used to bound members to the lineage head who hosted the worship of their common lineage ancestors led to the introduction of a new type of political relationship ensured by contract – the "Oath of Alliance" (*Meng*). During the Spring and Autumn period, such an "Oath of Alliance" was frequently taken at inter-state conferences by the state rulers as equals who swore their allegiance to the hegemon. Gradually, this practice of contractual political relationship was adopted into intra-lineage politics as a strategy to counter the increasing vulnerability of the lineages in the late Spring and Autumn period. In 1965, a large number of covenant inscriptions written in red color on jade or stone tablets were discovered outside the city of Houma in Shanxi, the Jin capital, and in 1976 an even larger number of such written tablets were found in Wenxian in northern Henan (Box 8.2). In the former, members of various minor lineages in the state of Jin swore allegiance to Zhao Jia, head of the powerful Zhao lineage prior to 424 BC.[21] It is above all interesting that the covenant enemy, against whom most of the oaths were sworn, was identified in the inscriptions as a person with the surname "Zhao," almost certainly the head of a minor branch of the same Zhao lineage. The social–cultural meaning behind these political contracts was profound and complex: on the one hand, the inscriptions undoubtedly speak about the lineage's attempt to preserve its status quo, or its traditional solidarity in competition with other lineages; on the other hand, this happened simply because the traditional bond could no longer guarantee the willing and unconditional support of the lineage members to their common head. Therefore, the head of the lineage needed to construct a much wider sociopolitical web including both the Zhao and non-Zhao members based on written contracts and to invite surveillance by the supernatural spirits as the only way to maintain the solidarity of the lineage. Ironically, the alliance so formed was aimed to bringing down certain rebellious elements of the lineage itself.

---

[21] According to Crispin Williams's new analysis, the covenant tablets from Houma were buried between 441 and 424 BC. See Crispin Williams, "Dating the Houma Covenant Texts: The Significance of Recent Findings from the Wenxian Covenant Texts," *Early China* 35 (2012), forthcoming.

Box 8.2   The Covenant Tablets from Houma

A total of some 5,000 jade or stone objects were excavated in 1965–6 from 326 pits in a small cemetery located about 3.5 km to the east of the Jin capital in Houma, Shanxi Province. These jade or stone objects were found buried in specially prepared small pits together with livestock including cattle, horses, and sheep, killed as sacrificial offerings during the covenant ritual. There are about 600 tablets with recognizable texts of covenants written in red that are concentrated in forty-three pits in the northwest corner of the cemetery (Fig. 8.2). The majority of these texts belong to a category that is called the "Loyalty Covenant" (example text 1.9 below) in which the covenantors, members or non-members of the Zhao lineage, swore personal loyalty to the covenant host Zhao Jia. Other categories include the "Pledge Texts" in which former allies of the enemy Zhao Hu declare the termination of their relations and pledge personal attachment to the new lord Zhao Jia (example text 156.20 below); the "Confiscation Texts" sworn for the purpose of preventing the minor lineages from incorporating into their possessions the people and properties of the dispersed enemy family; the "Curse Texts" that propose particular harms to those covenantors who would dare to violate the covenanted terms. These texts offer us fresh insights into the social relations as well as political dynamics of the late Spring and Autumn period.

TEX 1.9

[If] I, Hu, dare to fail to strip bare my heart and vitals in serving my lord; or dare to fail to thoroughly adhere to your covenant and the mandate granted in Ding Gong and Ping Si; or dare, in any respect, to initiate breaking of the faith, or dispersion [of the alliance], causing an interruption in the guardianship of the two temples; or dare to harbor the intention of restoring Zhao Hu and his descendants to the territory of the state of Jin or join in a faction to summon others to covenant [with them]; may our former rulers, far-seeing, instantly detect me; and may ruin befall my lineage.

TEX 156.20

[I], An Zhang, pledge myself at the dwelling place of my lord. Insofar as [I] dare to overstep the bounds [of this alliance] and communicate with Zhao Hu's camp, or with his descendants; or with [names of 22 enemies]; or join in a faction to summon others to covenant with them; [or if I], Zhang, physically harm Jia (you) or your descendants; [or] in any manner restore [the above-listed enemies] to the territory of the State of Jin; then, [may the

Box 8.2 (cont.)

far-seeing spirits] forever [stand ready to] detect me; and may ruin befall my lineage. Or if, after this pledge, [I] dare to fail to [cause] the sorcerers and seers, invokers and scribes to offer victims and other foodstuffs, and regularly sacrifice to the former rulers of Jin in their ancestral temples; then, [may the far-seeing spirits] forever [stand ready to] instantly detect me; and may ruin befall my lineage. I, as for the descendants of Men Fa, [if] meeting them upon the road, [I] do not kill, may the [former] rulers spy me out. *Modified from translations by Susan Weld*

Fig. 8.2 Covenant tablet 156: 20 from Houma.

Ethnic Relations and the Rise of the Huaxia Concept

The Spring and Autumn period was also a time during which the way the people in North China viewed themselves had been dramatically transformed by ongoing social and political changes. And this transformation is not unrelated to what was going on beyond the Zhou world. In fact, the Zhou dynasty down to the beginning of the fifth century BC paralleled in time the transition to pastoral nomadism that was taking place first in Central Asia and gradually spreading to Eastern Europe and East Asia. The collapse of the Western Zhou and the subsequent relocation of the Zhou royal court from the Wei River plain to Luoyang in the east had triggered waves of migration of the Rong (meaning warlike) peoples from the northwestern highlands into the central areas of the former Western Zhou. A number of such Rong groups were recorded to have occupied locations close to the confluence of the Yellow River and Wei River in eastern Shaanxi; some of these groups might have moved as far as western Henan near the royal capital in Luoyang (Map 8.1 above). In the north and northeast, groups identified as the Di people had moved down along the Taihang Mountain ranges and founded many small polities such as Wuzhong and Xianyu in Hebei and northern Henan after wiping the Zhou states Xing and Wey off the map. Some of the tribesmen, for instance, the Long Di people, who were probably very tall, might have occupied places in eastern Henan and western Shandong in the late seventh century BC.[22] Towards the end of the seventh century BC, even those states in the core area of the Zhou realm had come to find Rong and Di communities in their neighborhood; states on the periphery such as Qin and Jin were traditionally known to have been always surrounded by the various Rong people.

The relationship between these Rong or Di polities and the indigenous Zhou states was complicated to say the least. War was not the unvarying form of relationship between them – occasionally we find that certain Rong or Di groups were on campaigns along with their Zhou partners against other Zhou states. During the turmoil in the royal court caused by Prince Chao, the Rong people were among the troops from Jin that restored the Zhou king to the throne in 520 BC. A century earlier, another pretender to the royal throne, Prince Dai, employed the troops of Di to attack the Zhou capital and drove King Xiang out of the royal capital. There were also Rong or Di polities that carried out successful diplomacy, mediating between the Zhou states. Despite the regular contact between the Rong or Di polities

---

[22] For further reading on the migration of the various Rong and Di groups, see Jaroslav Průšek, *Chinese Statelets and the Northern Barbarians in the Period 1400–300 B.C.* (New York: Humanities Press, 1971), pp. 70–87, 119–149.

and the indigenous Zhou states, the ethnic and cultural distinction remained clear to both sides, and this is illustrated by the experience of a group of the Rong people identified as "Jiangshi." In the words of their chief transmitted in the *Zuo Commentary*, this Rong group was originally located in the far west. Driven out of their lands by the ambition of the state of Qin, they had migrated east to the Jin region and had lived there as clients of Jin, possibly in southern Shanxi. The Rong had different clothes and ate different food, making no use of money and speaking a different language. In 627 BC, the Rong supplied auxiliary troops to Jin and together they vanquished the Qin army in the famous battle at Xiao (Chapter 11). Despite their long-time association with Jin, in 559 BC, their right to take the "Oath of Alliance" along with Jin in the inter-state conference was boldly denied by Jin ministers, about which the Rong chief issued a serious protest.

It would be very interesting if such a condition of ethnic and cultural symbiosis could be found in the archaeological record. However, archaeology proves to be inadequate to demonstrate the scale and intensity of this cultural mixing in North China. The evidence that speaks about this historical process is mainly of two kinds. First, a tomb was discovered in Yimencun in Baoji at the western end of the Wei River valley, yielding a numbers of gold objects usually seen in nomadic cultures on the northern steppe, together with a number of iron tools and weapons, and horse gears. There is good reason to consider it as a burial of a horse-riding elite who had migrated into the Qin region. Second, a number of bronze objects, such as round-based cauldrons, ornate swords, and belt plaques of northern steppe styles were found in tombs from Qin and Jin territories. These are considered imported objects once appropriated or perhaps appreciated by Qin and Jin elites.[23] Although archaeology has yet to offer a large picture of the cultural and ethnic mixing up suggested by the historical records, it does offer us a rudimentary idea of the movement of populations during the Spring and Autumn period.

Whether "alien" cultural elements were appreciated or not by the population of the "Huaxia" stock, a term that referred to the indigenous people of the states of common Zhou heritage, there seems no doubt that the received textual sources document a widespread cultural prejudice against the Rong and Di people. The Rong were rudely regarded as birds and beasts who had no feelings for humanity, and who were born greedy. Even their blood and breath (*qi*) were configured differently from the regular human beings living in the Zhou world. However, underlying this explicitly expressed ethnic and cultural prejudice against the Rong and Di – two

---

[23] See Lothar von Falkenhausen, *Chinese Society in the Age of Confucius (1000–250 BC): The Archaeological Evidence* (Los Angeles: Cotsen Institute of Archaeology, 2006), 224–233.

terms which by the late Spring and Autumn period had come quite close to the meaning of "barbarians" in English – was a process of profound self-redefinition by the people who lived in North China. As the word "Xia" in the compound "Huaxia" represents the origin of the Chinese state, Hua refers to the Hua Mountain, located at the central point between the Zhou capitals in Shaanxi and the eastern capital in Luoyang in Henan. It was their common origin in the Western Zhou state that gave them a shared identity in a time when they had become geographically intermingled with the "barbarians" due to waves of migration. Viewed in this way, the Spring and Autumn period might have been a critical time in which the concept of a Chinese (Huaxia) nation was formed and articulated, though at the expense of a total conceptual exclusion of the "barbarians."[24]

SELECTED READING

Hsu, Cho-yun, *Ancient China in Transition: An Analysis of Social Mobility, 722–222 BC* (Stanford: Stanford University Press, 1965).
  "The Spring and Autumn Period," in Michael Loewe and Edward L. Shaughnessy (eds.), *The Cambridge History of Ancient China: From the Origins of Civilization to 221 BC* (Cambridge: Cambridge University Press, 1999), pp. 570–576.
Creel, Herrlee, "The Beginning of Bureaucracy in China: The Origins of the *Hsien*," *Journal of Asian Studies* 22 (1964), 155–183.
Blakeley, Barry B., "Regional Aspects of Chinese Socio-Political Development in the Spring and Autumn Period (722–464 B.C.): Clan Power in a Segmentary State" (Ph.D. dissertation, University of Michigan, 1970).
Weld, Susan Roosevelt, "*Covenant in Jin's Walled Cities: The Discoveries at Houma and Wenxian*" (Ph.D. dissertation, Harvard University, 1990).
McNeal, Robin, "*Acquiring People: Social Organization, Mobilization, and Discourse on the Civil and the Martial in Ancient China*" (Ph.D. dissertation, University of Washington, 2000).
Li, Feng, *Landscape and Power in Early China: The Crisis and Fall of the Western Zhou, 1045–771 BC* (Cambridge: Cambridge University Press, 2005), Chapter 6.
Falkenhausen, Lothar von, *Chinese Society in the Age of Confucius (1000–250 BC): The Archaeological Evidence* (Los Angeles: Cotsen Institute of Archaeology, 2006).

---

[24] On this point, see Li Feng, *Landscape and Power in Early China: The Crisis and Fall of the Western Zhou, 1045–771 BC* (Cambridge: Cambridge University Press, 2005), pp. 279–296; see also Falkenhausen, *Chinese Society in the Age of Confucius*, pp. 164–167.

9 The age of territorial states: Warring States politics and institutions (480–221 BC)

The overall political and military situation in the centuries following the eastward migration of the Zhou royal court can be characterized as big fish eating small fish. If the rulers, particularly those who had achieved the respectable status of "hegemon" in the Spring and Autumn period, still had at least some sympathy towards their brotherly states of common Zhou origin when coming to the matter of conquest, such feelings of affection would seem to have been a sign of misconceived political naivety in the face of the brutal military reality of the Warring States period. By the beginning of the fifth century BC only a little more than twenty of the original some sixty to seventy or so states seen in the record had survived the conflict of the previous three centuries. At the end of the century only about two dozen were still struggling for survival. Such a tendency to ruthless conquest and annexation was further intensified in the fourth century BC, and by the early third century there had emerged a relatively stable multipolar power structure in China dominated by seven powerful territorial states, Wei, Zhao, Hann, Qi, Qin, Chu, and Yan, together with a few much smaller polities sandwiched between them (Map 9.1).[1] The major states rose to dominance one after another through political and social reform, and all had become too large to be easily swallowed by their enemies. As China was irreversibly organized into seven gigantic killing machines, there had also developed a realization that, as expressively stated by philosophers and politicians of the time, such a condition was not desirable, much less ideal, to anyone, and indeed many rulers had entertained the dream of being the sole ruler to conquer all others. This was eventually achieved by the king of Qin in 221 BC, the year of the founding of the Qin Empire. Therefore, the Warring States can also be seen as a period during which the skills and institutions that supported the future empire were gradually developed.

---

[1] These were Zhou (further divided into Eastern and Western Zhou in 367 BC), Song, Lu, Teng, and Zhu.

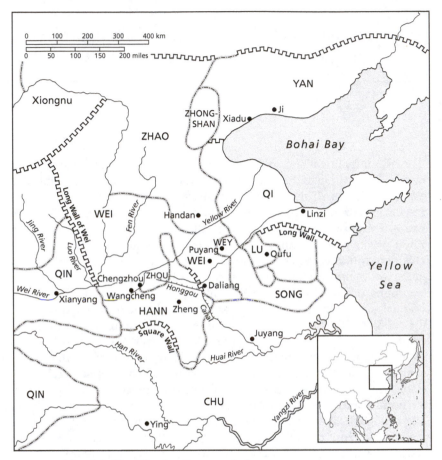

Map 9.1 The Warring States period.

The Concept of the "Territorial State"

At first glance, the term "territorial state" would sound conceptually repetitive since "territory" is an indispensable element associated with sovereignty in any definition of the state.[2] However, states as social–political organizations existed in different spatial forms, for instance, the Western Zhou states

---

[2] In the well-known anthropological studies of early states by Bruce Trigger, the "territorial state" was one of the two models of social–political organization (the other being "city–state") which developed out of the pre-existing chiefdom society. See Bruce Trigger, *Understanding Early Civilizations: A Comparative Study* (Cambridge: Cambridge University Press, 2003), pp. 94–113; *Early Civilization* (Cairo: American University in Cairo Press, 1993), pp. 10–12.

existed as layered clusters of settlements with no definite demarcating boundaries. Historians usually tend to envision the "territorial state" as the one developmental stage that preceded the empire, although they disagree, as in the case of Early China, on whether the "territorial state" emerged from a precondition that can be best characterized as the settlement-based state, or it was created through the expansion of the "city–state." This author is of the opinion that although a "city–state" system did probably exist for a short period of time during the early to mid Spring and Autumn period and only in the core area of the eastern plain, by and large the "city–state" model is unfit with regard to the political and economic situation of Shang and Western Zhou China.[3] In general, the "territorial state" as a higher stage of political and social development refers to a relatively large continuum of a territorial entity over which the relatively small core (the capital) exercised uninterrupted administrative control. It usually has clear boundaries defended by troops the passing through which is strictly checked and within which the political order is simplified/unified. Because of its territorial integrity and the control by an absolute political power usually imposed on its entirety, the "territory state" is the qualified pioneer of empire.

What had existed in Early China in the fifth to third centuries BC were actually such clearly demarcated territorial entities ruled by hereditary kings.[4] Moreover, particularly in China, the "territorial states" had one more defining physical characteristic – the earth or rock walls that ran hundreds of miles on the borders of these states. Historians and politicians in Early China did not fail to understand the political and military significance of such imposing structures and left behind them systematic records on their construction. The earliest one was the so-called "Square Wall" (*Fangcheng*) which defended the entrance from the Central Plain to the heartland of the state of Chu in the middle Yangzi region (Map 9.1). The wall began to be constructed in the Spring and Autumn period and gradually extended over 300 km to form three edges of a square until the early third century BC. The wall of Qi was the first structure to gain the name "Long Wall" (*Changcheng*) and was constructed during the late fifth and early fourth centuries BC, running over the ranges of the central Shandong Mountains for more than 400 km as far as the bank of the Yellow River, demarcating the south limit of the state of Qi in Shandong. Another long wall along the Luo River in Shaanxi was constructed in the mid fourth century BC by the state of Wei to defend its territory from the state of Qin to the west; Wei also constructed short sections of wall to protect itself from the state of Hann in central Henan.

---

[3] See Li Feng, *Bureaucracy and the State in Early China: Governing the Western Zhou (1045–771 BC)* (Cambridge: Cambridge University Press, 2008), pp. 284–287.

[4] The title of "King" (*Wang*) was adopted in 336 BC first by the territorial ruler of Wei; by 323 BC, all major states had adopted the royal title. The royal title was originally monopolized by the Zhou king who had by now descended to the status of only one among equals.

Fig. 9.1 The long wall of Qin in Guyuan, Ningxia Autonomous Region.

Other states such as Zhao, Yan, and the statelet Zhongshan had all constructed walls to defend strategic borders with others. Particularly those
states such as Qin, Zhao, and Yan which had borders on the northern steppe
constructed long walls in the north to protect themselves from the northern
nomads (Fig. 9.1), and these early sections of the walls made the foundation
for the construction of the Great Wall by the Qin Empire to defend its own
northern border after its unification of China in 221 BC. In the transmitted
literature from the Warring States period we frequently read stories of
politicians and diplomats who traveled through passes on the walls between
the states which usually required the payment of a toll. There seems little
doubt that the rise of the territorial states is the result of the inter-state
warfare in the preceding centuries already discussed in Chapter 8.

Thus, over the three centuries we see in China a very major geopolitical
transition from the Western Zhou model of state as layered settlement

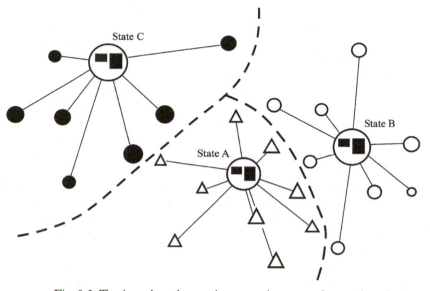

Fig. 9.2 Territory-based states in comparison to settlement-based states in Fig. 7.4.

clusters woven together by the power of the Zhou royal power (see Chapter 7, Fig. 7.3) to the new states with clearly defined territorial boundaries (Fig. 9.2). Certainly the counties (*Xian*) were the building-blocks of the new territorial state. As clarified already in Chapter 8, the counties were small territorial units with unitary administrative organization that emerged through the elimination of lineage structures as the result of the inter-state warfare and domestic conflicts. When the practice of counties became widespread and when the counties filled the peripheral regions distant from the previous state centers, the territorial state was the natural outcome. Therefore, the transition to territorial state was as much a process of military conquest as was the internal social reorganization through the expansion of the centralized administration of the state.

Political and Military Development

The most important objective of the territorial state was to acquire new territory and this was achieved almost exclusively through war. This overarching priority of the territorial state gave birth to an era whose main historical development was marked by a string of military victories, usually accompanied by large numbers of casualties, and we know from the excavated texts that famous military campaigns were used to mark the calendars of the time in a number of states. Statistical research identifies a total of 358 inter-state wars in the period of 535 to 286 BC, yielding a frequency of 1.37

wars per year.[5] The historical records show that, in fact, rarely did two years pass without a major battle between two or more territorial states, and there were many years that actually saw multiple military campaigns. Such an enormous frequency of war must have had a profound impact on the policies of the states and the mentality of the people.

The first 100 years of the Warring States period saw the supremacy of the state of Wei which was ruled by one of the three ministerial families which partitioned the former hegemonic state Jin. In 445 BC, under ruler Wen, the state of Wei employed the statesman Li Kui to carry out systematic reforms. Details of the reforms have not been transmitted in the contemporary records, but Han Dynasty texts indicate that it must have been wideranging with measures to regulate the use of land to maximize agricultural production, to stabilize market prices, and to establish a legal system based on the implementation of codified law. Empowered by the reform, ruler Wen dispatched the famous general Wu Qi to attack the state of Qin in 413 BC and captured from it the vast region lying to the west of the Yellow River. In the east, Wei combined its forces with those sent by the states of Hann and Zhao in a powerful strike on the Long Wall of the state of Qi, forcing its ruler to surrender in 405 BC. The sway of Wei's military power reached as far as the state of Zhongshan in northern Hebei; in order to conquer it, the Wei army actually had to transverse the territory of the state of Zhao in 406 BC. These victories had firmly established the hegemony of Wei that was to last well into the early decades of the fourth century BC.

However, the alliance between Wei, Hann, and Zhao collapsed when Zhao, envying Wei's territorial gains to the south of the Yellow River, attacked the state of Wey in northern Henan in 383 BC, thirteen years after the death of ruler Wen of Wei. Seizing on the opportunity of Wei's transfer of its main forces northeast to rescue Wey, Wu Qi, who had recently defected to Chu, directed the Chu troops on a swift campaign north, cutting Wei's main forces off from their capital Anyi in southern Shanxi and effectively breaking Wei into two halves. The conflict involved five major states which engaged one another in a series of battles that completely changed the balance of power in North China. Forced by the overall circumstances but more directly by another recent military catastrophe inflicted on it by the state of Qin in 364 BC to whom Wei is said to have lost as many as 60,000 human heads, Wei moved its capital from southern Shanxi to Daliang in eastern Henan in 362 BC, thus marking a watershed in Warring States history.

The waning of Wei power in the second half of the fourth century BC opened ways for the rise of Qin in the west and Qi in the east. For Qin, this was the age of great social and political transformation brought by the

---

[5] See Chiang Chi Lu, "The Scale of War in the Warring States Period" (Ph.D. dissertation: Columbia University, 2005), pp. 74–75.

reform of Shang Yang between 359 and 338 BC (see Chapter 11). In 340 BC, the reformer Shang Yang himself led the Qin troops to defeat Wei and captured Wei's Prince Ang; Wei was forced to cede the large area on the west bank of the Yellow River. After the fall of Shang Yang, Qin continued to conduct a series of battles against Wei and captured all towns that previously belonged to Wei in eastern Shaanxi. In other directions, Qin had conquered the "barbarian" polity Yiqu in the north, expanding its territory as far north as to the Lower Ordos, and added further to its proper the entire Sichuan region in the south by annexing the indigenous states Ba and Shu in 316 BC. By the closing of the fourth century BC, Qin had amassed a territory that was roughly equal to the three states Wei, Hann, and Zhao combined, and had become the indisputable superpower among the warring states. In the east, in two major battles the handicapped Qi commander Sun Bin devised superior strategies to first defeat the Wei armies in Guiling in 354 BC and then in Maling in 341 BC. Seizing on the opportunity of the domestic turmoil in the northern state of Yan, the Qi troops conquered the Yan capital in 314 BC.

   The inter-state politics in the late decades of the fourth century and early decades of the third century BC were guided by the dispute between two strategies of inter-state warfare known as the "Horizontal Alliance" and "Vertical Alliance." Simply speaking, this was a debate about the grand strategy which the many centrally located states should adopt in a world that had become increasingly polarized into the power of Qin in the west versus Qi in the east. The "Horizontal" strategy, viewed from the standpoint of any eastern state, proposed to embrace one of the superpowers (more often Qin) for its own security in fighting against other states; the "Vertical" strategy emphasized the unity of those relatively weaker states located in the middle in a joint effort to guard themselves against the threat from Qin in the west or Qi in the east. In reality, the "Horizontal" strategy was usually devised by Qin diplomats and better served Qin's territorial ambitions, such as manifested in the Qin–Wei alliance around 320 BC. An example of the use of the "Vertical" strategy was the joint attack on Qin in 318 BC by five states including Wei, Hann, Zhao, Yan, and Chu. But the Qin minister Zhang Yi was soon able to tear down the alliance and brought Wei and Hann over to Qin's camp, thus further developing his "Horizontal" strategy as a powerful weapon against the states of Chu and Qi. This led to the great military disaster for Chu in 312–311 BC which had weakened Chu power once for all. The "Vertical" strategy was also demonstrated by two later campaigns of the eastern states against Qin in 296 and 287 BC. But two years later, the same strategy was employed by Zhao, Yan, and Hann, with help also from Qin, to attack Qi, resulting in the complete ruin of Qi power. In the end, the manipulation of strategies by the warring states left Qin as the sole remaining superpower.

   In short, the Warring States period was an important page in the military history of the world. The sustained condition of war and the constant regrouping of powers gave rise to great political wisdom and military strategies; it also gave rise to some of the best pieces of diplomacy in Chinese history. The dynamics of the inter-state conflict in the multi-state system of the Warring States with shared cultural and language background resemble closely that of the politics of early modern Europe which gave rise to norms and diplomatic conventions that still govern international relations of the present time.[6]

Small Farmers as the Backbone of the New States

Perhaps the most important effect of the social transition of the seventh to fifth century BC was the complete reorganization of Chinese society into hundreds and thousands of households of small farmers. "Small farmer" refers to the family of a couple with their immediate kindred, namely parents and children, in a household of not more than ten people, who usually cultivated lands they owned or rented from others. Such nuclear families as independent social units were the economic foundation of the ancient Mesopotamian and the Mediterranean world, but they were a new phenomenon in China in the Warring States context.

Historians of ancient and modern times have talked a great deal about the so-called "Well Field" system as the model of land ownership attributed to the Western Zhou. In the early account of the system by Mencius, the second great master of the Confucian tradition (see Chapter 10), it entailed a piece of land divided into nine blocks in an arrangement that looked like the Chinese character 井 (jing) for "well" with eight families each cultivating an outlying block, and together jointly cultivating the central block as the "public" land that provided revenues for use by the lineage head and his family. This theory has been retold for 2,000 years in traditional Chinese historiography as the hallmark of economic relations in Zhou China. Thus, in Marxist historiography the social transformation in the Spring and Autumn period has been viewed as a shift from the "Well Field" system to private landownership by free peasant households. Given the information we now have about the Western Zhou period, there is little possibility that such a rigid land management system could ever have existed.[7] However,

---

[6] Victoria Hui, *War and State Formation in Ancient China and Early Modern Europe* (Cambridge: Cambridge University Press, 2005), pp. 54–108.

[7] Some scholars speculated that the Confucian imagination of such rigid land squares might have been inspired by the Warring States practice of the new state granting standard land units to free farmers in the counties, but this was anachronistically projected back onto the Western Zhou. See Mark Edward Lewis, "Warring States Political History," in Michael Loewe and Edward L. Shaughnessy (eds.), *The Cambridge History of Ancient China: From the Origins of Civilization to 221 BC* (Cambridge: Cambridge University Press, 1999), p.609.

the Confucian interpretation of the "Well Field" distantly and somewhat also accurately transmitted two aspects of what might have been real Western Zhou practice: (1) labor service was given instead of taxation in kind; (2) this took place in a system where land was owned by the lineage at least in theory and the lineage head assigned pieces of it to individual households belonging to the lineage while keeping a large portion of it for lineage use. This portion of land, cultivated collaboratively by the lineage members, provided for the maintenance of the "public" functions of the lineage including sacrifice in its ancestral temple.

Taking this as the starting point, significant changes must have taken place in land ownership and in the whole set of economic relationships surrounding the land. In the texts, when the Warring States politicians and philosophers talk about the condition of the peasantry of their time, it is clear that the small households of free farmers, the families that had recently won independence from their original lineages, are the ones in question. And this private land ownership by such small household farmers as the basic production units in agriculture was considered the economic foundation of the territorial states. In the transmitted agricultural theory of Li Kui, whose reform had empowered the state of Wei in the early fourth century BC, it is clearly said that a husband with a family of five mouths occupying a land unit of 100 *mu* should be made the foundation for tax calculation by the state. Historians have tried to calculate the size of such landholdings measured by the ancient unit, yielding roughly 5.14 acres (or 31.2 present-day *mu*) which seems to have been the common size of land a farmer could cultivate and a family of five could live on.

In some states, the size of the household of small farmers was strictly controlled by law as the basis for calculating tax revenue available to the state. During the reform that took place in the state of Qin in the middle of the fourth century BC, Shang Yang imposed double taxes on families that had two or more adult males; later, even a father (presumably still of socially productive age) and an adult son were prohibited from living in the same household.[8] Some scholars consider this to have been a method to break down the solidarity of the family in order to enforce a universal administrative order, but the economic advantage for the state invoked by the policy was unequivocal. From the standpoint of social history, this was probably the first time in Chinese history that the state used legislation to regulate the size of peasant families. In any event, the Qin practice strongly indicates the

---

[8] Derk Bodde, "The State and Empire of Ch'in," in Denis Twitchett and Michael Loewe (eds.), *Cambridge History of China*, vol. 1, *The Chi'in and Han Empires, 221 BC – AD 220* (Cambridge: Cambridge University Press, 1987), p. 37.

importance the state placed on the households of the small farmers as the cornerstones to support the superstructure of the territorial state.

Control of Farmers: Law, Taxation, and Universal Ranking

Discussed above are changes in the social standing of the farmers; what did this really mean for the state? The small farmers, unmediated by the traditional lineages, had become the new citizens of the state which regarded them as socially independent and capable of planning their lives, organizing their agricultural production, and being responsible for their own conduct. The state, by the same token, now entered into direct contact with individual farmers and had moral responsibility for their well-being. On the other hand, small farmers constituted a huge reservoir of manpower that the state was eager to draw on for its service to pursue supreme victory in war. The relationship between the state and the farmers was realized in a number of ways but most importantly through the promulgation of law, taxation, and military service. And the universal ranking system that was designed to reward such services created another long-lasting bond between the state and the individual farmers.

As discussed in Chapter 8, since the beginning of the sixth century BC we hear frequently that legal codes were composed and cast on bronze vessels displayed to the new citizens of the state. However, none of the statutes, if they existed at all, survived the centuries thereafter and made their way into the literary tradition that is available to us now. Since the discovery of the legal texts in a tomb at Shuihudi in Hubei in 1975 (see Chapter 11), dated around 216 BC after the unification of China by Qin, it has often been surmised by scholars that some of the statutes included in these legal texts of the Qin Empire might have already been in use in the state of Qin during the late Warring States period, if they were not actually originated in the reform of Shang Yang back to the mid fourth century BC. However, this can only remain a reasonable speculation. The fragments that have survived in the transmitted texts regarding legal practices in the previous centuries, for instance in the states of Zheng and Jin, seem to suggest that legal codes were constructed around the central concern for public security. The most unambiguous thread of this vague information attributes a text called *Canon of Law* to the reformer Li Kui in the state of Wei in the early fourth century BC. The canon is said to have been composed of six articles, dealing separately with offenses such as robbery, physical injury, and hiding from the government; it seems to have also included rules for handing out verdicts at the court, miscellaneous laws, and the increase and reduction of penalties. Some of these articles certainly have parallels in the laws of the Qin Empire from Shuihudi, but unfortunately no detail of any of the articles has been transmitted. In all, nothing like an actual legal statute or a synthesis of law has been passed down from the Warring States period. Nevertheless, the surviving information is enough to make the basic point that a legal system that was based on written laws was evidently in place in the pre-unification period.

Fortunately, concrete bits of information about the legal practice in the southern state Chu during the Warring States period were brought to light by the extraction in 1987 of bamboo strips from tomb no. 2 at Baoshan near Jiangling in Hubei Province, dating securely to 316 BC by the chronological records from the tomb. Most of the legal strips from Baoshan carry descriptions of actual legal cases and the so-called "date tables" which give dates for hearings after they were first filed with the government. For example, for most cases brought to the Chu central court, after their initial filing and acceptance a hearing was usually scheduled in about ten to ninety days depending on the location of the alleged crime. During this period local officers and sometimes special commissioners from the central court would be ordered to investigate the case before the court reopened. Both the plaintiff and defendant were allowed to enlist their witnesses to construct testimony but their close relatives were excluded from the groups. Sometimes, a previous case was given a chance for a second trial and when necessary could be transferred to another official by royal order. But there seems to have been a time limit before the officials eventually disposed of certain cases.[9] The strips from Baoshan show that legal procedures were well established in the state of Chu.

One other high concern of the state that we learn from the Baoshan strips was the accuracy of records of population registration as the basis for tax calculation by the state. Magistrates of the Chu counties were given orders to verify records on registers, and in cases where certain figures are missing from the records, particularly when the missing ones were of a young age, the minor officers in the local areas were liable to carry out an investigation in order to avoid their own punishment. The offenses of "keeping incorrect registers" or of "failing to register youths" had their close parallels in the Qin laws from Shuihudi; they also echo the name of an article dealing with people fleeing from the government included in the *Canon of Law* attributed to Li Kui. Certainly, accurate registration of population was critical to the new state for the purpose of mobilizing the maximum volume of resource, to support its expanding bureaucracy and military operations along the borders. There seems little doubt that this was important to all states.

---

[9] Susan Roosevelt Weld, "Chu Law in Action," in Constance A. Cook and John S. Major (eds.), *Defining Chu: Image and Reality in Ancient China* (Honolulu: University of Hawaii Press, 1999), pp. 87–95.

However, our information for a rough estimate of the actual figure of land tax is vague at best. In the transmitted agricultural theory of Li Kui, a 10% land tax payment in kind was taken as the basis for calculating the income and consumption of a household with five mouths. In an excavated manuscript text, Sun Wu, the master of war, is said to have remarked that the grade of land tax commonly imposed by the ministerial families on the lands they owned in the northern state Jin during the sixth century BC was 20%, a very high figure which Sun Wu considered would inevitably lead some of these families to fall.[10] To the other extreme, the political philosopher Mencius once remarked that the figure of 5% land tax was too low and it suited only the situation of the "barbarian" nations where the land yields were low and officials were few, but this was certainly insufficient to support the bureaucratic and ritual institutions in the competing states in the Chinese ("Huaxia") world. Based on this information, some scholars have suggested that, variations considered, the scale of taxation during the Warring States period was somewhere around 10%. But certainly this can only be taken as good speculation.

Military service was the responsibility of the small farmers. In fact, many of the earliest counties were created for the purpose of organizing the resident farmers in the local areas to fight in war. But gradually, as the scale of war increased, the unit called "Commandery" (*Jun*) which usually combined the areas of a number of counties had become the regular administrative structure to mobilize the peasants for military operations. There is no record telling us about the legal age or the terms of military service, but the number of casualties from the period indicates the possibility that in some cases, the entirety of the male population of a county or a commandery could be moved into battle. There is one case, for instance, in the famous battle of Changping between the states of Qin and Zhao in 260 BC, every male person of fifteen or above in the Henei Commandery (present-day northwestern Henan) was thrown into battle by the state of Qin. However, since this was reported as an unusual measure taken by the Qin state in facing an extreme situation in war, conscription of such young age was probably not normally practiced by the warring states. As in theory the entire male population was subject to conscription, they were also rewarded indiscriminately for military contributions. For instance, in the state of Qin, twenty ranks were created with the *gongshi* as the initial rank of foot soldiers. The merit of cutting off one enemy head was rewarded with a single rank along with 100 *mu* of land (about 5 acres).

---

[10] This is the text named "Questions by the King of Wu," one of the two lost texts with relation to Sun Wu that were discovered in 1972 together with the *Art of War* traditionally attributed to him in a tomb at Yinqueshan in Shandong Province, dating to the Western Han period (206 BC – AD 8).

Ranks can be accumulated over time and can also be used as payment for a fine in cases of legal offenses. In contrast to the traditional aristocratic ranks, these new ranks can be given to any commoner on account of his military contribution.

The Bureaucratization of the Governments and the Absolute Monarch

It was discussed in Chapter 7 that the central government of the Western Zhou state was gradually bureaucratized from the early ninth century BC, and that process created new dynamics in the political and social life of the royal domain in Shaanxi. However, the governments of the many regional states, though structurally replicating functional roles of the early Western Zhou central government, remained largely personal and unbureaucratic through the early Spring and Autumn period. Therefore, when the sway of bureaucratization took its second turn in China after the Western Zhou state had long gone to dust, bureaucracy manifested itself as a key technique for the creation and management of the territorial state.

During the Warring States period, the widely existing office in civil administration was invariably that of magistrate, though called by various names. In Qin, after the reform of Shang Yang, there were some 350 such magistrates. To assist the magistrate, a secretarial official named Assistant (*Cheng* as in Qin) or Secretary (*Yushi* as in Hann and Wei) was established in most states to handle land registration or other types of paperwork in the respective counties. In the more bureaucratic states like Qin, the office of Commandant was established to handle military and security matters and the office of Supervisor of Lawsuit (in Hann) was charged with responsibility for overseeing legal matters. Under them, there were certain subordinate officers down to those who had responsibilities at the village level. The military administrative unit commandery, usually headed by the Commandery Protector, was not universal and in states that had it, the commandery existed only in the border areas of military importance. The office of Grand Chancellor (*Xiang*) already appeared during the Spring and Autumn period and became a regular role during the Warring States period as the head of the central bureaucracy; in the southern state Chu, this role was played by the Chief Commander (*Lingyin*) who, originally a military officer, had by now come to bear both military and civil responsibilities in the central government.[11] There were other civil and military offices in the central government of the state such as the Scribe, Supervisor of Multitudes, and Supervisor of Horses,

---

[11] See Barry B. Blakeley, "Chu Society and State," in *Defining Chu*, p. 56.

all titles inherited from the Western Zhou bureaucracy, but their responsibilities varied from state to state and from time to time.

Besides the development of functional offices in many states, the Warring States was remarkable also for the creation of mechanisms to control the bureaucracy, an element that the Western Zhou bureaucracy lacked as far as we can tell on the basis of current evidence. One of the measures was the "Annual Report" which had become a standard administrative practice in most states during the Warring States period. A variety of elements were included in the content of such an "Annul Report": statistical numbers of land size, tax quotas, balances of the county granary, rosters of officials, scholars, and farmers with breakdowns for men and women, aged and young, and statements of local security. The document was produced presumably by the county secretary on wooden blocks and was personally brought to the capital by the county magistrate in the twelfth month of every year when it was due to be submitted for inspection by the king or the Grand Chancellor. The system effectively enabled the state to monitor the resources available to it and check on the performance of the bureaucracy. Certainly, throughout the year the kings frequently commissioned special inspectors and sometimes went on trips themselves to observe the situation in the counties as necessary.

Overall, the Warring States officials earned salaries in kind for their performance and were subject to standard systems of promotion and punishment. All officials down to the county level were appointed at the central court and could be removed at any time if found guilty of misconduct. There were master philosophers such as Shen Buhai and later Han Fei who advised the kings on how to exercise effective control over the officials by punishing them for not matching exactly what their offices required them to do (see Chapter 10). Such voices in the philosophical texts suggest perhaps a certain degree of cruelty in practice, but they highlight the issues that really concerned the Warring States kings. In general, the Warring States kings were more powerful than the rulers of the Spring and Autumn period, not measured by their title "King" (*Wang*) in contrast to the early "Duke" (*Gong*) as ruler of the state, and not measured by the size of armies that they could command, but by the degree of their grasp on power within the power structure of the state. Since the fortune of all officials now depended on the favor of the king (rather than, for instance, on their hereditary rights as in the early period),[12] the king had become the sole powerhouse in many states. Their power was absolute

---

[12] On this point, it is worth noting that the Warring States kings often preferred the appointment of "foreigners" to the top level of the state bureaucracy. Without social roots in their host states, these officials were overwhelmingly loyal to the kings who employed them and could be easily removed by the latter.

and unmediated, not only over the soldiers and farmers they ruled, but also over the ministers and officials who helped them to rule.

Transition in Warfare

As pointed out above, during the Warring States period, warfare was the most important aspect of social life, the principle of the state, and the compass that directed government policies. It is no exaggeration that by the late Warring States period (third century BC), war had escalated to the level that the entire state was organized for the very purpose of war, and this was true for all states. No other period in Chinese history was as militant as the fourth to third centuries BC. On the other hand, over the course of the nearly three centuries of the Warring States period, warfare itself as a social behavior conditioned by human and material factors had undergone fundamental changes both in terms of its objectives and in the ways in which it was fought.

During the Western Zhou through much of the Spring and Autumn period warfare was the privilege of the aristocrats who fought mainly from their chariots. Commoners sometimes fought in battles but they did so normally as attachments to the charioteers who were usually their lineage leaders. Therefore, in the Western Zhou inscriptions, besides the renowned Six Armies and Eight Armies, the standing royal forces, troops thrown into battle by the Zhou central court were often organized around or by lineages. Moreover, the maintenance of an army composed of a large number of horse-drawn war chariots was costly and the bronze weapons they used in combat were hardly affordable to commoners. These factors had significantly limited the scale of war which through much of the Spring and Autumn period remained as essentially an aristocratic exercise. However, the wide use of iron weaponry since the fifth century BC had made war economically more affordable to commoners, who by that time were largely free farmers living in the new counties. And the new states were eager to move the farmers into war to overcome the enemies (Fig. 9.3). Scholars have shown that the real purpose of the many reforms that took place during the early Warring States period was precisely to extend military service to the entire population, composed largely of small farmers.[13]

As a result of this change, the type of soldiers was dramatically changed and the size of armies greatly inflated. War was no longer the contest of fighting skills between warriors but rather was a matter of the large number of men a state could field to simply overwhelm its enemies. In the Spring

---

[13] Mark Edward Lewis, *Sanctioned Violence in Early China* (Albany: State University of New York Press, 1990), pp. 54–61.

Fig. 9.3 Battle scene engraved on a bronze *jian*-basin (h. 30.1 cm, diam. 54.6 cm) from Shanbiaozhen, northern Henan.

and Autumn period, war was very often fought by several thousand soldiers. The standing army of the state of Jin under Duke Wen was composed of three divisions (Upper, Middle, and Lower), and each was calculated to have had some 12,500 or more soldiers (or a total of 37,500 soldiers). The Chu royal army was also divided into three parts (Left, Center, and Right), massing a total power comparable to that of Jin. These were the most outstanding military forces of the Spring and Autumn period. With the arrival of the late Warring States period, the most powerful states Qin, Qi, and Chu are said to have each possessed an army close to 1,000,000 soldiers, and Hann, the smallest of the major states, had a total number of 300,000 troops.[14] It was not uncommon for 100,000 to 200,000 soldiers to be fighting on each side during a single engagement, and the number of soldiers killed in a battle could easily reach 30,000. Moreover, because the training required for such peasant–soldiers was minimal, a state could easily move its entire male population of fighting age into a major battle when necessary. The extreme case was the battle between Qin and Zhao in 260 BC. In the narrow valley called Changping in present-day southeastern Shanxi, the Zhao army comprising some 400,000 soldiers was forced to surrender after the death of their chief commander Zhao Kuo. The enormous number of prisoners caused major logistic problems for Qin. Thus, the Qin commander Bai Qi ordered the systematic murdering of all Zhao soldiers, leaving only 240 younger ones to spread fear in the eastern states. Although scholars have doubted the high figure of Zhao soldiers that the Qin army was able to murder, another broadly based statistical analysis shows that in the twenty-six major battles in the fourth to third centuries BC, a total number of some 1,800,000 casualties were suffered by the defeated states (exclusive of the death toll of the victorious states).[15]

Certainly the way war was fought also changed. The infantry was a more thoroughly destructive force compared to the chariotry of any time. The use of iron weapons not only enabled the massive participation of the farmers in war, but also improved killing efficiency. Furthermore, the killing capacity of Warring States armies was even elevated by the introduction of crossbows, a bow fixed on a central stock with a metal launching mechanism that enabled the archer to aim well, shoot farther, and launch multiple arrows each time (Fig. 9.4). The crossbow was invented in the south and first used by the armies of Chu, Wu, and Yue in the late Spring and Autumn period. By the mid Warring States period, it was commonly used in the northern armies. Another military "invention" was the cavalry, attributed to King Wuling of Zhao during the late fourth century BC who had actually introduced this nomadic style of horseback warfare during Zhao's

---

[14] Lewis, "Warring States Political History," pp. 626–627.
[15] Chiang Chi Lu, "The Scale of War in the Warring States Period," 107–110.

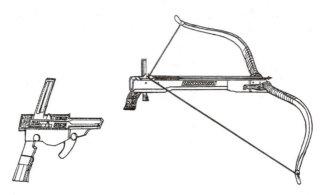

Fig. 9.4 A crossbow.

expansion onto the northern steppe. The horsemen, although their role was auxiliary compared to the infantry, certainly provided a powerful mobile force that could effectively break enemy defense and cut enemy supply lines. By the middle of the third century BC, cavalry had been introduced even to the southern state Chu which is said to have had some 10,000 horse-riders among its soldiers; the same figure was recorded for Qin and Zhao.

As the size of the armies had increased and efficiency improved, the objective of war had also changed. During the Spring and Autumn period, the main objective of the wars fought from the chariots was to subjugate the enemy. In fact, many well-known engagements by the major states in the seventh to sixth centuries BC had their sole purpose of winning more allies among the smaller states. During the Warring States period, however, war was fought to conquer new territories, and in cases where the conquered land could not be permanently occupied, the elimination of the fighting capacity, that is, the killing of enemy soldiers, was the goal of war. Therefore, war had become more deadly during the Warring States period, and the fear inspired by such destructive power was evidently in the calculation by the kings and strategists of their political advantage.

This had also led to significant changes in commandership. The old aristocrats were trained to direct themselves in battle, but the peasant–soldiers, many conscripted on short terms, were not. Many of them might not even know how to act as soldiers if they were left out by the army. Therefore, the Warring States armies were carefully constructed organizations with strictly defined ranks and the hierarchy of authority, commanded by professional military strategists who might not have been themselves physically competent in combat. The famous example was Sun Bin, a handicapped commander who led the Qi army to great victories in the late fourth century BC. The age of war certainly also gave

Box 9.1   The Story of Sun Wu and the Discovery of Military Texts at Yinqueshan

Sima Qian, the Grand Scribe of the Western Han dynasty, tells the story of Sun Wu (also known as Sunzi or Suntzu):

Sun Wu was a native of the northern state Qi, who had come to meet with the king of Wu and offered the king his Art of War *in thirteen chapters. The king after reviewing the text challenged him: "I have carefully read your chapters, but can you put your theory to a little test?"*

Sun Wu replied: "Yes!"

The king pursued: "Can you try it on women?"

Sun Wu replied again: "Sure!"

Thus, the king sent out 180 beautiful ladies from his palace and Sun Wu divided them into two teams with one of the king's most beloved consorts to be the captain of each.

Once at the start, Sun Wu asked the ladies: "Do you all know the difference between front and back, your right hand and left hand?"

"Yes!" The ladies responded.

Sun Wu continued: "When I say 'Eyes front,' you must look straight ahead. When I say 'Turn left,' you must face your left hand. When I say 'Turn right,' you must face your right hand. When I say 'Turn back,' you must turn round towards your back. Understood?"

"Understood." The ladies replied.

When the drums were thundered, Sun Wu gave his first order: "Turn right!"

The ladies burst out laughing. Sun Wu announced: "If the order was not sufficiently clarified, that is the fault of the commander."

The drill continued as Sun Wu gave his second order: "Turn left!"

The ladies burst out laughing again. Sun Wu said: "When the order was clarified, but it is not followed by the soldiers, this is the fault of the officers!"

Thus Sun Wu ordered the execution of the two captains. Stunned by Sun Wu's order, the king of Wu, watching from a high platform, hurriedly sent down his words: "I already know you are capable of commanding troops, but please spare the two concubines! Without them I won't be able to know the taste of my food."

Sun Wu replied, solidly: "Once commissioned by your majesty to command this army, I am now in the field, and I have no leisure to take your order!"

A text called *Audience with the King of Wu*, written on bamboo strips that parallels very closely the above narrative by Sima Qian, was excavated in 1972 in tomb no. 1 at Yinqueshan in southern Shandong, dating by the typological features of the ceramics and coins from the tomb to the early phase of the Western Han. From the same tomb, as many as 4,942 bamboo strips were excavated. Astonishingly, included among the texts on these strips are also two different texts both bearing the title *Art of War*. One is the *Art of War* of Sun Wu which parallels very closely the received version of the text, although the strips from the tomb offer only eight of the supposed

Box 9.1 (cont.)

thirteen chapter titles. The other *Art of War* is identified with Sun Bin, the handicapped general of the state of Qi who led the Qi army into great victories over the hegemonic state Wei. This text not only elaborates on the principles laid out by Sun Wu in the earlier *Art of War*, but also records the career of Sun Bin and his struggle with Wei. Other texts included in the corpus are the *Wei Liaozi, Yanzi, Six Secret Strategies, Shoufa shouling*, all texts of military nature known previously to have been produced in the Warring States period. These texts were published together in 1981.

When the second volume on the Yinqueshan tomb was published in January 2010, it offered an additional group of some fifty previously unknown essays on government and military affairs, together with other texts related to natural philosophy and divination. The nature of the texts from the tomb suggests that the person buried in the tomb might have been a professional military commander who died in an early year of Emperor Wu (*r.* 141–87 BC). Incidentally on the bottoms of two wine lacquer cups from his tomb is written the term "Supervisor of Horses" (*sima*), which was a well-known military title. Although these texts are written in Han clerical style and are Han Dynasty texts, many of them were doubtless transmitted from the Warring States period if not earlier.

The *Art of War* by Sun Wu, the *Wei Liaozi*, and the *Six Secret Strategies* are counted among the famous "Seven Military Classics" for which full-length English translations are available.[16]

rise to the composition of a long list of military texts in Early China, most famously the *Art of War* by Sun Wu, a commander in the southern state Wu during the late Spring and Autumn period (Box 9.1). The latter text has inspired generations of military commanders over the past 2,000 years and is taught in many military academies throughout the world today including West Point in the United States.

Transition in Bronze Culture

Despite the introduction of iron which was used to make agricultural tools and weapons, bronze remained the desired medium of expression of

[16] See Ralph D. Sawyer (trans.), *The Seven Military Classics of Ancient China* (Boulder: Westview Press, 1993).

the elite social order. The Spring and Autumn period began with the continuation of the elite bronze culture of the royal Western Zhou marked by the use of standard sets of vessels in elite tombs. As the use of such standard sets decorated with bold geometric patterns spread from the Wei River valley to the distant eastern states during the early Spring and Autumn period, for the first time the statuses of the elites in every corner of the Zhou realm can be compared through the material culture. Thus, despite the political fragmentation and the increasing chances of military conflict, a Zhou realm was preserved through the adoption of and adherence to the tradition of the Zhou bronze culture.[17]

The introduction of the lost-wax technology in the sixth century BC suddenly changed the image of the bronze culture in China. The new technology which simplified the casting process to produce more intricate shapes and patterns seems to have first appeared in South China, possibly in the Chu region. Since the same technology had been in use in Mesopotamia and South Asia since the fourth millennium BC, it is very likely that it came into the Yangzi region from the south. The earliest examples of bronzes produced by lost-wax casting have been found in the Chu tombs in Xichuan, dated around 552 BC, and the tomb of Marquis Yi of Zeng in northern Hubei, dated around 422 BC, contains multiple pieces of such bronzes. Some of these bronzes, for instance, the bronze table from Xichuan and the set of *zun*-container and *pan*-basin cast for Marquis Yi (Fig. 9.5), are technically very sophisticated, but judging from their general design and the inscriptions they bear, they were clearly locally produced. By the fourth century BC, the technology was clearly known also to the north as indicated by a *hu*-vessel, currently in the Nanjing Museum, which bears an inscription engraved by a Qi general who actually captured the bronze as a war booty from the northern state Yan during the Qi army's invasion of Yan in 314 BC, mentioned above.[18]

Further technological inventions were made to improve the surface look of the bronzes, usually cast by piece-mold technology. Before the end of the Western Zhou some sort of very hard metal had already been discovered and enabled the craftsman to incise inscriptions onto the surface of the bronze. Incision then became the mainstream technology to produce bronze inscriptions during the Spring and Autumn period. On the other hand, the content of the inscriptions in most cases had become simpler due to the disappearance of the Western Zhou royal institutions that once supported the creation of content-rich inscriptions. Gradually,

---

[17] On this point, see Lothar von Falkenhausen, "The Waning of Bronze Age," in *The Cambridge History of Ancient China: From the Origins of Civilization to 221 BC*, p. 543.

[18] This is the Chen (Tian) Zhang *hu*-vessel.

Fig. 9.5 Bronze *zun*-container (h. 30.0 cm, diam. 25.0 cm) and *pan*-basin (h. 23.5 cm, diam. 58.0 cm) from the tomb of Marquis Yi.

the use of the method of incision was shifted from inscription onto the decorative patterns of the bronzes. When this transition happened, it was not the traditional geometric patterns, but the more realistic depictions of social life, usually scenes of battle or elite banquet, that tested the creative power of the free hand of the craftsman (Fig. 9.3). Furthermore, when the technique of inlaying gold or silver was introduced, this had completely changed the image of bronzes from monochromic to polychromic. Besides the traditional types of bronze vessels inherited from the royal Western Zhou, the craftsmen in the late Spring and Autumn period and Warring States period took great interest in transferring images that they saw in the real world onto bronzes, creating an ingeniously dynamic and colorful new realm of bronze art as livelily exhibited by the masterpieces

Fig. 9.6 Bronze tiger (1.51.0 cm, h. 21.9 cm) from the tomb of the king of Zhongshan.

from the tombs of the king of Zhongshan, once conquered by Zhao in 296 BC (Fig. 9.6).

SELECTED READING

Lewis, Mark Edward, "Warring States Political History," in Michael Loewe and Edward L. Shaughnessy (eds.), *The Cambridge History of Ancient China: From the Origins of Civilization to 221 BC* (Cambridge: Cambridge University Press, 1999), pp. 587–650.
Sanctioned Violence in Early China (Albany: State University of New York Press, 1990).

Hui, Victoria, *War and State Formation in Ancient China, and Early Modern Europe*, Cambridge: Cambridge University Press, 2005).

Cook, Constance A., and John S. Major (eds.), *Defining Chu: Image and Reality in Ancient China* (Honolulu: University of Hawaii Press, 1999).

Falkenhausen, Lothar von, *Chinese Society in the Age of Confucius (1000–250 BC)* (Los Angeles: Costen Institute of Archaeology, 2006). Chapters 7–8, pp. 293–369.

10   Philosophers as statesmen: in the light of recently discovered texts

The period from the birth of Confucius (551–479 BC) in the middle of the sixth century BC to the closing of the Warring States period in 221 BC is usually designated as the "Age of Philosophers." Despite the ceaseless military conflicts staged by the large territorial states (analyzed in Chapter 9), China had at the same time also seen unprecedented intellectual developments with the *Shi* (discussed in Chapter 8) at the center of the stage. Those *Shi* who were able to systematically develop their theses, usually represented by a core group of texts, and in turn had them passed on to their disciples through the medium of private education were then remembered in history as the philosophers. The fundamental philosophical ideas developed by these late Spring and Autumn and Warring States period masters have since dominated the skyline of the Chinese intellectual life, and became the defining features of Chinese civilization over the next two millennia.

The phenomenon is interesting within the context of Chinese history and is also important for understanding the early development of the humanities in a global context. For this reason perhaps, the subject of early Chinese philosophy has always been at the heart of Western sinology. And this trend has only been increased with the discovery of critically important new philosophical texts from Warring States tombs, mainly in South China, over the past thirty years. It is obviously impossible to offer here a full discussion of the various propositions endorsed by the numerous philosophers and to trace the lines of their discourses across the extremely rich literature of the Warring States period, for which purpose good introductions have already been written.[1] Instead, as a unit of a concise survey of early Chinese civilization the present chapter will focus

---

[1] A widely read introduction to early Chinese philosophy for sinologists is Feng Yu-lan, *A History of Chinese Philosophy*, translated by Derk Bodde (Princeton: Princeton University Press, 1952–3); abridged edition: *A Short History of Chinese Philosophy*, edited by Derk Bodde (New York: The Free Press, 1966). But beginners are advised to read a new introduction by A. C. Graham; see *Disputers of the Tao: Philosophical Argument in Ancient China* (La Salle: Open Court, 1989).

on the process of formation of a few main philosophical traditions as a social and cultural phenomenon, along with the introduction of some fundamental concepts as their responses to the problems of their time and society. In this way, the chapter will also discuss some recent discoveries of philosophical texts and the significant new light they shed on the development of the early Chinese intellectual traditions.

Ideological Dilemma and the Global Context

Certain concepts, e.g. "Virtue" (De), had a much older origin in the Western Zhou period if not earlier. As discussed in Chapter 7, for many centuries the Zhou realm had been fixed on the concept of "Heaven" (Tian), and virtue was Heaven's superior gift to King Wen which was thereafter passed on to the succession of Zhou kings.[2] Thus, the Zhou kings were literally called the "Son of Heaven" and had exclusive access to this sacred realm, a status that met no challenge even centuries after Zhou royal rule had become ineffective; no other rulers in China had claimed this ritual paramount until probably the rise of the Han Empire. When the Zhou kings died, they became attendants in the court of High God, the anthropomorphic representation of Heaven. The military conquests carried out by the Zhou kings were propagandized as "Heaven's punishment," and the whole range of Zhou institutions indeed rested on the single point of support – Heaven's Mandate – for their legitimacy. However, as Robert Eno has pointed out, "it was the success of these institutions that had, in fact, anchored T'ien (Heaven)."[3] In a reciprocal relationship the continuing fortune of the Zhou state depended on the religious superiority of the Zhou royal house, and in turn, firm trust in Heaven as the root of Zhou's superiority rested on the good performance of the royal institutions. As a matter of fact, not only did the Zhou institutions perform badly, but they had come to a total collapse in 771 BC when the Zhou capitals fell to the hands of the invading "barbarians." Thus, the impact of the dynastic downfall in that year goes far beyond the political dissolution of the Western Zhou state; in a more profound sense, it marked the beginning of the collapse of the religious–ritual system that had so far supported the operation of the early Chinese royal state.

---

[2] On the concept of "Virtue" (De) in the Western Zhou context, with a paleographic root probably in Shang, see David Shepherd Nivison, "Virtue in Bone and Bronze," in Bryan W. Van Norden (ed.), The Ways of Confucianism: Investigations in Chinese Philosophy (Chicago: Open Court, 1996), pp. 17–30.

[3] See Robert Eno, The Confucian Creation of Heaven: Philosophy and the Defense of Ritual Mastery (Albany: State University of New York Press, 1990), p. 27.

Therefore, new sources had to be sought in order to legitimate the power of the new political states that rose from Zhou royal ruin. In a sense, it would even seem natural that any successor to the power of the Zhou house could, as once did the Zhou themselves, exploit the lucrative political profits that the theory of Heaven's Mandate could offer to their cause. But the very political reality that no regional state could hold onto military supremacy for more than a single century (usually it failed in only two to three generations) would have made such an argument less persuasive if not irrelevant; not to mention the continuing presence of the Zhou king, though a political figurehead, to a certain degree still religiously superior, in the small court in Luoyang until 256 BC. In this regard, the diverse philosophical traditions, Confucianism, Daoism, Mohism, Legalism, and so on, represented different ways to theorize an alternative ideological ground to answer this dilemma. And indeed all philosophers who had made their names known in the period had in the background of their thinking a default ambition to recover the coherent social order once promised by the Zhou royal house as the will of Heaven; the difference was only how to achieve it. This background had given early Chinese philosophy a common position, that is, philosophy was the method to solve problems in this world, rather than the inquiry into the relationship between man and gods as was frequently the case in Greek philosophy. Even the natural philosophy developed later was not after all purely the philosophy of the natural world, but was, as it turned out in the doctrine of Zou Yan (305–240 BC), closely concerned with the human world and its history.[4]

It is not difficult to find parallel intellectual developments in the global context and the concept of the "Axial Age" proposed by the German philosopher Karl Jaspers has served as an important vehicle for understanding reasons behind that parallel. In Greece, Socrates (469–399 BC) and Plato (428–347 BC) lived in the fifth to fourth centuries BC, roughly contemporary to Mozi (470–391 BC) and Mencius (372–289 BC) in China. In India, Buddha (563–483 BC) lived from the mid sixth to the early fifth century BC, being twelve years older than Confucius. In all three parts of the ancient world, the philosophers of these centuries had constructed fundamental concepts that came to define their respective civilizations, and no great civilization can survive without these fundamental ideas. Jaspers attributed the origin of the Axial Age to the common

---

[4] See Donald Harper, "Warring States Natural Philosophy and Occult Thought," in Michael Loewe and Edward L. Shaughnessy (eds.), *The Cambridge History of Ancient China: From the Origins of Civilization to 221 BC* (Cambridge: Cambridge University Press, 1999), pp. 818, 865.

sociopolitical condition in all three regions: (1) each region was politically divided into small states and small towns; (2) a politically divided age was engaged in incessant conflicts; (3) the misery caused by wars and revolutions in one place was accompanied by simultaneous prosperity elsewhere, since destruction was neither universal nor radical; (4) the previously existing condition was held up to question.[5]

For the historian, the striking similarity lies also in the very coincidence of time – in all three parts of the world, this is the period that can be regarded as "Post-Early Civilization." In Greece, the Mycenaeans and their Bronze Age contestants for power had long gone and their stories were heard only in later epic poems of Homer; even the recent hegemony of the Athenian Empire had reached its downturn by the time of Socrates. In India, the memory of a preceding Indus civilization was probably still kept alive in the regional traditions. In China, the memory of the past was crystallized in the legends of the royal dynasties Xia, Shang, and most recently the Western Zhou. The collapse of early civilization in each regional context posed fundamental questions over which the ancients had wondered and tried hard to answer: Who are we? Why we are here and where we are going? If the early civilization is not the answer to human happiness, then what is it? In China, be more specific, what is the alternative of the Zhou way?

Confucius and Confucianism

The Han Dynasty historian Sima Qian (c. 145–86 BC) narrated the life of Confucius with the same length and care he accorded to the hereditary kings; this reflects the growing importance of the Confucian agenda in the mid Western Han Empire. Modern scholars, willing to challenge the historian's account, take his narrative as merely a starting point of research to pin down some concrete bits of information about the philosopher in his own time context. One of the recent studies shows that Confucius was born close to the southern border of the state of Lu to an old warrior of the famous Zang family as his father and to a young girl of the indigenous Yan family as his mother. Since the Yan family was from a polity that was clearly known to have had its origin in the native "Eastern Barbarians" (Dongyi), this historical connection may suggest that Confucius might have been a cultural hybrid when he was young.[6] The patronage of the

---

[5] Karl Jaspers, *The Origin and Goal of History*, translated by Michael Bullock (New Haven: Yale University Press, 1955), p. 18.

[6] See Robert Eno, "The Background of the Kong Family of Lu and the Origins of Ruism," *Early China* 28 (2003), 1–11. The traditional records trace Confucius' ancestry to the state of Song in eastern Henan which was founded by descendants of the Shang people.

Zang family famous for maintaining ancient rituals must have been very important in affording him an early education, but Confucius was clearly unsuccessful as a young member of the elite and remained poor through most of his life. Scholars have debated about the highest bureaucratic level he was able to reach, but Warring States sources suggest that, though probably for a short period, Confucius was evidently a figure in the Lu court influential enough to be a strong opponent to the three powerful hereditary families that had long weakened the authority of the Lu ruler. He was likely to have been behind the plan, through the action of his student Zi Lu, to guide the three families into self-destruction of their bases, and he personally sent troops to crush the rebellion of the minister of the Mengsun family.[7] In 497 BC when he was fifty-four, possibly forced by the changing political circumstances, Confucius, in the company of his student group, embarked on a long journey which took him through most important states in China, reaching as far as the state of Chu in the south, not returning to his home state Lu until fourteen years later. Thereafter, it seems that Confucius devoted himself fully to learning and teaching in Lu.

This is about as much as we can say with certainty about the life and career of Confucius. In the received tradition, Confucius was credited with the editing of the *Book of Documents* and *Book of Poetry*, commentary on the *Book of Changes*, and the compilation of the *Spring and Autumn Annals* (see Chapter 7). Although modern scholars are eager to doubt as much as possible about this tradition, there seems little ground to question that Confucius was a scholar influential to his age and to later generations. Confucius is quoted either as the author of or the authoritative voice in the new commentaries of the *Book of Changes* discovered in the Han Dynasty tomb at Mawangdui, and one of the recently discovered manuscripts cites him commenting on the *Book of Poetry*.[8] His relation to the *Spring and Autumn Annals* is more plausible as he could well have copied the original materials out of the official chronicle of Lu.[9] The true importance of Confucius in Chinese history is that, besides his role as a philosopher, he was probably the most learned scholar of his time on these ancient works which he had doubtless taught in his classroom in his self-declared role as a mere "transmitter" of ancient institutions. Viewed from this perspective, we may even be allowed to speculate on a likely

---

[7] See Annping Chin, *The Authentic Confucius: A Life of Thought and Politics* (New York: Scribner, 2007), pp. 26–32.

[8] This is the text called *Confucius' Discussion of the Poetry* among the manuscripts in the Shanghai Museum. See below, n. 25.

[9] See David Shepherd Nivison, "The Classical Philosophical Writings," in *Cambridge History of Ancient China: From the Origins of Civilization to 221 BC*, p. 753.

"Confucian curriculum" in the terminology of modern academia as the core of education which Confucius provided his students with.

As such, we find no single essay written around a particular philosophical issue where Confucius may be expected to elaborate on his ideas in some detail. However, there are a number of recurring issues in the *Analects* that are corroborated by quotations of Confucius across other texts, providing us with at least a snapshot capturing of the mind of the philosopher. The *Analects* in twenty chapters is a collection of sayings of Confucius presented in the form of responses to the questions posed by his students. Although the final compilation of the *Analects* probably took place not far from the end of the Warring States period, at least some of its entries must have had much earlier origins. Therefore, the *Analects* has been considered core text to Confucius and Confucianism.[10] A very important issue for Confucius is the "Rectification of Names (*Zhengming*)," and Confucius saw this as the foundation of the state and government:

> When names are not correct, the words will not convey their meaning; when the words do not convey their meaning, affairs will not achieve success. Therefore, rites and music will not flourish and punishments would not fit the crimes. The people will not know what they should do.

Confucius' own explanation of "Rectifying Names" is found in *Analects* 12 where he answers the question posed by the ruler of Qi in the following words: "Let the ruler be ruler, subject be subject, father be father, and son be son." This certainly is not a word game of names – rather, he was concerned more with what is referred to by the names, and with whether the reality can properly match what the names require. Thus, if a ruler does not behave like a "ruler," and a subject like "subject," the state will definitely fall into chaos. In other words, names are a referential system to social political orders, and only the government in which each person does exactly what is required by his name can provide guidance for the people.

Interestingly, Confucius thought that this could be done not by imposing administrative orders but easily or willingly (in the sense of causing no harm to anyone) through the practice of "Ritual" (*Li*) which is rather natural to and even preferred by those who are engaged in it. The term *Li* by its origin in Western Zhou inscriptions referred to sacrificial offerings in ancestral worship which by the late Western Zhou had come to be associated with sets of sumptuary rules that determined the correct conduct of members of a religious–ritual community. By conducting oneself

---

[10] See Michael Loewe (ed.), *Early Chinese Texts: A Bibliographical Guide* (Berkeley: Institute of East Asian Studies, University of California, 1993), pp. 313–323.

correctly according to these rules, one is ritually reconfirmed of his status and duty in that community. The *Analects* itself does not give a clear definition of *Li*, but offers a number of cases where Confucius very seriously considered certain conducts as "Violation of *Li*," for instance, the use of dancers performing in eight rows in a ministerial family of Lu which was the ritual standard for state rulers. Confucius commented angrily: "If one can bear with this, what else is there one cannot bear with?"

As for the social effect of "Ritual," Confucius says:

Li promotes mutual visits. Therefore, if someone paid you a visit but if you do not pay a visit back, that is violation of *Li*. By the same token, if you visited someone but he does not pay you a visit back, that is also violation of *Li*.

For Confucius, everyday life is a performance in a wide social web where the interaction between people is not only inevitable but is desirable as the way to realize *Li*. Not only does an individual need to interact with others, but he must do so according to proper ritual rules which will naturally instill in him a sense of duty to fulfill his social obligations suitable to his status. Good social order comes as the result of each member of the society truthfully conducting his part as "ruler," "subject," "father," and "son"... as appropriate to their names in a predetermined social hierarchy. Confucius stresses that one should not only perform his duty, but needs to do so with sincerity and deep passion, and this relates to another important concept of Confucius – "Benevolence" (*Ren*), which he describes as more important than water or fire that people cannot live without it. Confucius' own interpretation of "Benevolence" is simply "to love people." He talks about the "Government of Benevolence," a proposition that the second great philosopher of the Confucian tradition, Mencius, was to elaborate on later. Confucius also suggested a method to determine whether one is benevolent or not – a Confucian "Golden Rule": "Do not do to others what you do not wish yourself!" In this formula, one should take one's own heart as the measurement of what is harmful and what is beneficial. Thus, *Ren* is not far from us.

Like most philosophers of the "Axial Age," Confucius perceived the world around him as essentially wrong. For him, the ideal social order existed only in the past, the Western Zhou, when the virtuous Zhou kings presided over a political system that was created under the Duke of Zhou, Confucius' own hero, and sustained through a ritual system that was in perfect order. For him, the solution to the current problems was to go back to the Western Zhou when royal authority was strong and subjects obedient; "Ritual" was the foundation for doing so and the "Rectification of Names" was the proper method to achieve this goal.

According to some accounts, the tradition once founded by Confucius was divided after the master's death into eight sects, among which that of Mencius was most influential. Since Mencius traced his intellectual inheritance back to Zi Si, Confucius' grandson, Zi Si and Mencius (372–289 BC) together represented a very important intellectual stream within the greater Confucian tradition. Mencius was born more than a century after Confucius' death, in a city that was possibly also very close to Confucius' birthplace. But he was apparently from a rich family and had good luck in finding rulers who would take delight in listening to his deliberations. In 320 BC, he was welcomed to the court of the state of Wei (Daliang) in eastern Henan where he stayed for some years. Then, he moved on to the state of Qi where he became a leading figure in the Jixia Academy sponsored by the Qi ruler.[11] His words are heard collectively in the long text of *Mencius* which most scholars agree to have been composed towards the end of his life, if not actually by Mencius himself.

Different from Confucius who was primarily concerned with the harmonious social order, Mencius, though with the same goal in mind, constructed his thesis at a more fundamental level by inquiring deeply into "human nature." According to Mencius, everyone was born with a good nature and everyone had the potential to become a sage. Mencius makes this case by pointing to the fact that everyone has sympathy towards a child who is about to fall into a well, as every child has an inborn love for his parents. The reason that some men became bad is because they starved their good qualities and therefore exposed themselves to bad influence. Common men will inevitably lose their good nature, only the gentleman, the *Shi*, can preserve it. This good nature of man is crystallized in four superior qualities which he termed "Benevolence" (*Ren*), "Righteousness" (*Yi*), "Manner" (*Li*), and "Wisdom" (*Zhi*). According to Mencius, the seeds of these four good qualities are already inborn within every person, and what he needs to do is to discover and further develop them. On this point, Mencius is very different from another Confucian master who came after him, Xunzi (310–220 BC), who argued that the nature of man is essentially evil, and only the proper practice of ritual and learning can set him apart from beasts. Mencius is particularly noticeable for his promotion of the concept of "Righteousness" as the principle of conduct in a time of no

---

[11] The Jixia Academy was a state-sponsored academy of learning located near the Jixia Gate of the capital of the state of Qi. The academy attracted hundreds of philosophers and scholars to its faculty and students who openly debated their philosophical theses under a proto-form of "intellectual freedom" guaranteed by the state. The academy was founded by King Wei of Qi close to the middle of the fourth century BC and was prosperous until the middle of the third century BC.

existing political–moral authority. On this point, he is uncompromisingly against political and moral utilitarianism. The concept of *Li* came to mean exclusively personal manners in Mencius' philosophy and lost its meaning as the superior "Ritual" order, the foundation that upholds proper social relations in Confucius' thought.

The natural extension of this basic understanding of human nature into political philosophy is the issue of "Good Government" with an army that acts in accordance with the principles of "Benevolence" and "Righteousness," a proposition which Mencius spent most of his energy to elaborate on. Living roughly 100 years after Confucius, Mencius was little bothered by the fact that the "Ritual" was violated, because such violation was just everywhere. Also unlike Confucius, Mencius had little interest in restoring the Western Zhou system because the Zhou house had long been proven hopeless, and by 323 BC, only three years before Mencius appeared in the court of Wei, rulers of all major territorial states had assumed the title "King" (*Wang*), thus being politically and ritually equal to the Zhou king. The issue for Mencius was to find a good ruler who was capable of conquering all others and re-establishing social order based on the concepts of "Benevolence" and "Righteousness," and it did not matter who he was. According to Mencius, the government of such virtuous kings would be the one that puts people to the center of concern. This is Mencius' answer to the most fundamental question of his time, the source of legitimacy of political power:

People are to be valued most, the altars of the grain and land next, the ruler least. Hence by winning the favor of the common people you become king; by winning the favor of the king you become lord of a fief; by winning the favor of the lord you become grandee. If the lord endangers the altars, replace him; if proper sacrifices were made at the altars but there is still drought and flood, replace the altar.

What if the king violates his people? Mencius did not say "replace the king" because he was talking to the king, but he says that there are the examples of three dynasties where evil kings were replaced by good ones. The critically important point here is that Mencius did not say that the king derived his power from Heaven, but from the favor given him by the common people. In this regard, Mencius was the first philosopher to have discovered a new source of legitimacy of political power in a time when Heaven's Mandate no longer conferred on a ruler the right to rule, thus coming quite close to the modern democratic political thought on the source of sovereignty. As the ruler derived the legitimacy of his power from the common people, as Mencius duly advises, he could enjoy it longer if he were willing to share his pleasure with the people.

On the final account of Mencius, he was thoroughly Confucian in the sense that he found the foundation of good government in the willing heart of the ruler, not as something which the ruler had no choice but to take on. This brings us to a conversation between Mencius and King Xuan of Qi who on a previous occasion had shown sympathy towards an ox that was about to be killed for sacrificial purposes. Mencius pointed out that this was an indication of the king's moral potential to become a virtuous king as long as he could extend his compassion from what he could see immediately to what he could not, and from what was close to him to what was far. If he could apply his love for his family to the families of others, and develop his compassion into a universal care for his people, he would be the one to bring good order to the world. In Mencius' view, this can be easily done because the good deed is already found in the king's heart. The issue is only that he needs to be willing to do so.

The Daoist Search for Natural Order

However, there were people who viewed the world in strikingly different ways and had a different remedy for the sociopolitical problems in China – philosophers whose theses were centered on one key concept: "Way" (*Dao*). According to the distinguished historian of Chinese philosophy, Feng Yu-lan, there were three stages in the development of Daoist philosophy: the early stage is represented by Yang Zhu, the middle period by the *Classic of Way and Virtue* (*Daodejing*, or more commonly known as *Laozi*), and the later stage by the philosophy of Zhuangzi.[12]

No date or life story is transmitted of the earliest Daoist philosopher Yang Zhu, but he must have lived sometime before Mencius. Since Mencius once lamented at the fact that in his days the world of philosophy was divided equally between the theories of Yang Zhu and Mozi, he must have been well known during the early fourth century BC. However, no works can be attributed to Yang Zhu and all that we know of him comprises a few lines of comments by other philosophers. Mencius said: "The principle of Yang Zhu is: Each one for himself. He would not pull off even a single hair from his shank if that can benefit the whole world!" By the Legalist philosopher Han Fei he was ridiculed in the same way. However, in the Daoist tradition Yang Zhu is respected as the one who had established the principle of "Preserving life and maintaining what is genuine in it." Since none would pluck out his hair for the benefit of the world, none would take the world as his gain. The real essence of Yang Zhu's

---

[12] See Feng Yu-lan, *A Short History of Chinese Philosophy*, pp. 65–67.

philosophy is to preserve one's genuine nature and not let it be entangled with and injured by worldly things. According to A. C. Graham, rather than Egoism, Yang Zhu's philosophy can be considered complete Individualism concerned with benefiting one's own body and simply leaving others to do the same.[13]

What we learn from the tradition about the philosopher "Old Master" (Laozi), the alleged author of the *Classic of Way and Virtue*, is entirely fictional. One piece of such accounts had Laozi as the archivist at the royal court of Zhou where he virtually lectured Confucius during the latter's visit to the Zhou capital in Luoyang. Feng Yu-lan felt that there may have been a historical Laozi who was a contemporary of Confucius, but the text *Classic of Way and Virtue* that came to bear his name was probably composed much later, likely towards the end of the Warring States period, if not after the unification by Qin in 221 BC.[14] However, the discovery at Guodian in 1993 has overturned this late date and suggests that the text must have had a much longer history of circulation in the fourth century and must not be later than 320 BC (see below). The text begins with the following lines:

Dao that can be spoken of is not the constant *Dao*; Name that can be named is not the constant name. Nameless was the beginning of Heaven and Earth; having a name is the mother of myriad of things. Always with no desire, we can see the subtlety (of things); always with desire, we can see their material outcome. These two things derived from the same origin but have different names. Profound and profound, this is the gate of subtleties!

The central teaching of the *Classic of Way and Virtue* is about *Dao*, the eternal "Way," the "non-being," but eternal existence which preceded "being" (see below). This is certainly not the way of the sages (as in Confucianism), but the cosmological way that existed long before the sage. *Dao* is the unseen, unspoken true "Way" of the universe. "Virtue" (*De*), the manifestation of *Dao*, is the quality which each individual thing received from it, and is what it naturally is. Despite the use of the same words, the concepts of "Way" and "Virtue" in Daoist philosophy depart radically from their meanings in Confucian philosophy. Although Daoism, at least in the received form of the *Classic of Way and Virtue*, has a very strong metaphysical if not naturalistic appearance when compared to Confucianism, it is fundamentally still a political philosophy.

---

[13] Graham, *Disputers of the Tao*, p. 59.

[14] See Feng Yu-lan, *A Short History of Chinese Philosophy*, pp. 93–94. Reasons for this are given in his earlier work where he suggested that the *Laozi* cannot be earlier than *Analects* and *Mencius*. See Feng Yu-lan, *A History of Chinese Philosophy*, translated by Derk Bodde, 2 vols. (Princeton: Princeton University Press, 1952), p. 170.

According to the text, the *Dao*, the superior "Way," has long been obscured in China:

When the great *Dao* is abandoned, therefore there are the doctrines of Benevolence and Righteousness; when wisdom and knowledge emerged, therefore there is perjury; when the six family relations were not in harmony, therefore there is the need for Filial Piety; when a state is in disorder, therefore there is the need for Loyalty. (Section 18)

Here, the world is perceived as being continuously declining from its original perfect condition, and as the result of the decline, if not the cause of it, there emerged a whole range of doctrines such as "Benevolence," "Righteousness," "Filial Piety," and "Loyalty," all moral values upheld by the Confucian philosophers. Thus, the real sage will be the one who would abandon all of these artificial wisdoms. He would not treasure valuables so people will not steal, and he would not promote goodness so people would not compete. He would always "empty the people's heart, fill their stomach, weaken their ambition, and strengthen their bones." Quite obviously much of this was written with Confucian doctrines as the targets because the latter's idea of a sage had given too much to be done to the world; the Daoist sage, by contrast, would have to undo all this, or he would not do anything in the first place. By "No Action" (*Wuwei*), all things will return in good order.

This is the Daoist answer to the issue of political order in China. Accordingly, the best government is the government that would not govern, and the ideal society is the primitive society where material goods were abundant, writing was put to no use, and people were strictly tied to their locales and would not communicate with one another. This is the perfect natural order of society to which the world should return, and this contrasts sharply with the Confucian (at least that of Confucius) ideal world as a layered social web with all relations in perfect harmony facilitated through the practice of ritual and music.

However, this concept of the "Way" (*Dao*) as the superior cosmological order and origin of the universe had clearly undergone significant transformation in the philosophy of *Zhuangzi*, a long Warring States text. Zhuangzi (369–286 BC), the reputed author of the text that goes by his name, or at least a core part of it, might have been a younger contemporary of Mencius, and perhaps well acquainted with the philosophical ideas of other thinkers of his own time. However, the text, particularly the outer-chapter group of it, contains materials of different origins and some of them apparently date long after his death. In *Zhuangzi*, the "Way" is no longer the "untouchable," the eternal "Way" which only the real sage, not even the ordinary sages, can possibly understand; instead, the "Way" has submerged into everything and everywhere reachable in the personal experience of each individual, if one does it right. As illustrated by the famous story of "Butcher Ding" and the story of the "Wheel-Maker," everyone, if he conducts himself correctly, may have the opportunity to experience the "Way." And the way to do so is to go beyond the level of technique to reach the realm of spontaneity which Zhuangzi describes as "Naturally So" or "Being Natural" (*Ziran*) – this is the way to nurture life. In fact, a parallel development can be found in Confucianism where "Ritual" (*Li*), which was the superior social order in Confucius, had become more or less a personal manner in Mencius.

This notion of "Naturally So" also relates to Zhuangzi's underscoring of "Virtue" (*De*) which is the "Nature" each individual received from the "Way" which, he argues strongly, is omnipresent. Different creatures possess different natures, and going against the Nature would inevitably lead to disasters. Thus, Zhuangzi tells the story of the ruler of Lu who wished to honor a seabird that happened to have stopped at his court. He placed it in the temple, slaughtered a bullock to feed it, and played grand music to entertain it. As the result, the seabird died in three days after its capture. A later chapter in *Zhuangzi* also tells the story of Zhuangzi himself being invited by the king of Chu to serve in his government. Upon hearing the message brought by two officers from the Chu court, Zhuangzi responded by asking: "I have heard that there is a sacred turtle in the state of Chu that had been dead for three thousand years. The king wrapped it with silk and kept it in his ancestral temple. Would this turtle like to be dead to leave its bones being treasured by the king, or would it like to live and drag its tail in the mud?" The officers answered that of course it would like to be alive. Then, Zhuangzi said in a strong voice: "Go! I will drag my tail in the mud!" These are instances that indicate that Nature may be violated by human interference, in the worst form of government, and human happiness is obtained only when one's distinctive Nature is fully preserved and properly entertained.

If there is anything in *Zhuangzi* that can be called a political philosophy, it is this notion of Nature which led the philosopher to "violently oppose the idea of government through the formal machinery of government."[15] Activist government, which Confucianism endorses, is particularly harmful and even resented because it represents the triumph of the artificial institutions over the given natural condition of mankind, and it is the source of misery and unhappiness:

---

[15] See Feng Yu-Lan, *A Short History of Chinese Philosophy*, pp. 106–107.

I have heard of letting mankind alone, but not of governing them. Letting alone springs from the fear that the people would pollute their innate nature and set aside their *De*. When people do not pollute their inner nature and set aside their *De*, then is there need for the government of mankind?

This notion of "No Do" in relation with "Do" is fully developed at the metaphysical level into the "Theory of Relativity" according to which the two things are actually one. Zhuangzi explicated this relationship in terms of "Usefulness" and "Uselessness" as he tells the story of the oak tree in the state of Lu. Once people thought about cutting it down to make timbers to be used to build a house, but they did not do so because the tree was not straight; another time people wanted to cut it down to make a coffin, but the tree was hollow inside. So they all took the tree to be useless and let it grow for three hundred years, to its age assigned by Heaven. So its *uselessness* is at the same time *usefulness*. A parable from Chapter 2 of *Zhuangzi* interestingly has the philosopher himself as the embodiment of this point:

Once upon a time Zhuang Zhou had a dream in which he became a butterfly. Flitting and fluttering as a butterfly, he was happy and going as he pleased! He did not know he was Zhuang Zhou. Suddenly he woke up, and was surprised to find that he was still Zhuang Zhou. He did not know if he was Zhuang Zhou who dreamed he was a butterfly, or a butterfly who dreamed he was Zhuang Zhou? Between Zhuang Zhou and a butterfly there must be a distinction. This is called the transformation of things.

To the modern mind that is used to rational thinking, this would appear as the demonstration of a mind that is in anarchy and cannot think by reasoning. But as pointed out by A.C. Graham, Zhuangzi had his reasons for not listening to our reason.[16]

The Discovery at Guodian and Its Place in Early Chinese Intellectual History

The above discussion highlights the radically different positions of Confucianism and Daoism with respect to the issue of social order and the proper ways to achieve it. These positions contrast still more sharply with the views of the third major intellectual stream of the Warring States period, Legalism, to be discussed later in this chapter. However, it should be noted that our understanding of these intellectual traditions has never been simple and static, fixed on the transmitted philosophical texts whose

---

[16] Graham, *Disputers of the Tao*, p. 176.

date and authorship are always open to question.[17] Instead, particularly over the last two decades, our view of the formation of the respective traditions in Early China has always been challenged and often improved by the new textual manuscripts excavated from tombs of the Warring States and Han periods. This is especially true and significant with regard to Confucianism and Daoism.

To offer a historical perspective, philosophical texts began to be discovered from underground not too long after they were buried. As early as AD 279, a version of the *Book of Changes* together with other smaller texts of philosophical nature had been excavated from the tomb of a Warring States king in northern Henan.[18] In modern times, the most famous case was the discovery in 1973 of three tombs at Mawangdui, Hunan (see Chapter 14). Although the texts from the tombs were buried in 168 BC during the Western Han Dynasty, many doubtless had had a long history of transmission before Han. The discovery made at Guodian in 1993 from a relatively smaller tomb that yielded as many as eighteen texts of exclusively philosophical nature, is such that we need to rethink not only some of the fundamental premises in Chinese philosophy, but also the prominent position of philosophy in the social life of Early China. The area has been home to numerous archaeological discoveries associated with the former capital of the state of Chu near present-day Jiangling in Hubei Province.

The significance of the discovery at Guodian arises first from the fact that the tomb was excavated by trained archaeologists and is securely dated to the late fourth century, falling somewhere between 320 BC and 300 BC, thus before the late Warring States period, the time-frame into which modern scholars conventionally put most transmitted pre-Qin texts, not just philosophical ones. This was the time, the mid Warring States period, when great philosophers like Mencius and Zhuangzi were still alive, and the two competing traditions represented by them were both still at their formative stage.[19] As such, the strength of the Guodian texts lies also in the fact that both philosophical traditions are evidently represented in them, although the balance in which the two traditions are present in the tomb is still debated among scholars. In fact, a few texts from the tomb seem actually to blur the distinction between the two traditions. But except for four that have their counterparts among the

---

[17] For a discussion of authorship of early Chinese philosophical texts, see Nivison, "The Classical Philosophical Writing," pp. 745–746.

[18] For a systematic account on this early finding, see Edward L. Shaughnessy, *Rewriting Early Chinese Texts* (Albany: State University of New York Press, 2006), pp. 131–184.

[19] See Sarah Allan and Crispin Williams (eds.), *The Guodian Laozi: Proceedings of the International Conference, Dartmouth College, May 1998* (Berkeley: Institute of East Asian Studies, University of California, 2000) pp. 31, 107, 118–20.

transmitted texts, the other fourteen are all new texts critical to any tradition to which they can be possibly associated at such an early time.

First, a core group of some six texts seems to have been associated with Zi Si, a grandson of Confucius and teacher of Mencius' own teacher, thus possibly providing a key intellectual link between Confucius and Mencius.[20] Within these texts, we can see a clear shift of focus in the Confucian tradition from the pursuit of superior social order to a persistent inquiry into the very quality and potential of man as individual agent. Concepts such as "Righteousness" and "Wisdom" that have been traditionally thought of as having characterized Mencius' philosophy were already the subjects of discussion in a text called the "Five Conducts" from Guodian. And the inquiry into the origin of "Nature" in the "Nature Derives from Mandate" both adheres to Confucius' belief in "Mandate" and anticipates the argument Mencius built around the concept to form the foundation of his philosophy. Because of this link, we now also have a new ground for understanding the goodness of "Human Nature" in Mencius because in Guodian it is said to have been derived from "Mandate" which commands a fundamental sense of righteousness and superiority, and it cannot be bad.

On the Daoist side, the most important elements have been three mid-fourth-century versions of the *Classic of Way and Virtue* together with a new text called "The Great One Gives Birth to Water" (*Taiyi sheng shui*) (Box 10.1). It is first of all significant that the Guodian *Classic and Way and Virtue* suggests that the so-called anti-Confucian sentiment seen in late Warring States to Han period versions of the text was likely a later addition to Daoism (which was the base for dating the text to the late Warring States period in previous scholarship) – in the three compilations of the *Classic of Way and Virtue* from Guodian, the targets of criticism were indeed certain qualities like "Wisdom" (*Zhi*), "Disputation" (*Bian*), "Craftiness" (*Qiao*), "Profit" (*Li*). And in one place these concepts are actually considered as opposing the ideas of "Benevolence" and "Righteousness," core Confucian concepts as they were understood in Daoism.[21]

"The Great One Gives Birth to Water," representing probably an even earlier stage of development of Daoism, offers what most scholars consider the first complete cosmogony in China that describes Heaven, Earth, Spirit, *Yin* and *Yang* (two opposing forces), the Four Seasons, and so

---

[20] This group includes the "Silk Garment" (*Ziyi*; traditionally attributed to Zi Si), "Five Conducts" (*Wuxing*), *Cheng zhi wen zhi*, "Revering Virtue and Propriety" (*Zun deyi*), "Nature Derives from Mandate" (*Xin zi ming chu*), and "The Six Virtues" (*Liude*), all written on bamboo strips of the same size and shape with the same method of binding. See Allan and Williams (eds.), *The Guodian Laozi*, pp. 109, 180.

[21] Allan and Williams (eds.), *The Guodian Laozi*, pp. 160–162.

Box 10.1   *The Great One Gives Birth to Water (Taiyi Shengshui)*

This is one of the texts written on bamboo strips, discovered in Guodian in 1993.

The Great One produced water. The water, in return, assisted the Great One, thus forming the sky. The sky, returning, assisted the Great One, thus forming the earth. The sky and earth again assisted one another, thus forming the numinous and the luminous. The numinous and the luminous again assisted one another, thus forming *yin* and *yang*. *Yin* and *yang* again assisted one another, thus forming the four seasons. The four seasons again assisted one another, thus forming cold and heat. Cold and heat again assisted one another, thus forming moisture and aridity. Moisture and aridity again assisted one another, formed a year and that was all.

Therefore, a year is that which moisture and aridity produced. Moisture and aridity are that which cold and heat produced. Cold and heat are that which the four seasons produced. The four seasons are that which *yin* and *yang* produced. *Yin* and *yang* are that which the numinous and the luminous produced. The numinous and the luminous are that which the sky and earth produced. Sky and earth are that which the Great One produced.

For this reason, the Great One hides in water and moves with the seasons. Circling and [beginning again, it takes itself as] the mother of the myriad living things. Waning and waxing, it takes itself as the guideline of the myriad living things. It is what the sky cannot exterminate, what the earth cannot bury, that which *yin and yang* cannot form. The gentleman who knows this is called [a sage]. (*Translation by Sarah Allan*)

---

forth . . . each giving birth to the next and ultimately the Great One giving birth to Heaven. While some scholars think that this new text was originally a part of or an appendix to one of the compilations of the *Classic of Way and Virtue* from Guodian, others think that this cosmogony was much earlier and was only later modified and incorporated into the received text of the *Classic of Way and Virtue*.[22] But none debates the close relationship of this new text with the Daoist tradition, and as such the critical point offered by it is: a cosmogonical model had already been developed by/before the time of Guodian, and the concept of "Way"

---

[22] For different positions on this relation, see Sarah Allan, "The Great One, Water, and the Laozi: New Light from Guodian," *T'oung Pao* **89**.4–5 (2003), 253; Donald Harper, "The Nature of *Taiyi* in the Guodian Manuscript *Taiyi sheng shui*: Abstract Cosmic Principle or Supreme Cosmic Deity?" *Chūgoku shutsudo shiryō kenkyū* **5** (2001), 16.

(*Dao*) which most scholars identify with the "Great One" must be understood within the dimensions of this cosmological paradigm.

It is true that scholars of early Chinese philosophy will continue to debate over the proper relationship between these newly excavated texts, either as individual works or as groups of works, and the philosophical traditions as they were understood in the Han period, and about the validity of "school" divisions determined by Han historians based on the transmitted texts,[23] which has been the starting point of modern studies of early Chinese philosophy. There is, after all, the question about whether a general philosophical or perhaps religious tendency or "belief" embraced by the tomb's occupant (some believe he was teacher to the crown prince of Chu) might have provided a common ground for the inclusion of the various texts in a single tomb.[24] Despite these uncertainties, any informed analysis of early Chinese philosophy can no longer stand without considerations of the texts from Guodian as well as the newer manuscript corpora that have surfaced after Guodian.[25]

The Legalist Measures

The Legalists were the helpers of the rulers and builders of the new "Territorial States" that had become the norm of political organization during the Warring States period. There was a long line of Legalist thinkers including Shang Yang (390–338 BC), Shen Dao (390–315 BC), Shen Buhai (385–337 BC), and Han Fei (281–233 BC). The first helped Duke Xiao of Qin to carry out the most thorough reform of the Warring States period (see Chapter 11), and the second and third were ministers of the state of Hann. The last, Han Fei, identified with the long text called *Hanfeizi* that bears his name, is traditionally considered the best synthesizer of the entire Legalist tradition. Han Fei was a member of the royal lineage of Hann, but on a diplomatic mission to Qin, he was hosted by the king of Qin, the future First Emperor of China, who much admired

---

[23] Allan and Williams (eds.), *The Guodian Laozi*, pp. 179–182.

[24] This possibility has been strongly argued by Kenneth W. Holloway; see *Guodian: The Newly Discovered Seeds of Chinese Religious and Political Philosophy* (New York: Oxford University Press, 2009), pp. 12–15, 102–103.

[25] There have been a number of new discoveries of Warring States to Han manuscripts since 1993. Most important among these more recent discoveries is a huge inventory of manuscripts purchased by the Shanghai Museum from the antique market of Hong Kong and published gradually between 2001 and 2007. The seven volumes include as many as thirty-four new texts of mostly philosophical nature. The manuscripts have already lost their provenance as the result of illegal looting from tombs, but it is likely that they were from the same cemetery at Guodian and date possibly to around the same time. Researches on these new texts are still in a preliminary stage.

his talent. But the king eventually did not use him; instead, on the advice of his minister Li Si, he executed the philosopher to prevent his talent from being used by another state.

Both Han Fei and Li Si were known as students of Xunzi, the best-known philosopher of the Confucian tradition after Mencius. In fact, Xunzi's famous doctrine that human nature is fundamentally evil provided a starting point from which Han Fei developed a theory radically different from his teacher's. According to Han Fei, in a year of good harvest people offer food to casual visitors on the road, but in a year of famine people do not even feed their own children – this is not because human nature is alternately good and bad, but because it depends entirely on the economic foundation of their lives. Therefore, there is no point for a ruler to try to make men good; he only needs to restrain them from doing evil. Nor should he try "to win the hearts of the people," because by nature everyone is selfish and concerned only with his immediate gains. For Han Fei, what the government should do is to provide sufficient economic foundation for the people, and to set up strict laws to keep them from doing wrong. Only this is the way to achieve superior social order.

On the issue of the source of legitimacy of political power, Han Fei's answer was typically positivistic, that is to accept it as it is. "Authority" (*Shi*) is the power that a ruler naturally has with him. Whatever a ruler's moral quality is and however he rules, the possession of "Authority" carries the undeniable rights to exact obedience. "Subject serving ruler, son serving father, and wife serving husband," this is not something that they can choose to do or not for a ruler; people simply have no choice. The ruler, on the other hand, exercises his "Authority" through "Law" (*Fa*), which once set up should be observed closely. Han Fei says that "the intelligent ruler makes the law to select men and makes no arbitrary appointment himself; he makes the law measure merits and makes no arbitrary judgment himself." He saw this as the foundation of the state and government. While adopting a positivist approach to "Law," Han Fei also gives examples to show the need to apply heavy punishment on small offenses. Cruel as it is, Han Fei argues that this is likely to eliminate fire before it spreads out. If you can prevent small crimes, people will not be in danger of committing worse crimes and being subject to capital punishment. So, in a sense, they would benefit from heavy punishment for small offenses.

Despite a ruler having the "Authority" to rule, he is in danger of losing it. Rulers of the Warring States period frequently found themselves victims of usurpation not by the lowly subjects they ruled, but by the ministers who helped them to rule in a political system that encouraged competition. Han Fei's answer to the problem is "Statecraft" (*Shu*), a concept that had been much stressed by Shen Buhai before him. According to Han Fei, after assigning an official duties the ruler should strictly demand the performance required by his office. If the official does less than required, he should be punished; if he does more by overstepping his power, he should also be punished. The punishment is not due to his excessive accomplishment, but due to that fact that he overstepped his power. Most importantly, as a ruler, he should never show laxity in taking personal responsibility of rewarding officials for their merits, and punishing them for their failures – the "Two Handles" by which the ruler exercises full control over his bureaucracy.

Han Fei's view of history is also distinctive from the Confucian idea about a past "Golden Age." Han Fei did not openly oppose the idea of a "Golden Age." But, for him, the matter is simply that each dynasty had its special circumstances, and it would be foolish to cling to the outmoded ways of the past kings. Therefore, political institutions must adapt to the special social condition of particular times, and must account for the prevailing patterns of human behavior, determined not by their internal moral standards, but by external conditions.

Further Reflections

Discussed above are three philosophical traditions that not only had a relatively long history through the Warring States period, but also exercised enduring influence on Chinese civilization thereafter. In the time context of their early history, they represented three main approaches to the social and political crisis that overtook China as the result of the collapse of the Western Zhou state and the ideology upheld by it. However, this does not mean that their positions were all strong in all times. In fact, Mencius once remarked that in his time the most popular philosophical schools were that of Yang Zhu, an early form of Daoism, and that of Mohism, seemingly suggesting a period of decline of the Confucian tradition after the death of Confucius' first-generation students.

The Mohist tradition was centered on a charismatic leader named Mozi who lived sometime after Confucius and probably died shortly before Mencius was born, although the exact years cannot be determined. He was likely the head of a band of some 100 warriors that played an active role in helping the attacked weaker states in their defenses. The text that bears his name, *Mozi*, is rich in information about military engineering, and is likely to have been written by someone who was actually engaged in such affairs. Taking Confucianism as his intellectual enemy, Mozi challenged it mainly on two counts. First, Mozi criticizes Confucians for their practice of luxurious ritual to entertain the dream of going back to the Western Zhou Dynasty. Instead, Mozi judged political and social institutions by their utilitarian value and by whether they would be beneficial to the people. Second, Mozi accused Confucianism of biased love, *Ren* or "Benevolence," based only on family relations in an existing social hierarchy. On the contrary, Mozi advocated "Universal Love." For Mozi, if everyone can love other people's families as he does his own, and other states as he does his home state, there will be no war. But this is reflected in Mencius' eyes as quite ridiculous because for one who cannot love his own kindred, there is no way for him to love all others beyond his family.

Another minor intellectual stream was that of the Sophists or Logicians whose main interests lay in the relationship between language and reality. Most of these people lived in the middle to late Warring States period, and two were most famous: Hui Shi (350–260 BC) and Gongsun Long (325–250 BC), both appearing in *Zhuangzi*. Zhuangzi took the former as a serious intellectual opponent and debated with him over the issue of the "Happiness of the Fish," but the latter is harshly ridiculed in *Zhuangzi*. In a sense, the Sophists are a group of philosophers who were least concerned with the ongoing social problems in China, and perhaps the ones who had given up hope of finding an orderly world. Perhaps they saw disorder as the order of the world, and on this basis they challenged the rationality of the ordinary mind. By the late Warring States period, another philosophical tradition, Naturalism, began to take roots in the intellectual soil of China. Embracing both the Dualist view of the world divided between *Yin* and *Yang* and a system of cosmological classification marked by the "Five Elements" (soil, wood, metal, fire, and water) which replaced each other in a circle, the Naturalist tradition reached its maturity in the philosophy of Zou Yan (305–240? BC). Zou Yan further developed the cosmological circle into a political theory and explained the fortune of each preceding dynasty with the virtue of one of the "Five Elements."[26]

As in the political–military arena of the Warring States that was marked by the rise and fall of the dominant states, in the cultural arena of the period it was just as natural to see the rise and demise of intellectual currents. Such a state of affairs has been termed the "Hundred Schools of Philosophy" which speaks well of a unique period of extremely vibrant intellectual activity in Chinese history. However, history has proven that the Legalist way was more effective in bringing forth a unitary social order in the face of the political division of Warring States China. In the

---

[26] See Harper, "Warring States Natural Philosophy and Occult Thought," pp. 818, 860–865.

intellectual realm, Naturalism became the most dominant philosophy in the early days of the Empire which came about by conquering the "Territorial States."

SELECTED READING

Feng, Yu-lan, *A Short History of Chinese Philosophy*, ed. Derk Bodde (New York: The Free Press, 1966).

Graham, A. C., *Disputers of the Tao: Philosophical Argument in Ancient China* (La Salle: Open Court, 1989).

Nivison, David Shepherd, "The Classical Philosophical Writing," in Michael Loewe and Edward L. Shaughnessy (eds.), *The Cambridge History of Ancient China: From the Origins of Civilization to 221 BC* (Cambridge: Cambridge University Press, 1999), pp. 745–812.

Harper, Donald, "Warring States Natural Philosophy and Occult Thought," in *The Cambridge History of Ancient China: From the Origins of Civilization to 221 BC*, pp. 813–884.

Allan, Sarah, and Crispin Williams (eds.), *The Guodian Laozi: Proceedings of the International Conference, Dartmouth College, May 1998* (Berkeley: Institute of East Asian Studies, University of California, Berkeley, 2000).

11 The Qin unification and Qin Empire: who were the terracotta warriors?

The rise of the Qin Empire (221–206 BC) was one of the greatest epics in human history. Like the Macedonians whose kingdom was dotted on the edge of a great civilization for centuries before they rose as a superpower, the Qin had a very long history that goes as far back as to the Western Zhou period. But this is a point that has only been recently testified by archaeological evidence. In June 1994, a pair of bronze *hu*-jar vessels appeared in the antique market in New York. The stylistic features of the vessels, clearly adherent to the standards of the Zhou mainstream bronze culture, suggest an indisputable early date close to the historical transition from the Western to the Eastern Zhou. Incidentally, both vessels are inscribed with six characters that read: "The Duke of Qin makes and casts this sacrificial *hu*-vessel." The inscription squarely identifies the bronzes with a ruler of the state of Qin, who had reigned some five centuries before the rise of the ultra-famous First Emperor of Qin (*r.* 246–210 BC). By early 1996, more bronzes bearing the same line of inscription have surfaced in the markets outside China and six were purchased and subsequently published by the Shanghai Museum (Fig. 11.1). It was found that all of these bronzes had been looted from a single site in the southeastern corner of Gansu Province, and their discovery opened a new era in the study of Qin, the creator of China's first empire. Coupled with the early discovery of the world heritage site, the "Terracotta Warriors," and a series of other recent finds, we now have a completely new ground to reinterpret the early development of Qin and the rise of the Qin Empire.

The Early History of Qin: The Archaeological Search

Compared to many other regional states in eastern China founded by the Zhou royal house during the early Western Zhou (discussed in Chapters 8 and 9), Qin was a relatively young state, established during the mid Western Zhou period. In a fairly detailed account, the Han Dynasty

Fig. 11.1   *Ding*-vessel (h. 38.5 cm, diam. 37.8 cm) cast by an early Qin duke, possibly Duke Xiang (*r.* 777–766 BC).

historian Sima Qian tells of the genesis of Qin people.[1] The forerunner of Qin was called the "Daluo Lineage," which had double marriages with the state of Shen, a long-time ally of Zhou on its western border. However, because Feizi, a secondary son of Daluo and direct ancestor to Qin, won the favor of King Xiao of Zhou, the king entertained the idea of substituting him for the legitimate heir of the lineage (given birth by a lady from Shen), and this was reflected in the eyes of the leaders of the Zhou state as a policy that only could jeopardize the security of Zhou's western border. As a political compromise, King Xiao granted Feizi the settlement of Qin in eastern Gansu, and the state of Qin thus was born as a subject of Zhou. In the following decades, the mother Daluo lineage was much weakened in the face of invasion by its neighboring groups, particularly

---

[1]   Sima Qian, *The Grand Scribe's Records*, vol. 1, *The Basic Annals of Pre-Han China*, edited by William H. Nienhauser Jr. (Bloomington: Indiana University Press, 1994), p. 89.

the people called Rong that eventually annexed its territory in the Xihan River valley. However, with military aid from the Zhou royal court, the Qin people were able to heroically reclaim the land of Daluo by defeating the Rong people and thereupon moved their center there in the upper Xihan River valley in the early years of King Xuan of Zhou (Map 11.1).

This narrow valley, located on the fringe of the Qinghai–Tibet Plateau, was remote from the Zhou center in Shaanxi, but was one of the important passes into the Sichuan Basin from North China. There is no doubt that the early Qin bronzes and golden objects that appeared in New York and other markets originated from a cemetery just off the bank of the Xihan River, confirmed by archaeologists later in 1994. The original center of Qin, instead, was located some 100 km to the east in the upper Wei River valley, much closer to the central region of the Western Zhou state. Archaeological study of the local pottery tradition suggests that no matter what ethnic origin the Qin might have had,[2] they arose from a cultural environment that, at latest by the mid Western Zhou period, was heavily influenced by the Zhou material culture centered on central Shaanxi.[3]

However, the inability of the Zhou elites themselves to hold their own capitals in central Shaanxi by 771 BC had left the Qin people completely encircled by the various Rong groups. In the decades that followed the Zhou withdrawal from central Shaanxi, the Qin people had to fight very hard to resist pressures from these Rong people, and gradually moved their political center east to the homeland of the Zhou people, and this allowed them to maintain contact with the eastern states as well as the Zhou royal court relocated in Luoyang. A half century had passed after their historical move to Shaanxi in 763 BC as the Qin people struggled to conquer the numerous Rong polities established on the ruins of Zhou, expanding their control as far east as the confluence of the Yellow and Wei Rivers. Transferring the newly conquered lands into counties, the Qin gradually emerged as a new territorial state on the western highlands of China. The Qin capital Yong in western Shaanxi from 677 BC to 383 BC has yielded rich archaeological materials uncovered since the 1970s. Archaeologists have not only confirmed the location of the city-wall enclosure and a few important architectural foundations within it, but

---

[2] It should be noted that the recently published manuscripts from Qinghua University, dating to the Warring States period, include a document that traces the origin of the Qin people to Shang. This has encouraged some scholars to reactivate an old hypothesis that the ruling house of Qin was ethnically related to groups in eastern China. But it seems that this point will remain hypothetical indefinitely.

[3] See Li Feng, *Landscape and Power in Early China: The Crisis and Fall of the Western Zhou, 1045–771 BC* (Cambridge: Cambridge University Press, 2005), pp. 262–273.

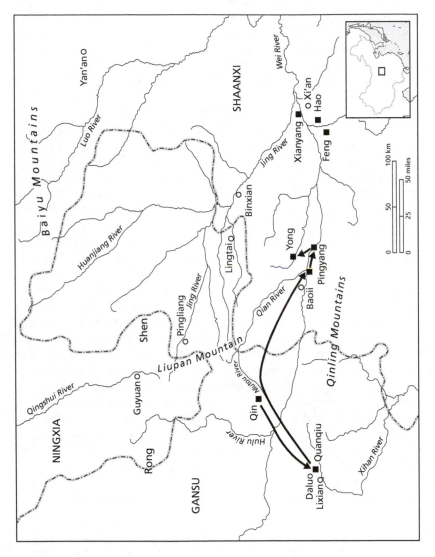

Map 11.1 Route of early Qin migration

Fig. 11.2 The excavation of tomb no. 1 in Fengxiang, possibly the grave of Duke Jing of Qin (576–537 BC). Above, archaeologists transporting wooden beams out of the tomb after excavation; below, bottom of the tomb with burial chambers of servants or concubines who accompanied the duke in death.

have also demarcated the cemetery of the Qin dukes including the largest and most well-known tomb no. 1, likely the burial place of Duke Jing of Qin (r. 576–537 BC), which archaeologists spent nearly ten years excavating during the 1980s (Fig. 11.2).

Politically, the Qin elites actively engaged in the affairs of the eastern plain and played an important role in installing Duke Wen of Jin to his home state, the future hegemonic Jin. However, in 629 BC, the army sent by Duke Mu of Qin (r. 659–621 BC) to attack the state of Zheng in the east was ambushed on their way home by the troops of Jin in the deep Xiao Mountains in western Henan where all Qin commanders on the campaign were captured. This serious military setback put a stop to Qin's growing ambition in the east, and the trend was not reversed until the ascendance of Duke Xian of Qin (r. 384–362 BC) in the early fourth century BC. Over the centuries, there had also developed in the Central Plain an elite culture that regarded the Qin people as culturally backward "barbarians." In the minds of these eastern elites, this anti-Qin sentiment could be fully justified with respect to the particular circumstances surrounding Qin's rise to power in the westernmost periphery of the Zhou realm, and even by the beginning of the Warring States period, Qin was still surrounded by the various groups of "barbarians" in western China.

However, the Qin elites clearly thought about themselves differently. They claimed to be the legitimate territorial heirs to the Zhou state to which Qin owed its political origin, and evidently the Qin dukes honored close contact with the Zhou court in Luoyang through diplomatic exchange and marriage. For instance, Duke Xian of Qin (r. 715–704 BC) took two wives from eastern China, the daughter of a Zhou king and the daughter of a ruler of the state of Lu in Shandong. This royal princess was politically very influential as evidenced by the bronze inscriptions.[4] The close tie with the Zhou royal house is also evident in the inscription engraved on a set of stone chimes excavated from tomb no. 1 mentioned above, which makes clear reference to the Son of Heaven (Zhou king) as the authority that was supposed to approve, doubtless only ritually, the succession of the Qin dukes. On the other hand, in early Qin ideology there was also a strong notion that the Qin were themselves recipients of Heaven's Mandate, thus their state has a cosmologically based legitimacy parallel to that of the Zhou. The inscription on a *gui*-tureen cast possibly by Duke Huan of Qin (r. 603–577 BC) says:[5]

The Duke of Qin said: "Greatly illustrious were my august ancestors; (they) received Heaven's Mandate and tranquilly dwelled in Yu's tracks. Twelve dukes

---

[4] She is the second voice speaking with authority in the inscription on a set of bronze bells cast by Duke Wu of Qin (697–678 BC), possibly her son. See Gilbert Mattos, "Eastern Zhou Bronze Inscriptions," in Edward L. Shaughnessy (ed.), *New Sources of Early Chinese History: An Introduction to the Reading of Inscriptions and Manuscripts* (Berkeley: Society for Study of Early China, 1997), pp. 111–114.

[5] Mattos, "Eastern Zhou Bronze Inscriptions," pp. 114–117.

are on God's mound (?). (They) reverently respected and revered Heaven's Mandate, protected and regulated their (state of) Qin, and vigilantly attended to the Man and the Xia...

Here, the duke of Qin claims that his ancestors received Heaven's Mandate to rule not only as successors to the Zhou, but as successors to the ancient legendary emperor Great Yu. It also mentions that Qin had vigilantly attended the affairs of both Xia, the Chinese world, and Man, the "barbarians." Given Qin's special location in the western periphery of the Zhou world, the inscription seems to explain well the cultural–political role of the early Qin state.

Shang Yang's Reform and the Reorganization of the Qin State

The reign of Duke Xian of Qin (r. 384–362 BC) saw the new trend of resurgence of Qin power. The duke himself spent thirty years in exile in the hegemonic state Wei and was quite impressed with Wei's reform and military accomplishments. Upon his return, Duke Xian prohibited the old Qin practice of burying companions in death and won wide support among the Qin populace. During his reign, the Qin also relocated their capital east in Yueyang to the north of present-day Xi'an and captured most parts of the land along the west bank of the Yellow River, turning them into new counties of the state. In 362 BC, the Qin struck east across the river and completely crushed the Wei army not far from its capital. The war virtually put a stop to Wei's hegemony and forced Wei to move its capital to eastern Henan only two years later (see Chapter 9).

However, what had really transformed Qin into a superpower and hence established the foundation for its future unification of China was a reform undertaken by the next ruler, Duke Xiao of Qin (r. 361–338 BC), with the Legalist hardliner Shang Yang (390–338 BC) as the chief engineer. Shang Yang was a descendant of the royal lineage of the state of Wey, and served in a minor office under the minister of the state of Wei who very much appreciated his talent. Tradition says that the same minister recommended Shang Yang to the Wei ruler as his successor and, when rejected, he then recommended Shang Yang's execution, but the Wei ruler did not listen to either suggestion. After the death of his patron, Shang Yang migrated to the state of Qin in the hope of gaining a better office under the new duke of Qin. Through the introduction of a servant, Shang Yang met with the ambitious young duke four times and finally succeeded in attracting him to his ideas of strengthening the Qin state through radical reform. Thus, the duke appointed Shang Yang

Chancellor of Qin and in the next twenty years, Qin carried out the most thorough political and social reform of the entire Warring States period.

The historical records on Shang Yang's reform are by no means systematic and some of the policies accredited to him might have been policies adopted by previous dukes long before Shang Yang's arrival on the scene. However, since his ideas are systematically expounded in the long text, the *Book of the Lord of Shang*, probably put together later by his followers, an outline of the reform can be learned without much difficulty.

Shang Yang began his reform by strengthening the social roots of the Qin state. A law announced in 356 BC after about three years of preparation required all peasant families be organized into "Five-Family Units," each with a head. The families were held mutually responsible for each other's conduct and for reporting any crimes committed in their area of residence. However, this corporate responsibility system was at the same time also a system of mutual assistance for if a family suffered a robbery the other four families were obliged to help if they heard the cry. New studies based on the Qin legal strips from Shuihudi in Hubei which include laws going back before the Qin conquest suggest that the head of a "Five-Family Unit" had more responsibilities as he would be held guilty in case of a crime regardless of whether he was home, while members of other families would not if they were not present.[6] The "Five-Family Units" were further linked to the state structure through the organization of *Li* (corresponding to natural village) and "District" (*Xiang*), although such larger units might have had a much longer history (Box 11.1).

On the top level of local administration was the "County" (*Xian*), the cells of the "Territorial State." Qin was well known for the early date of the establishment of counties in the early seventh century BC. The general scholarly consensus is that due to its history of migration and rapid territorial expansion in the seventh to sixth centuries BC, the Qin nobility was relatively underpowered (few of the Qin nobles are heard of in history) in comparison to those in the eastern states, and the Qin state had large portions of newly conquered lands under its control and leased lands to peasants living in the counties on short terms. No matter how developed the organization of the county was in the previous reigns, it was under Shang Yang's administration that the entire territory of Qin was organized

---

[6] See Robin D. S. Yates, "Social Status in the Ch'in: Evidence from the Yün-meng Legal Documents. Part One: Commoners," *Harvard Journal of Asiatic Studies* 47.1 (1987), 219–220; idem, "Cosmos, Central Authority, and Communities in the Early Chinese Empire," in Susan E. Alcock, Terence N. D'Altroy, Kathlean D. Morrison, and Carla M. Sinopoli (eds.), *Empire: Perspectives from Archaeology and History* (Cambridge: Cambridge University Press, 2001), pp. 636–637.

Box 11.1 Shuihudi and Qin Law

In December 1975, archaeologists from the Hubei Provincial Museum excavated twelve late Warring States to Qin tombs at Shuihudi in Yunmeng County. From tomb no. 11, 1,155 bamboo strips were excavated along with 75 other types of objects. The tomb was of rather modest size, but the writings on these strips, when fully published soon after the end of the Cultural Revolution, and made available in English by A. F. P. Hulsewé in 1985, opened a new era in the study of the Qin Empire, or in the study of legal history of China in general.

First of all, included in the materials is a chronicle which records the military advances of Qin from 306 BC to 217 BC, along with the personal history of Xi who had served as a legal officer in a number of counties in the jurisdiction of the South Commandery (present Hubei region) and died in the latter year or a year after at the age of 46, matching perfectly the physical age of the occupant of the tomb. The discovery of paramount importance is the eighteen articles of "Qin Legal Statutes," the only Qin legal codes that we know to date. Some well-known articles are the "Statutes on Land," "Statute on Inventory," "Statute on Labor Service," "Statute on Military Ranks," "Statute on Establishment of Offices," and "Statute on the Verification of Property," etc. Another important part of the material from Shuihudi is self-titled *Fengzhenshi*, which is composed of descriptions of legal procedures and legal case examples that might have served as a handbook for legal officers in the Qin Empire (Fig. 11.3). The sections on procedures describe rules with regard to interrogation (see example below), investigation, detainment, and report. Other materials from the tomb include a "Question/Answer"-style document explicating issues in Qin law, a document that states rules of official conduct, and an official statement issued by the governor of the South Commandery promoting the rule of law.

FENGZHENSHI:

Whenever questioning about a criminal case, always first listen to everything they say and write it down, each one laying out his statement. Even if you know they are lying, do not immediately question it. If, when the statement is completely written out, some matters are unexplained, only then question them with these questions. Question them completely, listening to and writing down the explanatory statement completely. Again look at those things not explained and question them about these. If the interrogation is done and they repeatedly deceive or change what they say and do not confess, or for those the statutes warrant beating, only then should you beat them. If you beat them, you must record it, saying in the report that because so-and-so changed his story repeatedly, or could not explain his statement, we beat and questioned him. (*Translation by Charles Sanft*)

Fig. 11.3   Terracotta statue of a civil/legal officer recently found in pit K0006 near the burial mound of the First Emperor of Qin. Right, statue no.1 (h. 189 cm); left, detail of representation of a knife and a bag hung from his waist in which is supposed to be placed a stone sharpener, essential accoutrements of a civil officer in Early China.

into some thirty-one (or forty-one) counties.[7] Through these reforms, the Qin state was thoroughly bureaucratized.

Not only was the entire population managed and controlled strictly through a pyramid structure of government, it was also subject to a universal ranking system. Certain terms and ranks existed before Shang Yang, but they were gathered into a single system only now. The system had some seventeen or eighteen levels, and the ranks were normally gained through military contributions – cutting off one enemy head brought a soldier the award of one rank along with the gift of one acre of land, and the right to use one government slave. Officials were rewarded on the number of heads taken by their subordinates. This practice subjected the entire population to a system of meritocracy that was designed to serve the purpose of war. There have been some doubts about the actual practice of the system because of the total number of heads hunted by the Qin army in the century before Qin conquest would have far exceeded the amount of land the Qin state could ever afford to reward its soldiers. It has also been pointed out by Robin Yates that the commoners could only reach degree eight, and a rank-holder could actually designate one of his heirs to inherit his title, implying that not everyone needed to start from the lowest degree.[8] The system could not be 100% fair, but it did grant the Qin state the best military power it could ever have.

Lands in Qin had been taxed since the time of Duke Jian in 408 BC, which is taken by some scholars as a sign of land privatization. In 350 BC, Shang Yang ordered the systematic destruction of the road grids on the state-owned lands, which were mostly re-demarcated as larger tracks to be given to individual families as private property. Certainly lands associated with ranks which soldiers received for their military contributions stayed as their family possessions. It is generally understood that from this time on, private land ownership was the norm in the state of Qin. In 348 BC, Qin is recorded as having imposed a poll tax for military purpose for the first time, separate from the land taxes that were collected according to the area of land a family possessed. Also, liable to such payment were merchants whose income did not come from land and landless farmers who had lost their lands. In order to keep the family size small so as to ensure the tax revenue due to the state, a law was issued that determined that a family with two adult males must be split or pay double the amount of the

[7] See Denis Twitchett and Michael Loewe (eds.), *The Cambridge History of China*, vol. 1, *The Ch'in and Han Empires, 221 BC – AD 220* (Cambridge: Cambridge University Press, 1987), p. 35 and n. 23.

[8] Yates, "Cosmos, Central Authority," p. 634.

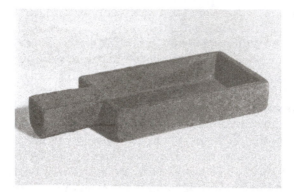

Fig. 11.4   Standard volume measurer commissioned by Shang Yang.

poll tax, and even a father could not live in the same household with his adult son of tax-liable age.

There were more specific measures such as the standardization of the units of length, weight, and volume used in the entire Qin state (Fig. 11.4), and more general guiding principles such as the discouragement of commercial activities and the equal application of punishment to all regardless of social status. As a part of the reform, in 349 BC, the Qin state began to construct a new capital on the north bank of the Wei River near present-day Xi'an and transferred its government there a few years later. Xianyang, this new site, then became the political center of Qin and the heart of the future empire.

The Han Dynasty historian Sima Qian remarked that in the first three years of the reform, Shang Yang's policies raised widespread discontent among both the old aristocrats and the commoners of Qin. After three years, the Qin people began to enjoy the new order and security brought about by the reform. Crime rates came down to the lowest level ever as the state's ruling apparatus was sufficiently improved. Shang Yang had rebuilt the state of Qin strictly along the Legalist path that aimed at strengthening the economic foundation of the state and promoted the rule of law. The reform served to transfer Qin into a new society that might have suddenly appeared dramatically different from the eastern states, causing them to denounce Qin as the "State of Tigers and Wolves."[9] However, when

[9] A recent study suggests that the reform of Shang Yang was responsible for the rise of a unique Qin "cultural identity," viewed both by others or the Qin elites themselves, as the single state beyond "All under Heaven." See Gideo Shelach and Yuri Pines, "Secondary State Formation and the Development of Local Identity: Change and Continuity in the State of Qin (770–221 B.C.)," in Miriam T. Stark (ed.), *Archaeology of Asia* (Malden: Blackwell, 2006), pp. 217–220.

Duke Xiao died in 338 BC, Shang Yang was accused of treason and was forced to rebel with a force he gathered from his own domain in Shang in southern Shaanxi. But he was instantly defeated and captured for execution with five chariots pulling him apart in the market of Xianyang.

Despite his disgraced fall at the hands of his political enemies, the policies implemented by Shang Yang over a course of some twenty years had taken deep roots in Qin society and political system, creating the foundation of the future Qin Empire. But more immediately, they had set Qin on a trend of rapid territorial growth in the century following Shang Yang, most importantly in two directions. To the south of Qin, the Sichuan Basin, rich in land and natural resources, was home to two indigenous polities, Shu and Ba. In the early fourth century BC, Shu extended its control north into the Han River valley. When war broke out between Shu and Ba in 316 BC, both states pleaded to Qin for help. Qin thus sent troops across the difficult Qinling Mountains, first conquering Shu, and then Ba. In the forty years after the conquest, Qin translocated 10,000 families from Shaanxi into the Sichuan Basin, building the region into a firm economic base for Qin's future success. The conquest of Shu and Ba not only expanded Qin territory to southwestern China, but also cast new pressures on the state of Chu from the west. In 278 BC, even the capital of Chu in present-day Jiangling was occupied by Qin troops that took the entire middle Yangzi River region under Qin control. In the north, Yiqu was a Rong state with some two dozen walled towns in the upper Jing River region to the north of Qin.[10] For centuries, Yiqu had played diplomacy between Qin and its eastern enemies, and had taken advantage of Qin's military setback to inflect further defeat on Qin. In 272 BC, the queen mother of Qin, who had been having affairs for years with the king of Yiqu, arranged his assassination in her harem, and this was followed by an overwhelming Qin attack to conquer Yiqu. The victory was very important because it enabled the Qin to occupy all of eastern Gansu and southern Ningxia, making a firm first step for incursion onto the northern steppe. In order to fend off the nomadic people on the steppe, Qin constructed a long wall stretching from the Liupan Mountains in southern Ningxia to the Hengshan Mountains in northern Shaanxi (see Fig. 9.1 above). The complete triumph of Qin power in the century following Shang Yang's fall fully proved the effectiveness of the policies he had implemented in Qin.

---

[10] Culturally Yiqu might have been closely related to the pre-existing Siwa culture in the upper Jing River region predating the Warring States; see Li, *Landscape and Power in Early China*, pp. 175–179.

The First Emperor and the Unification of China

Ying Zheng (259–210 BC), the future First Emperor of China, arrived on the scene in a time when Qin was already an indisputable superpower. The continuing growth of Qin in the preceding decades would have given everyone a sure answer – if China were ever to be unified, it was most likely that Qin would be the one to do the job. The fear for Qin power spread even farther and deeper after the battle at Changping in 260 BC, where as many as 400,000 soldiers from the state of Zhao were captured and reportedly buried alive on the order of the famous Qin general Bai Qi. Bai Qi, who had ruined the capital of Chu a decade earlier, typified the Qin use of terrorism to crush the confidence of the eastern states. Although the eastern states joined their forces to impede Qin power in 257 BC when the Qin armies attacked Zhao's capital Handan, they could not overturn the historical trend.

Ying Zheng was born in the capital of Zhao where his father lived in diplomatic captivity. In danger of being executed by Zhao with whom Qin was in constant war, the poor Qin prince met a rich merchant named Lü Buwei who was willing to invest in the prince for his own political future. It was told by Sima Qian that Lü had even yielded to the Qin prince his beloved concubine, and at that point she was already pregnant and afterward gave birth to Ying Zheng. In 250 BC, Merchant Lü eventually arranged for the return of the prince to Qin where he was established as King Zhuangxiang of Qin (*r.* 249–247 BC). But he died only three years later, leaving Ying Zheng to rule as king at the age of thirteen. Merchant Lü thus assumed the position of Grand Chancellor and became the most politically prominent figure at the Qin court. As the story continues to unfold, Merchant Lü now had everything under his control, met with the queen mother regularly and resumed their sexual relationship. However, as the young king was growing up, Merchant Lü gradually became scared by his own conduct. In order to pull himself out of the relationship, he introduced Lao-ai, a person of low status, to serve the queen mother's sexual desire. In order to hide from the young king, the secret couple moved their residence to the old Qin capital Yong, where the queen mother got pregnant by Lao-ai and gave birth to two sons. The secret was finally discovered in 235 BC when the king was twenty-four, and Lao-ai was captured for execution, and the Grand Chancellor Lü, because of his connection to Lao-ai, was ordered to commit suicide three years later.

Seemingly a palace incident, the event of 235 BC indeed put Ying Zheng to the center of Qin power at a young age with full control over the fiercest military machine in all of China. Due to the strange background of his childhood, Ying Zheng was naturally cruel, suspicious,

Fig. 11.5   A modern portrait of Ying Zheng as the First Emperor of Qin.

lacking affection, and willing to take risks. But he was also capable of good judgment, enterprising, and determined to pursue his goals (Fig 11.5). In fact, we are unusually fortunate to have a contemporary eyewitness, Wei Liao, a military strategist and the future Commandant of the Qin army, who, after his first audience with the young king, remarked on the king's personal character with the following words:

The king of Ch'in [Qin] was born with a prominent nose, elongated eyes, the breast of a bird of prey, and the voice of a jackal; he seldom extends favor and has the heart of a tiger or wolf. When in straits, he can submit to others, but when he has his way, he can easily eat you alive. I am a commoner. Nevertheless, when he received me, he always humbles himself before me. Once he really has his way in the world, the whole world will be held captive by him.[11]

[11] Sima Qian, *The Grand Scribe's Records*, vol. 1, p. 131.

The event of 235 BC had also provided a chance for Ying Zheng to reorganize the Qin government, readying it for the final conquest of China. Wei Liao was appointed Commandant and advised the king on military strategies. Among his advisors was also a hardliner Legalist named Li Si, recommended to the king by the Grand Chancellor Lü Buwei earlier. Li Si was a classmate of the Legalist theorist Han Fei, whom he advised the king to keep in Qin and then to execute. He and Wei Liao together helped the king of Qin to engineer the unification of China.

The program of final unification of China was carried out in 230 BC, only five years after Ying Zheng took power, when the Qin troops struck east, first conquering the weakest state Hann as a strategy to terrify other states. In 229 BC, General Wang Jian led the Qin troops on a march north into the Zhao territory and laid siege to the Zhao capital Handan; the following year, Wang Jian's troops captured the Zhao king and occupied the entire Zhao territory which was made a base for the conquest of Yan farther north. Fearing the inevitable fate of Yan, Prince Dan of Yan devised a plan in the last hope of stoping Qin's conquest campaign by sending the warrior Jing Ke to the Qin court in Xianyang where, witnessed by the high officials of this most powerful state, he attempted the assassination of Ying Zheng, the future First Emperor of China.

The Han historian Sima Qian narrates in detail the admirable warrior and his suicidal attack on the king of Qin. Jing Ke was a native of Wey who loved books and music in addition to the life of a swordsman. Prince Dan of Yan first discussed his plan with a respected old warrior of Yan named Tian Guang, patron to Jing Ke, to whom the prince requested the concealment of the secret. Considering himself too old to carry out the plan, Tian Guang committed suicide to demonstrate his determination and recommended Jing Ke to fulfill the mission. Arriving in the Qin capital with two presents for Qin, the head of a defected Qin general whom the king hated most and a territorial map of Yan important for Qin's upcoming campaign, Jing Ke was soon invited to an audience with the king. As the scroll of the map became fully revealed in front of the king Jing Ke suddenly took up the poisoned short sword there and stabbed the king seated across the table. Having survived the first strike the king of Qin stood up and fled around the pillars, chased by the assassin, but no official or the royal guards could come to the king's rescue (see Fig. 14.4 below). They could act only on the king's order which he was too busy to give. But it was fortunate for the king that his doctor happened to pass behind the scene and quickly threw his medical box right at the head of Jing Ke. This moment allowed the king to pull out his long sword and cut the assassin into pieces.

This was certainly one of the most breathtaking moments in ancient China, which could have effectively reversed the course of Chinese history.

As the assassination failed, the Qin troops moved north swiftly in 226 BC and completely crushed the Yan army and captured Prince Dan. With the land to the north of the Yellow River completely pacified, the Qin troops soon descended on the state of Wei and laid siege to its capital Daliang, where a century earlier Mencius had discussed philosophy with King Hui of Liang. In order to subjugate the enemy the Qin broke the bank of the Yellow River and flooded the Wei capital. The king of Wei saw no hope but to leave the capital and surrender to the Qin army. Now with most part of the Central Plain under control, in 224 BC, Ying Zheng sent the old general Wang Jian to take more than half of the entire Qin military forces south to conquer the vast and marshy territory of Chu. The next year, the Qin troops captured the last Chu king and forced his supreme commander into suicide. Finally, in 221 BC, the Qin troops crossed the Yellow River from the north and occupied the state of Qi, the last of the warring states except Qin.

One is only left to wonder why these states that had coexisted for more than five hundred years in an inter-state system marked by war and balance, or eight hundred years if counting from their establishment in the early Western Zhou, could suddenly be altogether destroyed by the single state Qin in only nine years. This was doubtless one of the most dramatic epics in human history and the most thorough change in the political landscape of Early China. The political and military preparation that Qin had undergone in the previous decades was key to its eventual success. But the political vision and determination of Ying Zheng, and the effectiveness with which his officials executed their jobs were also critical to ensuring a process that could not be reversed. After more than five centuries of political fragmentation and incessant warfare, China was finally brought under one power, the Qin Empire.

The Consolidation of the Qin Empire

Although the term "Empire" was derived from the Roman *imperium* with a semantic history usually traced through the European and Mediterranean experience, few have ever doubted that Qin China, brought about through conquest by Ying Zheng, would qualify as an empire.[12] And although scholars have had a hard time agreeing on a definition of "Empire," there are factors that seem to be common to most if not all empires understood as super social–political organizations – immense territorial size, a high degree of heterogeneity in terms of population and culture, absolute power invested in one hand (usually the emperor), a unitary political–

---

[12] See Alcock *et al.* (eds.), *Empire: Perspectives from Archaeology and History*, pp. 1–3.

administrative order to achieve direct rule, a history of conquest, and perhaps more importantly, an imperial ideology. The Qin Empire typified the organization of empire in all of these aspects.

The Qin Empire, as we have learned above, was the enlargement of a "Territorial State" through expansion over a century during which lands were added to its state core piece by piece. At the death of the First Emperor, the Qin Empire not only ruled the lands and populations of the six former territorial states, but had come to rule areas to the south of the Nanling Mountains inhabited by the various Yue groups, the Liaodong Peninsula in the east inhabited by the proto-Goguryo groups, and the Ordos Plateau in the north, the former base of the Xiongnu nomads.[13] The empire was, at least in the north, demarcated through the construction of the Great Wall which was partly rebuilt and partly connected the pre-existing walls of such northern states as Zhao, Yan, and Qin itself (Map 11.2). The complete wall runs 4,160 km from the mouth of the Yalu River to Longxi in the upper Wei River valley in southeastern Gansu, and it must have cost tremendous manpower. It thus was perceived by later historians as a source of resentment of Qin's harsh rule. Within the empire, a complex road system which had an accumulated length of some 6,800 km was constructed and was further integrated with the river system to connect the capital with the central city of every commandery. The most important was a superhighway called "Straight Road" which ran 800 km along the Ziwu Mountain ridge in north Shaanxi (Fig. 11.6), with various postal and military facilities built along it, connecting the Qin capital with the Ordos Plateau, the base of as many as 300,000 troops under command by the general Meng Tian.[14] The foundation of the road can still be seen even in modern times, and has been under archaeological investigation in recent years. Throughout the empire, all chariot axles were made to match the standard length of Qin in order to run on the empire's highway system.

In the process of Qin expansion, the administrative level of "Commandery" (*Jun*) was created in regions close to the front line so as to convene military coordination and to draw on local resources. After the conquest, the entire empire was divided into thirty-six commanderies. In this way the structure was transferred into a system of civil administration. The commanderies had under their jurisdictions as many as 900 counties of which about 300 are known by their names, according to a modern study. Each commandery was governed through a triumvirate structure comprising a Protector, a Commandant, and an Inspector. All counties were governed

---

[13] Twitchett and Loewe (eds.), *The Cambridge History of China*, vol. 1, pp. 64–67.

[14] *Ibid.*, pp. 61–62; for a map of the Qin road system, see Mark Lewis, *The Early Chinese Empires: Qin and Han* (Cambridge, MA: Belknap Press of Harvard University Press, 2007), p. 56.

Map 11.2   The Qin Empire

Fig. 11.6   The "Straight Road" of Qin in Fuxian, northern Shaanxi (arrow: excavation trenches, 2007).

by a Magistrate, assisted by a Secretary and a Commander in civil and military matters respectively. All of these officials were appointed at the imperial court in Xianyang and paid from the imperial treasury, and could be removed anytime on order of the central government. Clerks and minor officers in the county level and below, e.g. district and village, were in principle appointed locally. Further studies based on the legal strips from Shuihudi show that standard procedures were developed to govern the process of appointment and dismissal, as officials were strictly prohibited from stepping into a matter without an official appointment and, when facing a transfer, from bringing their assistants and scribes to the new post.[15] The Qin Empire was ruled through a carefully designed and closely supervised bureaucracy in which none was related to others or to the emperor in any other way except through the bureaucratic machine.

The unitary administrative order was also achieved through a series of policies that mandated standardization. This included first of all the issuing of standard units of length, weight, and volume necessary for the calculation of taxes throughout the empire and rations for its frontier armies as well as

---

[15] See Robin D. S. Yates, "State Control of Bureaucrats under the Qin: Techniques and Procedures," *Early China* **20** (1995), 342–346.

payment for officials. Such standardization had already been carried out in the time of Shang Yang's reform, but it was significant to expand the system over the whole empire. Old currencies used in the six eastern states before the Qin conquest were all destroyed, and the Qin currency was adopted for use in the whole empire. Most importantly, the unification of the writing system was attempted. Over the centuries after the fall of the Western Zhou state, the Zhou scripts had been variously modified, giving rise to the unique writing systems in the six states. The Qin Empire did not immediately implement their pre-conquest Small Seal scripts to the whole empire, but had its high official Li Si supervise the modification of them into a new system of writing, the Clerical Script, which featured more straight lines and allowed sharp turns, which made them much easier to write. While the pre-conquest Qin scripts continued to be used on monuments such as the stele inscriptions on the various famous mountains in the east whose creation were commissioned by the First Emperor, the new scripts were adopted as standards for government paperwork as well as registrations of the population. We do not know how fast or how thoroughly the Qin writing system had replaced the traditional regional writings in every corner of the empire, but the adherence to a single system of writing must have significantly improved the administrative efficiency of the empire. In fact, the new materials from Liye in Hunan show that even the transition from Small Seal to Cleric Scripts was probably a very mixed process.[16]

As pointed out by Robin Yates, the Qin Empire, or the Chinese empires in general, claimed to rule not on the basis of the concept of sovereignty, but on the personal dignity of the emperor and legitimacy of his patrilineal ancestral line.[17] The concept of "citizenship" had never been developed in Chinese civilization until modern times, and the pre-modern empire was essentially identified with dynasty, in sharp contrast to the Roman Empire which continued to flourish for centuries as the imperial throne traveled from one family to another. Therefore, the institution of emperor had a special meaning in China as the repository of imperial legitimacy. As soon as the unification was achieved, Ying Zheng adopted the deifying title *Huangdi* which combines the terms *huang*, "Mythical Ruler," and *di*, "God," although we conventionally translate it as "Emperor," which stressed instead his secular rule. Thus, certain words such as the first personal *zhen* (I) was strictly reserved for use by the emperor; *zhi* (edict) referred to orders originated

---

[16] In 2002, some 36,000 wooden strips were found in a well filled as deep as 15 m in Liye in western Hunan. The documents were part of the official archive of Qianling Country of Dongting Commandery of Qin, dating between 222 BC and 208 BC. They are the most important contemporaneous records of local administration of the Qin Empire.

[17] Yates, "Cosmos, Central Authority," p. 627.

from the emperor, and *xi* (stamp) referred to the seal the emperor used to sanction orders. On the other hand, the emperor's personal name was to be avoided by everyone in any public or private documents. The emperor dressed differently from all other people, and must also have eaten differently from all others. Furthermore, advised by a magician named Lu Sheng, the emperor adopted a strategy of deliberate secrecy. He traveled in tunnels and lived in hidden places, a condition said to be necessary for his intercourse with the immortals, and would execute anyone who exposed his location. By living as a ghost or shadow, the First Emperor purposely distanced himself from all humans who were basically his slaves.

The First Emperor ruled for eleven years during which he had six major tours through the many distant parts of his empire. He climbed most of the famous mountains in eastern China, offered sacrifices to Heaven, and erected inscriptions to commemorate the accomplishment of the empire and his own virtue. Six of these inscriptions were copied by Sima Qian into his *The Grand Scribe's Records*.[18] The imperial armies continued to win victories on the borders. In the north, General Meng Tian was sent with a force of 300,000 soldiers to attack the Xiongnu and drove the nomads out of this vast grassland at the north bend of the Yellow River. The Qin troops subsequently constructed a new section of the Great Wall to protect the conquered land which was made a new commandery with more than thirty counties under its control. In 211 BC, the Qin court transferred 30,000 households from central China to fill these northern counties. Even the crown prince Fu Su was sent north to assist Meng Tian to manage frontier affairs after a quarrel he had with his father. In the south, as soon as the conquest of central China was completed in 221 BC, the Qin Empire massed a huge invasion force of 500,000 soldiers, striking over the Nanling Mountains in five roads on a front stretching from Fujian all the way west to Guangxi. In order to support the two western divisions which aimed to conquer the present-day Guangxi region, the Qin Empire moved workers and engineers to open a canal to link the Yangzi River system with the Li River which flows south. By 214 BC, the Qin armies captured most areas in Fujian, Guangdong, and Guangxi Provinces, lands previously inhabited by the hundred Yue people, thus expanding the empire to the shore of the South China Sea.

Bringing the Empire to Afterlife

The First Emperor thus gained control over almost everything that he could possibly reach, except for his own destiny as a human being, a fact that he

---

[18] See Martin Kern, *The Stele Inscriptions of Ch'in Shih-huang: Text and Ritual in Early Chinese Imperial Representation* (New Haven: American Oriental Society, 2000), pp. 1–2.

tried very hard to deny. Facing the coming of old age, his strategy was twofold: on the one hand, he tried every means to stay in this world; on the other, he prepared to bring the empire to the afterworld which he could continue to rule. For years, the emperor entertained the dream of longevity by repeatedly sending magicians or occult specialists onto the high sea to seek herbs for immortality from such mythical islands as Penglai, and by holding personal sacrifices to the eight spirits worshipped previously in the state of Qi on the mountains in eastern Shangdong. He had also personally sailed on the high sea along the coast of the Shandong Peninsula in the hope of a spiritual encounter with the immortals. Failing to deliver herbs for immortality, some of the occult specialists such as Xu Fu simply fled overseas with rich provisions given by the emperor including reportedly hundreds of young boys and girls in his company.

However, when the emperor adopted the title "First Emperor," he must have envisioned a day when he could no longer rule and when the imperial throne would be passed on to the second emperor. With his time limited in this world, the emperor carefully planned to rule in the underworld. As soon as the unification was achieved, he commissioned 700,000 workers including many convicts to construct his eternal world at the foot of Lishan Mountain, some 40 km east of Xianyang, and the resulting underground complex, continuously excavated by archaeologists since the discovery of the terracotta army in the 1970s, is now counted among the seven wonders of the world (Fig. 11.7). Behind this huge project was of course the idea that the emperor's rule cannot simply end; it must continue into the afterlife and this can be facilitated through replicating as many features as possible from the life he used to live. In the past ten years, archaeologists in Shaanxi have made important progress in understanding the organization of this immense underground complex.[19]

At the center of the Lishan complex are two concentric walled enclosures. In the southern part of the inner precinct is the huge mound of 500 m on each side, sitting above the emperor's burial chamber which was intended as his living quarters, but the internal condition of the pit is still unknown. Located immediately at the north edge of the burial mound is what the archaeologists call the "Retiring Hall" which is a platform of approximately 60 m surrounded by corridors, a place where the emperor was supposed to retire to from his public life which should take place probably in the main chamber (Fig 11.8). In the back (west) of the mound, a number of structures have been found including a pit containing the well-known bronze chariot drawn by four horses, which the

[19] See Jane Portal (ed.), *The First Emperor: China's Terracotta Army* (Cambridge, MA: Harvard University Press, 2006) pp. 117–145.

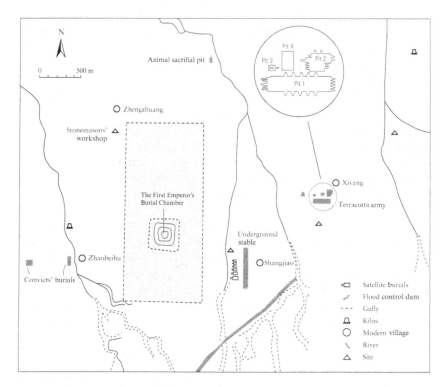

Fig. 11.7   The Lishan complex.

emperor would use on trips away from his underground palace. In the
northwest part of the inner precinct, four building foundations were found
arranged in a line covering an area measuring 600 m N–S and 200 m on
W–E. These were the temples where sacrifice was to be offered to nourish
the underground emperor. To the east of this area which actually forms a
smaller enclosure itself some thirty-four middle- or small-size tombs were
excavated, representing the minor officers and servants who once had
probably worked in the palace.

The outer precinct, which measures 971 m on W–E and 2188 m N–S, is
the site for a number of interesting features. Along the west wall from
north to south are located the site of an administrative building, and a site
that the archaeologists identified as the *Yigong*, grand inventory of food
supplies, based on inscriptions on the pottery jars excavated. Further
south across the west gateway of the city, two facilities were found: an
imperial stable where horses were buried together with miniature kneeling
human figurines of caretakers supplied with large plates, and a structure

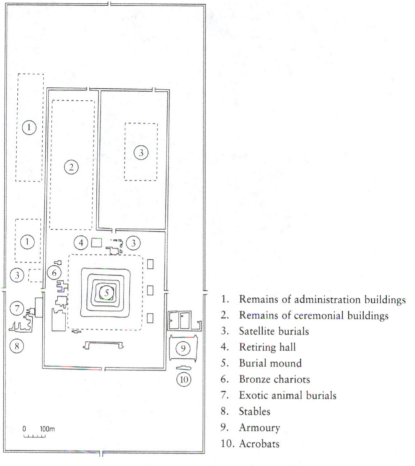

1. Remains of administration buildings
2. Remains of ceremonial buildings
3. Satellite burials
4. Retiring hall
5. Burial mound
6. Bronze chariots
7. Exotic animal burials
8. Stables
9. Armoury
10. Acrobats

Fig. 11.8   The underground city of the First Emperor.

filled with small pottery coffins that contain various birds and animals carefully selected from the imperial hunting park. Along the east wall, a large underground structure of 100×130 m is found, replicating the imperial armory, from which hundreds of sets of stone-made armor were excavated, representing different ranks in the Qin military. To the south of the armory is located the burial of an acrobat with a large number of terracotta figurines imitating the gestures of their performance for the amusement of the emperor. In addition, in 2001 a unique structure was found about 900 m from the northeast corner of the outer wall. The structure was actually an underground river system in F-shape,

Fig. 11.9   Bronze crane from the underground river constructed for the
First Emperor, to the north of his main burial mound.

continuing for about 60 m N–S, and was located close to a fish pond that
the archaeologists believe to have been in use as early as the First
Emperor's time. On the underground banks of the river, as many as
twenty swans, six cranes, and twenty wild geese, all in bronze, were
found in the company of a few human figurines (Fig. 11.9).

The various sites and objects from the complex suggest that the officials
who designed the Lishan project were careful to take into consideration
every need of the emperor and every public and private function he might
take charge of in his afterlife. They replicated not only his living quarters
and his servants, but also the natural features such as a river for him to bring
to the other world. One thing that was not included in the design of the
underground city was his army – these are found about 1 km to the east of
the city. To the south of the modern village called Xiyang, an estimated
total of 7,000 life-size terracotta warriors along with 600 terracotta horses
were found in four pits, covering a total area of more than 21,700 m^2. Pit
no. 1, from which as many as 6,000 individual warriors and horses were
excavated, is the main formation of the army and it combines infantry and
chariotry in eleven rows (Fig. 11.10). Pit no. 2 contains 2,000 warriors

Fig. 11.10   The terracotta army of the First Emperor, pit no. 1.

and horses in L-shape and their position in the formation is still debated. Pit no. 3, in U-shape, judged from the weapons and styles of the chariots, is apparently the commander headquarters of the whole formation.

Scholars have long debated the meaning of the terracotta army buried outside of the east gate of the First Emperor's underground city. But whether they represented the army the king of Qin sent to conquer the six eastern states, or the army the First Emperor brought with him on his tours to the east, or they replicated a selection of soldiers from all over China, as variously suggested by scholars, they were a source powerful enough to terrify enemies who would dare to stand in the way of the First Emperor, whether he was alive, or beyond life.

Regarding the First Emperor himself, much of what later generations know came through the lens of the historiography of the Han Empire which perceived itself as the enemy of the Qin Empire. There is the possibility that the First Emperor might not have been as vicious and ruthless as the Han sources have us believe. He was a great inventor of institutions and one who had the courage to test the power of the empire to its extreme. The empire he left behind provided the model for all later Chinese dynasties. But much of what the Han historians said about the

First Emperor was underscored by the fact that no matter how great the empire was it lasted only fifteen years. Thus, one wonders whether, had the First Emperor not brought the state of Qin to its conquest of all others, it might have lasted much longer indeed, as probably would all other states which Qin victimized.

SELECTED READING

Twitchett, Denis, and Michael Loewe (eds.), *Cambridge History of China*, vol. 1 *The Chi'in and Han Empires, 221 BC–AD 220* (Cambridge: Cambridge University Press, 1987), Introduction and Chapter 1, pp. 1–102.

Li, Feng, *Landscape and Power in Early China: The Crisis and Fall of the Western Zhou, 1045–771 BC* (Cambridge: Cambridge University Press, 2005), Chapter 5, pp. 233–78.

Portal, Jane (ed.), *The First Emperor: China's Terracotta Army* (Cambridge, MA: Harvard University Press, 2006).

Lewis, Mark, *The Early Chinese Empire: Qin and Han* (Cambridge, MA: Belknap Press of Harvard University Press, 2007).

Kern, Martin, *The Stele Inscriptions of Ch'in Shih-huang: Text and Ritual in Early Chinese Imperial Representation* (New Haven: American Oriental Society, 2000).

Loewe, Michael, *The Government of the Qin and Han Empires, 221 BCE–220 CE* (Indianapolis: Hackett, 2006).

12   Expansion and political transition
   of the Han Empire

If one is puzzled by the fact that the once great Qin Empire collapsed only fifteen years after it unified China, he is then bound to wonder why the once seemingly weak Han Empire lasted so long. The 411 years of the Han Dynasty, divided nearly equally into two halves by the reign (dynasty) of the usurper Wang Mang from AD 9 to 23, constituted a period of paramount importance in Chinese history and in the process of China's formation as a nation. This pattern of historical development that a short-lived dynasty was taken over by a long-lasting dynasty in which many of the former's inventions went through significant modifications is itself very interesting – it was repeated by the transition from Sui to the Tang Empire (AD 618–907). The Han Dynasty was both militant and culturally inspired, and its remarkable success instilled in China a deep sense of legitimacy granted to the imperial bureaucratic state backed by Confucian ideology. Particularly what happened between Han and the Xiongnu Empire in the second to first century BC was the struggle between two great empires using their full strength that occupied an important position in the world's military history. The victory the Han Empire was able to consolidate through a series of difficult engagements led it to pursue expansionist goals in regions far from the Han borders. Consequently the Han Dynasty was also a time of great geographical discovery as Han envoys reached nations and tribes in central and western Asia, where the West and the East first truly entered each other's sight. The discussion below of the Han Dynasty is divided into three parts: Chapter 12 reviews the political and military development under the Han Empire; Chapter 13 will discuss the internal organization and social orders of the Han Empire; the final chapter will analyze Han intellectual trends and highlight the splendors of Han material culture.

The Founding of the Han Dynasty

The First Emperor of Qin died in summer 210 BC, only eleven years after he unified China; in fact, he died on his last tour through the empire in eastern China, a thousand miles away from the capital. It was said that in order to disguise the odor of the imperial corpse to conceal his death, officials in his entourage decided to fill up ten carts with fish and carried the emperor back to the Wei River valley. In the process, they forged the emperor's letter in which he allegedly demanded the crown prince Fu Su, stationed for years on the northern border, to commit suicide, which he did, and upon arriving in Xianyang they established his younger son as the second emperor. But the people's fear for this vicious and godlike figure was finally gone.

In the summer of 209 BC, a group of 900 conscripts were marching north to guard the border. When they arrived in northern Jiangsu, formerly Chu territory before the unification, heavy rain delayed their movement and made it impossible for them to reach the guard posts on time; failing to do so would lead to capital punishment according to Qin law. Thus, Chen Sheng, leader of the group, forged highly provocative signs by putting a fabric written with words into the stomach of a fish which revealed Chen Sheng's kingship and by making someone scream in the bush in the voice of a fox: "The Great Chu will be restored, and Chen Sheng is our king!" Instantly, they killed the Qin officers watching them and attacked the county towns nearby. From northern Jiangsu, the rebels moved west into southern Henan where they declared the founding of a new Chu kingdom. By early winter when they attacked the Wei River valley, more than 10,000 farmers had joined them. For Chen Sheng, the goal was clearly to overthrow the Qin Empire, and indeed the empire itself opened ways for him to do so, for most of its legions were either stationed along the northern border or far in the south engaging in operations aimed at controlling the southeast China coast. With no time to pull these troops back, the Qin court armed the slaves and laborers working on the First Emperor's mausoleum and sent them to counter-attack the rebels. Chen Sheng's army was defeated about 60 km from the Qin capital and subsequently withdrew from the Wei River valley.

However, the Qin Empire survived this first blow only to meet more serious challenges – by early 208 BC, half the world had rebelled against Qin. These new rebels, all in eastern China, were composed of people of various social backgrounds. Some of them were farmers or local clerks at most, but many had real connections to the ruling houses of the former territorial states conquered by Qin. In fact, all of them rebelled in the name of the former kings but none of these could alone withstand the might of the Qin forces when they were remustered and put in field by the Qin court. After many defeats, the various rebel groups gradually merged into two stronger military forces, the first led by the former Chu general Xiang Liang and his nephew Xiang Yu who restored the Chu kingdom, and the second by Liu Bang, a county clerk from northern Jiangsu who had no significant family background. The armies were jointly defeated in a military catastrophe in western Shandong during which even Xiang Liang himself was killed by Qin troops.

However, when the Qin army then turned north to attack the restored kingdom of Zhao in Hebei, the defeated eastern rebels developed a clever strategy by sending the main body of the army led by Xiang Yu north to meet the enemy again at the Zhao capital, and at the same time sending a flank attack, led by Liu Bang, directly to the Qin heartland – the Wei River valley. Liu Bang was also aided by the cunning decision not to confront the Qin troops along the main roads through western Henan; instead, as totally unexpected by the Qin court, he traversed the Han River valley from Hubei and suddenly broke into the Wei River valley from the south. When Liu Bang arrived at the Qin capital in the tenth month of 206 BC, the last Qin emperor did not even put him up for battle but instantly surrendered to Liu Bang, putting a sudden end to the Qin Empire.

When Xiang Yu, the hero with unmatched muscle strength and an imposing personality, arrived in the Wei River valley after having crushed the Qin army near Zhao, he executed the Qin Emperor and carried out systematic destruction of the Qin capital, extending the damage probably to the accessible structures around the First Emperor's tomb, as archaeological evidence suggests. Furthermore, he decided to completely slice up the Qin Empire into eighteen independent kingdoms, all using state names of the pre-unification period; Xiang Yu himself then assumed the title of the "Hegemon King" and at the same time set himself up as the king of Chu. Liu Bang, because he had no connection to the Warring State kings, was given the Han River valley to rule as the "King of Han," locked deeply in the mountains of southern Shaanxi and cut off from all other kingdoms in eastern China. Xiang Yu's intention was clearly to prevent Liu becoming a major power to challenge his hegemony in the east.

However, Liu Bang succeeded in turning this strategy designed to contain him into the concealment of his real ambition – only four months after Xiang Yu returned to the east, Liu Bang's army suddenly broke into the Wei River valley, defeating all three local kings set up by Xiang Yu, and annexing the entire Wei River plain as his new base. In the next three years, China was virtually divided between two military camps with Liu Bang based on the Wei River plain in the west, and Xiang Yu centering on present-day northern Jiangsu. This was a long and difficult war for both sides. With continuing reinforcements sent by his able administers from the Wei River valley, Liu Bang eventually proved to be the more effective, and he forced Xiang Yu, the "Hegemon King," into suicide after a decisive defeat in northern Anhui in the twelfth month of 202 BC which left the latter with totally no chance for recovery. Thereupon, Liu Bang returned to the west and formally assumed the title "Emperor" of the Han Dynasty, posthumously called "Emperor Gaozu."

The Pivot of the Imperial Structure: Reorganizing the Empire

The heart of the empire was the Wei River valley again, where a new capital was constructed and named Chang'an, "Forever Peace" (Fig. 12.1). It was said that the layout of the imperial city embodied the formation of the constellation of the Northern Dipper with its stars falling exactly at the joints of walls of the city. However, studies show that the city was by no means a one-time project; therefore, there was little chance for it to have encoded a cosmological meaning in its general planning.[1] During Liu Bang's reign, only two major palace complexes in addition to the Armory located between them were constructed, each being surrounded by a walled enclosure. The outer wall of Chang'an was added during Emperor Hui's reign, and more units of construction were added even later, during the long reign of Emperor Wu, thus making up nearly 100 years of history of the construction of the imperial city. It was strictly an imperial city because almost the entire area was taken up by units of palatial architecture, allowing little space for residences outside the emperor's own home.[2]

However, beyond the imperial capital, the Han Empire was hardly a unified empire, not at least for its first half century. Side by side with the commanderies and counties located in the west centered on the Wei River valley, a state structure inherited from Qin, there were multiple kingdoms ruled by hereditary kings in the east, together taking up the larger half of the Han Empire (Map 12.1). This was certainly an institutional contradiction that had its historical origin in the previous age and which the Han had to work hard to overcome. This struggle between regionalism and centralization had profoundly influenced dynastic policies and guided the course of Chinese history.

In front of the Han emperor, there were two paradigms, that of Zhou and that of Qin. In the special historical context of the early Western Zhou, the "Fengjian" system implemented by the Zhou court was inevitable if the Zhou were to control a large geographical area such as the

---

[1] See Wu Hung, "The Monumental City Chang'an," in *Monumentality in Early Chinese Art and Architecture* (Stanford: Stanford University Press, 1995), pp. 143–187.

[2] On the archaeology of the imperial city Chang'an, see Wang Zhongshu, *Han Civilization* (New Haven: Yale University Press, 1982), pp. 1–10.

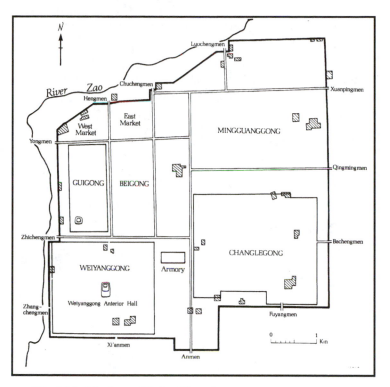

Fig. 12.1 The imperial city Chang'an.

middle and lower reaches of the Yellow River combined in an age when the imperial bureaucratic machine had not been invented, and it was indeed a great success. However, from the mid Western Zhou period, the system began to show its loose ends and the incessant wars in the 500 years after the fall of the Western Zhou capital completely destroyed the hope for political unity that the "Fengjian" system was designed to achieve. The Qin imperial system was created clearly with the Zhou model as its reference, and indeed as the remedy to Zhou problems, by putting all power in the single hand of the emperor who ruled through a strictly centralized bureaucratic system extending to the whole realm of the empire, which prevented larger territories from falling under control by the various local rulers. However, the early collapse of the Qin Empire revealed problems in the Qin system in which bureaucracy provided the only ties that bound officials to the emperor. When the center was struck down, the whole system was paralyzed overnight.

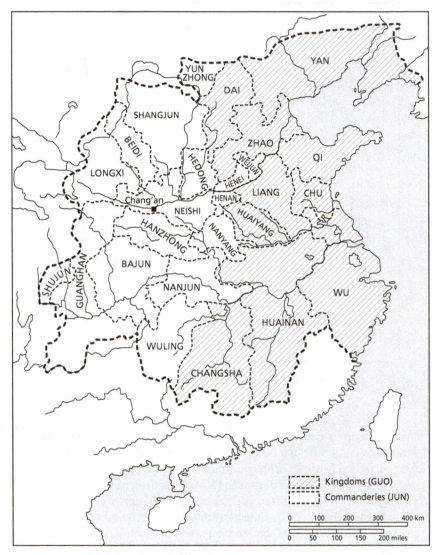

Map 12.1 The Han Empire in 195 BC.

The founders of the Han Empire found neither the Zhou nor the Qin system fully acceptable or indeed realistic. As a result, the Han imperial system was typically hybrid. In 201 BC, the Han court officially recognized the kingdoms of Chu, Liang, Hann, Changsha, Huainan, Yan,

Zhao, Qi, Dai, and Huaiyang. In fact, this trend to return to political regionalism, echoing the Warring States situation, gained its initial sanction by Xiang Yu, when the Qin model of empire was called into serious question.[3] Some of these kingdoms were ruled by Liu Bang's own generals or relatives, such as the kings of Qi and Dai, but many others were regional leaders who allied with Liu Bang in the war defeating Xiang Yu. Some kingdoms had a territory equal to a few commanderies combined, and the Han court simply could not rely on their kings to protect the interests of the empire because their backgrounds were various and ambitions unrestricted, being different from the regional rulers under Western Zhou. In reality, one after another, these kings rose against the Han court or were accused of doing so, as in the case of the King of Liang who was effectively forced into rebellion and was captured for execution. There were also kingdoms, particularly those located near the northern borders, that constantly swayed their alliance between Han and the newly rising nomadic empire on the northern steppe, the Xiongnu Empire.

On the whole, the struggle balanced in favor of the Han court when the kings were gradually replaced by members of the Liu family, and this process was completed in 195 BC. On his deathbed, Liu Bang swore an oath with his generals that if anyone who was not a member of the Liu family would again dare to assume the title of king, all people under Heaven should arise to eliminate him. Although the rule was soon broken by Empress Lü who had effectively ruled the Han Empire for fifteen years during which members of her own Lü family were entitled kings, in general it can be said that by the end of Liu Bang's life, the empire seemingly had returned to the Zhou system with the western half put under direct imperial administration and eastern half divided among nine kings who were personal relatives of the emperor. Liu Bang might have thought that by balancing the commanderies with regional kingdoms in the hands of the Liu family, the empire could last forever.

Ironically, even these Liu kings did not wait too long to strengthen themselves against the empire. The Han court had to fight very hard to maintain control over eastern China. Under Emperor Wen (r. 180–157 BC), the kingdoms of Zhao and Qi were divided and given to a number of princes of the two kingdoms. Under Emperor Jing (r. 156–141 BC), when a proposal was made by the emperor's close advisor Chao Cuo to further reduce the territory of the larger states Wu and Chu in the south, this caused widespread resentment among the regional kings who instantly

---

[3] See Mark Edward Lewis, *The Early Chinese Empire: Qin and Han* (Cambridge, MA: Belknap Press of Harvard University press, 2007), pp. 19–20.

decided to rebel and all together marched on Chang'an in 154 BC. Under pressure from the rebels, the emperor ordered the execution of Chao Cuo, but then, he sent troops east to crush the rebellious kings. Using the kingdom of Liang as a stronghold, whose king was brother by the same mother as Emperor Jing and hence remained loyal to the court, the Han forces were able to cut the supply lines of the enemies and eventually put down the rebellion after three months of war. This incident, though for bad causes, brought forth decisive destruction to the power of the regional kings and was an important watershed in Han imperial history.

During the reign of Emperor Wu (*r.* 140–87 BC), imperial power further crushed the conspiracy of the kingdoms of Huainan and Hengshan, converting their territories into new commanderies (Map 12.2). Meanwhile, in

Map 12.2 The Han Empire in 108 BC.

127 BC, the court adopted a new policy called "Extending Imperial Favor" (*Tuien*) which allowed the kings to grant their sons titles and territories to form secondary states, thus effectively slicing the kingdoms into even smaller pieces. New generations of the imperial offspring, when established kings, were allowed to receive a certain amount of the tax quota from the territory they were supposed to "rule," but they received no actual territories at all. This new system of regional "kings" without a territorial kingdom came as the result of the nearly century-long struggle between the imperial and regional powers and of the balancing between the Zhou and Qin political paradigms. It provided the empire with a pivot around which the imperial structure could revolve, and it was the key to the long-lasting stability of the imperial system itself. It was the marriage between "Empire" and "Dynasty" that could simultaneously satisfy the need to enforce imperial bureaucratic order throughout the empire and the need to build blood ties that could protect the empire's dynastic root. By granting imperial kinsmen ranks superior to all bureaucrats, a super-privileged class was formed, and this class would in turn secure the ruling position of the imperial family. But this superior class was in no position to run the bureaucracy which only the emperor could command.

Han and Xiongnu: A World Divided into Two Halves

The Han Empire was not alone. To its immediate north was the nomadic empire Xiongnu, which at the height of its power conquered the vast steppe region stretching from Manchuria in the east to Central Asia and southern Russia in the west. The southern periphery of this political–geographical landmass was formed by the grass-covered hill slopes and valleys straddling the great arch of the Yellow River in present-day northern Shaanxi, Shanxi, and southern Inner Mongolia, broadly called the Ordos region. To its immediate north was located the vast Gobi Desert across the current China–Mongolia national border. On the eastern edge of the Gobi is the grassland called "Hulun Baier," the home of the later Mongols. Crossing the Gobi Desert farther north the landscape gradually transforms into grassland in central and northern Mongolia and the forest-covered low hills in southern Russia (Map 12.3).

Despite their many known or unknown cultural or ethnic roots in this vast steppe region, current archaeology suggests that the Xiongnu (at least a part of them) might have been among the distant cultural descendants of a distinctive early Bronze Age culture in the Ordos region, contemporary with the late Shang state (1200–1046 BC) centered on Anyang. From the 1950s to the 2000s, more than twenty groups of bronzes were discovered in northern Shaanxi and across the river east in Shanxi. While tools and

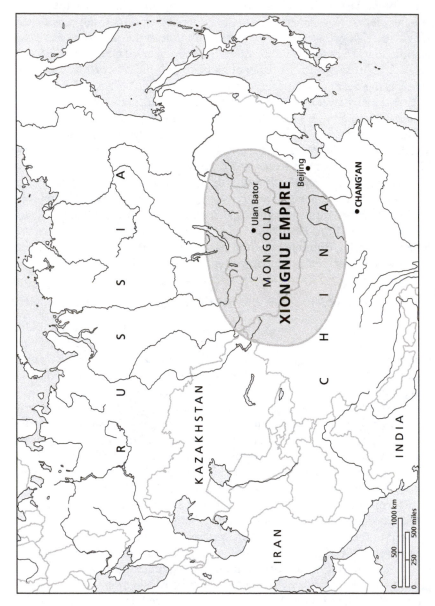

Map 12.3 The northern zone and the Xiongnu Empire.

weapons found in this region showed overwhelmingly northern steppe features, the bronze vessels found in the region included both distinctive local types and types apparently imported from the Shang culture. The subsistence system of the local communities was characteristic for the high degree of mixture of pastoralist life with widespread non-intensive agriculture. The later excavation in Zhukaigou in Inner Mongolia pushed the region's cultural horizon farther back in the late Neolithic period,[4] situating the region on the periphery of the sphere of agricultural life that had evolved centered on the middle and the lower Yellow River drainage basin since about 7000 BC (see Chapter 2). It also pushed the local history of bronze manufacturing back to around 1700 BC, contemporaneous with the early Shang.

There is still considerable debate as to whether the local bronze industry had its source of influence from the nearby Erlitou culture (1900–1500 BC) or received stimuli from farther west. What is clear is that during the eleventh century BC Ordos entered a period of sharp decline, and there is good reason to consider that this change was due to the rise of the Western Zhou state in the south. One of the long Western Zhou inscriptions, the Xiao Yu *ding*, records that the Zhou captured as many as 13,081 people, killing another 4,800, in a battle against the Gui Fang, very likely to have been located in the Ordos region.[5] On the other hand, the region seems to have been a participant in the broader social transition to nomadism that took place in the northern steppe regions during the tenth to the seventh centuries BC. When Ordos figures highly in the archaeological records again from the fifth century BC on, it was clearly integrated into a large steppe cultural complex that was at least partly associated with the ethnic Xiongnu. Such were the findings from a number of cemeteries located in Inner Mongolia contemporary with the late Spring and Autumn to the Warring States period in the middle Yellow River region. Weapons are the main items from these cemeteries, which also yielded various types of animal-shaped objects (Fig. 12.2), the most characteristic being bronze plates with zoomorphic designs, together with remains of animal and human skulls in their burials. The similar assemblage of bronze objects with typological variations has been found far north across the Gobi Desert in tombs excavated in the vast grassland

---

[4] For a substantial discussion of the Zhukaigou site and the broad context of cultural exchange between the northern steppe region and the middle to lower Yellow River regions down to late Shang, see Katheryn M. Linduff, "Zhukaigou, Steppe Culture and the Rise of Chinese Civilization," *Antiquity* **69** (1995), 133–145.

[5] This is the largest number of war captives ever recorded in Western Zhou bronze inscriptions; see Li Feng, *Landscape and Power in Early China: The Crisis and Fall of the Western Zhou, 1045–771 BC* (Cambridge: Cambridge University Press, 2005), p. 54.

Fig. 12.2 Bronze objects from the Ordos region, 400–200 BC.

in the central and northern Mongolia Republic and southern Russia, showing strong cultural links between the two zones of the vast steppe.

The earliest record in the Chinese sources points to 318 BC when the five eastern states, Hann, Zhao, Wei, Yan, and Qi, enlisted the Xiongnu in their forces and jointly attacked Qin. Whether this event had prompted the Qin to attack the Xiongnu is unknown; in the years that followed the Qin repeatedly attacked the Yiqu located to the north, and the eventual annexation of Yiqu territory would have inevitably brought the Qin into direct confrontation with the Xiongnu in the Ordos region. In fact, recent scholarship considers the formation of the Xiongnu Confederacy to have owed its origin to a precondition created by the continuous expansion of the Qin Empire onto the northern steppe, relevant particularly to a massive campaign led by Meng Tian in 214 BC.[6] Through this campaign the Qin captured the Ordos region from the Xiongnu, throwing the latter into a sudden social and political chaos that gave rise to a strong nomadic leadership. The person who represented this historical trend was Maodun who had come to unite the various Xiongnu tribes and assumed the title of *Shanyu* in 208 BC. In the following years, Maodun further conquered

[6] See Nicolas di Cosmo, *Ancient China and Its Enemies* (Cambridge: Cambridge University Press, 2002), pp. 178–179, 186–187.

tribes in western Manchuria, and tribes in northern Mongolia and southern Russia.

The newly founded Han Empire was apparently incapable of contesting the rising power of the *Shanyu*. As Han was internally weakened by the struggle between the central power and the regional kingdoms, this created a dangerous situation in which mishandling of the relationships with the regional kings could lead to serious intervention by the *Shanyu* from the north. Such was the case of the King of Zhao who under pressure from the Han court defected to the Xiongnu Confederacy in 201 BC. In order to punish him, Liu Bang personally brought his army north, only to fall hopelessly into the trap laid by the Xiongnu cavalrymen at Pingcheng in northern Shanxi. Losing most of his troops, Liu Bang narrowly escaped death by dressing up as a woman. In the next fifty years, knowing its own weakness, the Han court adopted a policy of appeasement in the name of "Peace and Affinity" (*heqin*) by sending a Han princess to marry the *Shanyu* along with a large quantity of gifts starting in 189 BC. The arrangement was made in the hope, at least in the words of those officials who defended this policy, that the Han princess would bear for the Xiongnu future leaders who might be sympathetic towards the Han Empire, but in reality the Han Empire had reduced itself to the status of a tributary state of the Xiongnu Confederacy.

However, the peace agreement did not ensure long-lasting peace. In 166 BC, under *Shanyu* Laoshang, the Xiongnu overran the Han pass in southern Ningxia and reached as deep into Han territory as 150 km from the capital. There were countless smaller attacks by the various Xiongnu tribal leaders on the long border which the Han simply could not defend. The rise of new leadership among the Xiongnu timely provided chances for war because the new *Shanyu* needed it to push the Han to enter new treaties with an increased amount of tribute with which he could purchase the loyalty of his supporters. But on a more general level, the problem was in the nature of the Xiongnu society which was simply not as centralized as the Han and could not be bound by a commitment to the whole.[7] The numerous Xiongnu kings decided the policies of their own tribes while remaining ceremonially loyal to the *Shanyu*, and war for booty was a part of the lifestyle on the northern steppe. In fact, they not only attacked Han; more often they waged war on each other for such purposes. From the perspective of global history, China as an agricultural society suffered as a result of the social transformation to nomadism on the northern steppe, a

---

[7] On this point, see Lewis, *The Early Chinese Empires*, p. 136.

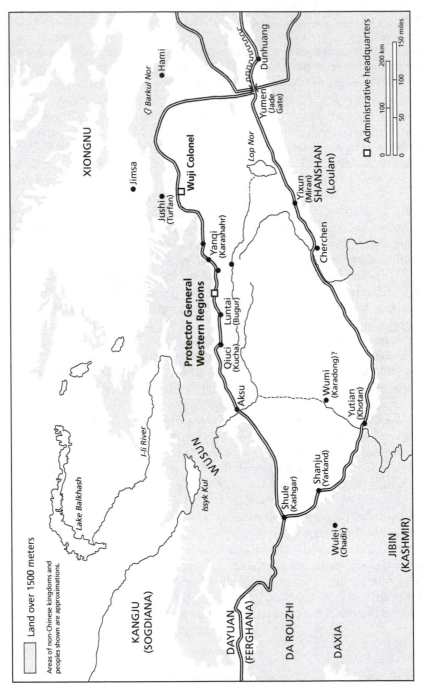

Map 12.4 The Central Asian city–states.

process that affected not only China but also agricultural societies located in Mesopotamia and Eastern Europe.

War with the Xiongnu and Han Expansion

The "Peace and Affinity" policy was criticized by some influential scholars as early as the reign of Emperor Wen, but the opposition was not able to really turn the table until the arrival of Emperor Wu (r. 140–87 BC). By then, the Han Empire was both politically and economically well consolidated, and it was in the hands of a young and ambitious emperor, assisted by a group of pro-war officials. More importantly, decades of overall peace had given the Han Empire time to develop a new style of army based on cavalry and the use of crossbows that could successfully engage the Xiongnu on the northern steppe.[8] But perhaps most important, the decades had also given the Han leadership enough time to conceive an overall strategy not to fight the Xiongnu on the Great Wall, but deep inside the Xiongnu territory.

The Han carefully planned the advances by first sending Zhang Qian on a diplomatic mission to Central Asia in the hope of finding allies among the Central Asian statelets (in particular the Rouzhi, forerunner of the Kushan Empire in India) in a common cause of war against the Xiongnu Empire. However, Zhang Qian was captured by the Xiongnu as soon as he left the Han border and spent the next ten years among the Xiongnu people, a period that actually prepared him well both in terms of language and of knowledge about the geography of Central Asia and about the customs of its people. Eventually Zhang Qian managed to escape from the Xiongnu Empire, but he did not return to Han immediately. Instead he went on a long journey to fulfill his mission to what turned out to be the most important geographical discovery in Early China. He visited most Central Asian states including Wusun in present-day Kyrgyzstan, Dayuan (Ferghana) and Da Rouzhi (Kushan) in Uzbekistan, Bactriana (Greek state) in Afghanistan, and Sogdiana in modern Kazakhstan to Uzbekistan (Map 12.4), and returned to Chang'an in 126 BC. Although he failed to convince any Central Asian state to pursue war against the Xiongnu, Zhang Qian brought back to China precious information about the Western Region which was a new world suddenly opened to the Han Empire with opportunities and endless wonders. More importantly, the Han Empire was convinced of the interest among these foreign people in

---

[8] *Ibid.*, p. 136.

Fig. 12.3 The Han–Xiongnu war depicted in a Han pictorial carving, Xiaotangshan, Shandong Province.

Chinese goods, especially silk, which later became the main item traded along the road paved by Zhang Qian in the second century BC.

Convinced that Zhang Qian must have been dead, the Han Empire set out to trap the *Shanyu* with a force of 300,000 soldiers near the frontier town called Mayi in 133 BC. However, the *Shanyu* discovered the plan and withdrew his horsemen before Han attacks. Although the operation failed before it ever began, it marked a complete shift of policy towards full-scale war with the Xiongnu. In 129 BC, five Han generals were sent out to attack the Xiongnu from five directions and each commanded an army of 10,000 cavalrymen. Two armies were completely defeated and the other two simply failed to engage the enemy. However, the young general Wei Qing made a sudden long-distance assault and captured Longcheng, the spiritual center of the Xiongnu. Two years later, Wei Qing led a large army unit going out from northern Shanxi and crossed the Yellow River from the north, suddenly falling on the Xiongnu. The Han forces totally crushed the Xiongnu, capturing two kings along with thousands of men and women, and retaking the Ordos region from the Xiongnu for the first time since the collapse of the Qin Empire. The victory not only eliminated the immediate threat to Chang'an, but served to decisively overturn the balance of power between Han and Xiongnu (Fig. 12.3). In order to consolidate the Han holdings on Ordos, 100,000 Han farmers were moved to populate the area, which was built up as a firm base for further Han operations on the northern steppe.

In the following years, the Han armies continued to search for chances to engage the Xiongnu who were essentially mobile. The Han generals had learned to use light cavalry that once characterized the Xiongnu forces and adopted the strategy of long-distance sudden attack, which had previously given the Xiongnu full advantage over the Han. From the standpoint of grand strategy, because the Han were holding a frontier stretching over 2,000 km against unexpected attacks, the sudden attacks launched by the Han forces could effectively offset the advantages enjoyed by the nomadic Xiongnu forces. In order to do so, the Han horsemen had to be better trained and better equipped, and they were indeed able to outmaneuver the Xiongnu even in cases where the Xiongnu outnumbered the Han soldiers. This was typical in the campaign of 121 BC when the light-cavalry general Huo Qubing led an army of 10,000 cavalrymen going west, traversing the territories of five Xiongnu tribes in six days and forcing King Hunye to surrender with 40,000 soldiers. Through a series of battles between 127 and 121 BC, the Han had gained complete control over the area to the south of the Yinshan Mountains and forced the Xiongnu to retreat to the north of the Gobi Desert.

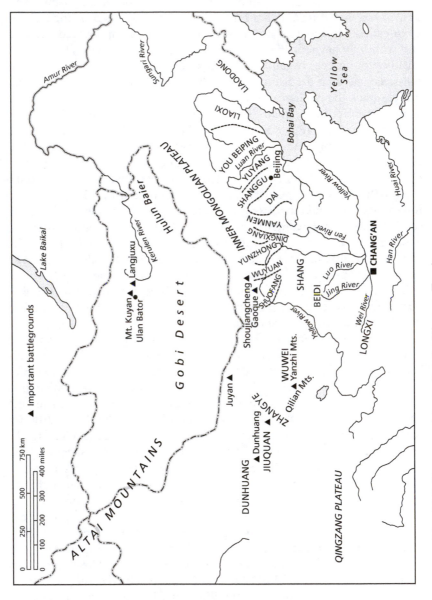

Map 12.5 Han campaigns against the Xiongnu Empire.

However, Emperor Wu was not satisfied with the victory; on the contrary, he planned an even more decisive and difficult engagement to completely destroy the Xiongnu Empire. In 119 BC, Wei Qing and Huo Qubing each commanded a force of 50,000 cavalrymen and 100,000 infantry troops marching north on two routes. In order to effectively support the war, the Han Empire further mobilized another 100,000 men who brought with them an additional 4,000 horses as reinforcement. The huge Han legions and various supply units crossed the Gobi Desert in a move of some 1,400 km in more than twenty days to meet the *Shanyu*'s forces for a decisive engagement near Mount Kuyan near today's Ulan Bator in northern Mongolia (Map 12.5). Given the logistic problems involved in supplying such a huge number of people over such a long distance through the desert, the Han were actually doing something nearly impossible. The Han troops demonstrated superior fighting skills and coordination, backed up by men and horses that continuously came out from the desert and arrived on the scene to join the battle. After a day of fighting, the *Shanyu* gave up hope and fled the field in darkness, leaving his troops in desperation. The campaign ended in complete victory for the Han, but it came only after the Han themselves also suffered a great number of casualties and the loss of some 100,000 horses. However, it is nevertheless true that the "North Desert Campaign" of 119 BC inflicted decisive damage on the Xiongnu Empire.

The war with the Xiongnu, measured both by the vast geographical space in which it took place and by the intensity of the campaigns and the level of human and material resources both sides threw into the confrontation, was unprecedented in world history.[9] After the "North Desert Campaign" in 119 BC, although the Han still had to fight the Xiongnu resurgences and lost some of the battles, this was never on a very large scale and most of the subsequent battles were fought far from the Han border. In the decades that followed, the Xiongnu Confederacy was further weakened by internal struggles between different factions, each having its own *Shanyu*. In 54 BC, Huhanye the *Left Shanyu* decided to accept the Han offer of tributary status and led his followers south to the Han border. On request of the Han court, Huhanye first sent his son as hostage to Chang'an, and was himself permitted to pay homage to Emperor Wu two years later. Zhizhi the *Right Shanyu* also sent a son to

---

[9] Alexander the Great was said to have conquered Asia with a force of 32,000 soldiers. The single largest concentration of Roman troops was at Actium in 31 BC, recorded to have involved a quarter of a million people or more, in comparison to the 300,000 soldiers the Han Empire sent north to attack the Xiongnu in 119 BC (exclusive of the 100,000 people in the supply units), if figures on both sides are reliable.

Chang'an, but he then continued fighting against the Han Empire in the west. In 36 BC he was killed in a battle by troops sent out from the "Protector General of the Western Regions" – the Han governor in Central Asia.

Dynastic Transition and the Founding of the Eastern Han Empire

Emperor Wu had left the empire behind him in an extraordinary way. By the end of his long reign, which lasted for fifty-three years, he had purged the crown prince and his faction, and had secured the succession of Emperor Zhao (r. 86–74 BC), an eight-year-old son by one of the last lovers in the emperor's life. In order to prevent the mother from interfering in the power of the future young emperor, Emperor Wu simply ordered her execution. On the other hand, he appointed two of his most trusted men as regents to safeguard the throne: Huo Guang, a brother of the victorious general Huo Qubing, and Jin Midi, a former Xiongnu prince who had come to Han as a war prisoner but had subsequently established himself as a model of virtue and discipline. Huo Guang married his daughter to Jin's son, and later another daughter to Emperor Xuan (r. 73–49 BC).[10]

In many ways, the reigns of Emperors Zhao and Xuan were clearly a transition in Han imperial history. During the next half century, three emperors ruled the Han Empire and all died very young. Because the emperors were young, real power fell almost constantly into the hands of their maternal uncles through the dowagers' personal influence, a situation that Emperor Wu was able to foresee but was unable to prevent. In contrast, the highest office in the empire, "Commander-in-Chief," was almost constantly occupied by the maternal uncles of the young emperors.[11] However, for decades, the maternal uncles operated in the existing system that was established in the early centuries of the Han Empire and under the fundamental legitimacy promised by the Han institution until the arrival of a new uncle, Wang Mang, who changed the rule.[12]

Wang Mang's aunt became a consort of Emperor Yuan in 54 BC and gave birth to Emperor Cheng. This lady enjoyed tremendous longevity,

---

[10] On the historical role of the Huo family, see Michael Loewe, *Crisis and Conflict in Han China,104 BC to AD 9* (London: Allen & Unwin, 1974), pp. 37–90, 114–153.

[11] On the power of the imperial in-laws, see Ch'u T'ung-tsu, *Han Social Structure* (Seattle: University of Washington Press, 1972), pp. 77–83.

[12] For a discussion of the reign of Wang Mang and the transition to Eastern Han, see Hans Bielenstein, *The Restoration of the Han Dynasty* (Stockholm: Elanders Boktryckeri Aktiebolag, 1953), pp. 82–165.

not only living through the reign of her son, but also through a part of that of her grandson, Emperor Ai. Her long life gave the Wang family enough time to accumulate political resources needed to overthrow the Han Empire. Wang Mang came to the office in 8 BC as the younger generation of the Wang family after his uncle and elder brothers had all served terms as Commander-in-Chief. Wang Mang apparently had a different approach to power and knew much better than his uncles and brothers about how to create favorable public opinion which could be used as an important political base. He sponsored public works and conferences on Confucian classics and established himself not only as the patron of the Han Empire, but also as the superior embodiment of Confucian values.[13] With continuing propaganda after the death of Emperor Ping, Wang Mang eventually declared the founding of the New Dynasty and himself emperor in AD 9. During the fifteen years of the New Dynasty, Wang Mang implemented a series of reforms to systematically change Han institutions, drawing up his plans largely based on illusions about the "Zhou institution" supposedly transmitted in the Confucian ritual texts.

As soon as the New Dynasty (AD 9–23) was inaugurated, he pushed forward the nationalization of land, setting limits on the area an individual family could own and prohibiting its sale. The policy apparently had its purpose to save the poor peasantry from the encroachment by the large land-owners. For the same purpose, the sale of slaves and retainers was also prohibited. He also created a mechanism to stabilize market prices, and installed a completely new currency system, while the state stepping in to monopolize the salt and iron industries as it did at the time of Emperor Wu. Some of Wang Mang's reforms were clearly designed to reduce the power of the nobility and the great official families who had by this time already been eating the lion's share of the social and economic resources needed to support the empire which he took over from the Liu family. As a way to further exploit the nobility, Wang Mang ordered the nobles of the rank of marquis and lower to exchange their gold for the new copper coins, and this caused widespread resentment of the New Dynasty. On the borders, to further secure imperial control, he reduced the kings of the various subjugated groups including the Xiongnu and Koguryŏ in eastern Manchuria and many others in Central Asia and southwestern China to the rank of "duke." The material manifestation of Wang Mang's reform is a group of distinctive religious ritual architecture found in the district of Chang'an, including the Nine Temples, the place where he worshipped

---

[13] Some even came to see him as the reincarnation of the ancient Duke of Zhou, a role Wang Mang had purposely worked to fit himself for. For the ground of Wang Mang's support, see Loewe, *Crisis and Conflict in Han China*, pp. 286–306, particularly p. 287.

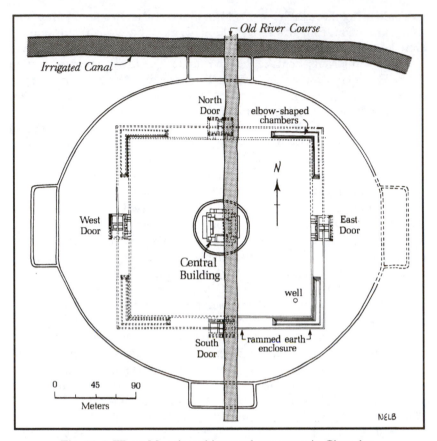

Fig. 12.4 Wang Mang's architectural structures in Chang'an.

the ancient sage kings (not the Liu kings), and the Bright Hall where the emperor (Wang Mang) observed the changes of seasons according to Confucian texts (Fig. 12.4).

Wang Mang's socialist and imperialist combined reform policies are subjects of controversy among modern scholars. Whether good or evil intentions might have been behind his decisions, there can be no doubt that their ultimate goal was to strengthen the roots of the New Dynasty regime which, if it had survived the destruction soon to come, would have made Wang Mang the greatest reformer in Chinese history. But his new regime faced the problem of legitimacy from the beginning, and even the credit that Wang Mang might have won from the farmers was soon offset by the hardship they had to endure caused by the natural disasters that spread over North China, which contributed to the downfall of the New Dynasty.[14]

In the chaos that brought Wang Mang's regime down, the Han Dynasty was restored by the local elites in southern Henan, led by Liu Xiu, a descendant of the Han imperial house. After a series of fierce battles, the new Han army broke into the Wei River valley in late September, AD 23. Wang Mang was forced to retreat and was killed by the local rebels before the Han army entered the capital. The following years saw the contest for power between the new Han Dynasty and the rebel army called the "Red Eyebrows," but in March, AD 26, when the "Red Eyebrows" moved out from the Wei River valley to the east, they were completely crushed by the Han army. In AD 37, Liu Xiu established his capital in Luoyang and therefore the restored Han Empire was referred to in history as the Eastern Han (AD 25–220). Liu Xiu was himself posthumously titled *Guangwu*, or the "Bright Marshal Emperor."

The Han Empire's Relations with the Roman Empire

The Han expansion into Central Asia during the two centuries before and after the beginning of the Christian era certainly raises questions about Han's relations with states and societies located farther to the west, most importantly the Roman Empire, master of the other half of the world that the Han shared. The Romans might have had a vague idea as to where silk came from, but when the Roman historian Florus used the word *Seres* he could have meant anyone who carried the merchandise into Rome along the "Silk Road." Beyond that there is simply not a single piece of reference in Roman sources that can be linked to China.

For the Han, although the Roman Empire lay beyond the world of their reach (once nearly reachable), it was located within the world they knew. As the Han had broad contacts with the independent states and kingdoms in Central Asia and the west who might have in turn had contacts with the Romans, the Han had come to be on a good footing to inquire about this great power in the Western world. In fact, the official history of the Eastern Han Empire includes a long essay about the Roman Empire which is called the "Great Qin Empire" (Da Qin) (Box 12.1). When that term is used, there can be no doubt that the Han historian was referring to a

---

[14] See Bielenstein, *The Restoration of the Han Dynasty*, pp. 154–156. Towards to end of Wang Mang's reign, the Yellow River flooded and took a new course, resulting in a great number of deaths among the poor farmers. Added to this were years of drought and ravages of locusts in North China. This happened first in eastern Henan and western Shandong, but soon spread to other parts of the Central Plain and into the Wei River valley in the west.

Box 12.1   The Roman Empire in the *History of the Eastern Han Dynasty*

Chapter 78, *"Chronicle of the Western Regions"*
Section 11, *"The Kingdom of Da Qin (Roman Empire)"*
History of the Eastern Han Dynasty,
by Fan Ye (AD 398–445)

The kingdom of Da Qin (lit. 'Great China' = the Roman Empire) is also called Lijian.[*] As it is found to the west of the sea, it is also called the kingdom of Haixi (lit. 'West of the Sea' = Egypt). Its territory extends for several thousands of *li*. It has more than four hundred walled towns. There are several tens of smaller dependent kingdoms. The walls of the towns are made of stone.

They have established postal relays at intervals, which are all plastered and whitewashed. There are pines and cypresses, as well as trees and plants of all kinds. The common people are farmers. They cultivate many types of trees, breed silkworms and grow mulberries. They shave their heads, and their clothes are embroidered. They have screened coaches [for the women] and small white-roofed one-horse carts. When carriages come and go, drums are beaten and flags and standards are raised.

The seat of government (Rome) is more than a hundred *li* (41.6 km) around. In this city are five palaces each ten *li* (4.2 km) from the other. Moreover, in the rooms of the palace the pillars and the tableware are really made of crystal. The king goes each day to one of the palaces to deal with business. After five days, he has visited them all. A porter with a sack has the job of always following the royal carriage. When somebody wants to discuss something with the king, he throws a note in the sack. When the king arrives at the palace, he opens the bag, examines the contents, and judges if the plaintiff is right or wrong. Each [palace] has officials [in charge of the] written documents.

[A group of] thirty-six leaders (or generals) has been established to meet together to deliberate on affairs of state. Their kings are not permanent. They select and appoint the most worthy man. If there are unexpected calamities in the kingdom, such as frequent extraordinary winds or rains, he is unceremoniously rejected and replaced. The one who has been dismissed quietly accepts his demotion, and is not angry.

The people of this country are all tall and honest. They resemble the people of the Middle Kingdom and that is why this kingdom is called Da Qin (or 'Great China'). (Translation by John E. Hill)

[*] Lijian is believed to have been the name of the earlier Seleucid Empire, much of it being incorporated into the Roman Empire.

The next section of the text offers an account of the products of the Roman Empire. It also mentions that in AD 166, envoys sent by Roman king An-dun (doubtless Marcus Aurelius Antonius, *r.* 161–180) arrived in the Eastern Han court. Curiously they came from the Vietnamese coast.

specific civilized nation that can be differentiated from all others he also mentions. The Roman Empire is said there to have been located to the west of the sea, embracing some four hundred cities in its territory, all built in stone. The capital of the Roman Empire is described as having a perimeter of more than one hundred *li* (41.6 km), including five main palaces, the king dwelling in one each day. The high court had thirty-six generals who together discussed matters of the state in a conference. The king was not hereditary; instead, the Romans chose a worthy man to serve in that position, being different from the Chinese practice. The second half of the essay then describes at length the products of Rome including, most importantly, glassware and golden and silver coins, symbols of Roman civilization.[15]

The essay shows a typical mixture of illusions with bits of information that might have had a genuine origin. Given the historical information available, we are even allowed a good guess as to how such information might have flown into the Han Empire. In AD 97, Gan Ying, a subordinate of Ban Chao, the "Protector-General of the Western Region," was sent on a mission that had as its sole purpose the establishment of diplomatic relations with the Roman Empire. According to modern studies, Gan Ying and his entourage departed from the kingdom of Qiuci (present-day Kuche in the Tarim Basin), traversing the territory of Anxi (Parthia, present-day Iran), and arrived at Tiaozhi (Characene and Susiana in present-day Iraq) on the shore of the Persian Gulf. However, the Parthians were unwilling to give the Han Empire direct access to the Roman Empire, in the fear that to do so might deprive them of the profit they made in the silk trade as middlemen. They greatly exaggerated the difficulties of crossing the sea and reaching Rome, and politely persuaded Gan Ying to return to the Han Empire. Although Gan Ying failed to reach Rome, the mission must have greatly enriched Han knowledge of the Western world.[16] There can be little doubt that stories about the Roman Empire must have been heard on Gan Ying's mission.

In the other direction, it is recorded too in the official history of the Eastern Han Empire, in AD 166, the king of the Roman Empire by the name "An-dun," doubtless Marcus Aurelius Antoninus Augustus (*r.* 161–180), dispatched envoys from beyond the frontier through the Han commandery in Vietnam to offer elephant tusks and rhinoceros horns to the Han Emperor.[17] The mission, whether of an authentic or

[15] See John E. Hill, *Through the Jade Gate to Rome* (Charleston: BookSurge, 2009), pp. 22–27.

[16] See Donald Leslie, *The Roman Empire in Chinese Sources* (Rome: Bardi, 1996).

[17] See Hill, *Through the Jade Gate to Rome*, p. 27.

faked origin, was apparently received at the Han court in Luoyang. But, unfortunately, this mission cannot be verified in Roman sources, which regrettably remain completely silent about East Asia.

SELECTED READING

Lewis, Mark Edward, *The Early Chinese Empires: Qin and Han* (Cambridge, MA: Belknap Press of Harvard University Press, 2007).

Bielenstein, Hans, *The Bureaucracy of Han Times* (Cambridge: Cambridge University Press, 1980).

Di Cosmo, Nicolas, *Ancient China and Its Enemies: The Rise of Nomadic Empire in East Asian History* (Cambridge: Cambridge University Press, 2002).

Twitchett, Denis, and Michael Loewe (eds.), *The Cambridge History of China*, Vol. 1, *The Chi'in and Han Empires* (Cambridge: Cambridge University Press, 1986).

Loewe, Michael, *Crisis and Conflict in Han China, 104 BC to AD 9* (London: Allen & Unwin, 1974).

Bielenstein, Hans, *The Restoration of the Han Dynasty* (Stockholm: Elanders Boktryckeri Aktiebolag, 1953).

Wang, Zhongshu, *Han Civilization* (New Haven: Yale University Press, 1982).

13 State and society: bureaucracy and social orders under the Han Empire

Although the Han elites portrayed themselves as the ideological opponents of the Qin Empire, there can be no doubt that much of Han's glory was owed to the foundation already built in Qin. By modifying Qin elements, the Han Empire created institutions and cultural patterns that were to exercise long-lasting impact on China. The Han Empire had a population of 59,594,978 men and women in the year of 8 BC as reported in the official history of the Western Han Dynasty, and quite a few of its most populated commanderies exceeded 1 million. In order to mobilize human and material resources to support operations by its armies and the various colonist groups in the vast space from southern Manchuria in the east to the Pamir Mountains in the west, stretching south to the southeastern China coasts, the Han constructed a huge bureaucratic machine, often regarded by historians as one of the most fully developed premodern bureaucracies in the world. Han society can be described as a typical rank society with its elite population divided into twenty ranks that enjoyed different degrees of privilege. The long process of expansion afforded tremendous opportunities for the young people of the empire to win military or civil merit and hence join the ranks of social elites. The rank system provided the basic social order of Han society which was enforced through the Han legal system. However, as time went on families of the upper ranks, which were usually hereditarily held, tended to consume an ever-increasing portion of social resources in competition with the imperial state. This in the long run inevitably served to undermine the economic foundation of the imperial state as the Han Empire was at the same time being weakened politically by a struggle between the imperial in-laws and the eunuchs surrounding the emperor.

The Yinwan Documents and the Han Bureaucracy

The Han imperial government had a relatively stable structure, referred to by historians as the "Three Excellencies and Nine Ministers," which lasted over 400 years with only some minor fixes. The system is considered by political scientists as the earliest government that came closest to Max Weber's model of *ideal* bureaucracy, and it was actually formed on strictly bureaucratic principles. At the top of the central government were three high offices, those of the Chancellor, Censor-in-Chief, and Grand Commandant. The role of the Chancellor had evolved gradually over the Warring States period mainly in the northern states into one that had general responsibility for the whole government. In other words, the Chancellor was one who was responsible only to the emperor and could in the emperor's absence command the entire bureaucracy to act, as did happen on a number of occasions in the history of the Han Empire. Because of his high authority and general influence, he was most helpful to the emperor but at the same time also posed a potential threat to the throne. Therefore, in Han practice the role was sometimes divided between two offices, Chancellor of the Right and Chancellor of the Left; the right was the senior, but the left was not subject to the right, both being responsible directly to the emperor. Censorial control of officials was an important feature of a fully developed bureaucracy and in the Han case this important function was embodied in the office of the Censor-in-Chief who as the emperor's watchdog made proposals for the promotion and punishment of officials (the actual terms of punishment were decided by the Commandant of Justice after further investigation). The last of these was called the Grand Commandant before 119 BC, representing the highest level of military authority under the emperor. Over time the role of the Chancellor was gradually weakened and much of its responsibility was taken over by the office of Commander-in-Chief which was created by Emperor Wu during the Xiongnu campaign and continued until its eventual termination in 8 BC.

The "Nine Ministers" covered a wide range of affairs involving the central government, but they were not directly subordinates of the Three Excellencies. They can be best considered the functionaries of the empire and the executive agents of the emperor. The construction of these nine offices reflected a general division between the sphere of administration directly related to the emperor and his home, the palace, and the administration of the wide empire; it also exhibits the principle of shared responsibilities. For instance, the financial administration was charged by the Grand Minister of Agriculture who was responsible for taxation and thus for the economic well-being of the empire, and by the Privy Treasurer who was responsible for the provision of the palaces. The Superintendent as the head of the imperial household also had responsibilities for the security of the palaces, but the Commandant of the Guards controlled guard posts at the gates of the palace compounds and along the wall of the capital Chang'an. Separate ministerial roles were also established for the tracking of imperial genealogy and for the reception of the visitors from the wide empire and the foreign lands beyond it (the Grand Herald). In the Western Han, particularly during the heightened military confrontation with the Xiongnu Empire, management of the horses was a critical matter; the Grand Coachman had a ministerial rank and was in charge of both the horses in the imperial stables and horses for the imperial carriages.[1]

The local administration of the Han Empire was divided into two tiers, commandery and county, following the model of Qin, added to which was the network of regional kingdoms whose number decreased over the first 100 years as the numbers of commanderies and counties grew. There were 57 commanderies and nearly 1,000 counties in the first decade of the empire, and the number increased to 103 by the end of the first century under which were 1,314 counties. These numbers reflect well the expansion of the empire and the growth of its bureaucracy. In a sense they also marked the greatest extent of Han local bureaucracy because there was a slow decline thereafter in both numbers, and this trend continued during the Eastern Han. Each commandery was governed by a Grand Administrator who enjoyed a salary level measured by 2,000 *shi* of grains, roughly equal to that of a minister in the central government (Box 13.1), and each county was governed by a Magistrate. However, since the time of Emperor Wu, special Inspectors were sent from the imperial court to oversee affairs in several commanderies in a large region of the empire, and this office became thoroughly localized during the Eastern Han, hence giving rise to some twelve Regions (*zhou*) which then formed the first tier of local administration, now divided into three levels.

The official history of the Western Han Dynasty (*Hanshu*) gives the total number of officials in the service of the Han Empire as 130,285 in 5 BC, including both local officials down to the level of county staff and those who were in the capital, starting with the Chancellor, the latter group being estimated to have been close to 30,000. Besides these civil servants, there were still a large number of military officers who spent their lives in various garrisons and camps throughout the Han Empire. If the above numbers are accurate, and there is no ground to suggest they are not, the total number of officials in service of the Han Empire would have been at least ten times larger than the number of officials employed by the Roman Empire, which only in its thoroughly bureaucratic later centuries had reached the level of Han officials in the capital alone. Looking at the comparison the other way around, while the Romans only needed to

---

[1] See Hans Bielenstein, *The Bureaucracy of the Han Times* (Cambridge: Cambridge University Press, 1980), pp. 7–69.

Box 13.1   Salary Scales of Han Officials

The salary scales of Han officials have been systematically discussed by Hans Bielenstein. Although the Han officials were subject to a system of abstract scales arranged in eighteen ranks as of the ending decades of the Western Han, the system did allow for comparison of statuses both vertically and horizontally. The top 10,000 *shi* was the salary level of the Three Excellencies, and 2,000 *shi* was the level of Ministers in the central government or Commandery Administrators (or Protectors) outside the capital. The Yinwan documents show that the Magistrates, depending on the size and population of the counties they governed are ranked between 1,000 *shi* and 400 *shi*. 100 *shi* was the level of leading clerks in the counties.

The payments that the Han officials actually received were related to this system but not directly calculated based on it. Sources suggest that officials at the level of 2,000 *shi* received some 12,000 coins annually, and officials at the level of equivalent to 800 *shi* received 9,200 coins in the later first century BC. A century later, in the early Eastern Han, the Three Excellencies received a monthly 350 *hu* of unhusked grain, and the payments for officials of 2,000 *shi* was 120 *hu*, 1,000 *shi* was 90 *hu*, 600 *shi* was 70 *hu*, and 100 *shi* was 16 *hu* of grain. Officials were allowed to receive a half of the amount in cash payment. Compared to the Western Han, the texts say that the payment for salary level of 1,000 *shi* and below was increased and for 2,000 *shi* and above was decreased. There was the debate as to whether the Han officials could live on their salaries, but Bielenstein concluded that at least by the scales of payment in early Eastern Han, they were adequately paid.

---

govern the semi-independent cities located on the sea coasts or along the main transportation lines in order to exercise indirect control over the largely rural population, the Han Empire had to put a huge bureaucracy in action in order to reach close to the villages. This was particularly true in the newly conquered inland regions such as the southwest inhabited by the various indigenous groups whose control virtually depended on the extension of the network of commanderies and counties.

Bureaucracy is not only the complex congregation of officials, but it is also defined by routine and standardized administrative procedures. An important archaeological discovery made in Yinwan in eastern Jiangsu in 1993 afforded us a keen view into the operation of Han bureaucracy at the local level through what might have been copied out of the governor's office in the Donghai Commandery between 16 and 11 BC. Among the documents written on wooden and bamboo strips totaling 156 pieces, was first of all a copy of a standard "Annul Report" submitted by the commandery to the central government in Chang'an. The report gives the number of counties and dukedoms as well as of administrative units at each of the three levels below the county including 170 districts (*xiang*), 688 sub-districts (*ting*), and 2,534 villages (*li*). Then the report describes the territory of the Donghai Commandery and gives the grand total of its officials as 2,203 and population as 1,394,195 with detailed age and sex breakdowns. The fiscal situation of the commandery is reported favorably as having a surplus of 1,120,859,115 coins, only slightly lower than the annual spending of the commandery. Accompanying the report were "Registers of Officials" which give detailed account of the number of individuals on the official payroll from the Grand Administrator to the heads of the sub-districts. For instance, Haixi County is reported to have had 107 officials in various roles who were paid out of the commandery's annual budget. What is even more interesting is a document named "Curriculum Vitae of Major Officials." This document records the career tracks of the three major officials in each county, the Magistrate, the Assistant, and the Commandant.

Scholars are free to debate the accuracy of some of the figures offered by these buried documents, but few can escape the conclusion that the Han Empire had indeed developed a highly elaborate system of bureaucracy that extended from Chang'an to each individual village in the corners of the empire, ensured by standard procedures to gather and deliver information to the capital. This information in turn enabled the Han central government to mobilize resources in the most efficient way to pursue its political and military goals. Basing himself on the figures provided by the documents from Yinwan and calculating by the number of commanderies and kingdoms reported in the official history, Michael Loewe concluded that the grand total of officials reported in the official history of the Western Han Dynasty for the year of 5 BC, cited above, was largely accurate.[2]

There were multiple sources that the Han Empire drew on to support its large bureaucracy. Each year, the Grand Administrator of a commandery was required to recommend a small group of young men of outstanding moral and personal quality, called the "Filial and Incorrupt," to the

---

[2] See Michael Loewe, "The Administrative Documents from Yinwan: A Summary of Central Issues Raised," posted on the website of the Society for the Study of Early China, www.lib.uchicago.edu/earlychina/res.

central government where after a short internship they would be appointed to serve in local administration. After the establishment of the Confucian curriculum by Emperor Wu in 136 BC, the imperial university in the capital began to produce an ever-increasing number of graduates qualified for official service and the number exceeded 10,000 each year by the beginning of the Eastern Han. Still on a constant basis, officials of the level of ministers in the central government or the Grand Administrators in the commanderies were allowed to place one of their sons in official service of the empire. But in a more general sense, the process of great expansion offered tremendous opportunities for young spirits to test their personal limits in military adventures or in civil service in the borderlands. It also offered an ever-growing number of offices added to the bureaucratic body of the empire. Without a doubt, the Han Empire was the most intensively governed area on the surface of the earth in the centuries before the Christian era.

The Zhangjiashan Legal Statutes and Social Orders under the Han Empire

Social order emerges from and was maintained through the implementation of the legal system, which in the Han case remained relatively stable over the four centuries. The official history of the Western Han Dynasty includes a chapter titled "Treatise of Law" which describes the origin of Han law. According to this, when Liu Bang arrived in the former Qin capital, he simply abandoned the harsh punishments practiced by the Qin Empire and promised "Three Articles" as basic rules for conduct which seem to have simply said that those who kill will be killed and those who injure or rob others will compensate their crimes. Then, it was his minister Xiao He who carefully examined the Qin statutes and selected and established the so-called "Nine Articles" which then served as the cornerstone of the Han Empire. Since none of these articles were transmitted in the received texts, the relevant account has been questioned by modern scholars.[3] The "Treatise of Law" was rooted in the intellectual soil of the early Eastern Han that had already been deeply plowed by Confucian values and ethics. In this respect, although it might not tell us much about the actual practice of the legal system in Han for which we now have better sources (see below), it can probably tell us about how the rule of law was understood by the Han government and Han elites in the largely Confucian mainstream, being different from the Legalist agenda.

---

[3] See Yongping Liu, *Origins of Chinese Law: Penal and Administrative Law in its Early Development* (Hong Kong: Oxford University Press, 1998), pp. 260–266.

There, law and punishment are likened to thunder and lightning of Heaven, thus gaining a divine and natural origin which justified their uses, similar to rites that are the manifestation of the natural orders. On the other hand, punishments are considered "regrettable necessities" to maintain social order, undesirable and even unappreciated, and the degree of virtue of a government can be measured by the number of laws it enacted and punishments it used to keep its citizens in order.[4] Therefore, good emperors are said to have concerned themselves mainly with the reduction of corporal, particularly mutilating, punishments rather than increasing them.[5] Thus, it is reported that under Emperor Wen, the punishment of amputation of the left foot was replaced by 500 strokes, and the amputation of the nose and tattooing of the face changed to 300 strokes, on the grounds that such punishments deprived offenders of the opportunity to reform themselves, and hence to return to normal lives. Under Emperor Jing, punishments of both degrees were further reduced by 100 strokes because many died before the right number of strokes was met. Despite its Confucian overtone, the "Treatise of Law" also offers bits of information about the number of Han laws in practice – under Emperor Wu, statutes and ordinances reached the total number of 359 articles, in which statutes related to the death penalty numbered 409, which included as many as 1,882 sample cases. These numbers seem to contradict the idea, suggested by the same text, that the Han legal system was set up for the minimum punishment of its people.

Overall it can be said that the Han legal system had its origins in the Qin Empire with the universal ranking system as its point of reference. Both systems went through modifications as necessary for adapting to the new reality in the Han Empire, such as the existence of a privileged aristocratic order. They provided the essential frameworks in which Han society operated.

In 1983–4, from a small tomb in Zhangjiashan in the district of the Jiangling City in Hubei Province, a total of 1,236 bamboo strips were excavated, including some 500 strips that carry Han legal statutes dating to the second year of Empress Dowager Lü (186 BC). The "Second-year Statutes" as they are commonly called by scholars include a total of twenty-seven articles, being the actual legal codes used in early centuries of Han (Fig. 13.1). Relevant to criminal offenses are the "Statutes on Murder" and "Statutes on Robbery" together with a number of articles about legal procedures such as the "Statutes on Reports," "Statutes on Arrest," "Statutes on Reduction of Punishment." An important group of

---

[4] *Ibid.*, p. 255.   [5] *Ibid.*, pp. 302–308.

Fig. 13.1 Strips of Han law from Zhangjiashan: 1, 2, "Statutes on Land"; 3, "Statutes on Currency"; 4, "Statutes on Robbery"; 5, unidentified; 6, "Statutes on Inspection."

the Zhangjiashan articles concerns the economic activities in the empire,[6] and another group of articles concerns rather the conduct of the government.[7] Related to the last group is a very interesting article called the "Statutes on Scribes" which describes the training and use of scribes at different levels of the government. Some articles have their counterparts

---

[6] These include the "Statutes on Transportation of Grain," "Statutes on Inventory," "Statutes on Land," "Statutes on Market," and most importantly, the "Statutes on Currency."

[7] These include "Statutes on Establishment of Offices," "Statutes on Awards," "Statutes on Exemption from Labor Services," and the "Statutes on Post Office."

among the Qin legal statutes from Shuihudi (discussed in Chapter 11), but doubtless the scope of the Zhangjiashan statutes is much wider.[8] It should also be noted that some of the terms were written with respect to the special circumstances of early Han such as terms regarding the defection of guards of local cities to the regional kings. On the other hand, it is likely that by all accounts the twenty-seven articles represent the core part, though maybe not the whole range, of Han laws that continued to be in use throughout the Han Dynasty.

A closer look at the "Statutes on Murder" offers us a good sense about the definition of crimes and the propriety of punishment. For instance, according to Han law, murder or killing during combat is subject to the punishment of public execution, but killing by mistake or during a game can be given parole on payment of a fine. If the victim was not dead, the offender would be punished by tattooing his face and convicting as a "Wall Builder" (chengdan) or "Grain Pounder" (chong);[9] but if dead, even the co-conspirator is subject to public execution. In cases of injuring people, if the injured died within twenty days, it is the same as killing. Injuring on purpose or self-injuring in order to avoid due services is punished by tattooing the face and turning into "Wall Builder" or "Grain Pounder." Injuring during combat, in the case where a weapon, hammer, or metal tool was used, leads to the punishment of having the hair shaved and turning into the two types of convicts mentioned above; in the case where a weapon or metal tool was not used, the punishment is shaving off the beard. In other words, in judging a case where the crime led to the physical injury or death of the victim, the offender's intention, the consequence, and the place and means by which the crime was committed all had to be carefully weighed.

For our main purpose in this chapter, the Zhangjiashan legal statutes offer a unique window through which we can see how social distinctions were constructed in Han society and what special rights and privileges were enjoyed by different social groups in front of Han law. The "Treatise of Law" lists four different orders in the lowest stratum of Han society from the bottom up as: (1) "Wall Builder" and "Grain Pounder," (2) "Gatherer of Fuel for the Spirits" (guixin) and "White-Rice Sorter" (baican),[10]

---

[8] But this point can be modified by the possibility that neither the Zhangjiashan nor Shuihudi statutes represent the whole corpus of Han or Qin law.

[9] These are the two types of convicts most commonly mentioned in Han sources. The male convicts were forced to labor in the construction of city walls; in the case of females, forced to labor in processing grain.

[10] "Gatherers of Fuel for the Spirits" were male convicts of lesser degree who were forced to gather firewood in the mountains; "White-Rice Sorters" were female convicts forced to pick a specific type of white rice. Both are for sacrificial purposes.

(3) male and female slaves, (4) commoners. In the Zhangjiashan legal statutes, the treatment of the four orders by law is clearly differentiated. An interesting point here concerns the social status of slaves, and hence the nature of slavery in the Han Empire, a long-debated question in the study of Early China.[11] For instance, the statutes state that if a "Gatherer of Fuel for the Spirits" or "White-Rice Sorter" attacked a commoner, they are punished by tattooing the face and convicting as one of the harsher type of laborers, "Wall Builder" or "Grain Pounder"; but if a slave attacked a commoner, he/she is punished by tattooing the face and being transferred to a different owner. Overall, the Zhangjiashan legal statutes suggest that slaves were of a significantly higher order than the two degrees of convicts forced to engage in hard labor. Their social dependence on their masters to whom they perform service is beyond question, but they are not criminals and could not be punished with forced labor. Once they are slaves, they abandon social responsibilities for their parents; therefore, the "Statutes of Report" say that when a slave is sued for "not being filial" such a report will be dismissed. The "Statutes on Miscellaneous Offenses" determine that when a free woman marries a slave, her children will be sent to another family as slaves; but children born from illicit sex between a male slave and a commoner woman can obtain the status as commoners. If a master had illicit sex with a female slave who is wife of another family's slave, children born of that relationship will be slaves of the other family. In a recent study Robin Yates redefined the slave in the early Chinese empire as a socially non-person (or socially dead person) who could not possess property of his/her own; all he/she possessed was the property of his/her master.[12] In this regard, the overall treatment or social perception of slaves in the Han Empire might have been very different from that in the Roman Empire, and the difference might have had much to do with the different sources of slavery. In the Han Empire the great majority of slaves were ethnic Han who were sold by their families or by themselves into slavery,[13] while in the Roman Empire, slavery was the fruit of Roman conquest.

The citizen body above the level of commoners (non-rank-holders) was differentiated by the so-called "Twenty Ranks" which provided the foundation of social order in the Han Empire. The system was

---

[11] See the long treatment of the issue by Clarence Martin Wilbur, *Slavery in China during the Former Han Dynasty, 206 BC – AD 25* (Chicago: Field Museum of Natural History, 1943), pp. 72–236.

[12] See Robin D. S. Yates, "Slavery in Early China: A Social–Cultural Approach," *Journal of East Asian Archaeology*, 3.1–2 (2001), 297–300.

[13] See Ch'u T'ung-tsu, *Han Social Structure* (Seattle: University of Washington Press, 1972), pp. 135–141.

completely taken over by the Han Empire from Qin. The "Statutes on Household" from Zhangjiashan stipulate specific areas of land and number of houses granted to rank-holders at each level with rank 1 (*gongshi*) at the bottom of the social ladder who received 150 *mu* of land and 1.5 residences, and rank 19 (*guanneihou*) and rank 20 (*chehou*) on the top who received, respectively, 9,500 *mu* of land plus 95 residences, and 105 residences (land area not specified for rank 20). It can always be questioned as to whether such rigid standards were implemented in Han society and whether, if the figures represent the maximum properties people at different ranks could possess, such figures were strictly guarded. But these stipulations in Han law could certainly be used by people who knew them to defend themselves against others in legal matters. And in law people of different ranks were not supposed to be treated equally. For instance, the "Statutes on Murder" state clearly that if a man of lower rank attacked a man of superior rank, the fine for the violation was four pieces of gold; the fine for violating a man of the same or lower rank was only two pieces of gold. The "Statutes on Reduction of Punishments" then determine that a person of rank 2 and his wife who had committed crimes subject to corporal punishments by tattooing the face and turning into a "Wall Builder" or "Grain Pounder" are allowed to receive the lighter degree of punishment – head-shaving and serving as "Gatherer of Fuel for the Spirits" and "White-Rice Sorter." But this privilege for reduction of punishment seems to have been given to families of rank 2 and above, but was not applicable to those of rank 1 and the commoners still below it.

In short, the Zhangjiashan legal statutes offer us a unique window to look into the social history of the Han Empire. In addition to the

---

Box 13.2   Example from the "Discussion of Crimes" (*Zouyanshu*) from Zhangjiashan

The *Zouyanshu* from Zhangjiashan tomb no. 247, discovered in December 1983, is a collection of twenty-two actual criminal cases that the respective commandery legal officers felt difficult to judge and therefore submitted to the office of Superintendant of Trial for verdicts. These cases were edited into a reference book around 195 BC and were widely circulated and studied by officials throughout the Han Empire. The cases included in the book offer important new insight into the workings of the Han legal bureaucracy.

Box 13.2 (cont.)

CASE 1

In the eleventh year [of Emperor Gao, 196 BC], eighth month which began on the *jiashen*-day (#21), on the *jichou*-day (#26), the Governor of Yidao (Barbarian Circuit), Jie, and the Assistant Jia dare to propose:

In the sixth month, on the *wuzi*-day (#25), the crossbow-soldier Jiu brought in an adult male [named] Wuyou who was called to serve as a garrison soldier under the Commander (Yao), but who, having already received the letter, had fled before reaching the post. Wuyou said: "As Manyi (barbarian) adult male [I] paid an annual poll-tax of 56 coins to be exempted from labor service, and I should not serve as a garrison soldier; therefore, when Commander Yao summoned me to serve as a garrison soldier, I fled before arrival. The rest are as Jiu [reported]." Yao (the Commander) said: "The Commandant of South Commandery has issued order to conscript garrison soldiers, and the "Statute on Barbarians" does not say not to enroll them as garrison soldiers; therefore [I] dispatched him, not knowing that he has fled. The rest are as Wuyou [said]." We interrogated Wuyou: "According to the Statute, male adults of Manyi [are allowed to] pay an annual tribute sum poll-tax for labor service, but it does not say not to enroll them as garrison soldiers. Even if you should not serve as a garrison soldier, once Yao dispatched you, you are a garrison soldier. Now you have fled, how [do you] explain?" Wuyou said: "Our chief has paid tribute money every year as poll-tax, and it is meant to be exemption from [labor service]. The [record] must have been kept by the officials. I do not understand?" [We] asked [the officials] and it was like he said. [We] inquire: "Wuyou is a male adult of Manyi who paid tribute sum every year as poll-tax for labor service. When Yao dispatched him to be a garrison soldier, [he] fled and was captured. All is clear. [We] suspect that he is guilty of crime, pending other arguments, and [we] dare to propose the case, and make this report."

The trial scribes opened the letter. The officials discussed about the verdict: Wuyou should be cut in halves; but some said that the case should be dismissed. The Superintendent of Trial reports: "[He] should be cut in halves!"

"Second-year Statutes," the same tomb also contained a collection of twenty-two cases of lawsuit that shed further light on the actual legal procedures of the Qin and early Han Empires (Box 13.2). In a more general sense, the Zhangjiashan legal strips provide us with a solid ground for understanding social values and distinctions in the Han Empire.

Peasantry versus Great Families: Social Problems of the Han Empire

The main social problem that had long-term impact on the Han Empire was the worsening condition of the peasants who were largely commoners below the rank-holders, but who shouldered the burden of the empire. At the upper levels of the social ladder were the descendants of kings, dukes, or prominent officials who occupied the highest ranks in Han society. The contrast between the two groups in terms of economic standing and social prestige was dramatic, to say the least. The potential threat posed by the landless peasants to the empire had been fully shown in the rebellions that brought down Wang Mang's regime. The fundamental issue is that farmers struggling for subsistence had minimum resources to cope with changing circumstances. Therefore, they were the most vulnerable elements of Han society. Facing bad years or emergencies poor farmers could easily fall into debt to their greater rank-holding neighbors who stood always ready to exploit such opportunities. When farmers could not recover from their debt, all they could do was to sell their children and eventually their land and themselves into the "Great Families" (*haozu*), hence disappearing as taxpayers for the state. The social history of the Han Empire, particularly during the Eastern Han, can be suitably seen as a process of gradual concentration of land and population in the hands of the larger land-owners.

As mentioned in Chapter 12, part of Wang Mang's reform was aimed at solving this problem by putting restrictions on the land area and the number of slaves a single family could own. But he failed hopelessly. On the other hand, the great disturbances caused by the rebellions against Wang Mang's regime and the war fought before the founding of the Eastern Han Empire had laid waste to a large amount of land previously owned by families of high ranks. Seizing on this opportunity, Liu Xiu, the first emperor of the restored Han Empire, ordered a systematic survey of land as a foundation for redistribution. Scholars have had serious doubts about how thoroughly the land survey ordered by Liu Xiu was carried out, particularly in areas where the imperial and aristocratic estates were concentrated. But at the same time, it is also likely that Liu Xiu did make some effort to ease tensions in the countryside, since it was reported that land tax was reduced from one-tenth to one-thirtieth. This trend of decline of the peasantry over the course of the Eastern Han can be viewed in the context of the decrease of population as demonstrated by a comparison of two maps showing changes in population density in AD 2 and AD 140 respectively (Fig. 13.2).

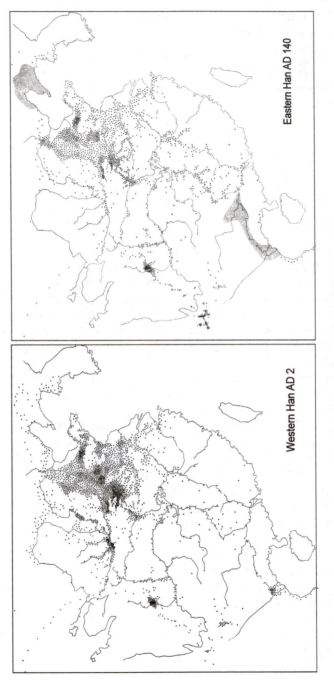

Fig. 13.2 Population decline in the Han Empire from AD 2 to AD 140.

The two maps in Fig. 13.2 show a dramatic decline in population over the course of 138 years from the end of the Western Han to the late century of the Eastern Han Empire. They meant an overall loss of some 8–9 million people from AD 2 to AD 140 in the Han Empire, and the census-based data are considered generally reliable.[14] There can be different explanations of this sharp decline in population, particularly in the formerly most populated North China, for instance by the natural disasters that occurred in the disturbed years of Wang Mang. In this regard, the impact of the flooding of the Yellow River has been well noted by scholars. But then it is difficult to explain why the population in North China did not recover substantially to reach the pre-Wang Mang level even under the favorable conditions of the first century of the Eastern Han Empire. Another plausible explanation is that, because the data for comparison were derived from statistics in the official histories of the Western and Eastern Han Empires based on information available to the central government, the change represents only a major decline in the number of registered taxpayers, not in the overall population. In other words, to a large extent the difference resulted from conversion by the great families of the free taxpayers of the small households by turning them into their own landless tenants or even slaves who in turn had to depend on them.[15] This must have greatly weakened the Han government's control over the peasants from whom it acquired tax revenues and labor services. Certainly, the process could have been more complex. For instance, given their increased monopolization of the local government, the great families could have effectively shifted their tax burden onto the households of the small farmers, hence forcing them into bankruptcy and to becoming their retainers.

The great families were the products of the Han social system discussed above. Many of the great families had their origins in the Western Han, being descendants of the local kings or dukes. In fact, Liu Xiu himself was from such a family. Others were descendants of high officials or families of rich merchants who could use their fortune to purchase ranks, a practice that went back to early Western Han. Over centuries,

---

[14] Although the increase of population in the south could somehow balance the decrease in the north (which is estimated at as many as nearly 18 million individuals), the overall population change is significant. See Hans Bielenstein, "The Census of China: During the Period 2–742 A.D.," *Bulletin of the Museum of Far Eastern Antiquities* (Stockholm) **19** (1947), 139, 144.

[15] Bielenstein, "The Census of China," 143. For a more systematic discussion of this process, see Denis Twitchett and Michael Loewe (eds.), *The Cambridge History of China*, vol. 1, *The Ch'in and Han Empires* (Cambridge: Cambridge University Press, 1986), pp. 556–559.

these families built their roots deeply into the local society and became strong competitors for the state by victimizing their weak neighbors. To give a sense of the economic power of the great families, it is recorded that the families of Ma Fang and Ma Guang, sons of the famous Eastern Han general Ma Yuan, each possessed more than 1,000 slaves, 100 million in cash, a large area of rich land in the suburb of the capital, and hundreds of guests who regularly lived in their houses. Liu Kang, king of Jinan in Shandong, is said to have owned as many as 1,400 male and female slaves and 1,200 horses in addition to 80,000 *mu* of land.[16] By Eastern Han standards, a family that had a few thousand people in its household was not rare in the local areas, and a family of some 300–400 people was the basic qualification for being called a "Great Family" (*haozu*). Certainly, a great family could not have been formed solely by people of the same ancestry. Instead, it took into its domain people of various surnames or origins for various reasons. Each great family was an independent social unit that had its own system of management and norms for conduct, posing important challenges to the commandery and county governments. Many great families also possessed their own armies composed of retainers. They could defend themselves against attacks in times of political and military turmoil, and they could also join local military powers in their war against one another, as frequently happened at the end of the Eastern Han.

In any event, the growing power of the great families and worsening conditions of the peasantry were doubtless two sides of the same coin. Seeing this from the standpoint of the great families in a broad historical perspective, the end of the great expansion achieved under the Western Han Empire and its inability to acquire new lands along the frontiers created for the Han social elites a condition where, in order to maintain their growing households, they had to exploit local resources. This was probably the most important dynamic in Han socioeconomic history.

Han Colonial Enterprise: With a Glimpse at Frontier Society

Sources are available for us to have a close look at the operation of the state and society, though in relation to military affairs, in specific regions along the frontier of the Han Empire. These are thousands of bamboo and wooden strips written with administrative documents buried in the

---

[16] Ch'u, *Han Social Structure*, pp. 202–209.

sands associated with the various Han Dynasty bases and facilities in present-day Gansu Province along the road leading into Central Asia.[17] Two initial campaigns into this region led by the general Huo Qubing took place in 121 BC. The alliance with the kingdom of Wusun in present-day Kyrgyzstan following 115 BC caused the Han Empire to take more aggressive actions in this region as a way to counter the influence of Xiongnu. By 72 BC four commanderies were deployed in the region west of the Yellow River with walls and defenses constructed extending into Central Asia; thus for the first time the region was taken into Han administration. By 59 BC, the Han colonial government, "Protector-General of the Western Region," was established in present-day Xinjiang to coordinate Han military and civil activities in Central Asia. The Eastern Han Empire owed much of its success in the western region to the great spirit of Ban Chao, who served for decades as the Han governor in Central Asia. Before he returned to Luoyang in AD 102, he is said to have been able to mobilize a force of 70,000 soldiers to serve the interest of the Han Empire in Central Asia.

A recent study by Chun-shu Chang based on the wooden strips excavated from fortresses in Jüyan helps us understand the administration as well as social life in the frontier communities of the Han Empire. In this narrow region of some 250 km along the Jüyan River, the Han developed a society that was managed through the coordination of dual systems. The garrison system was formed by four tiers, divided between two "Chief Commandants" (duwei) stationed in the two mains cities of the region. The second level of authority in each division was formed by seven commandants stationed in seven fortresses, under whom were forty captains who had under their control 260 watchtowers each guarded by two to five soldiers. This method formed the whole system of defense of the Jüyan region. The civil administration of Jüyan replicated the structure in the interior of the Han Empire divided into three levels: county – district – village. The two systems had independent authorities but worked in collaboration with one another. The total of military personnel including both guarding troops and the large units of farmer–soldiers is estimated at 4,066 and the civil population is estimated at 6,016.[18] There were also the transportation facilities equipped with carts and horses, and the postal

---

[17] Some of these materials are systematically discussed in Michael Loewe, *Records of Han Administration*, 2 vols. (London: Cambridge University Press, 1967).

[18] The official history of the Western Han Dynasty records the population of the Zhangye Commandery as 88,731; Jüyan was one of the ten counties belonging to the Zhangye Commandery.

service divided between the regular postal stations and the garrison establishments.[19]

The detailed information offered by the Jüyan strips allows us to glimpse some subtle aspects of the frontier society. For instance, about 42% of the soldiers in the region were from the Central Plain regions of the empire in the east, including a good number from the regional kingdoms, but very few from the Han capital region in central Shaanxi. All service-men were twenty years old and above, and no soldiers were over forty-five as no officials were over fifty.[20] In contrast to the guarding troops, the cavalrymen were predominantly from the local Zhangye Commandery which had ten counties including Jüyan; in other words, the cavalry forces were recruited locally from the frontier region. Another interesting aspect is about border control: three different types of passports were issued by the authorities for traveling through the frontier. The first was issued to individuals on government business and entitled them to accommodation at government facilities; the second was a travel permit issued to civilians and carried by the travelers themselves to the control points; the third type was issued to government or garrison personnel, usually split into two halves, one of which was delivered separately to the control points ahead of time to be used to match the other half in the traveler's hands.[21] The guarding soldiers in the numerous watchtowers, besides checking the passports of travelers, kept records of various signals that they handled each day, such as the origin and destination of the signals transmitted, time of signal reception and transmission, soldiers on duty, types of signals, and reasons for sending them, etc.[22]

The Weakness of the Imperial Institution and the Crisis of the Han Empire

The most important politics of the empire are those which surrounded the succession of the emperor. On this point, the Han Empire seems to have been on a stronger footing in comparison to the Roman Empire where the lack of rules governing imperial succession led to endless usurpation and murder that ended the lives of the majority of the Roman emperors. However, the strong unity of imperial rule and dynastic tradition in the Han Empire did not ensure that the emperor who thereupon came to rule was the best choice for the empire; in many cases, not even the better

---

[19] Chun-shu Chang, *The Rise of the Chinese Empire*, vol. 2, *Frontier, Immigration, and Empire in Han China, 130 BC – AD 157* (Ann Arbor: University of Michigan Press, 2007), pp. 23, 78, 107–118.

[20] *Ibid.*, pp. 53–73.   [21] *Ibid.*, pp. 135–142.   [22] *Ibid.*, p. 171.

choice. This opened ways for a different type of political struggle among the contending groups aimed at control, instead of takeover (which was certainly possibly as in the case of Wang Mang, but it was very difficult) of the emperor. This struggle centered on the central court served to disintegrate the Han social elites and eventually undermined the imperial institution in the face of strong, regional military leaders.

The rules governing the succession of Han emperors have been carefully analyzed by Anne Kinney. She shows that although two early Han emperors, Wen and Jing, did entertain the notion of appointing brothers to succeed them, the normal rule of succession established by Liu Bang who passed the throne onto his oldest son of the primary wife formed an important base for the rhetoric against such unorthodox attempts. And once an heir apparent was established, he was often hard to change, and the increasing influence of Confucianism at the Han court made straying from or manipulating the system more difficult and less attractive.[23] Therefore, the rule that the emperor was to be succeeded by his son, notwithstanding the usurpation by Wang Mang who was eventually unsuccessful, stood particularly firm through to the end of the Eastern Han Empire.

In fact, the founding of the Eastern Han Empire gave the imperial Liu family a chance to reinforce its dynastic rule. Liu Xiu, the "Bright Marshal Emperor," was himself well educated, enlightened in military strategy, and fond of Confucian values. Liu Xiu's intellectual quality was inherited by the next two emperors Ming and Zhang, whose succession caused no dispute. During their reigns, Luoyang was transformed into the center of culture and learning, and the empire as a whole enjoyed long-lasting peace and prosperity. The Eastern Han Empire had a total of fourteen emperors, and although dynastic rule remained strong, in almost no case was an emperor succeeded by his oldest son by his primary wife, except Emperor Shun. Since an emperor often had multiple sons by different wives, behind whose back were located different lines of family influence, there was enough room for manipulation of the succession by the interested parties. As a matter of fact, after Emperor Zhang died in AD 88 almost all Han emperors were established in their early teens, and quite a few in their infancy. There seems little doubt that in most cases this was the result of manipulation.

This condition of the emperorship gave rise to a recurrent pattern of political conflict between the eunuchs and the party formed around the imperial in-laws. When an emperor was young, the power was in the

---

[23] Anne Behnke Kinney, *Representations of Childhood and Youth in Early China* (Stanford: Stanford University Press, 2004) pp. 183–200.

hands of the dowager; in order to control the court, the dowager naturally relied on her father and brothers, as had already happened in the time of Wang Mang. In the long years during which a young emperor grew up, the only males he knew were the eunuchs who were both his emotional supporters and political allies, and who, because of their personal intimacy with the emperor, dangerously entertained the dream of taking over power from the in-laws, in most cases through brutal murder. Because there were always young emperors, over time the eunuchs had formed a deep root in court politics, and in AD 126 their heads began to possess titles of nobility. When a new emperor was established, a new group of in-laws would take over the court and drive the eunuchs back to the palace; but the same process would then be repeated. The worst case was the murdering of the Liang family which produced three empresses, six concubines, and fifty-seven ministers and generals. However, in AD 159 five eunuchs helped Emperor Huan to massacre the entire Liang family, for which they were granted the title of "Marquis" by the emperor. Later, the Confucian officials and students in the imperial university formed an association to counter the power of the five eunuchs and this led them to strike back, resulting in the deaths of 100 scholars and students in AD 168. During the subsequent purge over 10,000 people were brutally murdered.

The end of the Han Empire followed exactly the same course. In AD 189, the "Grand General" He Jin, half-brother of Empress Dowager He, was brutally murdered by the eunuchs in the palace. In revenge, He Jin's followers attacked the palace and killed all eunuchs therein. When Dong Zhuo brought his army from the northwestern frontier of the empire and attacked the capital, having been previously summoned by He Jin, the Han Empire was completely thrown into interregional warfare by local military leaders. In AD 220, the last emperor of the Han Empire was dethroned by the Cao family which established control over most part of North China, founding the Wei Dynasty (AD 220–265).

SELECTED READING

Twitchett, Denis, and Michael Loewe, *The Cambridge History of China*, vol. 1, *The Ch'in and Han Empires, 221 BC – AD 220* (Cambridge: Cambridge University Press, 1990).

Ch'u, T'ung-Tsu, *Han Social Structure* (Seattle: University of Washington Press, 1972).

Loewe, Michael, *Crisis and Conflict in Han China, 104 BC to AD 9* (London: Allen & Unwin, 1974).

Bielenstein, Hans, *The Restoration of the Han Dynasty* (Stockholm: Elanders Boktryckeri Aktiebolag, 1953).

Kinney, Anne Behnke, *Representations of Childhood and Youth in Early China* (Stanford: Stanford University Press, 2004).

Chang, Chun-shu, *The Rise of the Chinese Empire,* vol. 2, *Frontier, Immigration, and Empire in Han China, 130 BC – AD 157* (Ann Arbor: University of Michigan Press, 2007).

14   Ideological changes and their reflections in Han culture and Han art

The preceding two chapters discussed the political development and social conditions of the Han Empire. The 400 years of the Han Empire constituted a period of paramount importance in the cultural and intellectual history of China. In general, despite the great military glory of the Han Empire, Han society as a whole respected men of letters and the Han court had a deep interest in establishing the empire not only on military strength, but also on the basis of a carefully chosen ideology. The government itself was open for educated men to enter the service of state, and scholars had high standing in the Han bureaucracy. The great philosophers of the Warring States period deeply cultivated the world of thought in China; building on this early heritage, almost every aspect of Chinese culture was again profoundly modified and further developed under the Han. A bold outline of the intellectual trend over the course of the Han dynasty can go as follows: in the early years of the Western Han Empire, Naturalism, or more precisely the Huang-Lao school of thought, was favored by the Han court as its guiding philosophy. Incorporating both Daoist and Confucian ideas, the Syncretism of Dong Zhongshu (175–105 BC) became dominant towards the end of the second century BC. The study of the classics was revived under Emperor Wu, and Confucianism monopolized the intellectual sphere of the Han Empire, providing the empire with a new ideology. Near the end of the Eastern Han, Daoism was revived as a popular religion and Buddhism was introduced to China from India.

Huang-Lao Thought as State Ideology

Naturalism was a broad intellectual stream developed in the middle to late Warring States period, considered by some scholars as the fountainhead of the Chinese sciences and scientific thought.[1] Although this intellectual stream brought into its current both more theoretically oriented thinkers

---

[1] Joseph Needham, *Science and Civilization in China*, vol. 2, *The History of Scientific Thought* (Cambridge: Cambridge University Press, 1962), pp. 232–244.

like Zou Yan (305–240 BC) and other variously oriented practitioners of natural or supernatural magic or occult arts,[2] there was a common thread that was shared by all scholars and masters associated with the tradition. That is, they were all thoroughly interested in or truthfully play on the relationship between the human world and the world around, or broadly the relationship between culture and nature.

The core concepts of the Naturalist philosophy are *yin* and *yang* (two opposing forces of the universe), concepts that were borrowed from such Daoist texts as "The Great One Gives Birth to Water" or the "Classic of Way and Virtue" (*Laozi*), securely dated to the middle of the fourth century BC. Different from the concepts of *yin* and *yang*, the real invention of the naturalist tradition was the concept of "Five Elements." The theory argues that the external world is composed of (or can be classified into) five elements: metal, wood, earth, water, fire. The five elements conquer each other in order and the last element "fire" then conquers the first "metal" hence making a circle. The proof for this relationship is everywhere, and in a temporal fashion the five elements also represent "five phases" in a grand circle of time. Because of the last point, the "Five Elements" theory had in its foundation seeds for developing into a theory of history and this step was taken by Zou Yan who associated the "Five Elements" with five preceding dynasties each having the virtue of a single element. By the early Han, the "Five Elements" had come to be associated also with the four cardinal directions plus the center: west (metal) – east (wood) – south (fire) – north (water) – center (earth). Furthermore, the "Five Elements" were transferred into a color scheme that was used to classify the imperial cults of the gods: White Emperor (Metal) – Blue Emperor (wood) – Red Emperor (Fire) – Black Emperor (water) – Yellow Emperor (earth, center) (Table 14.1). In short, the "Five Elements" had become a common knowledge by the early Han Dynasty.

The maturity of the Naturalist philosophy in the late Warring States represents a strong inquiry into the unity of natural order and the position of human society in it. This tradition stood strong even under the Qin Empire although the guiding policies of Qin had much influence from Legalist philosophy. There is, in fact, no conflict between the Legalist agenda of the state and the Naturalist or Occult practices, as the First Emperor himself employed some of the occult practitioners to help him find chemicals for longevity. Instead, nature had come through to acquire

---

[2] For a discussion of this intellection tradition, see Donald Harper, "Warring States Natural Philosophy and Occult Thought," in Michael Loewe and Edward L. Shaughnessy (eds.), *The Cambridge History of Ancient China: From the Origins of Civilization to 221 BC* (Cambridge: Cambridge University Press, 1999), pp. 813–884.

Table 14.1 *The "Five Elements" and the correlative thinking of Han*

Five Elements	Directions	Colors	Imperial cults
Metal	West	White	White Emperor
Wood	East	Blue	Blue Emperor
Earth	Center	Yellow	Yellow Emperor
Water	North	Black	Black Emperor
Fire	South	Red	Red Emperor

a new meaning in Naturalist philosophical thought, differing from the "Nature" (*ziran*) in the Daoist view. It is no longer an eternal self-willed existence that is uncertain, unpredictable, and untouchable; instead, nature is understandable, analyzable, and even influenceable.

If Naturalism can be considered a science, then "Huang-Lao thought" would have to be called the "political science" of ancient China. In the early Han, a number of prominent officials at the imperial court, including the ministers Cao Cen and Chen Ping, are all said to have been followers of Huang-Lao philosophy. Both Emperor Jing and his mother Empress Dowager Dou had a strong Huang-Lao agenda. Particularly the dowager exercised long-lasting influence on the court after the death of her husband Emperor Wen until the maturity of her grandson Emperor Wu. Even Sima Qian's own father is reported to have studied Huang-Lao philosophy. There seems little doubt that in the early Han Empire, Huang-Lao philosophy was both dominant in the imperial court and widespread across the intellectual spectrum of Han society. However, for 2,000 years, no extant texts could be attributed to the Huang-Lao school. In the absence of authoritative texts, knowledge of the school, gleaned from a handful of citations in the historical records, was fragmentary and contradictory at best.

In December 1973, the famous tombs at Mawangdui in Hunan Province were excavated (see below). Among the treasures from the tombs are two well-preserved silk scrolls dating back to early Han. The two scrolls carry a total of more than 120,000 characters, and each offers a version of the complete text of the "Classic of Way and Virtue" (called *Laozi* A and B). On the same scroll with *Laozi* B, believed to have been written during the reign of Liu Bang on the basis of the character-taboo fashion displayed by the text, and indeed preceding the *Laozi* B text, there are four new texts: "Canonical Laws" (*Jingfa*), "Sixteen Classics" (*Shiliu jing*), "Weighing" (*Cheng*), and "Origins of the Way" (*Daoyuan*). A first study of the four texts published by the famous paleographer Tang Lan identified these texts with the so-called "Four Classics of the Yellow

Emperor" listed in the bibliography chapter of the official history of the Western Han dynasty, and traditionally believed to have been the core texts of the Huang-Lao school. Although this identification quickly met objections from other scholars, given the special intellectual context of early Han in which the texts were produced and entombed and their close relationship with the *Laozi* text written on the same scroll, there is a good possibility that they indeed belong to the large Huang-Lao tradition. But they might not be the so-called "Four Classics of the Yellow Emperor."

Working from assumption that these new texts are the so-called "Four Classics of the Yellow Emperor," R. P. Peerenboom provided what still stands as the most comprehensive analysis of the philosophical ideas of the Huang-Lao school in English.[3] Although it raised questions that have not been fully answered, there is no doubt that this study has opened up new ways for understanding the philosophy represented by the four texts as well as the overall intellectual climate of the early decades of the Han Empire. First, Huang-Lao thought starts with a three-tier cosmology and draws fundamental distinctions between the "Way of Heaven," the "Way of Human," and the "Way of Earth." The first is manifested through the movement of *yin* and *yang*, the change of seasons, and the celestial bodies; the second is represented by all human institutions including the kingdoms and the empire; the third is the earth, formed by the "Five Elements." Second, Huang-Lao is fundamentally Naturalism in the sense that the unquestionable cosmic order ("Way of Heaven") serves as the basis for everything, and is the foundation for human orders. It is the human's obligation to obey the Heavenly rules to construct political and social institutions that maximize the use of the "Five Elements," the "Way of Earth." Third, correlated to this foundational Naturalism is a natural-law theory – laws that govern human society are constructed as objective rules derived from a predetermined natural order.[4] Fourth, because the law has its origin in the predetermined heavenly order, there is a strong sense that the law is moral, something that humans are obligated to obey. In this regard, Huang-Lao thought, despite its sharing with Legalism the reverence for social order achieved through the implementation of law, is very different from positive law theory of Legalism. Fifth, there is a distinctive correspondence with epistemology in which natural order is predetermined and humans can directly discover and understand it by eliminating bias and subjectivity.[5]

---

[3] R. P. Peerenboom, *Law and Morality in Ancient China: The Silk Manuscripts of Huang-Lao* (Albany: State University of New York Press, 1993).

[4] In Peerenboom's interpretation, Huang-Lao thought indeed advocated a natural law based on the law of nature, but this point is being debated.

[5] For a critical review of Peerenboom's study, see Carine Defoort, "Review: The 'Transcendence' of Tian," *Philosophy East and West* 44.2 (1994), 347–368.

Apparently, Huang-Lao thought was not homogeneous. It seems most likely that, although taking Naturalism as its foundation, Huang-Lao thought absorbed elements from both Legalism and Confucianism, making it politically more appealing to the early Han Empire. The Han Empire perceived itself to be the ideological enemy of the Qin Empire and its Legalist method of government. However, the Qin laid the foundation for the political institution of the empire that the Han took over, so Han needed to legitimize itself on a new ideological basis. Huang-Lao thought timely answered this call by setting the empire in the framework of cosmological orders and on the basis of moral correctness. It is the new law of the empire that everyone has a moral obligation to obey, rather than being forced to comply as in the ideology of the Qin Empire. Moreover, in my view, Huang-Lao thought revolutionized the concept of *Wuwei* which had previously long been interpreted to mean "No Action" as it is used in the "Classic of Way and Virtue" and the *Zhuangzi*. "No Action" (*Wuwei*) is said to have been the highest guiding principle for the early Han Empire in adopting the policy of minimum interference in the lives of the people. But in reality, as the Zhangjiashan legal strips show, even in the early years of Empress Lü, the Han Empire implemented sets of laws and punishments that were often more strict than Qin laws. But from the perspective of Huang-Lao thought, and since the Chinese word *wei* could mean both "to act" and "to create," the Han founders could still have argued that they adhered to the principle of *Wuwei*, which did not mean "No Action," but meant "Not to Create by Oneself" in early Han contexts, because whatever they were doing was merely patterned on the "Way of Heaven." In short, Huang-Lao thought as an ideology suited the political needs of the early Han Empire extremely well, and this explains its popularity during early Han.

The Confucianization of the Han Empire and the Rise of Classical Scholarship

As Empress Dowager Dou (d. 135 BC) approached the end of her long life in the early years of Emperor Wu (*r.* 140–87 BC), Confucianism began to make heavy inroads in the Han court, supported by influential figures first of all among the imperial relatives. Under their advice, two scholars of the *Book of Poetry*, Zhao Wan and Wang Zang, were put in important positions in the government, with the former serving as the Chancellor. Thus, the change that took place in the early years of Emperor Wu marked both an intellectual shift and a political triumph of the faction of the younger generations at the Han court that took Confucianism as their guiding principle. As soon as the dowager died, Emperor Wu sponsored at least two open conferences attended by some 300 scholars for the purpose of bringing new light to the policies of the empire and discovering men of talent and virtue. Rising from these occasions were two important figures who both had their intellectual roots in the *Spring and Autumn Annals*, but represented different regional traditions of scholarship on the text. The first, Gongsun Hong, went on to serve as Censor-in-Chief and then Chancellor; the second, Dong Zhongshu, was less successful in officialdom and was sent, partly because of the jealousy of the first for his fine scholarship, to serve as advisor to two local kings. But it was Dong Zhongshu who was able to formulate a grand theory that provided the Han Empire with its new ideological foundation.

Dong was from Guangchuan Commandery in present-day Hebei Province, and had already been appointed Erudite (see below, p. 311) by Emperor Jing for his excellent scholarship. He is said in the official history of the Western Han Dynasty to have conducted himself strictly according to Confucian ritual and expounded from behind a screen during courses of instruction. After his return from the local kingdoms he devoted himself entirely to teaching and scholarship in the imperial university in Chang'an and was closely consulted by the emperor whenever there was a major policy discussion that took place at the imperial court, but he never appeared at the court in person. Dong left some 123 essays including the memoranda that he submitted to the throne, and a large part of his writing was gathered in the current version of the long text called "Luxuriant Gems of the Spring and Autumn Annals" (*Chunqiu fanlu*). However, the best statement of his philosophical views is found in the multiple memoranda which Dong had submitted to the emperor, copied into Dong's biography in the official history of the Western Han Dynasty.

These memoranda suggest that Dong had the fundamental belief that virtuous teaching is preferred to punishment, and in this regard he is thoroughly Confucian. In Dong's view, the reason that the people can still enjoy peaceful life in a time long after the sages had passed is precisely because of the teaching of rites and music which touched people's skins and sank into their bones. Therefore, "Teaching and Transforming" (*jiaohua*) by means of ritual and music is fundamental to the state and has the potential to reform people's nature and customs which will in turn reduce punishment to the minimum level. Furthermore, he interpreted the relationship between virtue and punishment in terms of *yin* and *yang*, as summer and winter that together make a complete year. But because misuses of punishment can lead to the accumulation of evil emotions among the people which can endanger the state, when a ruler received Heaven's Mandate to conduct government he relied on virtuous teaching and not punishment. To Dong Zhongshu, the worst scenario would be to punish people without teaching them. These are profound expressions of the fundamental belief of Confucianism.

Not only did Dong squarely borrow the concepts of *yin* and *yang* from the Naturalist tradition and use them to further explain a whole range of human relations such as that between ruler and subject, father and son, and husband and wife, but he also adopted the concept of the "Five Elements," interpreting them as the five highly esteemed Confucian values: benevolence, righteousness, rite, wisdom, and trustworthiness. Embracing all these is the concept of "Prime" (*yuan*) which he picked up from the *Spring and Autumn Annals* where the term is used to mark the first year of a ruler. But in Dong's theory, "Prime" gained a much more cosmologically conceived meaning as the origin of all things and the beginning of the universe. Confucianism before Dong Zhongshu remained essentially an ethical system, and it was Dong who had given the various Confucian values a cosmologically based framework that was initially developed in the Huang-Lao tradition. On the other hand, Dong continued the discourse on human nature which leads to the core of Dong's theory. According to Dong, "Human Nature" (*xing*) is the substance of a life, and "Emotion" (*qing*) is its desire. Human nature can be benevolent and can also be wicked, and only strict modeling and hammering can guide it to accomplishment; even so, it still cannot be perfectly good. Therefore, virtuous teaching is not only preferred to punishment, it is simply unavoidable.

Empire, in Dong's view, is the necessary institution set up for the purpose of educating the people to be good, and the emperor is the principal of the human university and the earthly embodiment of the cosmological "Prime" who, through correcting his own heart, corrects the officials who in turn would correct the nature of the people. In answering a question posed by an imperial edict that draws a distinction between the alleged non-activist governments of Emperors Yao and Shun, and the activist government of King Wen of Zhou (analogous to the profound political–philosophical change that was taking place at the Han court), Dong, without missing the real point, argued that the difference is only in time; as for their worrying about the welfare of the common people, seeking for virtuous men to serve the empire, and being cautious about the use of punishment, they were all the same. In Dong's view, emperorship is more a responsibility than a privilege. Furthermore, as the hardest-working and most worried man in the whole empire, the emperor was not only responsible to his people, but also stands to the call of Heaven in a relationship that Dong described as the "Interaction between Heaven and man" (*Tian ren gan ying*). For Dong, strange astronomical occurrences are warnings from Heaven; failing to heed the warning will lead to large-scale natural disasters such as floods and droughts which are the punishments inflicted by Heaven.

Dong Zhongshu's philosophy has long been characterized in Western sinology as "syncretism" or "eclecticism." It is true that he borrowed concepts from the pre-existing philosophical traditions, particularly Naturalism, or perhaps more directly from the Huang-Lao school, but his historical role was more than just a synthesizer. Instead, he built the concepts of various origins into a coherent system of thought in which Confucian values gained their basis in the cosmological order and both empire and emperor acquired their moral and legitimate roles. In other words, Dong was much more sophisticated and powerful, as is shown in his memoranda submitted to the throne. As recommended by Dong in his last memorandum copied into the official history of the Western Han Dynasty, Emperor Wu subsequently banned officials of all other philosophical affiliations from service in the central government and established Confucianism the sole guiding ideology of the Han Empire, and thereafter of all major dynasties in Chinese history.

Certainly, Confucianism as a scholarly enterprise was not just about Dong Zhongshu, but has a much longer history in the Han Empire. From the Warring States to the Han Empire China had experienced one of the most dramatic changes in her cultural history – the standardization of the Chinese writing scripts by the Qin. What was even more was that the First Emperor of Qin was reported to have systematically destroyed books particularly those Confucian texts such as the *Book of Documents* and *Book of Poetry*. So, the process by which the ancient texts were transmitted through Qin to early Han is one of the fundamental questions in Chinese history. It should also be noted that through this complicated process, Confucianism was itself transformed from a philosophy to a scholarly pursuit focused on the exposition of the meaning of the early texts, which laid the foundation for the long tradition of scholarship in China.

There were some intellectuals who apparently outlived the Qin Empire. The most famous was Fu Sheng, an Erudite of the Qin Empire who is said to have taught the *Book of Documents* in the Shandong region after the founding of the Han Empire. The Han court sent Chao Cuo, an imperial secretary, to learn from Fu Sheng and brought the text, evidently newly written in Han cleric scripts, to the imperial court in the west. Soon, the Han court carried out an empire-wide book campaign, and stories of discovery of ancient texts began to be circulated as books continued to flow into the imperial library in Chang'an. The most famous case was the discovery of a large number of books hidden in the wall of Confucius' home in Qufu, the previous capital of the state of Lu in Shandong, excavated when the local king incorporated a part of the original residence into his own palace. Another local king was also reported to have submitted texts which he had gathered in his territory in present-day Hebei Province.

The fundamental problem is that many of these rediscovered texts were written in archaic scripts of the Warring States period that had become no longer readable to the Han people. These texts were thus referred to as the "Ancient Texts," in contrast to the "Modern Texts" that were presumably passed down through a process of oral transition and then written down in Han clerical script. It is hard to trace the transmission of each text through the period, but for most known texts, two forms were simultaneously available by the end of the Western Han and they frequently differed from one another. Thus, clarifying the difference between the two textual traditions had been one of the fundamental issues in Han scholarship, but not fully accomplished in the next 2,000 years even down to modern times. In the case of the *Book of Poetry*, for instance, three lineages of transmission acquired official recognition in early Han, each based on a "Modern" version; besides, there was also the "Ancient" text transmitted by Master Mao, which is the text we have today but which was little recognized during Western Han. In 1977, archaeologists recovered another version of the *Book of Poetry* from an early Han tomb in Anhui Province, representing still another previously unknown tradition probably popular in the former Chu region.

In general, the "Modern Texts" had a clearer history of transmission and thus were officially endorsed by the Western Han Empire. In 136 BC, one position of Erudite was established in the imperial university for each of the five books: the *Book of Changes*, *Book of Poetry*, *Book of Documents*, *Book of Rites*, and *the Spring and Autumn Annals*, all based on their "Modern" versions. About ten students were assigned to study with each of the five masters, altogether called the "Erudites of the Five Classics" (*Wujing boshi*), and Dong Zhongshu was the instructor for the *Spring and Autumn Annals*. The event not only marked the establishment of a strict Confucian curriculum in the Han Empire, but also the canonization of texts transmitted from the pre-Han times. The imperial university where the five Erudites conducted their lectures then became the center of learning and scholarship in the Han Empire. By the end of the Western Han, the position of Erudite was increased to more than ten and enrollment expanded to some 300 students in the same grade. By the second century AD, the imperial university, relocated to Luoyang, enjoyed an enrollment of some 30,000 students (Box 14.1), squarely matching the enrollment of many modern top universities in the Western world.

Box 14.1 The Stone Classics

The creation of stone classics was an important moment in Chinese cultural history. The reasons behind the creation of the stone classics were relatively simple – to stabilize the texts in the face of continuing distortion and corruption that were indeed inevitable as the result of hand-copying in the long process of textual transmission. However, the meaning of stone classics must be understood in the wider context of proliferation of Confucian scholarship and the canonization of certain core texts by the imperial state. By engraving a selection of texts on stone set on the campus of the imperial university in the capital, excluding all other texts, the imperial state not only proclaimed the authority of these texts over others, but also asserted its own political and cultural agendas in a very prominent way.

The first set of stone classics, the "Xiping Stone Classics" (Xiping is the reign title of Emperor Ling), was carved in AD 175–183. The set comprised forty-six stone slabs on which were engraved seven texts beginning with the *Book of Poetry* and concluding with the Confucian *Analects*. The texts were carefully edited by a small group of famous literati led by Cai Yong and written in standard Han clerical script. The stones were covered with roof tiles and placed in front of the lecture hall of the imperial university in Luoyang (Fig. 14.1). However, during the chaos at the end of Eastern Han and particularly due to the burning of Luoyang by the tyrant Dong Zhao, the stone classics were completely destroyed. When the empire was reorganized under the Wei Dynasty, another set of stone classics was commissioned by the Wei emperor in AD 241. Since the texts in this set, including only the *Book of Poetry* and *Book of Documents*, were engraved in three calligraphic styles, the great seal, small seal, and the Han clerical script, it was also called the "Three-style Stone Classics."

After the Song Dynasty, fragments of the Xiping stone classics were collected and recorded. After centuries of effort, some 520 pieces of stone fragments carrying some 8,000 characters were systematically published and studied by Ma Heng in 1975. In addition, eight new pieces were found in the 1980s by the archaeologists who had also identified fourteen stone bases of the original slabs at the site of the imperial university in Luoyang (Fig. 14.1).

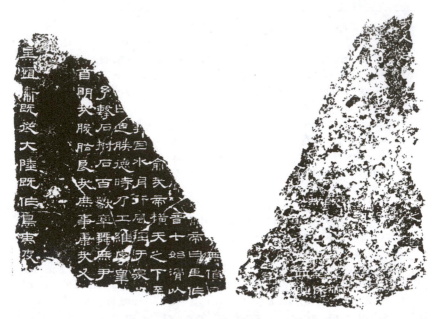

Figure 14.1 Fragment of the Xiping stone classics found in Luoyang: front (left), *Book of Documents*, Chapters "Gaoyao," "Yiji," and "Yugong"; back (right), Chapter "Qinshi" and the "Preface."

Gradually, the intellectual trend began to change, and scholarly interests shifted from the "Modern Texts" to the "Ancient Texts." By the middle of the Eastern Han, the scholarship based on the "Ancient Texts" began to yield some important results. Around AD 100, a major scholar named Xu Shen (AD 58–147) compiled China's first dictionary, the "Explaining Characters" (*Shuowen jiezi*), which systematically explains 9,000 characters and gives also their archaic forms that appear in the various "Ancient Texts." The book provides a key for modern scholars who strive to read and interpret inscriptions and manuscripts from before the Qin Empire, for instance, the bronze inscriptions of the Western Zhou period and the oracle-bone inscriptions of the Shang Dynasty, not to mention the various bamboo manuscripts from Warring States tombs. A scholar of his younger generation, Zheng Xuan (AD 127–200), synthesized the learning of previous scholars and produced systematic commentaries on the "Ancient Text" versions of the *Book of Changes*, *Book of Documents*, and *Book of Poetry*. It is well known that because Zheng Xuan chose to comment on the "Ancient Text" versions of these books which were then considered orthodox in medieval China, the "Modern Text" versions of these core texts were subsequently lost to history.

The Writing of History

Even in an age when archaeology has provided the essential pool of information for Early China as has been fully shown in this book, our understanding of China's early history, especially the 500 years before the Christian era, still cannot leave aside the great historical works produced during the Han Dynasty. Most important among these works are *The Grand Scribe's Records* (Shiji) by Sima Qian (135–86 BC), and the official *History of the Western Han Dynasty* (Hanshu) by Ban Gu (AD 32–92). The former author lived through the most glorious decades of the Western Han Empire and died one year after the death of its heroic Emperor Wu, and the latter author lived in the first century after the empire was restored by Liu Xiu. Sima Qian created the first ever universal history of China, and Ban Gu consolidated a style that has since been accepted as the orthodox form of dynastic historical writing in China.

Sima Qian was a son of the Grand Scribe whose role was akin to that of an astronomer in the court of Emperor Jing and early Emperor Wu. According to the accounts in his own autobiography, Sima Qian began to study ancient texts when he was only ten and set out on journeys when he was twenty that took him to almost every corner of the Han Empire. With his knowledge and extensive travel experience, Sima Qian became an attendant at the imperial court and participated in Han campaigns into present-day Yunnan Province in 111 BC. Returning from the campaign Sima Qian was met with the death of his father, the Grand Scribe, who in his last words told him to succeed him as Grand Scribe and, while in office, not to forget the book his father had wanted to write. Three years later, Sima Qian was officially appointed to the office at the age of twenty-eight. However, in 98 BC, after the revelation that the general Li Ling whom he had recommended had defected to the Xiongnu after a disastrous defeat, Sima Qian received the punishment of castration and was driven out from his office. Suffering from the humiliating punishment, Sima Qian lived on to accomplish this great work of history which in his own words would properly define the boundaries between Heaven and men and synthesize the changes from ancient times to the present. Among the many questions we can ask about this great work two are most important: (1) What makes *The Grand Scribe's Records* different from all written works before it? (2) Why did a work like *The Grand Scribe's Records* appear at the time it did? In order to answer the first question, we must first look at the contents of the book.

The whole book comprises 130 chapters, running to many volumes even in its modern punctuated paper version. Heading the book are twelve basic annals that provide the chronological framework for the book from the earliest time in history, the five legendary emperors, to the reign of Emperor Wu of Han. This is supported by ten chronological tables that provide concordance between political figures and historical events for the entire history covered by the basic annals. Following the tables are the eight treatises each synthesizing the whole range of human knowledge in one specific field of study including astronomy, measurement, calendar, rites, music, sacrifice, irrigation works, and economy. For later generations, these treatises provide the best field-specific introduction to early Chinese civilization. A large part of the book is then taken by thirty genealogical accounts of hereditary houses or lineages in China down to the Han Dynasty; these accounts are both histories of the aristocratic families and regional histories of China. They are followed by sixty-nine biographies of more than 100 eminent statesmen, military generals, scholars, and merchants. Included in this part are also accounts of foreign peoples and lands. The book is concluded by Sima Qian's own autobiography in which he narrates the history of the historian and explains the circumstances that gave rise to this monumental work of history.[6]

There can be no doubt that Sima Qian was not writing about a part or a period of the human experience but was writing about the totality of human history in the world known to him. As a universal history, Sima Qian created a system to present and analyze information that is much more sophisticated than the simple narrative of Herodotus (c.484–425 BC), as Sima Qian was better equipped as a scholar and more centrally placed in his own culture to produce such a work. Recent scholarship on Sima Qian has tried to determine the specific personal motives behind the creation of this monumental work. One such study sees the book as the manifestation of the joy and sorrow of the historian's personal life and suggests that by completing such a work Sima Qian intended to establish metaphorically for himself a historical role similar to that of Confucius.[7] However, we should not turn away from the much larger picture of the time which gave rise to the work or misunderstand the real political–intellectual inspirations for the book, together with the historical role of Sima Qian. The simple fact is that the project had already been initiated or at least planned

---

[6] Sima Qian, *The Grand Scribe's Records*, vol. 1, *The Basic Annals of Pre-Han China*, edited by William H. Nienhauser Jr. (Bloomington: Indiana University Press, 1994), Introduction, pp. x–xxi.

[7] Stephen Durrant, *Tension and Conflict in the Writing of Sima Qian* (Albany: State University of New York Press, 1995), pp. 1–27.

by his father, and by the time of the Li Ling incident Sima Qian had already been working on the book for some years. Reading Sima Qian's autobiography and his famously emotional letter to his friend Ren An, there are basic points that explain the purpose of writing *The Grand Scribe's Records*. First, Sima Qian had the clear understanding that rather than philosophy, the minute recording of historical events is the best way to illustrate the great principles, as exemplified by Confucius' writing of the *Spring and Autumn Annals*. Second, Sima Qian, and his father too, were well aware of the fact that they lived in the greatest time of the historically most accomplished empire ruled by its most enterprising and sometimes unpredictable emperor, and that they were writing from such a historical height that would allow them to understand fully the roles of the many great individuals who had contributed to this historical process. Being in such a position, he certainly had an intellectual ambition that goes far beyond his personal promotion or even the promotion of his family's social standing, and a heartfelt responsibility for his time and for the empire. In Sima Qian's own words, it would be a failure if not a crime for the historian not to be engaged in such a work.

The second great work of history, the *History of the Western Han Dynasty* was written a century after the death of Sima Qian. Its author, Ban Gu, was from a famous family of literati, and an older brother of Ban Chao, the long-time Han governor in Central Asia. Similarly prompted by his father who had already completed a few chapters, Ban Gu continued to write the book with the clear purpose of supplementing *The Grand Scribe' Records* which stopped at the end of Emperor Wu's reign. The family also produced the first female historian in Chinese history, Ban Zhao, younger sister of Ban Gu, who was responsible for the compilation of several tables in the book.[8]

Ban Gu was apparently a little less ambitious if not missionary than Sima Qian and had the limited goal of producing a general history of the greater half of the Han Dynasty (206 BC to AD 8) which was ended by the misrule of Wang Mang – in that regard, it is a nearly contemporary history of the Han Dynasty. Ban Gu adopted the basic structure of *The Grand Scribe's Records* as his model and composed the book in twelve basic annals, eight tables, ten treatises, and eighty biographies of the officials and military generals. In fact, for the period of the Han Dynasty already covered by Sima Qian, he simply used existing information and very often the copy was verbatim. However, there are no genealogical accounts of hereditary lineages because most such families had already vanished

---

[8] See Ban Gu, *History of the Former Han Dynasty*, vol. 1, translated by Homer H. Dubs (Baltimore: Waverly Press, 1938).

before the founding of the Han Empire. Some of Ban Gu's treatises are quite innovative and have been regarded highly by later generations. Among these the most important ones are the "Treatise of Art and Literature" which preserves the bibliography of the Han imperial library, and the "Treatise of Geography" which offers the very first real geographical survey of China.

Since ancient times, the royal court had kept scribes who would keep records of current political and military events. Such were the sources for historical texts like the *Spring and Autumn Annals* or the *Bamboo Annals*. The Han Empire was no exception. Not only did the Han imperial court employ a large number of scribes headed at one point by the Sima father and son, there developed strict rules and procedures for the training and promotion of scribes in the Han government, as we know from the statutes from Zhangjiashan. However, the task of synthesizing complex information and representing the grand historical processes in which individuals could then find their positions when turned into historical figures is the mission of great intellectuals. As such the works they produced may or may not truthfully represent the imperial view of history. However, the situation changed when Emperor Ming of Eastern Han commissioned officials to compile the history of his father's reign, which was subsequently carried down to the next ten reigns across a time span of some 180 years during which new records were gradually added. Since the work was conducted and kept in the eastern lounge, the imperial library of the Eastern Han Empire, the work was called the "Records of the Eastern Lounge." Although the book has been largely lost, its records are preserved in the *History of the Eastern Han Dynasty* by Fan Ye (AD 420–479), which then took over the position as the official history of the Eastern Han Empire.

Han Mortuary Art and Han Material Culture

Except for a few famous stone sculptures standing near the tombs of the Han emperors and generals, most of what we know about the visual culture of the Han Empire has come from burial sites. What people chose to bury in a tomb depends on what they considered important for the provision of the dead in the afterlife, and what could eventually be buried was also conditioned by the political and economic standing of the dead person and his or her family. But first, a few notes on the changes in the burial environment of Han tombs and their social contexts is necessary for understanding what has been unearthed.

During the Western Han, the practice of extravagant burial of the Warring States period continued to find favor with the Han nobility and

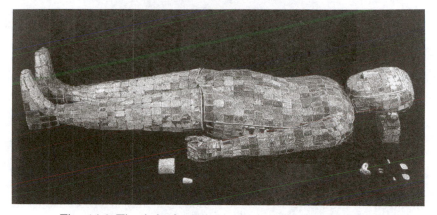

Fig. 14.2 The jade funeral garment of the King of Zhongshan in Mancheng.

social elites, particularly the numerous members of the imperial family and the high officials of the empire. Those tombs belonging to the regional kings were often dug deep into mountains or at least partly constructed by cutting cliff rocks. These mountain tombs usually have a long pathway leading to the spacious main chamber, which is surrounded by a circular hallway. On the two sides of the pathway multiple smaller chambers were opened to store burial goods. The construction of such mountain tombs cost a huge amount of manpower that only the kingdoms could afford to supply in early Han contexts. Typical examples are the tomb of the king of Zhongshan in Mancheng, Hebei Province, who was buried in 113 BC. From this tomb, as many as 10,000 articles were excavated including a large number of elaborate bronze vessels and implements in addition to the ultra-famous jade garment worn by the king himself. The garment was made of more than 1,000 pieces of jade stitched together with golden or silver wires (Fig. 14.2), and according to historical records, such garments were specially made in the imperial workshop in Chang'an and distributed to the regional kings as imperial gifts.[9]

On the next grade are the various large tombs with traditional wooden chambers, dug deep into the earth, such as the famous tombs at Mawangdui, though these are not the largest in the same category.[10] This type of large tomb had a long history in China, and in Han contexts,

[9] Wang Zhongshu, *Han Civilization* (New Haven: Yale University Press, 1982), pp. 181–182.
[10] The largest in this category is the tomb of the King of Guangyang, buried in 45 BC, in Dabaotai to the south of Beijing.

most of them were burials of nobles of secondary ranks such as dukes or marquises, or of high officials in the regional kingdoms. The so-called Mawangdui tombs include three burial pits, located side by side on the eastern outskirts of Changsha. Tomb no. 2 belongs to Li Cang, the chancellor of the kingdom of Changsha who held the rank of "Marquis," buried in 193 BC. Tomb no. 1 is slightly larger, from which the well-preserved body of Li Cang's wife was excavated. Tomb no. 3 belongs to their son, and it yielded a large number of bamboo strips as well as silk manuscripts that formed a small underground library, buried in 168 BC. The three tombs have yielded as many as 3,000 items featuring particularly 500 high-quality lacquer vessels including plates, drinking cups, jars, and musical instruments. Some of the types were clearly modeled on bronze vessels of the period, but they are more elaborate and show higher aesthetic standards. Particularly popular among their decorative patterns are the various finely executed thin-line clouds accompanied in their gaps by the ghostly presence of different types of zoomorphic imagery (Fig. 14.3). They depart sharply from the somewhat rigorous making of geometric patterns on Warring States period bronzes, and are probably associated with the belief in the paradise of immortal spirits.[11] But more fundamentally, they had roots in the unique Han appreciation of natural order that figured very highly in early Han intellectual thought. Such patterns also appear on silk fabric and clothes from the same tombs. One of the special items from Mawangdui tomb no. 1 is the earliest known painting on fabric from ancient China, which depicts the old lady's journey from the world of men to Heaven where she is greeted by two officials.

However, the luxurious ornaments and the aristocratic taste represented by articles from the tomb of the kings and high officials gradually became the target of social criticism by Confucian scholars in the first century BC as being too wasteful.[12] Ironically, in staging such criticisms against the practice of luxurious burials they were actually taking a position advocated by the Mohists against the Confucian practice of lavish ritual. In reality, the gradual disappearance of luxury items in burial contexts was the material reflection of the weakening power of the regional kings, already discussed in Chapter 12. At the beginning of the Eastern Han, the imperial court issued repeated orders to ban luxurious burials. The transition could not be straightforward, nor could it

---

[11] For a discussion of this type of ornaments and their religious and cultural meaning, see Martin J. Powers, *Art and Political Expression, in Early China* (New Haven: Yale University Press, 1991) pp. 76–84.

[12] *Ibid.*, pp. 2–5, 73–103.

d social
anied
nily

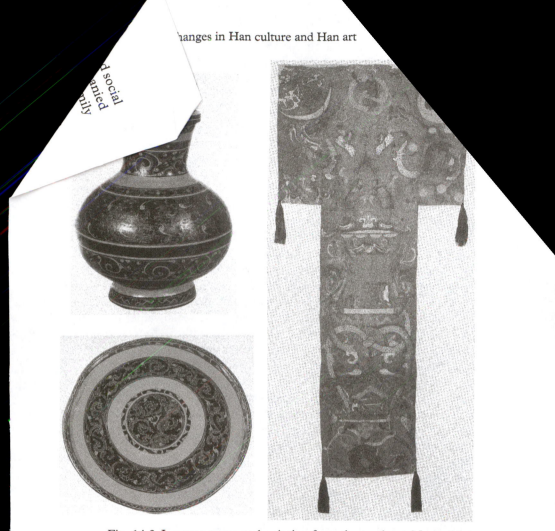

Fig. 14.3 Lacquer wares and painting from the tombs at Mawangdui, Changsha. Upper left, painted lacquer *hu*-vessel; lower left, painted lacquer *pan*-basin; right, painting on silk placed on the inner coffin of tomb no 1 (h. 205 cm, w. 92 cm) depicting the lady's journey to Heaven.

be synchronized everywhere in the empire. But in the material records, we do see during the Eastern Han a gradual shift from burials with wooden structures to underground brick chambers that contain mainly ceramic replicas which loosely imitate the previous living environment of the dead. This important change in tomb structure led to the shift of mortuary focus from what was buried there to what was to contain them, the interior surface of the tomb itself. This opened ways to the creation of

...d

...re the means of expression of Confucian values an...
...ie of these tombs are of considerable size and accomp...
...s constructed above ground as in the case of the Wu fa...
...omplex in Shandong.

...artin Powers's study shows that the construction of such brick o...
...ne chambers was based strictly on local economy, and the great major-
...ty of them that survived were sponsored by families of lower officials at the
county level. Since modular methods were used to produce such stone
slabs which reduced the overall costs, local families with good savings
could afford their construction.[13] Even high-ranking officials and kings of
the Eastern Han Empire gradually adopted similar funeral structures and
fashions, only making them much larger and more complex. But their
burials can in no way be compared with the lavish tombs of the Western
Han kings and nobles. Powers also shows that the styles of carving by the
craftsmen were associated with certain "schools" whose geographical
areas of representation were relatively small, and this indeed makes the
culture of funeral art strictly local, reflecting the social values of the local
elites as well as their level of education.[14] In fact, the funeral sites constituted an important arena of education for the young generations of the
local families that sponsored such tombs and shrines.

The best-known site is the Wu family cemetery in Jiaxiang in Shandong
Province, buried by AD 168. The funeral structures on the site included
both underground chambers and four aboveground stone shrines. Nearly
seventy stone slabs with pictorial carvings and inscriptions have been
gathered from the site, and those which belonged to the shrine of Wu
Liang, the second generation of the family, have been systematically
examined by Wu Hung. The entire surface of the shrine including the
four walls, two topped with gables, and the ceilings were decorated with
pictorial carving of auspicious images representing paradise and longevity.
The history panels, located on the three walls most visible from the opening of the shrine, are carved with a large number of historical figures
divided into four registers moving from the west to the east.[15] They
form a well-organized visual narrative of the historical past. There can
be no doubt that the Wu Liang pictorial carving program emerged for the
same reason that was behind Sima Qian's writing of history; that is to use
historical events, here illustrated on the slabs of Wu Liang, to manifest the
great principles. In the twenty or so years after the first generation of the
family was buried in the cemetery, the site must have been frequently

[13] *Ibid.*, pp. 129–141.   [14] *Ibid.*, pp. 124–125.
[15] Wu Hung, *The Wu Liang Shrine: The Ideology of Early Chinese Pictorial Art* (Stanford: Stanford University Press, 1989), pp. 142–144.

Fig. 14.4 The Wu Liang shrine: "Assassination of the First Emperor."

visited by members or relatives of the Wu family. To the youths of the family, each occasion afforded them a visual tour through the site approaching the shrines, and a rich experience of education about the human past and the glory of the Han Empire.

Starting with the images of Fuxi and Nüwa, ancestors to the human race, they would have been delighted to know the origin of the world in which they lived. They would encounter legendary rulers like the Yellow Emperor and Emperor Yao whose presentation could afford them a rudimentary sense about the time before history and civilization. They would then come across the stories of the Duke of Zhou, the reputed creator of institutions and ritual rules which they were told to obey by their parents. They would be intrigued to learn stories behind the breathtaking scene of the "Assassination of the First Emperor" (Fig. 14.4), and would be fascinated by the illustrations of "Two Peaches Killing Three Warriors," a story about wisdom and courage. Arriving at the present Han Dynasty, the youths would be exposed to the depiction of the Xiongnu prince Jin Midi who as a war prisoner had become a model of personal discipline and moral conduct in the Han Empire. From his story, the youths could further grasp some background about the Han Empire's war with the Xiongnu and about the world beyond Han.

Such a tour through history would necessarily help the young generations to experience the family's cultural heritage, immerse themselves in

Confucian values, and better understand the family's relation to the empire and the empire's position in the world. It is a tour that neither the family nor the empire should fail to give.

SELECTED READING

Harper, Donald, "Warring States Natural Philosophy and Occult Thought," in Michael Loewe and Edward L. Shaughnessy (eds.), *The Cambridge History of Ancient China: From the Origins of Civilization to 221 BC* (Cambridge: Cambridge University Press, 1999), pp. 813–884.

Peerenboom, R. P., *Law and Morality in Ancient China: The Silk Manuscripts of Huang-Lao* (Albany: State University of New York Press, 1993).

Durrant, Stephen, *The Cloudy Mirror: Tension and Conflict in the Writings of Sima Qian* (Albany: State University of New York Press, 1995).

Sima, Qian, *The Grand Scribe's Records*, vol. 1, *The Basic Annals of Pre-Han China*, edited by William H. Nienhauser Jr. (Bloomington: Indiana University Press, 1994).

Ban, Gu (trans. Homer H. Dubs), *History of the Former Han Dynasty*, vol. 1 (Baltimore: Waverly Press, 1938),

Powers, Martin J., *Art and Political Expression in Early China* (New Haven: Yale University Press, 1991).

Wu, Hung, *The Wu Liang Shrine: The Ideology of Early Chinese Pictorial Art* (Stanford: Stanford University Press, 1989).

Wang, Zhongshu, *Han Civilization* (New Haven: Yale University Press, 1982).

Index

activist government, opposed by Zhuangzi
    219–220
administration
    Han 漢 Empire 284–285, 287–288
    mid Western Zhou 周 147, 167–168
    Qin 秦 Empire 246–249
afterlife, First Emperor of China 250–256
"Age of Philosophers" 207
agriculture
    production in state of Wei 魏 188
    small farmer households 191–192
    Warring States period 190–192
    alcohol, Shang 商 Dynasty 83
Allan, Sarah
    Selected Reading 111
    Shang royal lineage 105
    Analects 212–213
ancestor worship
    pre-dynastic Zhou 117
    Zhou 147
"Ancient texts," Han Empire 312, 314–315
Andersson, Johan Gunnar 15, 17
animal bones, divination 92–93
"Annual Report," Warring States
    period 196
anthropology, meaning of "state" 42
Anyang 安陽
    twenty-first century discoveries 75
    area 69
    bone factory 75–78
    bronze casting site 75
    bronzes styles 77–78, 124
    construction process 71
    "cradle of Chinese archaeology" 66
    Creel, Herrlee G. 12
    cultural network 83–85
    economic life 75
    excavations 68–69
    oracle bones 67–68
        inscriptions 79, 113
        and shells 7, 9

palace complex 69–71
periodization 78–81
sacrificial activities 71
Sanxingdui *see* Sanxingdui 三星堆
Shang Dynasty excavations 9
spoken language 92
start of Chinese archaeology 9
Anyang Work Team of the Institute of
    Archaeology, CASS, Selected
    Reading 74, 89
"appointment inscriptions"
    bronze inscriptions 149–150
    Song *ding* 頌鼎 150
archaeology
    "complex society" concept 21–22
    discovery of Feng 豐, Hao 鎬, and
        Qiyi 岐邑 124
    dating standards 78–79, 116
    migration of peoples 181
    North China cultural mixing 181
    Ordos region finds 265–267
    start of Chinese 9
    Zhou regional states 132–134
Archer-Lords 109
architectural alignment
    Erlitou 二里頭 60
    Shang Dynasty 60
    Yanshi 偃師 60
armies
    composition in Warring States
        period 199
    Han cavalry 271, 273, 275
    Han crossbows 271
    Han innovations 271
    "Red Eyebrows" rebel army 279
    soldiers' composition in Warring States
        period 198–199
    standing army of state of Jin 晉 199
    in state of Hann 韓 199
    in state of Qi 齊 199
    in state of Qin 秦 199

armies (cont.)
Zhao 趙 cavalry 199–200
see also warfare
assassination attempt on Ying Zheng 嬴政
244
Austronesian people, Taiwan 4
"Authority," Han Fei 韓非 225
"Axial Age" 209–210, 213

Ba 巴, conquered by Qin 241
Bagley, Robert
late Shang writing 91–92
Selected Reading 89, 111
balance of power, Spring and Autumn
period 166
Bamboo Annals 49
Ban Chao 班超 299
Ban Gu 班固, *History of the Western Han
Dynasty* (Hanshu 漢書) 315, 318
Ban Zhao 班昭 317
Bao Si 褒姒 160–161
Baoshan 包山 bamboo strips, state of Chu 楚
193
Being Natural (*Ziran* 自然), philosophy
concept 219
Beixin 北辛 culture in Shandong 27
Beizhou 北趙 village burial-ground 133
Benevolence (*Ren* 仁), philosophy concept
213, 214, 215, 218, 222–223, 227
Bielenstein, Hans
Han officials' salary 286
Selected Reading 282, 302
Bin 豳 as home to Zhou people 113
Bingong *xu* 𤼌公盨 50
bipolar paradigm, Neolithic cultures 17
birds, mid Western Zhou bronzes 126, 127
Blakeley, Barry B., social transformation in
Spring and Autumn period 172
Boas, Franz, "Cultural Particularism" 20
Bohai Bay 165
bone factory, Anyang 75–78
Book of Changes (Yijing 易經) 157, 158, 211,
221, 312
Book of Documents (Shangshu 尚書) 49, 157,
158–159, 211, 312
destroyed by First Emperor of Qin 311
Shang–Zhou transition 143
Book of the Lord of Shang 236
Book of Poetry (Shijing 詩經) 49, 157,
159–160, 211, 312
destroyed by First Emperor of Qin 311
Han Empire versions 312
King Wen 文 117
Shang–Zhou transition 143
"The Birth of People" 144

Xianyun 玁狁 warfare with Western
Zhou 160
Book of Rites 311
border control, Han Empire 300
Bronze Age
bronze cultures contact with Shang
culture 86
centers in Erligang 二里崗 period 64–65
culture of Lower Ordos 89
first culture in China 46, 53
bronze casting sites
Anyang 75
Miaopu 苗圃 73
bronze culture
incision 203–204
inlaying gold and silver 204
lost-wax technology 203
mid Western Zhou 126–127
piece-mold technology 203
preservation of Zhou realm 202–203
real world images 204
bronze inscriptions
"appointment inscriptions"
149–150
Duke of Zhou's conquest of Yan 奄 and
Bogu 薄古 123
early Duke of Qin 229
Heaven's Mandate to Qin 234–235
King Cheng's 成 military campaigns in
east 120, 121
King Kang's 康 northern Zhou conquests
135
King Zhao 昭, expansion in Shandong
peninsula 136–137
legal statutes 176
Shang 8, 92
Shang military campaigns in Shandong
region 120
Western Zhou 8, 92, 140, 144
founding of regional states 129
legal matters 175
lineages 142
literacy 156–157
warfare 197
Yan 燕 state granted by Zhou king 133
Zhou 周
contact with Huai 淮 River region 138
inspection of regional states 132
land disputes 154
land grants of king 154
regional rulers' visits 134
royal cities 123
bronze technology
Erligang period 61
late Shang Dynasty 77–78

t 168–171
–174

to interior

125
–171   –125, 126

250

3, 124
overy 86

126–127
patterns 127
d regional and metropolitan

nd Shang styles compared
124–125, 126
dha 209
ddhism, Chinese civilization 5
Buku 不窋 113
bureaucracy
    Han Empire 265, 283–285, 287
    territorial state management technique 195
    Zhou Dynasty 112
bureaucratization
    mid Western Zhou government 147–152
    Warring States period 197
burial bronzes, mid Western Zhou 126–127
burial remains
    Jin 晉 rulers 133
    Sanxingdui 三星堆 87–88
    Sidun 寺墩 in Jiangsu 34
    Taosi 陶寺 32
    tomb of Lady Hao 好 76–77
    Yuanjunmiao 元君廟 28–29
    see also tombs
burial sites, Han Empire 318–322

Cai Yong 蔡邕 313
"Canon of Law," Li Kui 李悝 192, 193
"Canonical Laws" (Jingfa 經法) 306
Cao Cen 曹參, Huang-Lao follower 306
cavalry
    Han army 271, 273, 275
    Zhao 199–200
Censor-in-Chief, Han Empire 284
Central Asia
    contacts with 5, 136, 279
    Han Empire 299
    states visited by Zhang Qian 張騫 271
Central Plain, cultural development 18–20

Chancellor, Han
Chang Chun-shu 29
    Selected Reading 30
Chang, K. C. 65, 89
    "Chinese Interaction Sph
    Selected Reading 40, 111
    Shang royal government 106
    Shang royal lineage 105–106
    state formation 42
Chang'an 長安
    Han imperial capital 260
    Nine Temples 277
Changcheng 長城 ("Long Wall") of Qi 185
Changping 長平, Battle of 194, 199
charcoal samples
    Cishan 磁山 site, Hebei 23
    early Neolithic rice 24
    Peiligang 裴李崗 site, Henan 23
Chavannes, Édouard, book on Dunhuang
        strips 7–8
Chen Ping 陳平, Huang-Lao follower 306
Chen Sheng 陳勝 258
Chen 陳, state of 164
Chen Xingcan 陳星燦 65
    Selected Reading 40
Chengzhou 成周, Zhou administrative
        center 123–124, 163
Chief Commander (Lingyin 令尹), state of
        Chu 195
chiefdoms 21, 30
    comparison with states 37–40
    emergence of states 41, 53
    Longshan 龍山 society 37–40
China
    history of Sima Qian 司馬遷 315–317
    topography 1–2
    unification of 244–245
"Chinese League" formed by Qi 163
Cho-yun Hsu
    promotion of lower society
            members 172
    Selected Reading 139, 161, 182
Chu 楚, state of 165, 172
    archaeological discoveries 221–222
    Chief Commander office (Lingyin) 195
    conquest by Qin 241, 245
    counties 168
    Fangcheng 方城 ("Square Wall") 185
    legal procedures 193
    legal statutes 176
    military disaster of 311 BC 189–190
    population registration 193
    royal army 199

...ding 302

...l samples 23
...-裴李崗 culture 22,
...25–27

...tary service, Han Empire 288
...s, Warring States period 195–196
...ie, Spring and Autumn period
    171–172
...ns and clan names 140–141
Classic of Way and Virtue 217, 222–223, 305,
    306
Clerical Script 249
climate in early times
    North China 3, 22
    South China 3–4
Commandant, state of Qin 195
Commander-in-chief, Han Empire 276, 277
commanderies
    Han Empire 285
    Qin Empire 246
Commandery Protector, Warring States
    period 195
commoners on Han social scale 292
"complex society" archaeology concept
    21–22
concepts in philosophy *see* philosophy
    concepts
"Confucian Classics" 157, 312
Confucianism 311
    criticized by Mozi 墨子 226–227
    Dong Zhongshu 董仲舒 309–310
    Guodian 郭店 texts 222
    Han Empire 308–311
Confucius 157, 162
    ancestral family 174
    Book of Documents 159
    Book of Poetry 159
    dates of birth and death 207
    life and career 210–211
    parentage 210–211
    as philosopher 212–213
    as scholar 211–212
    Shi 士 status students 174
    in state of Lu 魯 211
    "Well Field" system 191
conscription 194–195
copper
    deposits south of Yangzi River 63
    mining in Tongling 銅嶺 63
cosmology, Shang Dynasty 99
counties
    bureaucratic inspections 196
    Han Empire 285

history and geopolitical c...
lineage system erosion 17...
military service 171
move from states' periphery...
    173
non-hereditary 171
numbers of in major states 170...
Qin Empire 246, 250
Qin's conquered lands 231, 236...
role of 168–171
taxation 171
territorial state's building blocks 18...
Xian 縣 derivation and meaning 168...
see also "County–Commandery" syste...
"County–Commandery" system 167–17...
    administration 167
covenant tablets
    Houma 侯馬 174, 177, 178–179
    Wenxian 溫縣 177
Craftiness (*Qiao* 巧), philosophy concept
    222–223
Crawford, Gray W., Selected Reading 40
Creel, Herrlee G. 12
    Anyang 12
    Selected Reading 14, 182
    The Birth of China 12
criminal cases, Zhangjiashan 293–294
crossbows 199
    Han army 271
currency standardization in Qin
    Empire 249

Da Qin 大秦 *see* Roman Empire
Daluo 大駱 230–231
Dan 丹, Prince of Yan 244–245
Daoism
    Dao 道 217–219
    search for natural order 216–220
    three stages of development 216
Dasikong 大司空 village, stratigraphy 78
dating
    archaeological method 78–79, 116
    bronzes 78, 79
    historical method 79–80
    Nianzipo 碾子坡 113–115
Daxinzhuang 大辛莊, literary evidence 83
Dayangzhou 大洋洲, bronzes discovery 86
defense system, Han Empire 299–300
deities, Earth, River, and Mountain of
    Shang Dynasty 100
"Desert North Campaign" 275
Di Cosmo, Nicolas, Selected Reading 282
Di 狄 people 180
    prejudice against 181–182
    relationship with Zhou regional
        states 180

Diaotonghuan 吊桶環, domestication of rice 24
dictionary, China's first 314
digitalization, modern sinology 13
ding 鼎 cauldron 124
Dinggong 丁公 pottery shard, early writing 36–37
diplomacy, Warring States period 189–190
Dirlik, Arif, Selected Reading 14
Disputation (bian 辯), philosophy concept 222–223
divination
    materials used 92–93
    non-royal 96–98
    non-Shang 98–99
    process of 93–96
    royal 93
    Shaanxi region 98
    Shang Dynasty 92–99
domestication
    of animals 27
    of rice 24
Dong Zhongshu 董仲舒
    career 309
    Confucianism 309–310
    empire and emperorship 310–311
    "Five Elements" theory 310
    historical role 311
    human nature 310
    instructor for Spring and Autumn Annals 312
    philosophy 309–311
    written works 309
Dong Zhao 董卓 313
Dong Zuobing 董作賓, grouping of oracle bones/shells 79–80, 96
Donghai 東海 Commandery 287
Dongyi 東夷 see "Eastern Barbarians"
dou 豆 high plate 127
"Doubting Antiquity" movement 10–11
    Erlitou culture and Xia Dynasty 52
    influence in North America 12–13
Duke Huan 桓 of Zheng 163
Duke Jian 簡 of Qin (414–400 BC) 239
Duke Mu 穆 of Qin (659–621 BC) 234
Duke 桓 of Qin (603–577 BC) 234–235
Duke of Shao 召 123
Duke Wen 文 of Jin (576–537 BC) 234
Duke Wu 武 of Zheng 163
Duke Xian 憲 of Qin (715–704 BC) 234
Duke Xian 獻 of Qin (384–362 BC) 234, 235
Duke Xiao 孝 of Qin (361–338 BC) 235–236
Duke of Zhou 121–123
    conquest of Yan and Bogu 123

"Five Announcements" 158
    Heaven's Mandate 144
    institutions and ritual rules 323
    southern states campaigns 138
Dunhuang 敦煌
    700 bamboo strips with writing 7–8
    medieval manuscripts inventory 7
Duoyou ding 多友鼎, Xianyun threat to Western Zhou 160
Durrant, Stephen, selected reading 324

Early China
    dates of 6
    floodplains 2
    importance of 1, 5–7
    integral period in Chinese history 5–6
    mining 63–64
    paleoclimatology 2–4
    philosophy 207–228
    studies in North America 12–14
Early China journal 12
early Chinese civilization
    Anyang archaeology 9
    East Asian indigenous 5
    evolution of 6–7
    external influences 5
"Eastern Barbarians" 136–137
    citizens of Qi 165
Eastern Guo 虢, state of 163
Eastern Han
    dates of Empire 6
    eunuchs 301–302
    mortuary art 321–323
    succession 300–301
    tombs of nobles 321–322
ecology, development of human society 2
Emaokou 鵝毛口, stone-tool workshop 22
"emperor," institution of 249–250
Emperor Ai 哀, of Han Dynasty 276
Emperor Cheng 成 of Han Dynasty 255
Emperor Jing 景 of Han Dynasty (156–141 BC) 263–264
    Huang-Lao follower 306
Emperor Ming 明 of Han 301
Emperor Ping 平 of Han Dynasty 277
Emperor Shun 順 of Han 301
Emperor Wen 文 of Han Dynasty (180–157 BC) 263
    punishment 289
Emperor Wu 武 of Han Dynasty (140–87 BC) 264, 271–276, 288
    Confucianism 308–309
    statutes and ordinances 289

Emperor Xuan 宣 of Han Dynasty (73–40
    BC) 276
Emperor Zhang 章 of Han 301
Emperor Zhao 昭 of Han Dynasty (86–74
    BC) 276, 277
"empire"
    definition 245–246
    definition of Chinese 249–250
    development from "territorial state" 185
empire and emperorship, Dong Zhongshu
    310–311
Empress Dowager Dou 竇, Huang-Lao
    follower 306, 308
Empress Lü 呂, Han Dynasty 263
Erligang 二里崗
    Bronze Age center 64–65
    culture 58, 61
    expansion 61–49
    influence on Wucheng 吳城 culture 86
    political system expansion 61–63
Erlitou 二里頭
    archaeology 43
    architectural alignment 60
    bronze 46–47, 61
    culture 42–47
    end of 53
    Longshan 龍山 culture influences 47–48
    luxury items 46–47
    organizational power 47
    relation with Xia 夏 Dynasty 51–53
    site
        description 43–46
        discovery 43
        location 43
        as state-level society 47–48, 53
        tombs 45–46
        transition to Yanshi 偃師/Zhengzhou 鄭
            州 60–61
Erudite, position of 311, 312
"Erudites of the Five Classics" (Wujing boshi
    五經博士) 312
ethnical differences of Rong 戎 181
ethnical relations in Spring and Autumn
    period 180–181
eunuchs in Eastern Han Empire 301–302
execution as punishment 291
Explaining Characters (Shuowen jiezi 說文解
    字) 314
"Extending Imperial Favor," Han Empire
    265

fabric, earliest known painting on 320
Falkenhausen, Lothar von, Selected
    Reading 40, 182, 206

families see "Great Families"
Fan Ye 范曄, History of the Eastern Han
    Dynasty 318
Fang 方 enemies, Shang state 109–110
Fangcheng 方城 ("Square Wall") 185
farmers
    poor see peasantry
    Spring and Autumn period 171,
        173–174
    Warring States period 192, 194, 198
farming
    in 6000–4000 BC North China 24
    Neolithic communities 22–25
    see also agriculture; farmers
Feizi 非子, secondary son of Daluo 230
Fen 汾 River valley
    state of Jin 165
    Taosi 陶寺 32
Feng 豐
    archaeology 124
    pottery assemblage 127
    Zhou capital 120
    Zhou royal city network 123–124, 155
Feng 灃 River 120
Feng Yu-lan 馮友蘭 216, 217
    Selected Reading 228
"Fengjian" 封建, Western Zhou state
    128–132, 142, 260–261
feudalism, inaccuracy re Western Zhou state
    129, 154
"Filial and Incorrupt" 287
Filial Piety, philosophy concept 218
fines as punishment 293
First Emperor of China see Ying Zheng, First
    Emperor of China
Fiskesjö, Magnus, Selected Reading 40
"Five Announcements" 158
Five Conducts, text from Guodian 222
"Five Elements" theory 227, 305
    cardinal directions 305
    color scheme 305
    composition of external world 305
    Dong Zhongshu 董仲舒 310
    five dynasties 305
    phases in circle of time 305
"Five Emperors" 48
"Five Cities," Zhou administration 123
"Five-Family Units," Qin 236
five-generation rule 142, 146
"Five Ranks," Western Zhou 167
floodplains in early China 2
Florus, Roman historian 279
forces see armies; warfare
fortified Longshan "towns" 30–32

bronze vessels
    dating of 78, 79
    Erlitou 46–47, 61
    Li *gui* 利簋 120
    Shang Dynasty 47
    Shang Dynasty wine vessels 124–125
    Western Zhou wine vessels 124–125, 126
    Zhengshou 鄭州 59
    Zhou elite tombs 152–153
bronzes
    Anyang period styles 77–78, 124
    Dayangzhou 大洋洲 discovery 86
    lineage sacrifice 146
    mid Western Zhou
        birds 126, 127
        burial bronzes 126–127
        geometric patterns 127
    Zhou period regional and metropolitan
        134
    Zhou and Shang styles compared
        124–125, 126
Buddha 209
Buddhism, Chinese civilization 5
Buku 不窋 113
bureaucracy
    Han Empire 265, 283–285, 287
    territorial state management technique 195
    Zhou Dynasty 112
bureaucratization
    mid Western Zhou government 147–152
    Warring States period 197
burial bronzes, mid Western Zhou 126–127
burial remains
    Jin 晉 rulers 133
    Sanxingdui 三星堆 87–88
    Sidun 寺墩 in Jiangsu 34
    Taosi 陶寺 32
    tomb of Lady Hao 好 76–77
    Yuanjunmiao 元君廟 28–29
    see also tombs
burial sites, Han Empire 318–322

Cai Yong 蔡邕 313
"Canon of Law," Li Kui 李悝 192, 193
"Canonical Laws" (*Jingfa* 經法) 306
Cao Cen 曹參, Huang-Lao follower 306
cavalry
    Han army 271, 273, 275
    Zhao 199–200
Censor-in-Chief, Han Empire 284
Central Asia
    contacts with 5, 136, 279
    Han Empire 299
    states visited by Zhang Qian 張騫 271
Central Plain, cultural development 18–20

centralization in Han Empire 260
Cernuschi Museum, Paris 78
Chancellor, Han Empire 284
Chang Chun-shu 299
    Selected Reading 303
Chang, K. C. 65, 89
    "Chinese Interaction Sphere" theory 18
    Selected Reading 40, 111
    Shang royal government 106
    Shang royal lineage 105–106
    state formation 42
Chang'an 長安
    Han imperial capital 260
    Nine Temples 277
Changcheng 長城 ("Long Wall") of Qi 185
Changping 長平, Battle of 194, 199
charcoal samples
    Cishan 磁山 site, Hebei 23
    early Neolithic rice 24
    Peiligang 裴李崗 site, Henan 23
Chavannes, Édouard, book on Dunhuang
    strips 7–8
Chen Ping 陳平, Huang-Lao follower 306
Chen Sheng 陳勝 258
Chen 陳, state of 164
Chen Xingcan 陳星燦 65
    Selected Reading 40
Chengzhou 成周, Zhou administrative
    center 123–124, 163
Chief Commander (*Lingyin* 令尹), state of
    Chu 195
chiefdoms 21, 30
    comparison with states 37–40
    emergence of states 41, 53
    Longshan 龍山 society 37–40
China
    history of Sima Qian 司馬遷 315–317
    topography 1–2
    unification of 244–245
"Chinese League" formed by Qi 163
Cho-yun Hsu
    promotion of lower society
        members 172
    Selected Reading 139, 161, 182
Chu 楚, state of 165, 172
    archaeological discoveries 221–222
    Chief Commander office (*Lingyin*) 195
    conquest by Qin 241, 245
    counties 168
    Fangcheng 方城 ("Square Wall") 185
    legal procedures 193
    legal statutes 176
    military disaster of 311 BC 189–190
    population registration 193
    royal army 199

Ch'u, T'ung-tsu, Selected Reading 302
circulating succession 105
Cishan 磁山 site, charcoal samples 23
Cishan–Peiligang 磁山-裴李崗 culture 22,
     23–24
   data difficulties 25–27
   rice 24
civil and military service, Han Empire 288
civil offices, Warring States period 195–196
civil strife, Spring and Autumn period
     171–172
clans and clan names 140–141
Classic of Way and Virtue 217, 222–223, 305,
     306
Clerical Script 249
climate in early times
   North China 3, 22
   South China 3–4
Commandant, state of Qin 195
Commander-in-chief, Han Empire 276, 277
commanderies
   Han Empire 285
   Qin Empire 246
Commandery Protector, Warring States
     period 195
commoners on Han social scale 292
"complex society" archaeology concept
     21–22
concepts in philosophy *see* philosophy
     concepts
"Confucian Classics" 157, 312
Confucianism 311
   criticized by Mozi 墨子 226–227
   Dong Zhongshu 董仲舒 309–310
   Guodian 郭店 texts 222
   Han Empire 308–311
Confucius 157, 162
   ancestral family 174
   Book of Documents 159
   Book of Poetry 159
   dates of birth and death 207
   life and career 210–211
   parentage 210–211
   as philosopher 212–213
   as scholar 211–212
   Shi 士 status students 174
   in state of Lu 魯 211
   "Well Field" system 191
conscription 194–195
copper
   deposits south of Yangzi River 63
   mining in Tongling 銅嶺 63
cosmology, Shang Dynasty 99
counties
   bureaucratic inspections 196
   Han Empire 285

history and geopolitical context 168–171
   lineage system erosion 173–174
   military service 171
   move from states' periphery to interior
        173
   non-hereditary 171
   numbers of in major states 170–171
   Qin Empire 246, 250
   Qin's conquered lands 231, 236, 250
   role of 168–171
   taxation 171
   territorial state's building blocks 187
   Xian 縣 derivation and meaning 168
   see also "County–Commandery" system
"County–Commandery" system 167–171
   administration 167
covenant tablets
   Houma 侯馬 174, 177, 178–179
   Wenxian 溫縣 177
Craftiness (*Qiao* 巧), philosophy concept
        222–223
Crawford, Gray W., Selected Reading 40
Creel, Herrlee G. 12
   Anyang 12
   Selected Reading 14, 182
   The Birth of China 12
criminal cases, Zhangjiashan 293–294
crossbows 199
   Han army 271
currency standardization in Qin
        Empire 249

Da Qin 大秦 *see* Roman Empire
Daluo 大駱 230–231
Dan 丹, Prince of Yan 244–245
Daoism
   Dao 道 217–219
   search for natural order 216–220
   three stages of development 216
Dasikong 大司空 village, stratigraphy 78
dating
   archaeological method 78–79, 116
   bronzes 78, 79
   historical method 79–80
   Nianzipo 碾子坡 113–115
Daxinzhuang 大辛莊, literary evidence 83
Dayangzhou 大洋洲, bronzes discovery 86
defense system, Han Empire 299–300
deities, Earth, River, and Mountain of
        Shang Dynasty 100
"Desert North Campaign" 275
Di Cosmo, Nicolas, Selected Reading 282
Di 狄 people 180
   prejudice against 181–182
   relationship with Zhou regional
        states 180

Diaotonghuan 吊桶環, domestication
    of rice 24
dictionary, China's first 314
digitalization, modern sinology 13
ding 鼎 cauldron 124
Dinggong 丁公 pottery shard, early writing
    36–37
diplomacy, Warring States period 189–190
Dirlik, Arif, Selected Reading 14
Disputation (*bian* 辯), philosophy concept
    222–223
divination
    materials used 92–93
    non-royal 96–98
    non-Shang 98–99
    process of 93–96
    royal 93
    Shaanxi region 98
    Shang Dynasty 92–99
domestication
    of animals 27
    of rice 24
Dong Zhongshu 董仲舒
    career 309
    Confucianism 309–310
    empire and emperorship 310–311
    "Five Elements" theory 310
    historical role 311
    human nature 310
    instructor for *Spring and Autumn
        Annals* 312
    philosophy 309–311
    written works 309
Dong Zhao 董卓 313
Dong Zuobing 董作賓, grouping of oracle
    bones/shells 79–80, 96
Donghai 東海 Commandery 287
Dongyi 東夷 *see* "Eastern Barbarians"
dou 豆 high plate 127
"Doubting Antiquity" movement 10–11
    Erlitou culture and Xia Dynasty 52
    influence in North America 12–13
Duke Huan 桓 of Zheng 163
Duke Jian 簡 of Qin (414–400 BC) 239
Duke Mu 穆 of Qin (659–621 BC) 234
Duke 桓 of Qin (603–577 BC) 234–235
Duke of Shao 召 123
Duke Wen 文 of Jin (576–537 BC) 234
Duke Wu 武 of Zheng 163
Duke Xian 憲 of Qin (715–704 BC) 234
Duke Xian 獻 of Qin (384–362 BC) 234, 235
Duke Xiao 孝 of Qin (361–338 BC)
    235–236
Duke of Zhou 121–123
    conquest of Yan and Bogu 123

"Five Announcements" 158
    Heaven's Mandate 144
    institutions and ritual rules 323
    southern states campaigns 138
Dunhuang 敦煌
    700 bamboo strips with writing 7–8
    medieval manuscripts inventory 7
Duoyou *ding* 多友鼎, Xianyun threat to
    Western Zhou 160
Durrant, Stephen, selected reading 324

Early China
    dates of 6
    floodplains 2
    importance of 1, 5–7
    integral period in Chinese history 5–6
    mining 63–64
    paleoclimatology 2–4
    philosophy 207–228
    studies in North America 12–14
Early China journal 12
early Chinese civilization
    Anyang archaeology 9
    East Asian indigenous 5
    evolution of 6–7
    external influences 5
"Eastern Barbarians" 136–137
    citizens of Qi 165
Eastern Guo 虢, state of 163
Eastern Han
    dates of Empire 6
    eunuchs 301–302
    mortuary art 321–323
    succession 300–301
    tombs of nobles 321–322
ecology, development of human
    society 2
Emaokou 鵝毛口, stone-tool
    workshop 22
"emperor," institution of 249–250
Emperor Ai 哀, of Han Dynasty 276
Emperor Cheng 成 of Han Dynasty 255
Emperor Jing 景 of Han Dynasty
    (156–141 BC) 263–264
    Huang-Lao follower 306
Emperor Ming 明 of Han 301
Emperor Ping 平 of Han Dynasty 277
Emperor Shun 順 of Han 301
Emperor Wen 文 of Han Dynasty
    (180–157 BC) 263
    punishment 289
Emperor Wu 武 of Han Dynasty (140–87
    BC) 264, 271–276, 288
    Confucianism 308–309
    statutes and ordinances 289

Emperor Xuan 宣 of Han Dynasty (73–40 BC) 276
Emperor Zhang 章 of Han 301
Emperor Zhao 昭 of Han Dynasty (86–74 BC) 276, 277
"empire"
    definition 245–246
    definition of Chinese 249–250
    development from "territorial state" 185
empire and emperorship, Dong Zhongshu 310–311
Empress Dowager Dou 竇, Huang-Lao follower 306, 308
Empress Lü 呂, Han Dynasty 263
Erligang 二里崗
    Bronze Age center 64–65
    culture 58, 61
    expansion 61–49
    influence on Wucheng 吳城 culture 86
    political system expansion 61–63
Erlitou 二里頭
    archaeology 43
    architectural alignment 60
    bronze 46–47, 61
    culture 42–47
    end of 53
    Longshan 龍山 culture influences 47–48
    luxury items 46–47
    organizational power 47
    relation with Xia 夏 Dynasty 51–53
    site
        description 43–46
        discovery 43
        location 43
    as state-level society 47–48, 53
    tombs 45–46
    transition to Yanshi 偃師/Zhengzhou 鄭州 60–61
Erudite, position of 311, 312
"Erudites of the Five Classics" (Wujing boshi 五經博士) 312
ethnical differences of Rong 戎 181
ethnical relations in Spring and Autumn period 180–181
eunuchs in Eastern Han Empire 301–302
execution as punishment 291
Explaining Characters (Shuowen jiezi 說文解字) 314
"Extending Imperial Favor," Han Empire 265

fabric, earliest known painting on 320
Falkenhausen, Lothar von, Selected Reading 40, 182, 206

families see "Great Families"
Fan Ye 范曄, History of the Eastern Han Dynasty 318
Fang 方 enemies, Shang state 109–110
Fangcheng 方城 ("Square Wall") 185
farmers
    poor see peasantry
    Spring and Autumn period 171, 173–174
    Warring States period 192, 194, 198
farming
    in 6000–4000 BC North China 24
    Neolithic communities 22–25
    see also agriculture; farmers
Feizi 非子, secondary son of Daluo 230
Fen 汾 River valley
    state of Jin 165
    Taosi 陶寺 32
Feng 豐
    archaeology 124
    pottery assemblage 127
    Zhou capital 120
    Zhou royal city network 123–124, 155
Feng 灃 River 120
Feng Yu-lan 馮友蘭 216, 217
    Selected Reading 228
"Fengjian" 封建, Western Zhou state 128–132, 142, 260–261
feudalism, inaccuracy re Western Zhou state 129, 154
"Filial and Incorrupt" 287
Filial Piety, philosophy concept 218
fines as punishment 293
First Emperor of China see Ying Zheng, First Emperor of China
Fiskesjö, Magnus, Selected Reading 40
"Five Announcements" 158
Five Conducts, text from Guodian 222
"Five Elements" theory 227, 305
    cardinal directions 305
    color scheme 305
    composition of external world 305
    Dong Zhongshu 董仲舒 310
    five dynasties 305
    phases in circle of time 305
"Five Emperors" 48
"Five Cities," Zhou administration 123
"Five-Family Units," Qin 236
five-generation rule 142, 146
"Five Ranks," Western Zhou 167
floodplains in early China 2
Florus, Roman historian 279
forces see armies; warfare
fortified Longshan "towns" 30–32

"Four Classics of the Yellow Emperor"
    306–307
Franke, Herbert, selected reading 14
frontiers, Han Empire 298, 300
Fu Sheng 伏生 311
Fu Su 扶蘇 258
Fuxi 伏羲 and Nüwa 女媧 323

Gan Ying 甘英 281
Gansu
    partial occupation by Qin 241
    site of Qin 229, 230
"Gatherer of Fuel for the Spirits"
    on Han social scale 291–292
    as punishment 293
geometric patterns, mid Western Zhou
    bronzes 127
Gobi Desert 265, 275
God see High God of Shang Dynasty; High
    God of Zhou religion
gold inlay in bronze 204
Gong Fang 舌方 110
Gongsun Hong 公孫泓 309
Gongsun Long 公孫龍 227
Good Government, philosophy concept
    215, 216
government
    mid Western Zhou 147–152
    Shang Dynasty 106–107
Graham, A.C., Selected Reading 228
"Grain Pounder"
    on Han social scale 291–292
    as punishment 291, 293
Grand Chancellor (Xiang 相), Warring
    States period 195
Grand Commandant, Han Empire 284
Grand Scribe's Records (Shiji 史記)
    composition of 316
    importance of 315–317
    motives for 316–317
    Sima Qian 司馬遷 315
Grand Secretariat, mid Western Zhou
    government 147–148
"Great Families"
    economic power in Han Empire 298
    Liu Kang 劉康, King of Jinan 濟南 297
    origins in Han Empire 297–298
    vs. peasantry in Han Empire 295–298
Great One Gives Birth to Water (Taiyi sheng
    shui 太一生水) 222–224, 305
Great Wall, Qin Empire 246, 250
Gu Jiegang 顧頡剛, "Doubting Antiquity"
    movement 10, 13
gu 觚 wine vessel 124
Gui Fang 鬼方 110, 135

defeat by Zhou 267
gui 簋 tureen 124–125, 127
Guo 虢 (Henan), Zhou regional state 132
Guo Moruo 郭沫若, refuge in Japan 11
Guodian 郭店 221
    philosophical texts discovery 221–222,
    224
    texts re Confucianism 222
guoren 國人, Spring and Autumn period
    176

Han 漢 Dynasty
    dynastic transition 276–279
    founding of Eastern 279
    founding of Western 257–260
Han 漢 Empire
    administration 284–285
    "Ancient Texts" 312, 314–315
    army innovations 271
    border control 300
    bureaucracy 265, 283–285, 287
    burial sites 318–322
    cavalry 271, 273, 275
    Censor-in-Chief 284
    Central Asia 299
    Chancellor 284
    Chinese intellectual history 304
    civil and military service 288
    commanderies 285
    Confucian university curriculum 312
    Confucianization 308–311
    counties 285
    defense system 299–300
    discovery of ancient texts 311–312
    emperors' in-laws 301–302
    end of 302
    eunuchs 301–302
    "Extending Imperial Favor" 265
    frontier
        record-keeping 300
        society 298–300
    Grand Commandant 284
    "Great Families"
        economic power 298
        origins 297–298
        vs. peasantry 295–298
    imperial kinsmen 265
    intellectual trend outline 304
    law 288–294
    legal statutes 289–294
    maternal uncles' role 276
    military strategy against Xiongnu 271,
    273
    "Modern Texts" 312–314, 315
    "Nine Ministers" 284–285

Han 漢 Empire (cont.)
  number of officials in service 285, 287
  passports 300
  "Peace and Affinity" policy 269
  peasantry 276, 294, 295–297
  population 283, 295–297
  punishment 289, 291, 293
  Qin input 283, 308
  as rank society 283, 292–293
  regional kingdoms 262–264
  regionalism vs. centralization 260
  Roman Empire 279–282, 285–286
  salaries of officials 286
  scribes 318
  Shanyu 單于 relations 269
  social problems 295–298
  society 291–293
  succession rules 300–301
  "Three Excellencies and Nine Ministers"
    283–285
  university 312, 313
  Zhang Qian 張騫 271–273
  Zhou vs. Qin ruling system 260–261, 265
Han Fei 韓非
  "Authority" (Shi 勢) 225
  history 226
  human nature 225
  importance of punishment 225–226
  Legalism 224, 225–226
  source of legitimacy of political power 225
  "Statecraft" 225–226
Han 漢 River, Zhou military defeat 138
Hangzhou Bay, early rice cultivation 24
Hann 韓, state of
  army size 199
  enlistment of Xiongnu forces 268
  Supervisor of Lawsuit 195
Hao 鎬
  archaeology 124
  pottery assemblage 127
  Zhou capital 155
  Zhou royal city network 123–124
Hao 好, Lady 75–78
Harper, Donald, selected reading 324
He Jin 何進 302
Heaven and God, Zhou religion 145, 208
Heaven (Tian 天), a Zhou discovery 143, 208
Heaven's Mandate 143–144, 154, 208,
    209, 309
  Qin 234–235
Hegemon, Duke Huan 桓 of Qi 165
hegemon, institution of 166–167
hegemony
  state of Chu 166
  state of Jin 晉 165–166
  state of Wei 魏 188
  state of Wu 吳 166
  state of Yue 越 166
Hemudu culture in Yangzi Delta 27
High God
  of Shang Dynasty 99–100, 143
  of Zhou religion 144–145
historiography in China 7, 9, 10–12, 167
  Han historians re First Emperor 255–256
  "Well Field" system 190
history
  depicted in mortuary art 322–323
  Han Fei's view of 226
History of the Eastern Han Dynasty, Fan Ye
    318
History of the Western Han Dynasty (Hanshu
    漢書)
  Ban Gu 班固 315, 318
  composition 317–318
  importance of 318
  motives for 317
  officials in service 285
Honey, David, Selected Reading 14
Hongshan 紅山 culture 27
"Horizontal Alliance," Warring States
    period 189
Houma covenant tablets 174, 177,
    178–179
house remains, Jiangzhai 姜寨 27, 29
households, Han stipulations 293
Hu Fang 虎方 110, 138
Hua 華 Mountain 182
"Huai 淮 Barbarians" 121
Huai 淮 River
  groups threatening Western Zhou 160
  wars with Zhou 138, 160
Huan 洹 River 69, 73
Huanbei 洹北 Shang City
  archaeological finds 81–82
  discovery 81
  size 81
  time-frame 82–83
Huang-Lao 黃老 philosophy 306–308
  compared with Legalism 307, 308
  early Han period 306, 307
Huangdi 皇帝 Ying Zheng 249
Huangpi 黃陂, Zhou culture 138
Huaxia 華夏 nation, formation of 182
Huayuanzhuang 花園莊 oracle bones
  discovery 96–97
  distinctiveness 97–98
  importance 98
  non-royal divination 97–98
Huhanye 呼韓邪, the Left Shanyu 275
Hui Shi 惠施 227

Hui, Victoria, Selected Reading 206
human life-size bronze statue, Sanxingdui
    三星堆 87
Human Nature, philosophy concept
    Dong Zhongshu 310
    Han Fei 225
    Mencius 214–215
human sacrifices, Shang Dynasty
    102–103
"Hundred Schools of Philosophy" 227
Hunye 昆邪, King 273
Huo Guang 霍光 276
Huo Qubing 霍去病 273, 275, 276, 299

imperial university, Han Empire 312, 313
incision, bronze culture 203–204
Individualism, philosophy concept 217
inlaying gold and silver in bronze 204
Inner Mongolia, topography of China 2
Inter-state conferences, Spring and Autumn
    period 165, 166–167, 181
iron
    introduction to China 168, 169
    weaponry 197, 199

jade garment, King of Zhongshan 中山 319
jade production, Longshan culture 34
Japan, a birthplace of modern sinology
    11–12
Jaspers, Karl 209–210
Ji 紀, state of 165
jia 斝 wine vessel 124
Jiahu 賈湖 24
Jiang Yuan 姜嫄 145
Jiangzhai 姜寨
    compared to Pingliangtai 30–31
    domestication of animals 27
    matrilineal society 27–29
    Yangshao 仰韶 village 27–29
Jin Midi 金日磾, Xiongnu prince 276, 323
Jin 晉 rulers, burial remains 133
Jin 晉, state of
    counties 168, 171
    end of lineage system 172–173
    legal codes 192
    legal statutes 176
    overview 165–166
    political struggle 172–173
    standing army 199
    as Zhou regional state 132–133, 180
Jinan 濟南, Bronze Age center 64
Jing Ke 荊軻 244
Jing 涇 River valley 113, 115, 161, 163
Jixia 稷下 Academy, Mencius 214
jue 爵 wine vessel 124

Jüyan 居延
    defense system 299–300
    strips 299–300

Karlgren, Bernhard, Swedish sinologist 8
Keightley, David 12
    divination inscriptions 96
    late Shang writing 91
    Selected Reading 111
    Shang governance 106
    Shang proto-bureaucracy 147
Kern, Martin, Selected Reading 256
King Cheng 成, 121–123
    eastern military campaigns 120, 121
    Zhou regional states 135
King Kang 康
    expansion in Shandong peninsula 136
    temple 145–146
    Zhou geographical perimeter 135
King Mu 穆, change in Zhou ritual tradition
    153
King Wen 文
    Book of Poetry 117
    break from Shang regime 119–120
    construction of Feng 123
    death 120
    highlights of rule 120
    recipient of Heaven's Mandate 143, 144,
        154
King Wu 武 of Chu 168
King Wu 武 (the Marshal King)
    battle of Muye 120–121, 123
    construction of Hao 123
    death 121
King Xuan, 宣 political struggle with King
    You 161
King You 幽
    factual end of Western Zhou Dynasty 161
    mythical end of Western Zhou Dynasty
        160–161
King Zhao 昭
    expansion in Shandong peninsula 136
    legacy 138
    middle Yangzi region warfare 138
King Zhuangxiang 莊襄 of Qin (249–247
    BC) 242
kings
    in Shang Dynasty 104–105
    in Warring States period 196–197
Kinney, Anne Behnke, Selected Reading
    303
Kuai 鄶, state of 163
Kuiqiu 葵丘, inter-state conference 165,
    166–167
Kurakichi, Shiratori 白鳥庫吉 11

Lady Hao 好 75–78
    tomb 76–77
Lai 萊, state of 165
Lajia 喇家, Neolithic earthquake site 38–39
land ownership
    lineage 191
    private 191–192
    Qin 239
land tax
    Han Empire 295
    Qin 239–240
    Warring States period 194
language spoken in Anyang 92
Lao-Ai 嫪毐 242
Laozi 老子 217
late Shang period 107–110
Laufer, Berthold 12
law
    codified 175, 176, 188
    Han Empire 288–294
    Qin 237
    Spring and Autumn period 175–177
    see also "Treatise of Law"
legal statutes
    bronze inscriptions 176
    Han Empire 289–294
    pre-Qin Empire 192–193
    Qin 237
    state of Chu 176
    state of Jin 176
    state of Zheng 176
"Legal Statutes," Zi Chan 子產 176
legal system
    lineage-based 175–176
    Spring and Autumn period 175–177
    Western Zhou 175–176
Legalism
    Han Fei 224, 225–226
    and Huang-Lao philosophy 307, 308
    law and punishment 289
    philosophy concept 224–226, 228
legislation, pre-Qin Empire 192–193
Lewis, Mark Edward, Selected Reading
    256, 282
Li Cang 利倉, family tomb 320
Li Feng, Selected Reading 139, 161, 256
Li *gui* 利簋, bronze vessel 120
Li Kui 李悝, Wei statesman 188, 191, 194
    "Canon of Law" 192, 193
Li Si 李斯 225, 244
"*li* 鬲 tripod + *guan* 罐 jar" 127
Liang 梁 family massacre 302
Liangzhu 良渚 culture
    archaic states 37

disappearance of 34
    Yangzi Delta 34
Linduff, Katheryn, Selected Reading 139,
    161
lineage system 141–143
    decline of 171–174, 176
    land management 191
    legal system 175–176
    primary and derivative lineages 142–143
    sacrificial bronzes 146
    segmentary 21, 29
    segmentation
        five-generation rule 142, 146
        Zhou elite 142
    temples 146–147
    warfare 197
Lishan 驪山 complex 251–255, 258
    armory 253
    bronze chariot 251–252
    design 254
    layout 251–254
    "Retiring Hall" 251
    stable 252
    temples 252
    tombs 252
    underground river system 253–254
    Yigong 252
literacy
    Shang Dynasty 90–92
    Western Zhou Dynasty 140, 156–160
    Zhou Dynasty 112
Liu Bang 劉邦
    "King of Han" 259–260
    rebel against Qin 259
Liu Bang, Emperor of Han Dynasty 260,
    263, 269
    rules of succession 301
Liu E 劉鶚 67
Liu Kang 劉康, King of Jinan, "Great
    Families" 298
Liu Li 65
    Selected Reading 40
Liu Xiu 劉秀, Han Emperor 301
    land survey 295
Liulihe 琉璃河 133
Liye 里耶, writing systems evidence 249
Loehr, Max 77
Loess Plateau, topography of China 2
Loewe, Michael 287
    Selected Reading 161, 256, 282, 302
    "Long Wall" (*Changcheng* 長城)
        of Qi 185
Longqiu 龍虯 pottery shard, early writing
    36–37

Longshan 龍山 culture
  discovery 17
  influences on Erlitou culture 47–48
  pottery 30
Longshan millennium 30
  fortified "towns" 30–32
  high-quality pottery 35
  metallurgy 36
  social stratification 34–35
  societies
    as archaic states 37
    as chiefdoms 37–40
  "town" culture 30–37
lost-wax technology, bronze culture 203
Lower Erligang 二里崗 Phase 58, 59
Lower Ordos
  bronze culture 89
  contact with Shang culture 89
  migrations after collapse of 135
Loyalty, philosophy concept 218
Lü Buwei 呂不韋 242, 244–245
Lu 魯, state of 164, 172
  Confucius 211
  as Zhou regional state 132
Luo Zhenyu 羅振玉 67
Luoyang 洛陽 163, 165
Luxuriant Gems of the Spring and Autumn
    Annals (Chunqiu fanlu 春秋繁露) 309

Ma Heng 馬衡 313
magistrates, state of Qin 195
"Man-eating Tiger" bronze 78
Manchurian Plain, topography of China 2
Mandate of Heaven see Heaven's Mandate
Manner (Li 禮), philosophy concept 214
Maodun 冒頓, Shanyu 268
Marquis Yi 乙, tomb of 203
Marxism 11
  and Western theories, Neolithic China 20
maternal uncles, role in Han Empire 276
matrilineal society, Jiangzhai 27–29
Mawangdui 馬王堆, Han Dynasty tombs
    211, 221, 306
  layout and contents 319–320
May Fourth Movement (1919) 10
measurements standardization, Qin 240,
    248–249
medieval manuscripts inventory,
    Dunhuang 7
Mencius 214
Mencius
  good government 215, 216
  Guodian texts 221
  human nature 214–215, 216, 222
  land tax 194

legitimacy of political power 215
life of 209, 214
as philosopher 214–216, 226
Shi 士 175
in state of Wei 214
"Well Field" system 190
Meng Tian 蒙恬, General 250
Merchant Lü 呂 see Lü Buwei
meritocracy, Qin 239
metallurgy
  Erlitou 46–47
  Longshan millennium 36
  sectional mold casting 46–47
Miaopu 苗圃, bronze casting foundry 73
mid Western Zhou
  administrative officials 147, 167–168
  bronze
    "appointment inscriptions" 149–150
    birds 126, 127
    culture 126–127
    geometric patterns 127
  bureaucratization 147–152
  burial bronzes 126–127
  early Qin 229–231
  foreign relations 153
  government bureaucratization 147–152
  Grand Secretariat 147–148
  military administration 148–149
  promotion in government 149–150
  ritual system 153
  Royal Household management 147–148
  royal succession abnormality 153
  Three Supervisors 147
  transition 152–154
Middle Shang, discovery of 78–83
migration of peoples 154, 180, 182
  archaeology 181
military
  administration in mid Western Zhou
    148–149
  campaigns of Shang state 109–110, 120
  campaigns in Warring States period
    187–188
  forces in Spring and Autumn period
    197–199
  offices in Warring States period
    195–196
  texts of Warring States period 201–202
military service
  in "Commandery" unit 194
  in counties 171
  of entire population 198
  in Warring States period 194–195
Ming and Qing archival documents
    reclamation (1909) 7

mining in Early China 63–64
"Modern Texts," Han Empire 312–314,
    315
Mohism 226–227, 320
Morgan, Louis Henry 28
mortuary art
  depiction of history 322–323
  Eastern Han 321–323
"Mother Wu," cauldron cast for 78
Mozi 墨子 209, 226–227
Mozi 墨子 226
multi-region model of development,
    Neolithic cultures 17–19
Muye 牧野, battle of 120–121

Nanjing Academica Sinica, Anyang
    excavations 9, 10–12
Naturalism 227, 228
  core concepts 305
  Huang-Lao 307
  maturity of 305–306
  relationship between culture and nature
    304–306
Nature Derives from Mandate 222
Neo-evolutionism 21
Neolithic China
  bipolar paradigm 17
  cultural development 15–20
  early farming 22–25
  marks as early writing 36
  Marxist and Western theories 20
  multi-region model of development
    17–19
  products of particular regions 15, 17
  regions of culture 17
  social development 20–22
  three critical inventions 22
New Dynasty
  founding of 277
  reforms 277–279
"nexus ancestors" 146–147
Nianzipo 碾子坡, dating of 113–115
Nienhauser, William H. 65
  Selected Reading 65
"Nine Articles" of Han law 288
"Nine Ministers," Han Empire
    284–285
Nine Temples, Chang'an 277
Ningxia, partial occupation by Qin 241
Nivison, David Shepherd, Selected
    Reading 228
No Action (*Wuwei* 無爲), philosophy
    concept 218, 220, 308
nomadic culture, Yimencun tomb 181

Nomadism, northern steppe regions 267,
    268–269
North America, Early China studies
    12–14
North China
  climate in early times 3
  farming in 6000–4000 BC 24, 25–27
North China Plain
  pre-Qin texts 2
  topography of China 2

"Oath of Alliance," Spring and Autumn
    period 165, 177
offerings, to Shang royal ancestors
    100–103
oracle bones
  earliest writing system 90
  first publication 67
  inscriptions
    Anyang 79, 113
    developmental history 90–91, 92
    the "Four Lands" 107–108
    pre-dynastic Zhou 117
    Shang mention of Zhou 113
    Shang military campaigns 109–110
    sudden emergence of 90–92
  Shang 商 Dynasty 8–9, 51
  and shells
    Anyang 7
    five-period scheme 96
    Huayuanzhuang discovery 96–97
    King Wu Ding 武丁 96
    non-Shang divination 98–99
  Zhou 118–119
Ordos region
  archaeological finds 265–268
  bronze manufacturing 267
  conquered by Qin 268
  extent of 265
  period of decline 267
  see also Lower Ordos
organizational power, Erlitou 47
Oriental Archaeology Research Center of
    Shandong University, selected
    reading 89
"Origins of the Way" (*Daoyuan* 道原) 306

paleoclimatology in China 2–4
paleography 6
Pang 莘, Zhou royal city network 123–124
Pankenier, David W., astronomical
    historian 33
Panlongcheng 盤龍城 63
passports in Han Empire 300

"Peace and Affinity" policy of Han Empire 269
peasantry
    Han Empire 295, 297
    selling themselves 295
Peerenboom, R.P. 307
    Selected Reading 324
Peiligang 裴李崗 site, charcoal samples 23
periodization, Anyang 78–81
philosophical texts
    archaeological discoveries 221
    see also Guodian
philosophy
    Confucius 212–213
    see also Confucianism; Confucius
    Dong Zhongshu 309–311
    early Chinese 209
    Han Fei 224, see also Han Fei
    Mencius 214–216, see also Mencius
    Mohism 226–227, 320
    Naturalism 227, 305
        see also Huang-Lao philosophy;
        Naturalism
    Sophists 227
    traditions 209
    Warring States period 304, 305
    Zhou Dynasty philosophers 112,
        207–228
    Zhuangzi 莊子 218–220, see also Zhuangzi
philosophy concepts
    Being Natural (Ziran 自然) 219
    Benevolence (Ren) 213, 214, 215, 218,
        222–223, 227
    Confusianism 212–213, 222, 226–227,
        311
    Craftiness (Qiao) 222–223
    Dao 道 217–219
    Daoism 216–220
    Disputation (Bian) 222–223
    Filial Piety 218
    "Five Elements" 227, 305
    Good Government 215, 216
    Huang-Lao 黃老 306–308
    Human Nature 214–215, 225
    Individualism 217
    Legalism 224–226, 228
    Loyalty 218
    Manner (Li 禮) 214
    No Action 218, 220
    No Action (Wuwei) 308
    "Prime" 310
    Profit (Li 利) 222–223
    Righteousness (Yi 義) 214, 215, 218,
        222–223
    Ritual (Li 禮) 212–213, 214–215, 219

source of political power legitimacy 215,
    225
    "Teaching and Transforming" (jiaohua 教
    化) 309
    The Way see philosophy concepts, Dao
    Universal Love 227
    Virtue (De 德) 208, 217
    Wisdom (Zhi 智) 214, 222–223
    yin 陰 and yang 陽 227, 305
piece-mold technology, bronze culture 203
Pingcheng 平城 269
Pingliangtai 平糧台 early fortified "town"
    30–31
Plato 209
Pleistocene Epoch 3
political
    contracts
        social–cultural meaning 177
        Spring and Autumn period 177
    economy, meaning of state 42
    power
        legitimacy according to Han Fei 225
        legitimacy according to Mencius 215
    science, meaning of "state" 41
    struggle in state of Jin 172–173
poll tax, Qin 239–240
polygamy, Zhou elite 141
population
    Han Empire 283, 295–297
    migration 154, 180, 182
    registration in state of Chu 193
"Post-Early civilization" period 210
pottery
    assemblage during Shang and Zhou 127,
        134
    development in Zengpiyan 24–25
    high-quality Longshan 35
    invention of 24–25
    pre-dynastic Zhou 113–116
    Western Zhou 127
        localized types 127
Powers, Martin J. 322
    Selected Reading 324
pre-dynastic Zhou 112–117
    ancestor worship 117
    oracle-bone inscriptions 117
    pottery 113–116
pre-Qin texts, North China Plain
    marshes 2
prejudice against Rong and Di peoples
    181–182
"Prime," philosophy concept 310
primogeniture 141, 145
    Shang Dynasty 103, 104
Profit (Li 利), philosophy concept 222–223

promotion, mid Western Zhou government
    149–150
punishment
    in Han Empire 289, 291, 293
    Han Fei 225–226

Qi 契, ancestor of Shang people 54
Qi 齊, Duke Huan of 165, 166–167
Qi 齊, state of 164, 165, 172
    army size 199
    battles, fourth- and third-century BC 189
    Changcheng ("Long Wall") 185
    conquest by Qin 245
    enlistment of Xiongnu forces 268
    Mencius 214
    as Zhou regional state 132, 153
Qiang Fang 羌方 110
Qin 秦
    "barbarians" 234
    capital transferred to Yueyang 櫟陽 235
    "County" (*Xian* 縣) reformed by Shang
        Yang 商鞅 236–239
    early culture 231
    early history 229–235
    in eastern Gansu 241
    "Five-Family Units" of peasants 236
    foundation of Han Empire 283, 308
    genesis of Qin people 230–231
    Heaven's Mandate 234–235
    land ownership 239
    long wall construction 241
    meritocracy 239
    population ranking system 239
    private land ownership 239
    in Shaanxi 231
    Shang Yang's reforms 235–241
    Shuihudi 睡虎地 laws and statutes 237
    in southern Ningxia 241
    succession to be approved by Zhou king
        234
    taxation 239–240
    Xianyang 咸陽 as capital 240
    Zhou relationship 234
Qin conquests
    Chu 245
    Fujian 250
    Guangdong 250
    Guangxi 250
    Ordos region 268
    Qi 245
    Shu 蜀 and Ba 巴 241
    Sichuan Basin 241
    Wei 245
    Yan 244–245
    Yiqu 義渠 241, 268

Qin Empire
    administration 246–249
    civil officials 246–248
    commanderies 246
    consolidation of 245–250
    counties 231, 236, 246, 250
    creation of 245
    currency standardization 249
    dynasty 6
    extent of at death of First Emperor 246
    founding of 183
    Great Wall 246, 250
    highway system 246
    measurements standardization 240,
        248–249
    northern demarcation of 246, 250
    overthrown 257–259
    writing systems 249, 311
Qin, state of 180
    army size 199
    battles, fourth-century BC 188–189
    border walls 186
    Commandant, office of 195
    conscription 194–195
    counties 168
    "Horizontal" strategy 189
    magistrates 195
    rise to superpower among warring states
        188–189
    small farmer households 191–192
    as Zhou regional state 132
    see also Qin; Qin conquests; Qin Empire
Qinghai–Tibetan Plateau, topography of
    China 1–2
Qiyi 岐邑
    archaeology 124
    pre-dynastic Zhou capital 117
    Zhou capital 155
    Zhou royal city network 123–124

rammed earth wall, significance of 30
rank society, Han Empire 283, 292–293
Rawson, Jessica, Selected Reading 138
"Rectification of Names" (Zhengming) 212,
    213
"Red eyebrows" rebel army 279
reforms, New Dynasty 277–279
regional
    kingdoms of Han Empire 260, 262–264
    rulers of Western Zhou 154–155
    states *see* Zhou regional states
"Regional Systems and Cultural Types"
    theory 17–18
religion
    role of writing 91

Sanxingdui 87–88
    Shang Dynasty 99–103
    Zhou 143–147
Ren Fang 人方 110, 120, 121
    Shang military campaigns against 120
rice
    Cishan–Peiligang culture 24
    cultivation 24
    domestication at Diaotonghuan 24
    Hangzhou Bay 24
Righteousness (Yi 義), philosophy concept
    214, 215, 218, 222–223
Ritual (Li 禮), philosophy concept 212–213,
    214–215, 219
Roman Empire
    Han description of 279–281
    Han Empire 279–282
        comparison 285–286
Rong 戎 peoples 180–181
    early Qin 231
    ethnical differences 181
    prejudice against 181–182
    relationship with Zhou regional states
        180–181, 231
    Zuo Commentary 181
royal
    ancestors in Shang Dynasty 100–103
    divination 96
    lineage in Shang Dynasty 103–106
    succession rules in Shang Dynasty
        103–104, 105–106
Ruler Wen 文 279–281

sacrifices, Shang Dynasty 99–103
sacrificial
    activities at Anyang 71
    bronzes of lineage system 146
"sacrificial circle" = one year 102–103
Sahlins, Marshall 21, 29
salary scales of Han officials 286
Sanxingdui 三星堆
    Anyang 110
    burial remains 87–88
    human life-size bronze statue 87
    religion 87–88
    Sichuan 86–88
Schneider, Laurence A., Selected
    Reading 14
scribes, Han Empire 318
scripts
    Clerical Script 249
    Small Seal 249
    stone classics 313
    see also writing systems
seafaring in early times 4–5

seashells, Western Zhao currency 136
"Second-year Statutes" 289–294
sectional mold casting 46–47
segmentary lineage system 21, 29
Selected Reading
    Allan, Sarah 111
    Anyang Work Team of the Institute of
        Archaeology, CASS 74, 89
    Bagley, Robert 89, 111
    Bielenstein, Hans 282, 302
    Blakeley, Barry B. 182
    Chang, Chun-shu 303
    Chang, K. C. 40, 65, 89, 111
    Chen, Xingcan 40, 65
    Hsu, Cho-yun 139, 161, 182
    Ch'u, T'ung-tsu 302
    Crawford, Gray W. 40
    Creel, Herrlee G. 14, 182
    Di Cosmo, Nicolas 282
    Dirlik, Arif 14
    Durrant, Stephen 324
    Falkenhausen, Lothar von 40, 182, 206
    Feng, Yu-lan 228
    Fiskesjö, Magnus 40
    Franke, Herbert 14
    Graham, A. C. 228
    Harper, Donald 324
    Honey, David 14
    Hui, Victoria 206
    Keightley, David 111
    Kern, Martin 256
    Kinney, Anne Behnke 303
    Lewis, Mark Edward 205, 256, 282
    Li, Feng 139, 161, 256
    Linduff, Katheryn 139, 161
    Liu, Li 40, 65
    Loewe, Michael 161, 256, 302
    McNeal, Robin 182
    Nienhauser, William H. 65
    Nivison, David Shepherd 228
    Oriental Archaeology Research Center of
        Shandong University 89
    Peerenboom, R. P. 324
    Powers, Martin J 324
    Rawson, Jessica 138
    Schneider, Laurence A. 14
    Shaughnessy, Edward 139, 161
    Sima Qian 324
    Thorp, Robert 65, 89
    Twitchett, Denis 282, 302
    Underhill, Anne 40
    Wang Zhongshu 282, 324
    Weld, Susan Roosevelt 182
    Wu Hung 324
    Xu Pingfang 徐蘋芳 40

Service, Elman 21
"Seven Military Classics" 202
Shaanxi region, divination 98
shamanistic power, Shang Dynasty 106
Shandong region
  Shang military campaigns 120
  Zhou expansion in 120, 136–137
Shang 商 Dynasty 6
  alcohol 83
  Anyang *see* Anyang
  architectural alignment 60
  bronze
    casting advancements 77–78
    production end 127
    styles compared with Zhou 124–125,
      126
    vessel types 47
    wine vessels 124–125
  cosmology 99
  cults
    royal ancestors 100–103
    winds 100
  dates of 51
  deities of Earth, River, and Mountain 100
  divination 92–99
  Document Maker 147
  founding of 54
  government 106–107
  human sacrifices 102–103
  kings
    mainline and collateral 104
    names 104–105
    oracle-bone divination records 67–68
    shamanistic power 106
    tombs at Xibeigang 71–73
  literacy 90–92
  oracle bones 51, 54, 56
    kings' divination records 67–68
    mention of Huan River 73
    mention of Zhou 113
  pottery in Western Zhou period 127, 134
  power retention by king 102
  primogeniture 103, 104
  religion 99–103
  religious offerings 100–103
  relocation of capital 54–56
  royal
    genealogy 54, 67
    lineage 103–106
    sacrifices 99–103
    succession rules 103–104, 105–106
  sacrificial activities 71
  "sacrificial cycle" = one year 102–103
  shamanistic power of king 106
  Shang Jia 上甲 54

Tang 湯 (Da Yi 大乙) 54, 60
  temperature drop 3
  Wang Hai 王亥 54
  Zhong Ding 仲丁 60
  see also Anyang; Shang state
Shang Jia 上甲, Shang Dynasty 54
Shang 商 state
  conquests by Zhou 117–123
  cultural network 83–85, 89, 109
  Fang enemies 109–110
  the "Four Lands" 107–109
  geographic area 109
  hunting trips 108–109
  military campaigns 109–110, 120
  political network 83, 85
  proto-bureaucracy 147
  relationship with Zhou 117
  Shandong region campaigns in bronze
    inscriptions 120
  see also Shang Dynasty
Shang Yang 商鞅, Qin reformer 189, 191
  Chancellor of Qin reforms 235–240
  counties reform 236–239
  death of 240–241
  early life 235–236
  land reform in Qin 239
  Legalism 224
  reform in Warring States period 224
  reforms' importance 240–241, 249
Shang–Zhou transition 143–144
Shanxi Longshan culture, Taosi 31–32
Shanyu 單于 relations, Han Empire 269
Shaughnessy, Edward, Selected Reading
  139, 161
shaving as punishment
  beard 291
  hair 291, 293
Shen Buhai 申不害, Legalism 224, 226
Shen Dao 慎到, Legalism 224
Shi 士
  good nature 214
  intellectual developments 207
  leaders of society in Spring and Autumn
    period 175
  lower elites in Spring and Autumn period
    172, 175
  as a social group 175
  status explained 174–175
Shu 蜀, conquered by Qin 241
Shuihudi 睡虎地 legal texts
  discovery 192–193
  Qin "Five-Family Units" 236
  Qin law 237
  Qin officials' appointment/dismissal 248
Shun 舜, last of the "Five Emperors" 48

Sichuan Basin, conquered by Qin 241
Sidun 寺墩, burial remains 34
Silk Road in early times 5
silver inlay in bronze 204
Sima Qian 司馬遷 49
　assassination attempt on Ying Zheng 244
　genesis of Qin people 230
　Grand Scribe's Records 48, 54, 67, 103, 250
　Grand Scribe's Records (Shiji) 315
　his life 315
　life of Confucius 210
　Lü Buwei 242
　motives for writing *Grand Scribe's Records*
　　316–317
　Selected Reading 324
　Shang Yang's policies 240
sinology
　China, Japan, the West 13–14
　digitalization and electronic publication
　　13
　French and Swedish influence 7–8
　Japanese influence 11–12
　Marxist influence 11
　"Sixteen Classics" (*Shiliu jing*) 306
slaves on Han social scale 291–292
Small Seal scripts 249
social
　groupings in Han Empire 291–293
　history
　　changes in social standing of farmers
　　　190–192
　　legislation on size of peasant families
　　　191–192
　organization in Yangshao village 27–29
　problems in Han Empire 295–298
　stratification
　　in Longshan millennium 34–35
　　in Taosi 32
　transformation in Spring and Autumn
　　period 172
sociology, meaning of "state" 42
Socrates 209, 210
solar observatory at Taosi 32, 33
soldiers *see* armies; military service; warfare
Song *ding* 頌鼎, example of "appointment
　inscriptions" 150
Song 宋, state of 164, 172
Sophists 227
South Asia, early contacts 5
South China, climate in early times 3–4
Spring and Autumn Annals 162, 211, 312
Spring and Autumn period
　balance of power 166
　concept of Chinese (Huaxia) nation 182
　creation of *guoren* 176

　decline of lineage system 171–174
　ethnical relations 180–181
　farmers 171, 173–174
　importance of historical development
　　166–167
　influence of Zhou periphery states
　　164–166
　interstate conferences 165, 166–167, 181
　legal system 175–177
　military forces 197–199
　nature of warfare 197
　"Oath of Alliance" 177
　political contracts 177
　rise of ministerial families 172
　rise to office of lower society
　　members 172
　Shi
　　as leaders of society 175
　　as lower elites 172, 175
　　as a social group 175
　social transformation 172
　transition from Western Zhou 162–163,
　　166–167
　wars and civil strife 171–172
"Square Wall" (*Fangcheng*) 185
state
　establishment of royal state system 49
　formation questions 42
　meanings of 41–42
　"territorial state" concept 184–187
"Statecraft," Han Fei 225–226
states
　ascendancy over chiefdoms 41, 53
　see also states by their names; territorial
　　states
statutes *see* legal statutes
"Statutes on Household," Han Empire 293
"Statutes on Murder," Han Empire 291,
　293
"Statutes on Reduction of Punishments,"
　Han Empire 293
Stein, Aurel, Dunhuang strips 7
steppe region, extent of 265
stone
　chimes 234
　classics 313
　tool workshop 22
"Straight Road," Qin Empire highway
　system 246
stratigraphy, Dasikong village 78
Su Binqi 蘇秉琦 17
succession *see* circulating succession;
　　Eastern Han Empire, succession;
　　Han Empire, succession rules; Shang
　　Dynasty; royal succession rules

Sun Bin 孫臏, Qi commander 189, 200
The Art of War 202
Sun Wu 孫武
    land tax 194
    The Art of War 201–202
Supervisor of Lawsuit, state of
        Hann 195
Supervisors *see* mid Western Zhou,
        administrative officials; Warring
        States period; functional offices

Taiwan, Austronesian people 4
Taixi 台西, Hebei 83
Tang 湯 (Da Yi 大乙), founder of Shang
        Dynasty 54, 60
Tang Jigen 唐際根, discovery of Middle
        Shang 82
Tang Lan 唐蘭 306
Taosi 陶寺
    burial remains 32
    copper bell discovery 36
    social stratification 32
    solar observatory 32, 33
    town of Shanxi Longshan culture
        31–32
    waning of power 41
    tattooing face as punishment 291
taxation, Qin 239–240
taxation in counties 171, 173
temples
    clusters in Zhou Dynasty 145–146
    five-temple group 145–146
    Grand Temple 145
    Kang Temple 145
    lineage 146–147
    Lishan complex 252
    Temple of Zhou 145
    Zhou 145–146
Ten Heavenly Stems 104–105
Teng 滕 (Shandong), Zhou regional
        state 132
terracotta warriors 254–255
"territorial state" concept 184–187
territorial states
    border walls 185–186
    bureaucracy 195
    main objective of 187–188, 197
    transition to 187
    warfare 187–188, 197
The Art of War
    Sun Bin 202
    Sun Wu 201–202
The Way *see* philosophy concepts, *Dao*;
        philosophy concepts, Daoism
Thorp, Robert, Selected Reading 65, 89

"Three Articles," Liu Bang's rules for
        conduct 288
"Three Excellencies and Nine Ministers"
        283–285
Three Supervisors, mid Western Zhou
        government 147
"Three-style Stone Classics" 313
Tian Guang 田廣 244
tombs
    Baoshan bamboo strips 193
    burial of Duke Jing of Qin 233
    contents in Western Han period
        318–320
    Erlitou 45–46
    Guodian 220
    King of Zhongshan 319
    Li Cang family tomb 320
    Lishan complex 252
    lost-wax casting bronzes 203
    luxury contents decline 320–321
    Mawangdui 211, 221, 306, 319–320
    mountain 319
    nobles of Eastern Han 321–322
    nobles of Western Han 319–320
    Qin and Jin territories 181
    Shang kings at Xibeigang 西北崗 71–73,
        106
    Shuihudi legal texts 192–193
    steppe culture 267
    Western Han social elites 318–319,
        320–322
    Yimencun 益門村, Wei River
        valley 181
    Yinqueshan 銀雀山 military texts
        201–202
    Zhangjiashan 289, 293–294
    Zhou elite bronze vessels 152–153
Tongling 銅嶺, copper mining 63, 64
Tonglushan 銅綠山, ancient mining site
        63–64
topography of China 1–2
    Inner Mongolia 2
    Loess Plateau 2
    Manchurian Plain 2
    North China Plain 2
    Qinghai–Tibetan Plateau 1–2
"Treatise of Law"
    Han society 291
    origin of Han law 288
tribal organization 21
troops *see* armies; warfare
turtle shells, divination 92–93
Twitchett, Denis, Selected Reading 282,
        302
"Two Peaches Killing Three Warriors" 323

Underhill, Anne, Selected Reading 40
unification of China 244–245
Universal Love, philosophy concept 227
universal taxation, counties 171
university of Han Empire 312, 313

"Vertical Alliance," Warring States
    period 189
Virtue (*De*), philosophy concept 208, 217

"Wall Builder"
    on Han social scale 291–292
    as punishment 291, 293
walls bordering territorial states 185–186
Wang Guowei 王國維 8–9, 10, 67
Wang Hai 王亥, Shang Dynasty 54
Wang Jian 王翦, General 244, 245
Wang Mang 王莽, Emperor of New Dynasty
    276–279, 295
Wang Yirong 王懿榮, inscribed bones
    66–67
Wang Zang 王臧 308
Wang Zhongshu 王仲舒, Selected Reading
    282, 324
warfare
    army composition in Warring States
        period 199
    battle-ready male population 199
    changes during Warring States period
        197–202
    commandership changes 200
    fighting methods 199–200
    frequency of wars during Warring States
        period 187–188
    goals of war changes 200
    lineages 197
    soldiers' composition in Warring States
        period 198–199
    Spring and Autumn period 197
    Western Zhou 197
Warring States period
    agriculture 190–192
    alliances 189
    "Annual Report" 196
    bureaucratization 195–197
    composition
        of army 199
        of soldiers 198–199
    diplomacy 189–190
    farmers 190–192, 194, 198
    frequency of war 187–188
    functional offices 195–196
    "Horizontal Alliance" 189
    kings' absolute power 196–197
    land tax 194

Legalism 224–226
military
    service 194–195
    texts 201–202
    overview 183
    philosophy 304, 305
    Qin's rise to superpower 188–189
    small farmer households 190–192
    state control of farmers 192
    supremacy of state of Wei 188
    territorial states *see* territorial states
    "Vertical Alliance" 189
    warfare changes 197–202
    Zhou states list 131
"Way of Earth" 307
"Way of Heaven" 307
"Way of Human" 307
Wei 魏 Dynasty, founding of 302
Wei Liao 尉繚, Commandant of Qin army
    243–244
Wei Qing 衛青 273, 275
Wei 渭 River plain
    Zhou city network 123–124
    Zhou lineage centers 142
Wei 渭 River valley
    elites relocation 163
    Han army reconquest 279
    Han Empire heartland 260
    population transfer from 154
    pottery 127, 134
    Qin rebel attacks 258, 259
    Qin's original center 231
    Rong group occupation 180
    Yimencun tomb 181
    Zhou people 113–117, 120, 141
Wei 魏, state of
    agricultural production 188
    battles, fourth-century BC 188, 189
    border walls 185
    hegemony 188
    legal codes 192
    Li Kui *see* Li Kui, Wei statesman
    Mencius 214
    Qin conquest 245
    supremacy in Warring States period 188
    Xiongnu forces enlistment 268
"Weighing" (*Cheng* 稱) 306
Weld, Susan Roosevelt, selected reading
    182
"Well Field" system 190–191
Wenxian 溫縣 covenant tablets 177
Western Han
    tombs
        of nobles 319–320
        of social elites 318–319, 320–322

Western Han Empire 6
    administrative documents 7
Western Zhou
    bronze
        culture changes 126–127
        inscribed objects dispersal 156–157
        inscriptions 129, 140, 144, 175
        styles compared with Shang 124
        wine vessels 124–125, 126
    cultural development 134
    end of 160–161
    "Five Ranks" 167
    founding of Dynasty 121
    legal matters 175–176
    literacy 140, 156–160
    pottery 127
    regional rulers 154–155
    regional states 129, 184
    social order 147
    temperature drop 3
    texts 49
    threats
        from Huai River groups 160
        from Xianyun people 160, 161
    transition
        to Spring and Autumn period 162–163
        to Warring States period 186–187
    war and warfare 138, 197
Western Zhou state 154–156
    central Shaanxi royal domain 155–156
    "Fengjian" 128–132, 260–261
    geopolitical description 155
    government and society developments
        153–154
    security 132
    weakening of 132
Wey 衛, state of 132, 164, 165, 180
"White-rice Sorter"
    on Han social scale 291–292
    as punishment 293
winds, Shang Dynasty 100
wine vessels see bronze vessels
Wisdom (Zhi 智), philosophy concept 214,
    222–223
writing
    Dinggong pottery shard 36–37
    Dunhuang 700 bamboo strips 7–8
    early 36–37
    Longqiu pottery shard 36–37
    Neolithic marks 36
    on perishable materials in Western Zhou
        157
    religious role 91
    social contexts 91–92
    see also literacy; scripts

writing systems
    "Ancient Texts" 312
    Liye evidence 249
    Qin Empire 249, 311
    see also scripts
written evidence, importance of 90
Wu Ding 武丁, Shang king 75, 76, 104, 109
    oracle bones/shells 96
Wu 武 Family cemetery, Jiaxiang 嘉祥
        322–323
Wu Hung 322
    Selected Reading 324
Wu Liang 武梁, shrine of 322–323
Wu Qi 吳起 188
Wu 吳, state of 121, 166
Wucheng 吳城 culture 64
    influenced by Erligang 86
Wugeng 武庚 121
Wuwei 無為 308

Xia 夏 Dynasty
    debate about 48–53
    kings list 49–51
    origin of 48
    relation with Erlitou culture 51–53
Xi'an 西安, Bronze Age center 65
Xian 縣 system see "County–Commandery"
        system
Xiang Liang 項梁
    rebel against Qin 258–259
Xiang Yu 項羽, rebel against Qin 258
    "Hegemon King," King of Chu 259–260
Xianyang 咸陽, capital of Qin 240
Xianyun 鮮于 people, threat to Western
        Zhou 160, 161
Xiao 崤, battle of 181
Xiao Yu ding 小盂鼎 267
Xibeigang 西北崗 71–73
    sacrificial activities 71, 103
    tombs of Shang kings 71–73, 106
Xihan 西漢 River valley 231
Xing 邢 (Hebei), Zhou regional state 132
    pottery 134
Xing 邢, state of 165, 180
Xiongnu 匈奴 250
    capture of Zhang Qian 271
    defeats by Han forces 273
    fighting for five eastern states 268
    Han military strategy against 271
    Han war with 271–276
    king reduced to rank of duke 277
    origins 265
Xiongnu 匈奴 Confederacy 268, 269
    internal struggles 275
    tribal autonomy 269

Xiongnu 匈奴 Empire 263, 265–271
"Xiping 熹平 Stone Classics" 313
Xipo 西坡, Yangshao settlement 29
Xu Pingfang 徐蘋芳, Selected Reading 40
Xu Shen 許慎 314
Xunzi 荀子 214, 225

Yan 燕, state of
    attack by Rong people 165
    border walls 186
    conquest by Qin 244–245
    enlistment of Xiongnu forces 268
    pottery 134
    state granted by Zhou king 133
    as Zhou regional state 132, 133
Yan Wenming 嚴文明, Central Plain 19–20
Yang Zhu 楊朱, Daoist philosopher
    216–217
Yangshao 仰韶
    discovery of culture 15, 17
    Jiangzhai 27–29
    pottery 27
    social organization of village 27–29
    society 25–30
    Xipo 29
    Zhudingyuan 鑄鼎原 29–30
Yangshao 仰韶 Era 27
Yangzi Delta
    Hemudu culture 27
    Liangzhu culture 34
    topography of China 2
    Zhou's relationship with 137–138
Yangzi River
    canal link to Li River 250
    copper deposits 63
Yanshi 偃師 56, 57, 60–61
    architectural alignment 60
    layout 56–57
    start of construction 59
    transition from Erlitou 60–61
Yates, Robin 239, 249
    slaves 292
Yellow River
    flooding of Daliang 245
    occupied by Rong groups 180
    Qin conquests 235
    sites contemporary to Cishan-Peiligang
    23–24
Yihou Ze gui 宜侯夨簋, inscription 129
Yimencun 益門村 tomb, nomadic culture
    181
Yin Weizhang 殷瑋璋 17
Yin 陰 and Yang 陽 227, 305
    Dong Zhongshu 309–310
Ying 應, Zhou regional state 132

Ying Zheng 嬴政, First Emperor of China
    242, 249–250, 323
    afterlife 250–256
    assassination attempt 244
    death 257–258
    early life 242
    personal character 242–243
    unification of China 244–245
Ying Zheng 嬴政, Huangdi 249
Yinqueshan 銀雀山, discovery of military
    texts 201–202
Yinwan 尹灣 documents 286–287
    "Annual Report" 287
    county magistrates' ranking 286
    "Curriculum Vitae of Major Officials"
    287
    "Registers of Officials" 287
Yiqu 義渠, state of, conquered by Qin 241,
    268
Yoffee, Norman, "complex society" 21
Yong 雍, Qin capital, archeological
    importance 231–233
Yu 禹, legendary founder of Xia Dynasty
    48–49, 50
Yuanjunmiao 元君廟 cemetery 28–29
Yue 越, state of 166
Yueyang 櫟陽, Qin capital relocated to 235
Yunmeng 云夢 Marsh 4, 63

Zengpiyan 甑皮岩, early pottery 24–25
Zengzi 曾子, disciple of Confucius 174
Zhang Changshou 張長壽, analysis of
    bronze vessels 80
Zhang Qian 張騫 271–273
Zhang Zhongpei 張忠培 37
Zhangjiashan 張家山
    criminal cases 293–294
    Han legal statutes 289–294
    legal procedures 293–294
Zhao 趙, cavalry 199–200
Zhao 趙, state of, enlistment of Xiongnu
    forces 268
Zhao Wan 趙綰 308
Zheng 鄭, state of 163–164, 172
    legal codes 192
    legal statutes 176
Zheng Xuan 鄭玄 314–315
Zheng 鄭, Zhou royal city network 123–124,
    163
Zhengzhou 鄭州 56, 57–58
    archaeology 58–59
    bronze vessels 59
    time-frame 59–60
    transition from Erlitou 60–61
Zhizhi 郅支, Right Shanyu 275–276

Zhong Ding 仲丁, Shang Dynasty 60
Zhongshan 中山, King of
   jade garment 319
   tomb 319
Zhongshan 中山, state of 205
Zhou 周
   1059 BC 117–120, 143
   ancestor worship 147
   battle against Guifang 267
   bronze
      art changes 152
      culture tradition preserved 202–203
      styles compared with Shang 124–125,
         126
   bureaucratic administration 112
   Central Asia contact 136
   collapse in 771 BC 208
   conquests of Shang 117–123
   contact with external world 136
   expansion in Shandong peninsula
      136–137
   genealogical relationship of king and
      regional rulers 131, 132
   geographical perimeter 135
   Heaven 143, 145, 208
   Heaven's Mandate 143–144, 154, 208,
      209
   historical location 113–117
   Huai River region contact 138
   India contact 136
   land grants and disputes 154
   literary culture 112
   northern conquests 135
   oracle bones 118–119
   overview of dynasty 112
   people's mixed origins 116–117
   periphery states 164–166
   philosophers 112, 207–228
   pottery assemblages 134
   pre-dynastic see pre-dynastic Zhou
   regional and metropolitan bronzes 134
   religion 143–147
   see also Heaven; Heaven and God;
      Heaven's Mandate
   royal
      ancestor Buku 113
      cities 123
      city network 123–124
      clan 141
      court relocation 163
      house "nexus ancestors" 147
      lineage 142–143
   Shandong peninsula expansion 136–137
   Shang kingdom relationship 117
   temples 145–146

   territorial control expansion 121–123,
      135–138
   wars in Huai River region 138
   Wei River valley people 113–117, 120,
      141
   West Asia contact 136
   Yangzi delta relationship 137–138
   see also mid Western Zhou; Western Zhou;
      western Zhou Dynasty
Zhou, Duke of see Duke of Zhou
Zhou 周 elite
   changes in tomb bronze vessels 152–153
   clans and clan names 140–141
   lineages 141–143
      primary and derivative 142–143
      segmentation 142
   polygamy 141
   preservation of bronze culture 202–203
   ritual system 153
   social organization 140–143
Zhou 周 regional states
   archaeology 132–134
   contact with Zhou king 132, 134
   distribution 131
   establishment 131
   functioning of 129–132
   inspection of 132
   King Cheng 135
   listed in Warring States period 131
   periphery states 164–166
   political control of Zhou king 132
   Rong and Di relations 180–181
   rulers' visits to 134
   weakening of royal power 153
Zhou 周 state 172
   border walls 186
Zhuangzi 莊子 218–220
   activist government 219–220
   "Being Natural" or "Naturally So" 219
   Guodian texts 221
   "The Way" 218–219
   usefulness and uselessness 220
Zhuangzi 莊子, Warring States text 218–220
   parable of butterfly dream 220
   Sophists 227
Zhudingyuan 鑄鼎原, Yangshao settlements
   29–30
Zhukaigou 朱開溝 culture 267
Zi Chan 子產, "Legal Statutes" 176
Zi Si 子思, Guodian texts 222
Zou Yan 鄒衍 305
Zuo Commentary (Zuozhuan 左傳)
   description of county 167
   Rong group of people 181
Zuoce Ban's 作冊般 Turtle 74, 89